Copyright © 2023 by Chandidas Mohanty

All rights reserved.

This book or any portion thereof may not be reproduced or used in any manner whatsoever without the express written permission of the respective writer of the respective content except for the use of brief quotations in a book review.

The writer of the respective work holds sole responsibility for the originality of the content and The Write Order is not responsible in any way whatsoever.

Printed in India

ISBN: 978-93-6045-056-4

First Printing, 2023

The Write Order
A division of Nasadiya Technologies Private Ltd.
Koramangala, Bengaluru
Karnataka-560029

THE WRITE ORDER PUBLICATIONS.

www.thewriteorder.com

Edited by Ridham

Typeset by MAP Systems, Bengaluru

Book Cover designed by Keerthipriya

Publishing Consultant - Vaishnavi Nathan

Kaleidoscopic Life

Chandidas Mohanty

Dedication

This gift of literary creation is dedicated to the three most important guiding lights in my life. I humbly pray for my parents, Gokulananda and Nirmala, and my wife, Rashmi, for their ever-peaceful rest at God's abode.

Chandidas Mohanty.

Baba

Maa

Rashmi

Preface

In the past, I have authored two books. One of them, titled "Bouquet of Wild Flowers," focused on English poetry and was published in 2006. The other, "Financial Management for Managers," was centered around management and was published in 2016. However, my wife's serious health decline due to Alzheimer's disease compelled me to put a halt to all my writing endeavours starting in 2014.

Following the passing of my wife in early 2019, I found myself completely devoid of enthusiasm for life. I was on the brink of depression. Thankfully, my three loving children, Mona, Dimpy, and Dev, were always by my side. They served as my unwavering sources of support. Their dedication, affection, and love gradually helped me return to the routines of everyday life.

At this point, all of them persistently encouraged me to document the tapestry of my life through the written word. Their aim was to keep me engaged in a meaningful endeavour and, at the same time, create a written account of my life for my children, as well as the numerous friends, fans, and well-wishers who follow my journey.

Title of the book Kaleidoscopic Life symbolises the ever dominating human spirit. It symbolises the blessings of the Lord that gave strength to Chandidas to confront vagaries of living with a dominant spirit. The book represents my sincere effort to chronicle the events of my life as they unfolded over the span of eight decades. These events are specific to their respective times and places. Throughout the narrative, I subtly incorporate the significance of emotional, sociological, psychological, and historical perspectives to make the reading engaging, even though there may be some occasional repetition.

Only time will reveal the extent of my success in this endeavour. Nearly the entire narrative has been crafted from memory, as I never maintained written notes before. The idea of documenting the events of my own life, especially when they involved unpleasant or avoided episodes, never occurred to me.

The account of my life story is genuine and based on my best recollections of the facts. The actions and behaviours of the individuals involved have not been altered in any way. However, I have changed some names to protect individuals' privacy. I extend my sincere apologies to anyone who may have been upset or offended by this narrative.

Recalling events from childhood to old age is a highly challenging task. Its accuracy may lead to differing opinions and interpretations. But that's the nature of life itself! Just as people have diverse personalities, their perspectives can also vary, sometimes even to the extreme. Nevertheless, this hasn't swayed me from staying committed to the path of truth. I hope readers will appreciate and understand this.

This is the tale of an ordinary Indian from the middle class, born with a dream. I hail from a state abundant in natural resources but plagued by poverty, a place that was overlooked during the 19th century yet rich in historical heritage and cultural legacy. Looking ahead, I genuinely envision a future where my beloved state can reclaim its past glory.

Jai Jagannath
February 2023

Prelude

The narrative commences with its central character, Chandidas. The name itself, quite literally, translates to "servant of the goddess Chandi." Chandidas is often affectionately referred to as Chandi. Throughout this story, whenever necessary, I will use this shorter name to refer to myself.

I came into this world in 1935, within the borders of what is now known as Odisha. My place of birth was Cuttack. Even after living for eighty-six eventful years, my affection for both the state and the city of my birth remains unwaveringly close to my heart. *I derive immense pleasure from reminiscing and recounting the rich historical splendour and cultural heritage of my state and birthplace on numerous occasions.*

Cherished Memories

My State Of Birth

I had a deep affinity for delving into the history of my home state, Kalinga (present-day Odisha). The story of Odisha's origins stretches back to the Lower Palaeolithic Era, with tools from that time period unearthed in various locations throughout the state. The early history of Odisha can be traced through references in ancient texts such as the Mahabharata and various Hindu Puranas (scriptures).

Kalinga, once an independent region, came under the rule of the Mauryan emperor Ashoka in the 3rd century BC. He was profoundly affected by the immense loss of life among the Odia Paikas (warriors) during the Kalinga War, which took place near the Daya River, located ten kilometres from Bhubaneswar, the present-day capital of Odisha.

The violence and suffering endured during the Kalinga War had a profound impact on Ashoka, leading him to embrace pacifism and convert to Buddhism. He dispatched peace envoys to neighbouring nations, indirectly spreading the influence of Buddhism throughout Asia. During this time, Odisha was already known to other kingdoms in the East Indies region due to maritime trade relations.

Following the decline of the Mauryan empire, the region fell under the rule of Kharavela, who held the title of Supreme King of Kalinga. From the 4th century BC to the 15th century AD, several dynasties governed Kalinga, which was also known as Kosala and Utkala. Between the 11th and 15th centuries, the Gangs emerged as the dominant power in the region and assumed the title of Kalingadhipati. They relocated their capital to Kataka, modern-day Cuttack. During this era, Kalinga was ruled by a succession of kings who not only treated their subjects with benevolence but also provided steadfast support during challenging times when external threats brought immense suffering.

I found great enjoyment in learning about the earlier Kalinga monarchs, including Bhanu Dev II, Bhanu Dev III, Narasingh Dev IV, and Bhanudev IV, who reigned over the region from 1306 to 1434 AD. I took immense pride in the achievements of Kapilendra Dev, the visionary behind the 'Suriyavanshi Dynasty,' who not only expanded the kingdom but also laid the foundation for the Kalinga Empire.

This empire stretched from the Ganges in the north to Trichinopoly in the south, and from the Bay of Bengal in the east to a significant part of Madhya Pradesh in the west. Kapilendra Dev held the prestigious title of Gajapati as the ruler of this burgeoning Kalinga Empire from 1435 to 1467 AD. It was during this period that the Odia Mahabharata was penned by Sarala Das, and trade and commerce reached their zenith. Goods from the empire were traded in distant places like Java, Sumatra, Borneo, and more.

While the Sun Temple of Konark was initially constructed during Narasingh Dev's reign, a multitude of other temples, boasting exquisite design and architectural brilliance, began to grace the region. Each of these temples was a testament to the artistic and poetic expression etched in stone. This era also witnessed a cultural renaissance, encompassing music, dance, literature, the arts, and crafts. This era of progress persisted for another century, despite the change in ruling dynasties, transitioning from the Bhoi dynasty to the Chalukya dynasty.

However, during the rule of Mukunda Dev, the empire gradually succumbed to Mughal influence, starting in 1568. To this day, I have observed that children in villages sing songs that mock the destruction of temples and the tampering of Kalinga's cultural heritage by 'Kalapahad,' the commanding officer of the Mughal army.

After 1568, the region experienced a gradual decline, and Odisha ceased to exist as an independent kingdom. Over time, the once-vast empire was fragmented into smaller kingdoms, and by 1617, Raja Todarmal divided Odisha into Moghulbandi and Gadajat.

Between 1590 and 1707, which marked the death of Aurangzeb, the region was under the rule of the Mughal Empire. In 1751, it became a part of the Maratha Empire, and in 1803, the British conquered the area.

In less than a year, in 1804, a rebellion erupted against British rule in Odisha, led by the Paika warriors under the guidance of Jayee Rajguru, who served as the royal preceptor to Raja Mukunda Dev II. This marked the first uprising against British rule in Odisha. The British authorities, with the assistance of some disloyal locals, brutally quelled the rebellion, leading to the imprisonment of both Rajguru and the Raja.

Subsequently, on December 6, 1806, Rajguru faced conviction in Midnapur. He was subjected to a gruesome execution where his legs were bound to two separate branches of a Banyan tree, which were then released, tearing him apart. In a remarkable act of sacrifice, the Raja was released in 1807, as Rajguru had willingly shouldered the entire responsibility for the uprising. This made Jayee Rajguru the first Indian martyr in the early struggle for freedom against British rule. His sacrifice was not in vain; it served as the foundation for a significant revolt known as the Paika Mutiny, which erupted eleven years after his martyrdom.

In 1817, the British managed to suppress the Paika Mutiny after considerable effort. The Paikas were a landed militia exempted from land taxes in exchange for their services. They became discontented with the new British land laws and were led by Bakshi Jagabandhu, who served as a commander for the king of Khurda. This rebellion was extensive, with the Kandhas of Ghumsar also supporting the rebels in their cause.

Due to the early resistance against British rule, Odisha remained under the governance of other regions for an extended period. Initially, it was administratively linked with Bengal and Bihar as part of the Bengal Presidency. It wasn't until March 22, 1912, that Bihar and Odisha were separated from the Bengal Presidency. However, it took another 24 years for Odisha to achieve independent provincial status, which occurred on April 1, 1936, following its separation from Bihar.

I also discovered that in 1920, numerous leaders in Odisha threw their support behind the Indian National Congress (INC) resolution to reorganise provinces based on linguistic boundaries. Thanks to their persistent efforts, the six districts of Cuttack, Puri, Balasore, Ganjam, Koraput, and Sambalpur came together to form the State of Odisha in April 1936.

Following the conclusion of World War II, in the post-war climate of 1946, elections were conducted for the Odisha Provincial Legislative Assembly, resulting in a majority for the Congress party. Dr. Harekrushna Mahatab, the leader of the Congress party in Odisha, assumed the role of Prime Minister on April 3, 1946. During the same year, the Cabinet Mission visited India, and Mahatab pledged to bring up the matter of merging the Gadajat states with the new Odisha province before the Mission.

Shortly after India gained independence, the situation in Nilgiri state grew increasingly tense. The ruling Raja instilled fear among the population in an attempt to subdue them, leading to a rebellion. The people of Nilgiri reached out to Mahatab, who promptly engaged with the Home Minister, Sardar Patel, in New Delhi. Mahatab secured permission for the merger of Nilgiri with Odisha. On November 14, 1947, Nilgiri was merged into the Balasore district through police action, marking the first instance in independent India's history when a princely state was integrated.

On December 24, 1947, Mahatab convened a meeting in Cuttack that brought together all the Rajas of the Gadajat states in Odisha. The purpose of the meeting was to discuss the amalgamation of their respective states. He advised the kings, subtly cautioning them that with India's independence, there was no longer any room for the native princely states to remain autonomous; their integration with Odisha was an inevitable course of action. Sardar Patel also shared his counsel, emphasising that signing the merger agreement would demonstrate their maturity.

Thanks to the efforts of Sardar Patel, Harekrushna Mahatab, and VP Menon, the merger of the Gadajat states into Odisha became a reality. In 1949, the Central Government transferred the administration of all 26 merged princely states to the Government of Odisha. Unfortunately, for political reasons, the other two states, Seraikela and Kharsawan, were not incorporated into Odisha and instead were merged with Bihar.

Following the merger of states, seven new districts were established: Mayurbhanj, Keonjhar, Dhenkanal, Phulbani, Bolangir, Kalahandi, and Sundargarh. These districts, along with the existing six districts of Cuttack, Balasore, Puri, Ganjam, Koraput, and Sambalpur, brought the total number of districts in Odisha to thirteen. Subsequently, some of these districts were further divided, and the current count now stands at thirty districts.

I came to realise that Odisha's genuine development began after India gained independence. Significant initiatives, such as the construction of the Hirakud Dam in Sambalpur and the establishment of the Rice Research Institute in Cuttack, were carried out vigorously starting in October 1947. In 1948, decisions were also made to create a new capital in Bhubaneswar, establish an All India Radio Station, and set up a High Court in Cuttack. The capital was eventually shifted to Bhubaneswar in 1949.

The groundwork for the Rourkela Steel Plant was laid in 1953, while the establishment of an agriculture college in Bhubaneswar followed in 1954. Subsequently, this college transformed into the Agriculture University of Odisha. The years between 1955 and 1959 saw the commencement of an engineering college and a medical college in Burla. Additionally, during this period, the Orissa Sahitya Academy and the Orissa Lalitkala Academy came into existence.

In 1953, I left Odisha for an extended journey and pursued my higher education from 1953 to 1959. My professional career primarily took me outside Odisha, which kept me occupied and prevented me from closely observing other significant developments in the state. These events coincided with the inauguration of several universities. Another noteworthy milestone in Odisha's modern development was the construction and operation of Paradeep Port, along with its associated industrial complex.

The groundwork for the Rourkela Steel Plant was laid in 1953, while the establishment of an agriculture college in Bhubaneswar followed in 1954. Subsequently, this college transformed into the Agriculture University of Odisha. The years between 1955 and 1959 saw the commencement of an engineering college and a medical college in Burla. Additionally, during this period, the Orissa Sahitya Academy and the Orissa Lalitkala Academy came into existence.

In 1953, I left Odisha for an extended journey and pursued my higher education from 1953 to 1959. My professional career primarily took me outside Odisha, which kept me occupied and prevented me from closely observing other significant developments in the state. These events coincided with the inauguration of several universities. Another noteworthy milestone in Odisha's modern development was the construction and operation of Paradeep Port, along with its associated industrial complex.

I discovered that Dr. Harekrushna Mahatab is also recognised as the "Lion of New Odisha," and his remarkable work and dedication to the territorial integration and consolidation of the state are fondly commemorated. Subsequently, the father-son duo of Biju and Naveen further propelled the state's growth by implementing rapid industrialization and infrastructure development. All Odias will forever hold these three figures in special regard.

The founding figures, such as Madhusudan Das, Gopabandhu Mishra, and a host of other notable Odia politicians, artists, writers, educators, and scientists, will always be warmly remembered for their invaluable contributions. There is a substantial gap between what Odisha was like at the time of its establishment in 1936 and its present state. Visible progress can be observed across all sectors—cultural, social, and economic. This transformation represents a significant achievement for a state that was considered backward in several aspects for many years.

The account of modern Odisha would remain incomplete without acknowledging the significant contributions of pioneering Odia figures like Madhusudan Das, Dr. Harekrushna Mahatab, and Biju Patnaik. The recounting of their actions and positive endeavours for a stronger and more prosperous Odisha stands as a cherished chapter in the contemporary history of the state. Even today, they are held in affectionate remembrance by all Odias, serving as a source of inspiration for generations of residents committed to building a resilient and thriving Odisha.

The following narratives about these illustrious Odia personalities are of particular significance:

Madhusudan Das: In 1870, he achieved the distinction of becoming the first Odia to earn a graduate degree, securing a Bachelor of Arts from Calcutta University. Subsequently, in 1873, he furthered his academic pursuits by attaining a Master of Arts from the same university. After obtaining his law degree in 1878, he became actively engaged in politics. His move from Calcutta to Cuttack in 1881 marked a turning point. In 1882, he established the Utkal Sabha, initiating political activities in Odisha. In 1888, the Utkal Sabha presented the idea of consolidating all Odia-speaking territories under a single administration, marking the inception of the Odisha state's formation. Mr. Das will forever be remembered for this pivotal contribution. He is also remembered as the first political leader who advocated for the empowerment of women, with his daughter playing a key role in establishing the first women's college in Cuttack.

Harekrushna Mahatab: Dr. Harekrushna Mahatab was a versatile and beloved figure, often affectionately referred to as the 'Utkal Keshari' or the Lion of Odisha. He embodied a multitude of roles, encompassing a great freedom fighter, politician, administrator, historian, writer, social reformer, and journalist, all seamlessly woven into one remarkable persona. His entire life narrative stands as a testament to his unwavering convictions, unwavering determination, boundless self-assurance, and resolute perseverance.

He drew significant influence from eminent personalities such as Swami Vivekananda, Mahatma Gandhi, and Madhusudan Das, embarking on his political journey under their inspiration. As time progressed, he, in turn, became a source of inspiration, influencing thousands of his followers. Mahatab played a pivotal role in shaping the profound political transformation in Odisha during the freedom movement. He transcended the status of an individual to become an institution in himself.

Sardar Patel held a deep admiration for Mahatab's remarkable personality, describing it as "Himalayan". He wrote, "While history will always remember you as the architect of modern Odisha, the country will hold you dear as one of its courageous and dutiful sons." To put it succinctly, Mahatab possessed an exceptional personality marked by splendid qualities. He was not only a distinguished historian, having authored works like "History of Orissa" in both Odia and English but also a unique writer of Odia novels. His journalistic talents were evident in Odia daily newspapers.

Leaders with such diverse and exceptional qualities are exceedingly rare. Mahatab's unwavering dedication to the betterment of Odisha and its people remained the most cherished objective close to his heart, serving as an enduring wellspring of inspiration throughout his life.

Biju Patnaik: Similar to Mahatab, Biju (Bijayananda Patnaik) was also a multifaceted personality. He is rightfully hailed as the father of Odisha's industrial development.

He excelled as a pilot, a seasoned politician, a visionary, and an industrialist. His character was always characterised by a fearless and daring attitude. Despite hailing from a middle-class background, he departed from his studies at Ravenshaw College, Cuttack, to pursue a career as a pilot. At the onset of World War II, he left his position in a private airline to join the Royal Indian Air Force, ultimately rising to become the head of the Air Transport Command.

During his service, Biju developed an interest in national politics. He utilised air force transport planes to distribute subversive literature to Indian troops, although he remained committed to the fight against the Axis powers. He was jailed by the British for disseminating political leaflets to Indian soldiers who were serving under British command in Burma. The British charges also suggested his involvement in clandestine flying missions, which involved transporting Congress Party leaders from hidden locations across India to secret meeting places. These missions played a significant role in shaping the course of the independence struggle and earned him the trust of Jawaharlal Nehru.

His contributions during World War II in Russia, his involvement in Indonesia's fight for freedom, and his role in safeguarding Kashmir are immortalised in the annals of history. Subsequently, he embarked on a varied political journey, despite having served as the Congress Chief Minister of Odisha for a brief period during Indira Gandhi's tenure. Eventually, he found his own regional political party.

The initiatives led by him encompassed several notable projects, including the Paradeep Port, the Orissa Aviation Centre, Bhubaneswar Airport, and the Cuttack-Jagatpur Mahanadi Highway Bridge. He played a pivotal role in the establishment of institutions such as the Rourkela Regional Engineering College, Sainik School, and the Odisha University of Agriculture and Technology. Additionally, due to his tireless efforts, projects like the National Aluminium Company, Talcher Thermal Power Station, Balimela Hydel Project, HAL Sunabeda, and the industrial zones of Choudwar and Barbil were successfully set up.

Five years prior to his passing in 1997, Bijayananda Patnaik imparted the following quote to the people of Odisha:

"In my dream of the 21st century for the state, I would have young men and women who put the interest of the state before them. They will have pride in themselves, confidence in themselves. They will not be at anybody's mercy, except their own selves. By their brains, intelligence, and capacity, they will recapture the history of Kalinga."

The above message, on recapitulation, fills me with intense emotions.

India currently rests as a sleeping giant among nations, with the potential to become a formidable and highly developed nation in the near future. Odisha, in this context, is poised to claim the top position among all the states in this future superpower, driven by its comprehensive developmental framework and abundant natural resources. The state boasts substantial reserves of iron ore, coal, bauxite, and precious gems, and the possibility of significant oil and gas reserves in the Mahanadi basin and the vast coastal areas.

The cultural legacy of Lord Jagannath, a unique heritage of Odisha, has already taken root in numerous countries. The grand 'Car Festival' of Lord Jagannath can be witnessed even in cities like London and New York. Odisha's art and crafts are gaining recognition and influence in foreign lands. Just as the ancient Kalinga culture, art, and craft left a mark in Far Eastern countries in the past, present-day Odisha is poised to bring about even more profound changes in the traditions, lifestyles, and ideologies of many countries around the world.

Historically, it held a central role as a centre for Buddhist emissaries who disseminated Buddhism throughout Asia. Today, it is rapidly emerging as a focal point for the IT industry and the export of marine products. It stands as the stronghold of the world's finest reserves of iron ore, bauxite, coal, and rare-earth minerals. It offers vast expanses for exploration, potentially containing substantial deposits of yet-to-be-discovered precious gems, hydrocarbons, and other valuable minerals. In the future, it is poised to undergo a remarkable resurgence, akin to the mythological Phoenix rising from the ashes. Chandi eagerly awaits that Greek miracle to happen!

Odisha is undeniably poised to become a haven for future tourism, boasting a wealth of natural wonders. Its extensive coastline features exquisite beaches, while the Eastern Ghats offer rolling hills cloaked in dense forests, a diverse range of vegetation, mountain streams, and cascading waterfalls, all contributing to its remarkable geographical heritage. Its protected forests teem with a variety of wildlife, including tigers and elephants, along with rare species of flora and fauna. Some regions even witness snowfall during the winter months.

The coastline serves as a favoured nesting ground for foreign sea turtles, which journey thousands of kilometres from the Pacific Ocean to lay their eggs. Deep gorges in the region also serve as breeding grounds for crocodiles, as exemplified by Satkosia Gorge near Angul. The expansive Chilika Lake, which welcomes rare birds from Siberia during the winter, houses dolphins and various other exceptional marine life. It offers opportunities for water sports and is dotted with small islands that host temples and picturesque spots perfect for picnics.

The state is adorned with an abundance of temples, some of which date back to periods earlier than the 3rd century BC. The capital city of Bhubaneswar alone boasts over a thousand temples, adorned with exquisite stone carvings that represent priceless works of art meticulously crafted by skilled sculptors. Notably, the Konark Sun Temple has earned a place on the UNESCO World Heritage List. Other temples, like the Jagannath Temple in Puri and the Lingaraj Temple in Bhubaneswar, are exceptional examples of rare artistic mastery. The carvings found in the Khandagiri and Udayagiri caves, inscribed in the ancient Pali language, serve as invaluable exhibits showcasing the ancient art of stone carving dating back to the BC era. It is indeed a remarkable and astonishing heritage.

When contemplating the ancestors of the Odia people, it becomes apparent that they were not only courageous but also culturally affluent. Their trading prowess in bygone eras facilitated profitable exchanges in distant markets across the seas. In essence, they embodied the finest qualities of both Aryans and Dravidians, whose descendants they are believed to be. They possess the resilience of the Dravidians and the agility and intellect of the Aryans. The doctors, engineers, educators, scientists, and administrators from Odisha consistently make their mark of excellence not only in India but also on the global stage.

Another intriguing aspect of the state pertains to its language. Supported by historical evidence spanning 2,500 years, the magnificence and richness of the Odia language find solid validation. As one of the oldest languages in the country with roots in Sanskrit, it is spoken by approximately 84% of the state's population. Odia achieved the distinction of becoming the first language from the Indo-Aryan linguistic group to be recognised as the sixth classical language of India. Odisha is also celebrated as a multilingual state where linguistic diversity thrives without any instances of intolerance towards languages such as English, Hindi, Urdu, Bengali, or Telugu.

I took great pride in the fact that my homeland, while preserving its original splendour in all its facets, seamlessly incorporates modern amenities that harmonise with its long-standing tradition of warm hospitality. A visual feast of vibrant colours, steeped in values and diversity, embarking on a cultural journey through this land transports one to one of the world's most ancient civilizations. If Kashmir is renowned as 'Heaven on Earth' for its breathtaking landscapes, Odisha can undoubtedly compete for a similar distinction, thanks to its blend of religious, cultural, ethnic, and scenic treasures.

I hailed from a conventional middle-class family that harboured no biases related to caste, creed, or religion. This land, epitomising the principle of "Vasudev Kutumbakam," which means that the entire world is one family, provided me with a solid foundation in life. From a young age, I acquainted myself with the realities of the outside world and confronted them with courage, self-assurance, and an independent spirit. Later in life, my career led me to serve in various regions across India, including Assam, Bengal, Bihar, Uttar Pradesh, Punjab, Andhra Pradesh, and many other parts of the country. In these roles, I acted as an ambassador for Odisha. During my tenures in these places, I endeavoured to alter the perceptions, knowledge, and understanding of a significant number of individuals from other states and regions, fostering a greater appreciation for Odisha and its people.

Following India's independence, as recruitment for various central services commenced, a multitude of young and talented Odia youths found their way into these services. These bright and diligent young officers, possessing a keen understanding of the evolving times and an unwavering commitment to their respective roles, played a pivotal role in reshaping the perspectives and attitudes of influential figures within India's bureaucratic and political spheres. Gradually, the state began to receive its rightful share from the central government, propelling it ahead of other states in numerous critical domains such as healthcare, education, mining, telecommunications, industrial development, and economic progress. I now hold a strong belief in the potential for a transformation akin to a Greek miracle to unfold in my state.

My City of Birth

I was born in Cuttack, which is the second-largest city in Odisha, trailing only behind the current capital, Bhubaneswar. My early childhood and a significant portion of my school and college years were spent in this city. Following my father's retirement from government service, our family permanently relocated to Cuttack, bidding farewell to our ancestral village of Pasulunda in Mahanga tehsil, Cuttack district.

Even during my bustling years in Allahabad for my undergraduate and postgraduate studies, as well as throughout my career in various locations in India and abroad, I never missed an opportunity to visit Cuttack. My affection and attachment to this place were unwavering. I would often delve into the city's eventful history, its strategic location, its picturesque surroundings, and its unique arts and culture.

What deeply resonated with me was the enduring fact that this city, much like in ancient times, remained the cauldron for all significant developments in the state. It served as a constant reminder of the love of my parents and my siblings. Cuttack was the stage where many pivotal moments of my life unfolded and concluded. It's a place where memories evoke both tears of happiness and heart-wrenching sorrow. This city is where numerous vibrant dreams of my life took shape, with some realising their potential and others slipping away during the turbulent phases of life.

Coming into contact with the soil of the city filled me with enchantment. Its streets and narrow lanes stirred memories of my joyful childhood spent with dear friends. Even the harrowing sights of the swollen Mahanadi and Kathjori rivers during the monsoon season fascinated me, despite the shivers of fear they induced. The angelic vision of *kasatandi* flowers (Saccharum spontaneum) during autumn, scattered across the dry riverbed of the Mahanadi, has left indelible impressions that I can vividly recall to this day. These vast expanses of feathery, long-stalked, white blossoms resembling brooms against the backdrop of the azure sky grace the landscape throughout this season. My parents told me that these flowers are associated with Durga Puja. During the two-week-long festival, the fields come alive with these lovely grasses, swaying in the gentle breeze and filling the air with their delightful fragrance.

The cherished memories of Barabati Fort and its adjacent moat, my frequent visits to Cuttack Chandi Temple (especially during exam periods), and the grandeur of the Cuttack *medhas* during Durga Puja are all firmly etched in my mind. Cuttack's delightful sweets fostered my enduring love for them. The recollection of savouring the delightful street food, '*Dahibara*' and '*Aludum*,' in Cuttack with my college friends filled me with pure joy. Even amidst extravagant gatherings at seven-star hotels in later years, I found myself yearning for such simple pleasures.

It's hard to put into words the unforgettable childhood memories of enjoying Odia dramas with my parents at 'Odisha Theatre' by Kali Charan Das and 'Annapurna Theatre' by Bauri Bandhu Mohanty. The arrival of cinema halls marked the decline of both of these theatres, much like many similar venues across India. I distinctly remember that my parents were quite religious during my childhood. My mother used to observe many festivals, and I eagerly awaited their arrival solely to savour the variety of delicious *pithas* (homemade Odia sweet cakes) she would prepare. I've missed this for many decades now; nothing could quite match the quality and flavour of *Maa's pithas*!

I think it's prudent to delve into the intricacies of Cuttack city, both its historical past and its present state. I'm pleasantly amazed by its rich historical heritage and the turbulent yet fascinating events that have shaped its current position. The areas in and around Cuttack have historically served as a crucial hub for political, economic, trade, and cultural activities within the mighty Kalinga empire. This significance persisted even during the period when Odisha was under British colonial rule. Cuttack's strategic location, surrounded on three sides by mighty rivers and extending towards the sea on the fourth side, made it an ideal center of power and prestige in ancient times. Remarkably, this importance endures even today, as evidenced by the establishment of a Police Commissionerate for the twin cities of Bhubaneswar and Cuttack in the early part of the current century.

Founded in 989 AD by King Markat Keshari, Cuttack served as the administrative centre of Odisha for nearly a millennium. Over the centuries, it witnessed the rule of various foreign powers, including the Mughals, Marathas, and the British. In the year 1002, King Markat Keshari constructed stone embankments along the surrounding rivers to shield the capital from floods. The city's name, an Anglicised version of "Kataka," translates to "The Fort," referring to the ancient Barabati Fort around which the city originally developed. Cuttack is renowned as the Millennium City and the Silver City, reflecting its thousand-year history and famed filigree craftsmanship. Additionally, it holds the status of the judicial capital of the state, housing the Odisha High Court.

Under Maratha rule in 1750, Cuttack experienced rapid growth as a prominent trading hub, bolstered by its accessibility from Nagpur, the Marathas' seat of power. Following the British conquest in 1803, it was designated as the capital of the Odisha division in 1816, a status it retained until 1948, when the capital was relocated to Bhubaneswar.

Cuttack encompasses an area of 192 square kilometres and is divided into 59 wards within the Cuttack Municipality. Geographically, it extends from Phulnakhara in the south to Choudwar in the north and from Kandarpur in the east to Naraj in the west, situated within the river delta of the Mahanadi.

In addition to the Mahanadi River, Cuttack is traversed by three of its tributaries: the Birupa, Kathjori, and Kuakhai rivers. The Mahanadi flows along the northern boundary of the city, creating a division between the main city and the Jagatpur Industrial Area. The Kathjori River forms an island known as Bayalis Mouza, comprising 42 wards, which acts as a natural barrier between the main city and this region. The Kuakhai River bisects the southern part of the city into two distinct sections: Pratap Nagari and the newly developed Narainapur township. Flowing southward, the Kuakhai runs along Phulnakhara before entering Bhubaneswar. To the north of the Jagatpur Industrial Area, the Birupa River courses through, creating a demarcation from Choudwar.

Finally, I seemed to have unravelled the mystery of these four rivers, which bestow a distinct character on the city—a feature that sets it apart from any other city in India.

The Mahanadi River serves as the primary source of drinking water for the city. Recent urban expansion has led to the city's growth extending across the Kathjori River. A new township, known as Markat Nagar or CDA Bidanasi, has emerged at the delta's head, situated between the Kathjori and Mahanadi rivers. This township covers an expansive area of 2,000 acres. Within the CDA, there are 15 sectors, 11 of which are residential, housing a population exceeding 150,000 residents. Additionally, Jagatpur and Mahanadi Vihar serve as two satellite townships, complementing the broader city of Cuttack, akin to other satellite areas like Narainapur and Trishulia.

As of the 2011 census, the city's population was recorded at approximately 606,000. Considering an average annual population growth rate of 1.22% for Cuttack, the estimated population in 2020 is around 665,000. This increase in population has led to continuous congestion on the city's roads. Unfortunately, there is limited room for road expansion, particularly in the perpetually congested old areas within the city limits, resulting in narrow roads.

During my childhood, I used to enjoy exploring the old market areas of the city, such as Buxi Bazar, Chandni Chowk, Marwari Patti, Chaudhry Bazar, Mangala Bag, and Ranihat. However, the relaxed demeanour of shopkeepers and their assistants, along with the carefree and joyful attitudes of their customers, have gradually disappeared in this fast-paced era of perpetual busyness. This transformation saddens me, and as a result, I now tend to avoid visiting these areas.

I typically visit my relatives in CDA by travelling from Bhubaneswar. I enter the city using the peripheral Ring Road, which runs along the embankments of the Mahanadi and Kathjori rivers. Interestingly, this road was conceived and constructed by my old classmate Basanta Biswal, who held a prominent ministerial position in the state cabinet from 1965 to 1985. Due to this significant achievement, the people of Cuttack fondly refer to him as 'The Modern Markat Keshari,' drawing a parallel to the historical figure King Markat Keshari, who had built the embankments in the past to protect the city from recurrent floods.

Another aspect of the city that I take pride in is its current status in terms of literacy rates and the harmonious coexistence of various religious groups among its residents. Cuttack boasts an impressive average literacy rate of 91.17%, with a male literacy rate of 97.87% and a female literacy rate of 84.49%. This positions Cuttack among the top cities in India with high literacy rates. In terms of religious demographics, approximately 89.5% of the city's population follows Hinduism, while Muslims make up 8.5%, and the remaining 2% belong to other religious groups. Notably, Cuttack is home to the largest Christian population in the state.

Throughout its long history, Cuttack has never experienced any instances of religious discord. The entire population of the city wholeheartedly participates in each other's religious functions and festivals, fostering an atmosphere of unity and harmony. Whether it's Dussehra, Moharram, Dole Jatra, or Christmas, the entire city comes alive with vibrant colours and festivities, resembling a joyous bride. Cuttack stands unparalleled in India, both in its communal harmony and the spirit of celebration.

The city is blessed with numerous pilgrimage sites representing various faiths, including Hinduism, Jainism, Sikhism, Islam, and Christianity, enriching its ancient heritage and modern practices. The residents enthusiastically engage in the festivities associated with these places of worship. Some of the noteworthy religious sites and festivals include Cuttack Chandi Temple, Jagannath Temples at Chandni Chowk and Dolamundai, Dhabaleswar Temple, Paramhansa Nath Temple, Baba Ramdev Temple, Qadam-e-Rassol, Jama Masjid, Bukhari Baba Dargah, Guru Nanak Gurdwara, Digambar Jain Mandir, and The Church of Epiphany. During my childhood, I had the opportunity to visit most of these sites with my parents and friends, and their images still resonate vividly in my memory. Unfortunately, due to constraints during later periods of my stay or visits to the city, I couldn't explore the remaining pilgrimage sites. However, at this advanced age, I do aspire to make a second visit to these unexplored sites if time permits during my future sojourns to Cuttack. In sharing these experiences, I hope to pique the interest of future visitors and tourists in Cuttack's rich religious tapestry.

The Cuttack Chandi Temple stands in close proximity to the Mahanadi River's banks and serves as a significant religious site in Cuttack. Goddess Chandi is the primary deity revered in Cuttack, and the temple takes on central importance during the renowned Durga Puja and Kali Puja festivals in the city. Interestingly, the Gada Chandi Temple, located within the Barabati Fort premises, is one of the oldest temples in Cuttack and is believed to have been the original site of Cuttack Chandi before her relocation to the temple's present location.

The Jagannath Temple at Chandni Chowk was a later addition to the city's architectural landscape. Positioned closer to the banks of the Kathjori River, this temple was constructed as a smaller replica of Lord Jagannath's temple in Puri. The worship facilities and the provision of 'Mahaprasad' (sacred food offering) closely resemble those in Puri. During the Ratha Yatra, this temple also becomes a prominent centre of celebration.

Another renowned pilgrimage site is the Dhabaleswar Temple, dedicated to the worship of Lord Shiva. This temple is located on a picturesque island in the Mahanadi River and boasts intricate stone carvings that trace back to the early 10th and 11th centuries. The island is connected to the mainland, specifically the Choudwar side, by a suspension bridge, the first and only one of its kind in the state. Alternatively, residents of Cuttack can reach the temple by taking a boat ride on the Mahanadi River from the Chata Ghat. During my childhood, I had the opportunity to visit this temple multiple times with my parents and siblings, embarking on boat rides from the riverbank near our home in Tulsipur, Cuttack.

The Paramhansa Nath Temple is another remarkable monument in Cuttack, proudly standing for over a millennium at a height of eighty feet. It was constructed in the 11th century and is located on the banks of the Kathjori River. To reach the temple, one can follow the path along the river bank from the Panchmukhi Hanuman temple on Khapuria Road. This temple comprises five chambers and features exquisite sculptures of the Navagraha on the Vimana and Bhogamandapa. The plinth areas of the temple depict scenes from battles, while the sanctum houses a Patal-Phuta Shiv Lingaa. Surrounding the temple, you'll find other deities such as Parvati, Kartikeya, and Ganesh. Additionally, images of Rama abhiseka are present on the northern wall, and two Vishnu images adorn the temple's outer walls.

Situated along the Cuttack-Bhubaneswar national highway, there is another temple known as the Baba Ramdev Temple. This unique temple is entirely constructed of white marble. Ramdev *Pir*, a Hindu folk deity hailing from Rajasthan, India, is the central figure of worship in this temple. Ramdev is revered as an incarnation of Lord Krishna and is believed to possess extraordinary miraculous abilities. According to legend, five *pirs*, who were Islamic religious leaders from Mecca, visited Ramdev to test his divine powers. Even today, numerous devotees visit this temple to seek the fulfilment of their wishes through prayer and devotion.

In the heart of Cuttack city, there is a significant historical pilgrimage site known as Qadam-e-Rasool. This place originated from the belief in the veneration of the Prophet Muhammad, where it was believed that his footprints left an imprint when he stepped on a rock. This belief, although not accepted by orthodox branches of Islam, was widely disseminated, leading to the creation of several shrines commemorating the imprint of the prophet's footprints around the world. Cuttack's Qadam-e-Rasool is one such shrine among them. Unfortunately, I do not have any information about who constructed this shrine or when it was built in the city of my birth.

Cuttack is also home to a Jama Masjid, which was constructed during the Mughal era. Previously, there was a *madrasa* within this mosque, but it has since been relocated to a different location. Throughout the city, there are numerous shrines dedicated to Muslim *pirs*, and people from all religions gather at these shrines on specific dates to seek their blessings.

One of the prominent *dargahs* in the Silver City is the Bukhari Baba *Dargah*, which attracts a large crowd, especially on Thursdays. People of various faiths come here to offer prayers and seek the fulfilment of their wishes. This ancient *dargah* is dedicated to the Sufi saint Sayeed Ali Saheed Bukhari, known as Bukhari Baba. The *dargah*, characterised by its white-domed structure, is a fine example of Mughal architecture and was constructed in 1468. It draws devotees from across the state, including those from different religious backgrounds. Approximately two lakh devotees visit this sacred shrine each year, and during the peak winter months, interesting and vibrant *mushairas* (poetry recitals) are held to entertain visitors.

Cuttack also takes pride in hosting a significant historical Sikh shrine, known as the Daatan Sahib Gurudwara. This sacred place served as an overnight halt for the first Sikh Guru, Shree Guru Nanakji, during his journey to Puri. It is also referred to as Gurudwara Guru Nanak Daatan Sahib. The legend says that a tree branch planted by the Guru after using it as a tooth cleaner, flourishes here, which is why it is named 'Daatan Sahib.'

During British rule, a considerable number of people from the Jain sect migrated to Cuttack from Uttar Pradesh and Rajasthan. They primarily settled in areas like Nua Bazar, Jaunliapattty, and Choudhury Bazar. This Jain community consisted of both the 'Digambar' and 'Swetambar' sects.

They erected four Jain temples in Choudhury Bazar, Jaunliapattty, Alamchand Bazar, and Kaji Bazar, each housing images of Tirthankara. The Choudhury Bazar temple, built in the 20th century, stands out for its remarkable artistic design. I personally visited this temple when I went shopping with my parents in the vicinity for clothing and was deeply impressed.

Another notable religious landmark in Cuttack is the Church of Epiphany. It is the oldest of several churches in the city, including the Holy Rosary Church and Odia Baptist Church. The Epiphany Church was constructed in 1865 and is located on Cantonment Road. Its iconic brick structure serves as an example of colonial architecture from the British era.

In addition to the aforementioned pilgrimage sites in Cuttack, the city boasts many other renowned temples, including the Gada Chandi Temple, Khannagar Sai Mandir, Amareswara Temple, Raghunath Jew Temple, Ramakrishna Mission, Maa Jhanjiri Mangala Temple, Dolamundai Jagannath Temple, Chahata Rama Mandir, Badambadi Siddhivinayak Temple, Khannagar Kali Mandir, Kaliaboda Shani Temple, and more.

I was elated to experience the diverse fragrances of different religions in Cuttack. Moreover, witnessing the spirit of coexistence, harmony, and unity among all communities in my city of birth filled me with pure and divine joy!

No one can easily forget the grand celebrations in this city I hold dear. Cuttack is renowned across the nation for its extravagant Durga Puja festivities. Various puja committees in the city craft over two hundred clay idols of Goddess Durga for worship. What sets Cuttack's Durga Puja apart is the elaborate 'Chandi' and 'Sona' *medhas* (silver and gold mandaps) in which the idols are adorned with copious amounts of silver and gold. These *medhas* are not only structurally impressive but also exceptionally artistic and captivating. Different neighbourhoods in the city strive to outdo one another by creating more alluring idols and mandaps.

The city embraces its Durga Puja with utmost vigour, activity, and entertaining programmes, spanning Maha Saptami, Maha Ashtami, Maha Navami, and Vijaya Dashami (Dussehra). On the final day of Dussehra, effigies of Ravana are set ablaze before large, festive gatherings in vibrant attire. This festive period attracts a significant number of people from Odisha and neighbouring states, who come to Cuttack to savour the puja and create unforgettable memories.

Following this is the festival of Kali Puja, dedicated to the worship of Goddess Kali. Some of the earlier Durga Puja mandaps showcase Kali *medhas* during this time, although the number of *medhas*, the intensity of the festival, and its spirit of enjoyment are comparatively lower than those of Durga Puja. Soon after, Kartikeswar Puja is organised by local puja committees. Lord Kartikeya, the eldest son of Lord Shiva, is the deity of this puja. Except for Sabarimala, Kartikeswar Puja is celebrated with exceptional enthusiasm nowhere else in India.

Bada Osha is another distinctive festival celebrated with deep religious fervour at the Dhabaleswar Temple dedicated to Lord Shiva. Devotees observe a fast for nearly twenty-four hours, eagerly anticipating the special *bhoga* (Gaja and Taran) that marks the end of their fast. Another significant festival in

Cuttack is Mana Basha, known as Lakshmi Puja or the worship of the goddess of wealth in other regions. While this puja originated in Cuttack district, it has since spread to coastal districts and parts of western Odisha.

A classic and noteworthy festival in Cuttack is Boita Bandana, observed on the final day of the holy month of Kartik (Kartik Purnima). On this auspicious day, people take an early morning bath in the Mahanadi or Kathjori River and offer prayers before setting afloat miniature boats or model boats on the rivers. These boats are specially crafted for the occasion, serving as a tribute to the ancient Kalinga Kingdom merchants who ventured to distant eastern destinations by sea, trading in places like Bali, Java, Sumatra, Borneo, and others.

This day also marks the commencement of Bali Jatra, a festival akin to Bali's Masakapan Ke Tukad festival and Thailand's Loi Krathong festival, both of which involve the ritualistic floating of model boats around the same time of the year. It's no surprise that Thailand, Java, Sumatra, and Borneo still retain some aspects of Odia culture and tradition. There are also similarities and resemblances in the architecture and carvings of ancient Odisha temples that can be found among the remnants of their heritage sites.

I remember the childhood tantrums I used to have during Kartik Purnima days, especially an incident that occurred in late 1945. My mother would wake me up early in the morning to take a bath in the cold waters of the Mahanadi River before floating a miniature boat as part of the Boita Bandana celebration.

I have vivid recollections of those early mornings when I used to wake up and accompany my parents from our rented residence in Mohamadia Bazar to Gada Gadia Ghat. At that time, our family was residing in a rented house while awaiting the official quarters allotted to my father. I also recall that, after taking a dip in the river, I would release the boat and offer my prayers at the Gada Gadia Mahadev temple.

These boats were crafted from materials such as cork, the bark of plantain tree trunks, bamboo, or wood, and adorned with colourful plastic flags. They were available in the markets in the days leading up to the Boita Bandana celebration. It was a delightful experience, one that still holds a cherished place in my memories. Many years later, I had the honour of being invited to the dais at Paradeep Port during Boita Bandana. I sat alongside the Chief Minister of Odisha and the Chief of Paradeep Port for the inauguration of the Boita Bandana festival at the port. The grandeur and colourful spectacle of that port festival remain etched in my memory to this day.

Coinciding with the Boita Bandana festival, a large fair is organised on the banks of the Mahanadi River every year, lasting for a fortnight. This fair is famously known as the Bali Jatra. It serves as an annual reminder to the people of Odisha about the adventurous voyages undertaken by their ancestors to the distant lands of the Far East across the sea. These intrepid mariners from Kalinga carried their goods for trade in the overseas countries of the Far East, and their visits have left lasting influences on the culture and arts of those distant lands.

The rich blend of Odisha's arts and culture, which was transported to far-off lands by these courageous traders, now lies buried in the sands of time. Legend has it that upon their return from these foreign journeys, the traders would exhibit the exotic goods they had acquired at the very place where the Bali Jatra is now held. This was quite fitting, as Cuttack was the capital of the kingdom at that time. People from various parts of the Kalinga kingdom would visit the fair to marvel at and acquire these foreign treasures.

Even today, much like in the past, Bali Jatra is celebrated annually on the banks of the Mahanadi River, situated opposite the Barabati Fort. In the vicinity, the Barabati Stadium has also been erected. Over the years, the area of the fairgrounds has expanded, now encompassing a portion of the dry riverbed of the Mahanadi during the month of November. Presently, the nature of goods available at Bali Jatra has undergone remarkable transformations. The items on display encompass a wide array of consumables, including artefacts, engineering products, electrical and electronic items, household goods, agricultural equipment, and industrial products.

Traders from all corners of India come to this place to showcase their wares to customers from all over the country. The activities at Bali Jatra have evolved in keeping with the changing times. Bali Jatra offers entertainment options for both children and adults, featuring large Ferris wheels, rotating round canopies with wooden horses, magic shows, bioscopes, video parlours, and stalls selling best-selling books in various languages, providing a diverse range of options for everyone to enjoy.

Eateries offering cuisine from various other states, alongside Odisha's cuisine, which dominates in terms of the number of stalls, can be found at every corner of the fairground. There's a noticeable crowd at stalls serving famous Odia dishes, sweets, and a variety of *pithas*, or Odia cakes.

It's indisputable that Cuttack holds the title of being the street food capital of Odisha, and Bali Jatra abundantly provides all such culinary delights. Visitors to the stalls can savour *dahibara aloodam* and indulge in the renowned *chena poda* and *rasgulla* from Bikala Kar of Salepur. Other popular street foods like samosa, chaat, and panipuri are also abundantly available here.

If someone desires to savour traditional Odia rural cuisine, dishes like *dahi-pakhal* (known for its cooling properties), *badichura*, and *saag*, along with fish fry and *alubharta*, can also be found at a few stalls. The people of Cuttack, known as Katakis, eagerly await the annual availability of *thunka puri*, a beloved rural Odia dish that's exclusive to Bali Jatra and can only be enjoyed once a year. Additionally, Mughlai dishes such as biryani, tandoor items, and sheer kurma, highly favoured by many visitors, are also in demand.

Being a passionate foodie, I always looked forward to visiting Bali Jatra whenever I returned to Odisha during that time.

While some of Cuttack's significant festivals remain etched in my memory, I also recall the celebration of other regular Indian festivals that are observed with great enthusiasm by the city's residents. These include Ratha Yatra, Raja, Ganesh Chaturthi, Vasant Panchami, Holi, Diwali, Eid, and Christmas. They serve as occasions for reverence, respect, and enjoyment for the city's inhabitants. I have had the pleasure of celebrating these festivals with friends from diverse communities, a cultural tradition instilled in me by my parents and one that I continue to hold dear to my heart.

My place of birth has been the residence of numerous notable individuals who have made significant contributions to the culture and history of modern Odisha. Cuttack, in the past, held a prominent position in the realms of art and literature. Annapurna Theatre is recognised as a trailblazer among Odia Theatre Company. Located in Buxi Bazar, it is the oldest theatre in Odisha. Additionally, Kala Vikash Kendra, situated in Cuttack, serves as a leading institution for dance, drama, and music in the state. Annually, it hosts the International Theatre Olympiads, attracting artists from various countries to join alongside local talents.

Sarala Sahitya Sansad and Utkal Sahitya Samaj are a couple of other organisations that have made significant contributions to the cultural richness of Odisha. Cuttack has historically served as a hub for various literary endeavours, with several renowned poets and writers, including Radhanath Roy and Gopinath Mohanty, residing and creating their work here. Additionally, the city hosts several important libraries in Odisha, such as the Kanika library and the Madhusudan library. CMC Sahid Bhawan features a spacious art gallery for exhibitions, and Cuttack is home to several prominent auditoriums, including the Town Hall and Shatabdi Bhawan, among others.

Cuttack is often regarded as the heart of Odia culture, both in the past and the present. It has also become the home of the Odia Film Industry, commonly referred to as 'Ollywood,' a fusion of Odisha and Hollywood. In 1974, the Odisha government officially recognised filmmaking and the establishment of cinema theatres as an industry within the state. Subsequently, in 1976, it established the Odisha Film Development Corporation (OFDC), with its headquarters located in Cuttack.

As a result, one of the regional offices for the Central Board of Film Certification began operating from Cuttack. The city boasts several cinema halls that screen Odia, Hindi, and English movies. Historically, Cuttack once accounted for nearly half of the total number of cinema halls in the state, although this number has gradually declined. In the 1920s, the city had five single-screen movie theatres and two multiplexes.

One year following my birth, in 1936, the second cinema hall, known as Capital Cinema, was constructed at Tinkonia Bazar, close to Ravenshaw Girls School, where my wife Rashmi received her education. She had many fascinating stories to share about her time at that school. I also recalled that my initial school in Cuttack, Pyari Mohan Academy, where I attended classes in the sixth and seventh grades, was situated in the nearby vicinity.

Additionally, I remembered that my younger brother, Durgadas, was actively involved in the Odia film industry for a significant portion of his career. Initially, he held the position of Odisha Chief at the Eastern India Motion Picture Association (EIMPA) and later served as the second-in-command at OFDC, right after its Managing Director.

To this day, the members of the Odia Film Industry fondly recall his contributions to the field. His affection for the industry blossomed during his time with EIMPA and through his friendship with Mitra Babu, the owner of Capital Cinema. This friendship developed in the early days of his career, and Mitra Babu, whose understanding and knowledge of the Odia film industry were extraordinary, also became his mentor. He played a pivotal role in helping him gain a deeper understanding of the nuances of the Odia film industry.

The allure of Cuttack remains so strong that its residents, whether they were born there or not, can never forget their memories of the city. Its rich heritage, vibrant culture, and camaraderie among its diverse residents, regardless of their colour, creed, or religion, leave such a lasting impact that the fondness endures throughout one's life, whether they continue to reside in Cuttack or not!

The 52 Bazar (markets) and 53 Gali (lanes) of Cuttack have become integral to Odia folklore. In the post-independence era, a female Chief Minister of Odisha took significant steps to enhance the city's infrastructure. She oversaw the surfacing of all 53 lanes with metal roads, a substantial improvement. Additionally, she initiated beautification projects in Cuttack, including the creation of Deer Park, the construction of a modern bus stand along the wide Link Road, and the enhancement of Gauri Shankar Park in Tin Konia Bazar.

Furthermore, she facilitated the resurfacing of some of the city's major roads. Her efforts also contributed to the development of the Khapuria Industrial Area and the strengthening of Cuttack's hub for the filigree industry.

Individual opinions about Cuttack may vary, as some may love it while others may not, but one thing is certain: nobody can forget it. This city has been the birthplace and home to the maestros of Odia music and Odissi dance, who not only lived here but also significantly contributed to the promotion of these art forms. The unique "Sahi Culture" of Cuttack brings its residents together, transcending differences in caste or religion. A true "Kataki" (resident of Cuttack) never relocated to the new capital, Bhubaneswar. Cuttack holds a special place in the hearts of Odias, perhaps even more so than Kolkata does for Bengalis. My famous slogan always remains: "Long live Odisha and long live Cuttack!"

Family Get-together, December 9, 2013

Parents

I had a deep affection for both my parents. They were very precious to me, although I felt a stronger connection to my mother. Like my siblings, I referred to them as Baba and Maa. In my writing, I will always use these terms to address them. My father's name was Gokulananda, and my mother's name was Nirmala.

Father

Baba was born in October 1901 into a Zamindar family in the village of Kuanpal Pasulunda, located in the Cuttack district. His father, Udayanath, was a compassionate individual who cared for all the subjects (prajas) within his Zamindari. The Zamindari covered nearly thirty surrounding villages in the Pasulunda-Kuanpal region.

The Zamindari system originated during the Mughal period and persisted during the British Raj. Under this system, the Zamindar typically served as a prominent landlord in the area. They were appointed by the rulers and entrusted with the administration and tax collection of a specific set of villages. The local residents paid their taxes to the Zamindar, who, in turn, paid a portion of these collected taxes as royalties to the ruling authorities. This annual royalty payment was a fraction of the taxes collected and was submitted to the rulers upon demand.

A few years after Baba's birth, his sister Tulsi (Tuli) came into the world in 1903. Tragically, during Tulsi's birth, their mother passed away when Baba was just two years old. In 1905, my grandfather lost his Zamindari, which was a fate shared by many other Odia Zamindars in the Cuttack district. These unfortunate events were orchestrated by certain Bengali officials in the Revenue Department of the Calcutta Presidency. They falsely alleged that, despite several reminders sent to these Zamindars, they had not paid their royalties. These accusations were completely unfounded and untrue. These scheming officials managed to allocate these Zamindaris to individuals of their acquaintance through arranged auctions.

Udayanath, unable to cope with this dire situation, succumbed to it. He had lost his wife two years earlier, and now he had lost the Zamindari as well. He passed away prematurely in early 1906. At that time, Baba was just five years old, and his sister Tuli was only three. Consequently, both children had to reside in their large ancestral house with their aunt and other relatives.

The house was quite spacious and comprised several additional blocks attached to the main structure. These blocks were inhabited by distant relatives and farm laborers. There were also facilities like a cattle shed and a stable for the horses. The homestead itself occupied an area of approximately two acres.

Towards the rear of the house, there were extensive fruit orchards featuring various fruit-bearing trees such as mangoes, guavas, bael, bananas, coconuts, and other fruit-bearing trees and shrubs. The combined area of these orchards exceeded 18 acres. Furthermore, there was a two-acre bamboo plantation located along the Gobari rivulet. This bamboo plantation was primarily established for commercial purposes, as bamboo is commonly used in the village for repairing the thatched roofs of local houses.

In the vicinity of the house, spanning the front and other sides, there were more than forty acres of agricultural land used for cultivating crops like paddy and other crops.

Following the passing of their grandparents and the loss of the Zamindari, the family continued agricultural activities, particularly the cultivation of paddy and various other crops, through a sharecropping system known as "Bhaga Chasa." The income generated from these agricultural ventures was sufficient to maintain a comfortable rural lifestyle. However, the family consistently faced a shortage of liquid cash.

Baba's aunt (referred to as Dadi Ma), who was the spouse of Udayanath's elder cousin, played a significant role in the family and resided in the house. They cared for Baba and Tuli as if they were their own children, including Bira, who was a year younger than Baba. Baba spent the following six years growing up in this supportive environment.

As a child, Baba developed a deep fondness for birds, butterflies, and small animals. He would spend hours wandering through the orchards, eagerly searching for the nests of nightingales (bulbul), woodpeckers (katha hana), cockatoos (kakatua), and weaver birds (baya chadahi). Whenever he managed to catch these creatures, he would later release them after a day or two. Baba would often engage in spirited pursuits, such as chasing squirrels, rabbits, and mongooses in the village.

Unfortunately, there were no quality schools available in the vicinity of the village for his formal education. To bridge this gap, his uncle provided him with basic lessons in subjects like Odia, English, arithmetic, and more. During his early years, roughly between the ages of 7 and 10, Baba demonstrated a keen interest in his studies, alongside his passion for birds and animals.

Around that time, another uncle named Kinu, who resided in Dhenkanal, came to visit the village. Upon learning that there was no suitable school in the village to provide Baba with an education, Kinu made the decision to bring Baba with him to Dhenkanal. There, Baba would live with Kinu and attend the high school in Dhenkanal, marking the end of his close ties to the village. This significant change in his life would shape his future in profound ways.

Uncle Kinu and his wife had no children of their own, and they embraced Baba as if he were their own son. Surrounded by their genuine love and care, he managed to overcome the emotional wounds of parental loss and focus wholeheartedly on his studies. Despite starting his formal education later than most, Baba excelled academically, and at the age of 18, he successfully passed his matriculation examination in 1919. This examination was conducted by Patna University.

At that time, Dhenkanal did not offer opportunities for further college-level education. The nearest place to pursue higher studies was Cuttack, where the renowned educational institution Ravenshaw College had been established in 1868. Uncle Kinu was keen on providing Baba with a college education and shared that a relative of theirs had a house in Cuttack. This relative also held a position as a professor at Ravenshaw College. Learning of this opportunity, Baba became even more determined to pursue higher education.

The relative in question was named Artaballabh, and his residence was situated in the Sheikh Bazar area, near the Cuttack Chandi temple. Baba received his matriculation results in March 1919, and he had approximately three months before he could enrol in Cuttack College.

In mid-May 1919, Baba departed from Dhenkanal and arrived in Cuttack. Upon his arrival, he proceeded directly to Artaballabh's house and introduced himself, explaining the purpose of his visit. Artaballabh, the professor, inquired about Baba's matriculation marksheet. After reviewing the marks, the professor informed Baba that while admission to college was feasible, securing hostel accommodation for new admissions was challenging. He also pointed out that Cuttack was an expensive place to reside, and pursuing studies without access to affordable housing would be difficult.

In response, Baba proposed that he could support himself financially by offering private tutoring to schoolchildren in the mornings and evenings.

However, he needed a suitable place to live for this endeavour. He requested permission from the professor to stay in the outhouse of his residence, even offering to pay rent for the accommodations. Regrettably, the professor declined this request and instead advised Baba to seek a suitable position in one of the government departments, given his qualifications. This response left Baba deeply disheartened, as his aspirations for a college education were prematurely dashed.

After a span of thirty years, the same professor found himself in a position where he needed to request a favour from Baba based on their familial relationship. His son, Hemendra, who had received education abroad and was working as the Chief Engineer in the Odisha Irrigation Department, was facing imminent arrest by the Vigilance Department on charges of corruption. By that time, Baba had risen to the rank of senior officer, overseeing the district police.

Baba reached out to his friend, Sripati Nanda, who was the Superintendent of Police (SP) and in charge of the state's vigilance department. Through their collaboration, they managed to reduce the severity of Hemendra's charges on a technicality, leading to his honourable exoneration. In gratitude, both the father and son visited Baba to express their heartfelt thanks. Baba, always gracious, responded by emphasising that it was his duty to assist everyone, including family members. This episode highlights Baba's magnanimity and lack of resentment, serving as a form of poetic justice in the eyes of some.

Returning to the events of May 1919, Baba did not lose hope after being denied the opportunity for a college education. He possessed a resilient spirit and was determined to be self-reliant, forging his own path towards a promising and independent future. His determination paid off when he spotted an opportunity on the horizon. He successfully passed the recruitment examination for the police department, emerging as the top-ranked candidate. Among the successful candidates, the majority were graduates and intermediates. However, there was a twist in his success: Graduates were appointed to the position of Sub Inspector (SI), while non-graduates, like Baba, were appointed to the role of Assistant Sub Inspector (ASI).

The selected candidates were required to undergo a one-year training programme, and in August 1919, the entire batch was sent to Patna for their training. Upon the completion of their training, at the passing-out parade held in October 1920, Baba was honoured with the title of best cadet of the year. It was a remarkable birthday gift as he celebrated his 19th birthday.

Following his training, Baba was assigned to the Cuttack Police Lines in the role of an Assistant Sub Inspector (ASI). He was entrusted with the responsibility of overseeing the district armoury and also took charge of training newly recruited constables. In a short span of time, he earned a reputation as an exemplary figure among his peers. His keen attention to detail, ability to anticipate future events, and innovative ideas for the department earned him praise from juniors, colleagues, and superiors alike.

His passion for the English language and his avid interest in reading books and acquiring knowledge remained his most valuable assets throughout his life. While serving at Cuttack Police Lines, he had the opportunity to meet Mr. Clerici (IP), who held the position of Superintendent of Police (SP) in Cuttack. Clerici was deeply impressed by Baba and took special measures to ensure that he received a promotion to the rank of Sub-Inspector (SI) in less than three years. Subsequently, Mr. Clerici went on to become the head of the State Police (Inspector General, or IG) in 1945.

Baba was promoted to the rank of sub-inspector in June 1923. His posting was at Lal Bagh Police Station, located in Chandni Chowk, Cuttack. This police station held great significance as its jurisdiction covered most of the VIP areas of Cuttack. Situated opposite the Governor's House, it was also in close proximity to the offices of the District Magistrate, Superintendent of Police, and High Court. Additionally, it served as the primary policing presence in the main economic hub of Cuttack.

The Lal Bagh Police Station was managed by an inspector who oversaw two Sub-Inspectors (SIs), four Assistant Sub-Inspectors (ASIs), and 15 constables. The inspector had his residence on the eastern side of the station, adjoining the station's compound. There were two family quarters designated for the SIs as well as barracks for the rest of the staff, all of which were situated within the station's compound. On the western side, adjacent to the police station, was the Chandni Chowk Post Office.

While Baba held the position of third in command at the police station, he played a pivotal role. He successfully resolved numerous longstanding cases and achieved a significant breakthrough by apprehending the elusive Dacoit Kubera, who had evaded capture for over seven years. Baba not only arrested Kubera but also meticulously prepared a charge sheet to ensure his prosecution. Consequently, the dacoit was convicted and sentenced to life imprisonment.

He rarely spent much time at his residence, as he was primarily stationed at the police station. This dynamic officer, who remained a bachelor and was widely regarded as a man of impeccable character and integrity, became the subject of interest for fathers with eligible daughters. One such individual was Raju Babu, the postmaster of the Chandni Chowk Post Office. Raju Babu hailed from a former Zamindar family and was a native of the nearby village of Balipadia, situated close to Kuanpal Pasulunda. He had a daughter and a son. His son, Jogi, was older than his daughter, Nirmala. Both children would visit during holidays and stay with their father, whose residence was located within the post office compound adjacent to the police station. However, they primarily resided in their village home for their education.

Raju Babu was known for his sense of humour but also possessed a strong determination, which was a characteristic often associated with individuals from old Zamindar families. Eventually, he succeeded in his efforts to arrange the marriage between Nirmala and Baba in 1929. At that time, Nirmala (Maa) was only 15 years old, making her 13 years younger than Baba. She exhibited a very childlike demeanor. Following their marriage, she came to live with Baba in his residence at Lalbagh Police Station. Adjacent to their quarters was a Jamu Rola tree, bearing sweet and tasty fruit, which Nirmala would secretly climb to pick. Baba soon became aware of this childlike behaviour, and to instill some maturity and proper domestication in Nirmala, he brought Dada Maa from the village to stay with them for six months.

In 1930, Baba was transferred from Chandni Chowk Police Station to Cuttack Police Lines, where he assumed the position of a senior SI. His responsibilities included reorganising the police armoury and overseeing the newly recruited constabulary. These were significant tasks, and authorities believed that Baba was the right person for the job due to his prior experience and excellent work as an ASI at the same location. He demonstrated his competence and succeeded in these endeavours, with the systems he devised and implemented still being referenced to this day.

However, there was a challenge associated with this posting. There were no official quarters available for the person in charge. As a result, Baba had to rent a residence nearby. In Buxi Bazar, there was a double-story house, and its owners, an elderly couple, resided on the ground floor. They agreed to rent out the first floor to Baba and Maa.

The owner of the house was known as Kashim Saheb, and he belonged to the Suni Bohra Community. He had relocated to Cuttack from Bombay (Mumbai) with whatever remained of his wealth. In Bombay, he had been a prominent merchant who owned a couple of large dhows. Using these dhows, he conducted trade and exports with Arab countries. Kashim Saheb had a son, a daughter-in-law, and two grandchildren. On one occasion, his son, along with his wife and children, sailed on those dhows with merchandise destined for the Middle East. Unfortunately, a severe cyclonic sea storm struck during the journey, causing the ships to sink. All the passengers, along with the cargo, were lost at sea. This tragic event led Kashim Saheb and his wife to move to

Cuttack. They were a deeply religious and pious couple, and they developed a strong bond with Baba and Maa. Perhaps they saw a connection between their late son's family and Baba's family. For the next ten years, until 1940, when he was promoted and transferred, this house became the residence of Baba and his family. Many cherished memories and significant events were associated with this house.

In this residence, the first child of the family came into the world. My eldest sister, Promila, was the initial addition to the family, born here in 1931. Approximately a year and a half later, a son joined the family, but sadly, he lived only for a few months. The loss of this child deeply saddened both Maa and Baba. To cope with their grief, they resorted to fasting and continuous prayers at temples, with a particular focus on the Cuttack Chandi temple.

Their sorrow eventually came to an end with my birth in early 1935. They considered me a divine gift from Goddess Chandi and named me Chandidas, signifying my role as a servant of the goddess. To ensure my well-being as I grew up, they hired a 14-year-old helper named Ramesh to look after me.

Ramesh remained a part of our family for six years, until we relocated from Cuttack. Baba took it upon himself to help Ramesh secure a job with the owner of a renowned sweet shop known as Purna Chandra Mistan Bhandar. Over time, Ramesh became well-known for making the sweet son papdi and even started his own business selling it. In 1951, he visited our home and treated me to his deliciously prepared son papdi.

On April 1, 1936, Odisha was officially separated from Bihar and established as an independent province. Consequently, Baba became a member of the Odisha Police, and the "Bihar" affiliation was removed from the cadre.

In our Buxi Bazar residence, my second sister, Urmila, was born in October 1939. When she was just over a year old, Baba received a promotion to the rank of inspector and was transferred from Cuttack to Angul in late 1940.

Angul, located 60 miles (96 kilometres) away from Cuttack, was known for having the largest coal reserves in Odisha. It had a notably hot climate compared to Cuttack. To combat the intense summer heat, most houses in the area had thatched roofs. Even Baba's official bungalow, which was quite spacious, had a thatched roof with false ceilings underneath.

The township of Angul, being close to dense forests and the gorge of the 'Saat Koshia Ganda' in the Mahanadi River, attracted a variety of wildlife during the night. The region also had a significant population of snakes, including the venomous 'Chiti Sapa' (common Indian Krait), which often inhabited the roofs of the thatched houses in Angul. Baba's bungalow was no exception in this regard.

The police station where Baba served as the in-charge was located nearby. Most of the staff at this station were from the western region of Odisha, with one exception: SI Gyana Babu, who was originally from Cuttack. Gyana Babu held the second-highest position at the police station but was not particularly competent, which added to Baba's workload.

Gyana Babu's ineffectiveness in field investigations meant that Baba often had to travel outside of Angul. In an effort to reduce the delays and travel time, Baba purchased a new motorcycle during one of his visits to Cuttack. However, Maa had reservations about the bike due to concerns for Baba's safety. She tried to persuade him to sell the motorcycle, and when he didn't heed her advice, she became so angry that she severely damaged the fuel tank of the bike by striking it forcefully. This marked the end of the 'Motorcycle Saga.'

In Angul, Dada Maa came to stay for a few months as Maa was expecting her fourth child. My brother, Durgadas, was born in January 1941. About a year after his birth, Baba received a transfer to Jeypore, a town located in the Koraput district. Koraput is a hilly region that includes parts of the Eastern Ghats and shares its border with Andhra Pradesh. During this time, the area had become a focal point for armed tribal groups that were inspired by the freedom movement of the era. The British government aimed to deploy capable police personnel in these areas to effectively manage the situations. This was the reason behind Baba's transfer from Angul to Jeypore within two years.

Baba initiated the move from Angul to Jeypore in early 1942. Jeypore was a considerable distance away, and the journey could only be made via long and challenging road travel. Transporting a family of six, including a one-year-old child, was not an easy task. Baba planned the journey meticulously, with two short breaks of a day each before reaching the district headquarters in Koraput. He also arranged for the family to rest for three more days upon reaching Koraput. The journey covered the Dandakaranya area, passing through Nayagarh, Phulbani, and other treacherous terrains. Dense forests, teeming with wildlife, including tigers, deer, and elephants, covered a significant portion of the travel route.

The family's first stop was at Tapta Pani, a location known for its hot water spring, near Nayagarh. They spent the night at a government Dak bungalow there. Their second break was at a place between Nayagarh and Koraput, although the exact name of this place seems to have escaped my memory. Early the following morning, the family embarked on a nearly five-hundred-kilometre journey that took almost twelve hours to reach Koraput.

Upon arriving in Koraput, they headed to the Government Circuit House for a three-day stay. The next morning, Baba visited the office of Mr. Smith, who served as the Superintendent of Police (SP) for the Koraput district. During their meeting, Baba informed Smith that he would be going to Jeypore to assume his post in two days. Smith provided Baba with information regarding crime and other relevant activities in the district that were of concern to the police. He also sought Baba's insights on important matters. Smith was highly impressed by Baba's responses, particularly regarding the remedial actions that the department needed to take to address these issues.

There was an immediate and positive connection between Baba and Smith, reminiscent of his previous British supervisor, Clerici. This rapport remained strong throughout Baba's tenure in Jeypore and continued beyond. Following their meeting, Smith suggested that Baba return to the Circuit House for lunch with his family and also recommended showing them the picturesque locations in Koraput. The family had the opportunity to appreciate the natural beauty of the hills, valleys, and plantations that adorned the town.

Koraput, both in the past and at present, is a splendid town. From the Circuit House, I had a view of the lush surroundings. Vast expanses of dense forests stretched out for miles and miles. The Circuit House was situated atop an elevated platform on a hillock. The town was encircled by interconnected layers of hills, many of which featured extensive coffee plantations.

Seeing such plantations for the first time filled me with excitement. Among these hills, one could also spot a few small waterfalls. The pure air and the refreshing breeze that persisted throughout the day were revitalizing. Baba informed the children that Odia poet Radhanath Ray had described Koraput as a poet's dream, the finest citadel.

During those days, travelling from Koraput to Jeypore was not as convenient as it is today, thanks to the construction of National Highway 26 (NH 26). Back then, one had to navigate the treacherous Sunki-Salur ghat road, which was quite perilous and sent shivers down the spine throughout the journey.

I can vividly recall my initial impression of that time. The ghat road was so narrow and elevated that looking down from it sent chills down the spines of travellers. It was an exhausting journey, taking four to five hours to cover the distance to Jeypore at snail's pace. This experience remains stored in my memory, especially when I consider how easily people can travel on that route today.

Another noticeable feature of those ghat roads was the type of passenger buses in operation. These buses were open, with only railings enclosing the seating area on all three sides. They had a metal roof on top and a front windshield for the driver. These buses ran on coal gas, and during the entire journey, a helper at the rear continuously operated a hand-driven centrifugal pump that emitted a humming sound to supply the necessary fuel.

Upon their arrival in Jeypore, Baba and his family were greeted by the police station staff, who escorted them to the official residence of the inspector. The entrance to the house from the main road was connected via a culvert. The house itself was quite spacious and had a sizable compound that extended to the police station's compound. Baba would frequently walk down to the police station and spend long hours assessing various situations.

During this period, the Non-Cooperation movement of 1942 was in full swing, and its impact on the area's law-and-order situation was quite evident. It became Baba's primary duty to maintain control, particularly in dealing with the activities of agitating mobs. As a response to these circumstances, additional armed constabulary forces were deployed to control violent protests, a measure typically reserved for district headquarters. However, due to the unique situation at that time, a portion of these forces were temporarily stationed in Jeypore.

The government regarded this area as a potential hotspot for violent protests that needed to be controlled, even if it meant resorting to the use of firearms. This assessment by the government was accurate, and it was also corroborated by Baba. Smith, the Superintendent of Police (SP) in Koraput, maintained regular communication with Baba and sought daily updates on the situation.

Baba consistently carried out his official duties in accordance with both work ethics and personal principles. Despite having a sympathetic disposition towards the freedom struggle, he never allowed this sentiment to interfere with his commitment to fulfilling his official responsibilities in accordance with government guidelines and the directives of his superiors. In retrospect, I came to understand that this quality is a hallmark of all honest and principled officers who refrain from abusing their authority due to personal biases.

The critical moment arrived in Jeypore when a large group of protesters surrounded the police station, intent on setting it ablaze. Inside the police station, there was a sense of unease among those present, including the magistrate, the armed constabulary, and numerous constables armed with batons. They anticipated that Baba would order the use of firearms to quell the situation. However, Baba, armed with a well-thought-out strategy and unwavering mental resolve, had a different plan in mind. He instructed his personnel that, upon hearing a blank shot from his revolver, they should initiate a heavy lathi charge.

Despite the discouragement of others who advised him against approaching the agitators, Baba stepped outside and engaged them with a resounding voice. Maintaining eye contact with their leaders, he questioned why they were resorting to violence when their national leader, Gandhi, advocated nonviolence. He conveyed his reluctance to harm anyone but made it clear that if they persisted in breaking the law, he would not hesitate to use force. The agitated crowd began to calm down, although they did not disperse entirely. After a few minutes, Baba fired a blank shot from his revolver, signalling the commencement of the lathi charge. This effectively dispersed the crowd, and the situation was brought under control, eventually returning to normalcy.

There were several instances of a similar nature, occurring two or three times. However, crowd dispersal always took place without resorting to firing or causing fatalities. In one of these incidents, during a lathi charge, some of the agitators sought refuge under the culvert near Baba's official residence in an attempt to escape the beatings. I observed that the orderly constable on duty at the house managed to catch the two of them. He gave them a sound thrashing after tying them to a post. I, too, gave them a few blows. When Baba returned home, he released them, and no charges were filed against the duo.

Following the conclusion of the agitation, Baba was honoured with the prestigious Imperial Police Medal in 1943 for his courageous actions. In that year, a significant portion of the recipients in India earned this medal through encounters that resulted in casualties among agitators. Mr. Smith held Baba in high regard due to his effectiveness, integrity, and dedication to his duties. He also noted that no other police officer enjoyed such extensive public trust. Baba received unwavering support from his superior. Both Mr. and Mrs. Smith visited Jeypore personally to express their gratitude. They were treated to a delightful lunch prepared by Maa at their residence. Baba's reputation within the department was so exceptional that securing early promotions became his strength.

As anticipated, in June 1945, Baba received a promotion to the position of Deputy Superintendent of Police (Dy. SP) and was transferred from Jeypore to Cuttack. Prior to his promotion, my youngest sister was born in April 1944 in Jeypore, and she was named Lakshmi. It was believed that her birth brought prosperity to the family, which seemed to be confirmed by Baba's subsequent promotion.

Baba arrived in Cuttack in July 1945, and since there were no official quarters available, he rented a spacious house in Mohamadia Bazar. This house was situated near the intersection of Chandni Chowk Road and Kathgadia Sahi Road. It was in this house that Chandi learned how to ride a bicycle on these very roads.

Upon his arrival in Cuttack, Baba resumed his duties. His office was situated in the same building as the office of the Superintendent of Police (SP) of Cuttack, near the Kathjori River bank. This building was an integral part of the main administrative complex for Cuttack district. As always, Baba was deeply engrossed in his work, leaving home at 0930 hours in the morning and returning late, often around 2200 hours.

In July 1945, I was enrolled in Class VI at PM Academy School in Cuttack. My admission was based on the school transfer certificate from the government High School in Jeypore, where I had completed classes IV and V. I used to walk to school in Cuttack, which was approximately 2.5 kilometres away from our house. I spent a year at this school and successfully completed Class VI in July 1946. To facilitate this, I had to stay alone for three months (May, June, and July) with Bata Babu, who was a trusted associate of Baba and had previously worked under his supervision in Angul. This arrangement was necessitated by Baba's unexpected transfer.

After serving in Cuttack for just ten months, Baba received a transfer to Balasore in May 1946. This transfer came at a time when World War II was still ongoing. Following Japanese bombings in the vicinity of Balasore, the order for Baba's transfer was swiftly issued. He had to relocate immediately with our family and commence his duties in Balasore.

His official residence in Balasore was quite spacious, featuring a substantial compound with numerous fruit trees and an attached porch to the main house. Additionally, there was a large shed or stable for cows and horses on the premises. The main entrance of the house's compound opened onto a road parallel to the main road leading to the railway station, situated around fifty feet to the south.

I eventually reunited with the family at the end of July. I enrolled in Balasore Zila School, starting in class VII. The school was located three kilometres away from our residence, and I would often go there on foot. Sometimes, the home orderly constable would give me a ride to school on his bicycle. After persistently requesting a bicycle of my own, one was purchased for me when I advanced to class VIII. By that time, I had also earned the title of District Athletic Champion. Balasore holds a special place in my memories due to numerous unforgettable incidents, which I will describe later in this book.

Following the end of World War II on September 2, 1945, rumours of Indian independence filled the air. With the Labour Party taking power in England in 1946, British Prime Minister Clement Attlee made a significant announcement regarding Indian independence. It was slated to occur within a year and a half, leading to various administrative changes throughout India. This was also one of the reasons for Baba's early transfer from Cuttack to Balasore, where he remained until his next promotion in 1948.

During the period leading up to independence, state assembly elections were conducted, resulting in the formation of a Congress government under Harekrushna Mahatab. Following India's independence on August 15, 1947, efforts were initiated to integrate the princely states, a process that unfolded in 1948. This integration made Odisha a larger state, necessitating the creation of eight additional districts. Consequently, more administrative positions were required at the top level in all districts.

To facilitate promotions within the state cadre and selections for All India Services, both the Departmental Promotion Committee (DPC) and the UPSC selection committee were activated. Baba was approved by the DPC for consideration by the UPSC for promotion to the next rank of Superintendent of Police (SP) within the Indian Police Service (IPS) cadre.

He was scheduled to appear before the UPSC in Bhubaneswar for his interview. Some members of the committee were hesitant to allow Baba to participate in the interview because he lacked a formal degree. However, Mr. Clerici, who served as the head of the state police (IG) and was also a member of the UPSC committee, firmly advocated for Baba's inclusion. He emphasised that he had observed Baba's performance since his entry into the police department in 1921. Clerici highlighted Baba's knowledge, understanding, and clarity of thought, which he believed made him one of the finest officers in the state. He argued that many graduates couldn't match Baba's capabilities and suggested that the committee should assess him during the interview before making a decision.

As a result, Baba went on to appear for his interview and left a strong impression on all the committee members. They were so impressed with his performance that he received unanimous praise and a high rating for selection. Baba was officially inducted into the Indian Police Service (IPS) cadre in February 1948. This may have been a unique and possibly the first and last occasion in all of India where an individual with a matriculation qualification was selected for a prestigious All-India Central Services Grade One position (IPS).

Following his selection, he was assigned to the role of Superintendent of Police and transferred to Keonjhar. In February 1948, he assumed his new position, taking over from NK Ray (IP), who had joined the Imperial Police (IP) cadre in 1945 before India's independence. NK Ray was the son of BK Ray, who served as the Chief Justice of the Odisha High Court at that time. Baba moved to Keonjhar with his family, except for me. I remained in a hostel to complete my eighth-grade studies.

The Superintendent of Police's (SP) residence in Keonjhar was quite impressive and spacious. It had previously served as the residence of the Dewan of the Keonjhar King. Situated along the main road leading to the palace, the SP's bungalow featured a large compound. The front of the bungalow had a well-maintained lawn with flower beds, while the rear portion boasted a substantial area filled with various fruit trees. Beyond the rear compound, extensive agricultural lands stretched out, bordered by dense forests and lush green hills. On the opposite side of the road, about three hundred metres away, stood the residence of the King's younger brother, known as the Kothi. A bit further from the Kothi was the bungalow of the District Magistrate (DM), who would join the district a few days later. It was only later on that his family became connected to mine through my wife's family.

In April 1948, Baba acquired his first vehicle while stationed in Keonjhar. It was a Ford V8 station wagon, obtained through an auction of vehicles that once belonged to the former Maharaja (King) of Keonjhar. The purchase price was three thousand rupees, and an additional fifteen hundred rupees were invested in modifying and upgrading the vehicle. This station wagon remained in use until 1952 when it was replaced by a new Ford Zephyr car.

Upon my return from Balasore in June 1948, after successfully completing my eighth-grade examination, I was thrilled to see the station wagon. It was accompanied by a police havaldar driver named Gajapati Singh, who was a Sikh, and four home orderly constables, which was in line with the entitlement for the position of SP.

Driver Gajapati, unlike the typical image of Sikhs, was small in stature and appeared fragile. It was known that he had migrated to Keonjhar from Patiala with his parents. Their move was associated with the entourage accompanying the princess, who was the daughter of the King of Patiala after her marriage to the King of Keonjhar. The Keonjhar King and the Princess of Patiala had crossed paths while studying in London. At the age of fourteen, I had the opportunity to learn the basics of driving a car from Driver Gajapati.

During this time, Baba was deeply engrossed in the establishment of new police stations and enhancing the capabilities of existing ones throughout the district. This necessitated long tours for inspection and oversight. His absence from home was felt by the family, and there was no alternative but to endure it.

Baba, as a loving and affectionate husband and father, frequently organised family outings to scenic locations to keep the family in high spirits. The district boasted several beautiful tourist destinations, and the family explored these places of interest using their newly acquired vehicle.

Gaja was the one behind the wheel during these trips to various destinations. Some of the noteworthy places we visited included the Ghatagaon Tarini Temple, Sanaghagara Falls, Gonasika Temple, Baldevjew Temple, Khandadhar Waterfall, and many others. The renowned Maa Tarini is considered an incarnation of the goddess Durga. Gonasika is the place where the Baitarani River originates, and Khandadhar is the twelfth-highest waterfall in India, with water cascading from a height of over five hundred feet. These experiences left a lasting, magical impression!

In June 1948, I began my studies in Class IX at Gibson High School in Keonjhar. This was a coeducational institution. My younger sister, Urmila, also enrolled in Class IV at the same school. However, within a year, as they progressed to their next classes, both of them had to bid farewell to this school due to Baba's transfer from Keonjhar to Bolangir in May 1949.

The official residence in Bolangir, although spacious, lacked the aesthetic appeal and layout of the one in Keonjhar. It featured a large courtyard with a central well, and the main building connected to a section containing a store, kitchen, and servants' quarters. Next door was the residence of Bolangir DSP Gadanayak, who was nearing retirement. The main road was situated approximately five to six feet higher than the ground level of both houses.

Baba assumed his duties in Bolangir district in June 1949. I enrolled in class X at PRHE School Bolangir, while my sister Urmila joined class V at Bolangir Girls School. During our journey to Bolangir via Cuttack, Maa brought along her brother's daughter, Pari, who was nearly the same age as Pramila. Maa's intention was that she would give a company to Pramila. Pari, like Pramila, had discontinued her education after completing Class VII, a common occurrence among girls in conservative Odia families during that era. However, Baba later ensured that this did not happen to my other two sisters, despite Maa's conservatism.

In January 1950, Baba and Maa travelled to Cuttack for a three-day annual conference. This left the six children, including Pari, alone with the orderly constables responsible for their meals and care. On the second day of their parents' absence, there was a slight rainfall during the night, leaving the courtyard wet and slippery. While Pramila was on her way to the storeroom to fetch some food, she slipped on the wet courtyard and fell into the well, emitting a loud cry and a heavy thud.

All the children, along with the orderly constables and Gadanayak Babu, immediately rushed to the well. Taking Pramila out from the well proved to be a challenging task. She had lost consciousness as her head had struck the well's side rings. Fortunately, the well had relatively little water, preventing her from drowning. However, the impact on her head had a severe effect on her brain. This incident left an indelible scar on the family, particularly the parents, haunting them endlessly throughout their lives. Pramila's lifelong struggles became an unbearable burden for the entire family, especially her parents.

I completed my classes X and XI, and Urmila finished her classes V and VI by the end of 1951. Following my successful test examination in class XI, I was eligible to sit for the Matriculation Examination of Utkal University, which was scheduled for February or March 1951. However, due to Baba's transfer, my examination centre was changed from Bolangir to Cuttack. In January 1951, Baba was reassigned as SP to Cuttack and relocated with the family. Back in Bolangir, the family had employed a maid named Shankari and a servant named Keshav, both of whom also moved to Cuttack.

Shankari remained with the family for the entirety of my parents' lives, providing significant assistance and service until Maa's last moments. However, Keshav's tenure was relatively short. When Shankari declined his marriage proposal, he decided to leave his job.

Baba served as SP of Cuttack for three years, from 1951 until the end of 1953. In the subsequent two years, 1954 and 1955, he held the position of SP in Balasore district. His final phase of service was as the SP of Mayurbhanj district, with its headquarters in Baripada. During his time in Baripada, he oversaw the construction of a large and splendid Shiva temple at Baripada Police Lines.

During his postings at different places in varied posts, he was very popular among the public. People had never seen before a police officer so dedicated to his service responsibility. He was a police officer who was honest to the core; a police officer who was always ready to extend friendly assistance to victims; a police officer who disciplined his juniors and inculcated in them the spirit of service and true help for the public.

Baba retired in October 1958. Before that, during the years 1956 and 1957, he had built a bungalow for the family at Cuttack. The house was on a plot of one acre. The boundary of the plot touched the embankment of the Mahanadi River at Tulsipur, a locality of Cuttack city.

It was a posh neighbourhood in the city. The house's layout closely resembled that of the SP Cuttack bungalow, where he and his family had resided for three years. He had arranged for a coal wagon to deliver bricks for the construction of the house. At the back of the property, a section of land was excavated to create a pond, which also supplied soil for the bricks. This pond was intended to serve as a water source for irrigating the vegetable garden and for potential fish farming in the future. Baba had a knack for making the most of his limited resources, always striving to provide maximum comfort for the family at minimal cost. The house was completed by the end of the first quarter of 1958.

Following Baba's retirement, the family permanently relocated to the house in mid-November 1958. The front of the house featured a spacious area adorned with extensive flower beds. On both sides of the pathway leading from the front gate to the car porch, there were diverse flowering plants such as Kerata (Plumeria), Ganga siuli (Coral Jasmine), Golap (Rose), Jai Phula (Daisy), and others. Towards the rear of the property, in addition to the pond with fish and vegetable gardens, there was a substantial collection of fruit trees, including mango, guava, jackfruit, papaya, plantain, and elephant apple. A small room at the back provided a resting place for the gardener during breaks from his daily work.

Baba added a second floor to the house in 1965, and it closely resembled the main block on the first floor. The house also became the venue for the solemnisation of important family events, including the marriages of both daughters, Urmila (in 1961) and Lakshmi (in 1971), as well as the marriages of both sons, Chandi (in 1963) and Durgadas (in 1973).

Following the completion of my higher education at Allahabad University, I returned to this house in March 1959, although my stay here was brief. I relocated to Balasore for a few months to take up my first job as a lecturer in the Odisha Education Service. Meanwhile, my younger brother, Durgadas, continued to reside with our parents in Cuttack, providing me with peace of mind regarding our parents' well-being as long as he remained there.

Following the marriages of all their children, the parents fulfilled their family responsibilities. However, due to her brain injury, their eldest daughter, Pramila, had no choice but to continue living with her parents. Her condition brought ongoing pain, sorrow, and stress to Baba and Maa. Additionally, a relative living with them added to the family's stress.

Suddenly, Baba became highly stressed due to a family matter, and this stress triggered a stroke in 1979, causing him to fall into a coma. After 24 hours, he was revived from the coma, but it was evident that he had lost his ability to speak and was paralysed on one side. During this critical time, I was posted in Bhubaneswar, and I had left for Bombay with my family a day before this incident occurred, taking advantage of the Leave Travel Concession (LTC) and travelling by car.

Upon receiving the news of Baba's stroke upon my arrival after a three-day road journey, my family and I immediately began our journey back the next morning. Once back in Cuttack, I arranged for a nurse and had Baba's condition examined by the top neurologist at Cuttack Medical College. I made sure to be by Baba's side almost every day, travelling daily from Bhubaneswar in the afternoon. This continued until 1981, when Baba miraculously regained his speech and recovered from the paralysis, thanks to the neurologist's efforts and Baba's strong determination.

During my posting in Bhubaneswar from 1974 to 1983, I regularly sent my car to Cuttack to bring Baba and Maa to Bhubaneswar once or twice a month. However, they always preferred to return to their house in Tulsipur due to their deep attachment to it.

Rashmi and I, along with our three children, Mona, Dimpy, and Dev, used to visit Baba and Maa every weekend, spending the night at the Tulsipur house. These were the happiest moments for my wife and me, and our children have lasting memories of the boundless love and affection they received from their grandparents.

In July 1983, I received a transfer to Lucknow after nearly nine years in Odisha. My parents were deeply saddened upon hearing the news of my transfer. It was the first time in my life that I saw tears in Baba's eyes.

Three months later, Baba suffered another stroke and passed away, leaving this mortal world forever. Thus, the life of a saintly man who had endeared himself to all during his lifetime came to an end. His departure left a void in the lives of all family members that could never be filled, and the grief remained constant. For Maa, it was an immeasurable loss, as she had lost her loving companion of 58 years. My mourning for Baba will persist until my last breath.

In his memory, I wrote a few lines in the form of an Ode:

To Baba - An Ode

At an early age, he lost his parent
And matured amidst ample diversity
Amongst all his kin, he couldn't connect
But bravely endured fate's adversity.

Began his studies in a small town,
Full of foliage and chirping birds.
Nature's scenes never frowned.
Days in school had finally passed.

He, a lonely circumspect teenager,
His own destiny bravely charted.
Barriers crossed without any fear,
God bestowed on him a modest start.

Hope became his only companion.
He espoused the saga of simplicity.
The poor were his hub's champion;
Never would he pamper a celebrity.

Truth and honesty, he never shook.
Criminals—he would quickly book.
Innocent—protected without fear.
The primacy of justice remained dear.

Life was an open book without cess
Strongest tool was fairness,
Always had the fairest look.
Cancers of society, he would hook.

Immensely loved his dearest family;
Like a cocoon, shielded them totally.
Dictums ensured courage for death.
Provision for justice wasn't a myth.

Children grew and found their way.
Baba never remained too far away
Blessings ensure total protection;
No scope of filial love for detection.

Kaleidoscopic Life

Forever he was like a saintly hermit,
Had no place for mundane pleasure.
Anger of others that could never hit
Or break his mind's strongest cover.

Let the lord fondly keep and rest his soul;
Lasting abundant peace be the goal,
His story of life remains an ideal.
Be bacon of inspiration to people all.

Mother

Maa, whose name was Nirmala, was born on a Kumar Purnima day in October 1914 at their ancestral home in Balipadia village. This day was considered highly auspicious in accordance with the Odia calendar (Madala Panji) and the prevailing customs of that era. Her family belonged to the old aristocracy of Zamindars and was renowned for their benevolence in their area and the neighbouring villages.

However, by the time she was born, their Zamindari had already been seized by unscrupulous individuals based in Calcutta, a fate similar to that of my paternal grandfather. Nirmala's maternal grandfather and her family had to rely on the income from their landed property. To supplement this income, he took up government service in the postal department.

Nirmala was the younger of two siblings, with an elder brother who was three years older than her. As the youngest and only daughter, her parents showered her with abundant love and granted her complete freedom from a very young age. During those times, granting freedom to a girl child or providing her with an education was more of an exception than the norm. Such progressive actions were not tolerated in the conservative society. However due to her father's prominent social standing, no one in the village dared object to the way Maa was raised.

As a result, Maa enjoyed her childhood thoroughly. She displayed a rather tomboyish demeanor in her attitude, clothing, and activities, which even included climbing fruit trees. She received her initial education up to class V in a nearby "Minor School," where classes extended up to class VII. However, she later moved to Cuttack, where her father was posted, and completed her remaining education in classes VI and VII.

Her father had been promoted to the position of Senior Post Master by then and was in charge of a larger post office, namely the Chandni Chowk Post Office in Cuttack. Interestingly, at that time, it was the second-largest post office in Odisha, second only to the Buxi Bazar Post Office in Cuttack.

Her formal education came to an end after she completed Class VII like that of many girls from affluent backgrounds during that era. However, her pursuit of knowledge continued within the confines of her home. She immersed herself in the study of various sacred Hindu scriptures, sparking an early passion for religion. In the subsequent years, she dedicated a minimum of three hours every day to religious worship in the puja room at home.

Following the customs of the time, Maa was married off at a tender age, just 15 years old, in the year 1929. After her marriage, she had to relocate to Baba's official residence, as mentioned earlier, which was situated within the premises of the Lalbagh Police Station in Cuttack.

Adjacent to their residence, there stood a fruit tree known locally as "Jamu Rola." In English, it bore the name "Tree of Green Water Apple." This tree was laden with an abundance of delicious fruits, and it captured Maa's heart, for she still retained a childlike spirit within her. The tree became her primary target for her climbing antics, a skill she had perfected on many trees around her village home.

Despite her marriage and her transition into a demure bride, she couldn't suppress her tomboyish desire to climb trees at that time. With persistent persuasion from her father, Baba, and Dada, Maa finally gave up her tomboyish habit. She ultimately embraced her role as a coy bride, bringing a great relief and putting an end to any embarrassment for Baba.

She swiftly acquired the skills necessary for managing household affairs and became adept at preparing delicious dishes. This marked the beginning of her renowned culinary prowess, as she learned to prepare a wide variety of foods.

Maa welcomed her first child, Pramila, into the world in 1931. Her second child, a son, was born in 1933, but unfortunately, he passed away after only a few months. The loss of her son deeply affected her, leading her to become profoundly religious during this period. Alongside her newfound piety, she also developed a 'quicksilver temper', a characteristic that would persist in her behaviour throughout her life. Everyone, including Baba, held a certain fear of her temper and carefully avoided provoking her when she was in anger, as she seemed like a completely different person during those moments.

Maa's world revolved around love, affection, concern, welfare, and care for only six individuals: her husband and her five children. Despite occasional disagreements, Baba always viewed her as his primary source of strength. He held her in high regard for her simplicity, her boundless care for the family, and her ability to manage the household and family with limited financial resources. She had a remarkable talent for budgeting and ensuring that neither her children nor her husband felt the constraints of their financial situation. She seemed like a financial wizard when it came to managing the household finances.

Baba would be deeply moved at the sight of tears in her eyes, and he consistently made every effort to bring her comfort and happiness throughout their entire life together. They were a couple perfectly matched in compatibility and boundless love for each other. Their children had never witnessed their father raising his voice against Maa, and they also observed the anguish their mother experienced when their father fell ill or was overwhelmed by the pressures of work.

Maa had an abundance of love for her family and excelled as a housewife and household manager. She was incredibly possessive, not only about her children but also about her husband. At times, her possessiveness towards her husband bordered on embarrassment at social gatherings, especially when other women were present. However, her heart was pure, and she had unwavering faith in her husband. This possessiveness was the primary reason for limiting the family's social interactions.

The family didn't have much time for socialising due to Baba's work-related pressures. His dedication to his duties left limited room for social activities. Maa, too, avoided mingling with people, even distant relatives. This avoidance might have stemmed from her marriage at a young age, which left her feeling insecure despite her husband's loving and protective nature. As the years passed and she was surrounded by her five children, she became more caring, composed, and calm. She never made anyone feel neglected, and her attachment to her children was so strong that no one dared mistreat any child for their wrongdoings.

Her husband, an honest and upright police officer, earned an income that was not sufficient to provide a comfortable life for the family in relative terms. Managing the household with this income and ensuring her children never felt discomfort was nothing short of a miracle. However, Maa performed this miracle day in and day out. In the drama of life, she was a courageous, inspiring, and beloved true companion to Baba.

Maa's culinary skills knew no bounds. Her dishes and cuisine bore the skilled touch of her hands. The variety of dishes and the *pithas* she prepared were so delectable and flavourful that they were beyond imagination. I could never taste such delicacies elsewhere. The children eagerly awaited festivals because it meant they could devour the various *pithas* prepared by Maa on such occasions. Moreover, every child's birthday would turn into a festive celebration filled with delicious dishes and a joyous, caring spirit. All her grandchildren had immense love for her.

Similar to Baba, Maa always showed great concern for her eldest daughter, Pramila. Both parents showered equal love and affection on all their children without any discrimination, making it a harmonious and loving family.

After Baba's retirement in 1958, the family moved from Baripada to Cuttack and settled into their new house. During these fifteen years, until 1973, when all their children got married, significant changes occurred in the surroundings of their house. A substantial portion of the rear land was sold to finance the marriages of their two daughters. The rear pond and the land used for vegetable cultivation were sold to new owners. The total compound where the house stood was reduced from an acre to less than half an acre. Additionally, several acres of village land and orchards were also sold for the same reason. The loss of landed property and the use of Baba's Provident Fund did not sit well with him. On top of this, there was the commutation of his pension after retirement, which added to Baba's financial burdens. Durgadas' income seemed to primarily support his own family's needs and did not significantly contribute to household expenses. I was posted outside Odisha and did provide some financial assistance to my parents to the best of my ability, even at the cost of sacrificing some of my own family's needs. This provided a bit of relief and comfort to my parents, but life at home continued to be worrisome due to financial constraints and certain family members' behaviour.

As the tension escalated within his home, Baba suffered a fatal second stroke that ended his life on August 10, 1983. This was a devastating blow for Maa, and it triggered severe arthritic attacks. I tried to persuade and motivate her to come and live with me in New Delhi, but she consistently refused, using excuses such as the need to care for Pramila. She was accustomed to living in a larger, independent place like a bungalow, and the idea of living in a flat in Delhi seemed daunting to her. Even after Pramila's death in 1987, she remained unwilling to move and cited her attachment to Baba's memories in the Cuttack house.

After Baba's passing, she continued to live for another 17 years. Her life was consistently lonely and filled with sadness. Despite the presence of Durgadas and his family, she often felt isolated and uncared for. Her sole companion, until her last breath in that house, was the maid Shankari. During my frequent visits to see Maa, I noticed her sitting for hours on the front verandah, staring blankly at the front gate of the compound. It appeared as if she were waiting for Baba, a sight that often brought tears to my eyes.

I made several requests to my brother to spend more time with Maa and engage in conversations to lift her spirits. It appeared that Arun, Durgadas's son, often brought her joy during his visits from Bhubaneswar. Arun had a deep affection for his grandmother, and during that time, he was pursuing his post-graduate studies.

During the last two years of her life, she became completely bedridden and developed bedsores, which led to septicemia, an extremely painful condition. Her suffering finally came to an end in the year 2000. Rashmi and I travelled from Delhi and were by her side during the last week of her life. It seemed as though she had been waiting for me before taking her final breath!

Her passing was an immense emotional ordeal for me. I found it impossible to contain my emotions and wept profusely. Filled with profound sorrow, I conducted her cremation at Puri's "Swarga Dwara." With Maa's departure, an era came to a close. Losing my parents was the most significant blow to the happiness, unity, and zest for life within my family. Rashmi and the children were utterly devastated. Even after returning to New Delhi, my eyes frequently welled up as I remembered Maa. She held the deepest love for me among all her children and was the one closest to my heart among all other family members. During this period of mourning, I composed a heartfelt ode to express my emotions for Maa and convey what she meant to me.

An Ode To Maa

Holding your finger, I learnt to walk,
And your voice inspired me to talk.
Seeing the sweet smile on your face,
My pleasure glowed in total solace.

Wiped my tears to drive fears away.
A look of yours gave me the strength.
Passage of time not able to destroy
All the facets of my dear mother's faith.

Kaleidoscopic Life

Time's tyranny has not diminished.
The memory of the concern does chime.
Endearing affection never finished,
Nor it vanished with the tide of time.

Sadly, I recall your persistent denial
To being near me with your cool stay.
Liked not the place of my duty's call,
Failed to put your objections away.

I missed your smile and patience.
We all missed your loving company,
My wife was depressed in your absence
Life was an opera without a symphony.

Work and my life's varied tasks vilified
And kept me away; Mom couldn't come.
The wish of Dad, I could not fructify;
She refused to leave her old home.

Years after years it continued to roll,
Many visits of mine only to see her.
Looking at her would make the happy tears fall;
Love for my dear mom grew further.

A severe cyclone once beat our town,
My presence there was consolation.
Storm awaiting her life yet unknown,
I bid her adieu unaware of the transition.

In a few months, her end appeared sure.
I had to return to our ancestral home.
She was lying in pain, full of bedsores.
Her look at me gave the sign of welcome.

The physical pain in her last few days,
She suffered it all with heroic grace.
In her, I watched life's flickering rays,
Holding my hand, she was in trance.

She could not gauge the tears I shed.
Spirit was passing her sorrowing son,
Grief for all, as our mother was lying dead.
All tasks for the funeral had begun.

The flames covered her mortal frame.
With sorrow, I gazed at the turbulent sea.
Remembrance of my childhood came;
Old memories appeared and flipped and fled.

The thought reminds me of thy kindness.
You protected the child from harm.
All periods—good and bad—were priceless.
Your teachings made life warm.

The constant flow of love from your end,
Never stopped for any gifts to return.
Can see your face at life's every bend.
Bereft of you, I feel lost and forlorn.

May your august soul rests in eternal peace,
Thoughts of you, fill all of us with joy,
Not having the angel look on our face.
All are painfully lost in anger's foray.

* * *

Siblings

As I previously mentioned, in addition to my older sister Pramila (Kuni), I had two more sisters named Urmila (Menki) and Lakshmi (Lakhi). My younger brother, Durgadas (Budha), was born between these two sisters. This chapter delves into the individual stories of each of my siblings.

Pramila (Kuni)

She was born at the Buxi Bazar house in Cuttack in March 1931. Dada Maa had arrived a few months earlier to take care of Maa and manage the household. Kuni, as she was affectionately called, was a chubby and fair baby when she was born. Dada Maa welcomed her as a gift from the goddess Lakshmi to the family.

From the very beginning, she held a special place in the hearts of Baba and Maa; they loved her deeply. Despite the challenges she faced in later years, she continued to be the most cherished and cared-for child of her parents until their last days.

As she grew, she transformed into a cute, fair, and remarkably beautiful child. Both Maa and Dada Maa regularly massaged young Kuni with turmeric paste and oil to maintain her radiant complexion and strengthen her bones. Baba was so attached to her that he dedicated nearly all of his time at home to her.

The family's sorrow over the loss of their second child, a son, was significantly alleviated when they witnessed the enchanting sight of three-year-old Kuni crawling like a small kitten and attempting to stand and walk like an unsteady angel. Day by day, she was growing into a little doll, and to Baba's great delight, he affectionately began calling her his little fairy, his "Snow White."

When Kuni reached the age of four, Baba took on the role of her home tutor. He taught her the fundamentals of the Odia and English alphabets, as well as numbers. Kuni, being a highly intelligent child, quickly grasped these lessons. Due to Baba's limited free time, an external tutor named Kanhu Babu, who taught at Victoria High School in Cuttack, was hired to provide Kuni with further education at home. Kanhu Babu was a quiet and amiable person, well-liked by his students. He eventually became the permanent home tutor for the other children whenever Baba's posting was in Cuttack. I remember him as a tall, thin man with a dark complexion and prominent, hairy ears. Later, he also tutored me, Menki, and Budha at home.

At the age of five, Kuni began her education in the "Sishu Shreni" (nursery) of a nearby primary school in Cuttack Municipality. She successfully completed her classes II, III, IV, and V at this school by the end of 1940. When Baba was transferred to Angul in July 1940, Kuni enrolled in Angul's girls' school. There, she passed her class VI and VII exams by the end of March 1942.

However, following Baba's transfer in April 1942 to Jeypore in the Koraput district, the family had to relocate from Angul. Unfortunately, this marked the end of Kuni's formal schooling, as Maa opposed her further education in school. Despite Baba's strong objections, Kuni didn't seem too eager to continue her formal education. She was content to stay at home and care for her younger brother, Budha, who was around a year and a half old at the time.

While the family resided in Jeypore, a private tutor was hired to provide me with additional lessons for admission to Class IV at the local government high school. This same teacher also offered tutoring sessions to Kuni, focusing on Sanskrit and advanced Odia literature.

Baba had a strong desire for Kuni to study various scriptures in both Odia and Sanskrit. Kuni possessed an exceptional memory, capable of reciting passages from these scriptures after just one or two readings. If she had been given the opportunity to pursue further education in schools and colleges, she could have become a genius within the family. It's also possible that such a path could have shielded her from future misfortunes. Indeed, the workings of destiny are mysterious and often beyond human comprehension.

The family resided in Jeypore for over three years, during which time Kuni assisted Maa with various household tasks. Maa also tried to impart her culinary knowledge to Kuni, particularly when it came to making traditional Odia *pithas*. When Maa was occupied in the kitchen, Kuni spent time with Menki and Budha, keeping them company and ensuring they stayed out of mischief. I sometimes played pranks on my younger siblings, leading to disagreements and occasional fights with Kuni, which often incurred Baba's disapproval.

Jeypore boasted numerous picturesque locations in the surrounding areas. On one occasion, the family embarked on a picnic near the Kolab River. This river, originating from the Srikaran Hills of the Eastern Ghats in the Koraput district, flowed swiftly over a rocky bed near our chosen spot. Its strong current posed a constant danger, and a moment of carelessness could lead to disaster. During our outing, Kuni and Menki were collecting pebbles near the river's embankment, enjoying their playful antics. Suddenly, Menki slipped and fell into the river. Kuni immediately called out for Maa's help. Without hesitation, Maa bravely leaped into the river, despite its strong current. She swam towards Menki, grabbed her by the hair, and pulled her to safety on the shore. It was a miraculous rescue!

Subsequently, the family learned that the Kolab River was infested with venomous, large snakes. These snakes had slim, round bodies exceeding four metres in length. They used to enter their victims through the nostrils, ultimately reaching the brain, and kill them by eating their brain tissue. This incident left a lasting impression on the family, and Maa received well-deserved praise for her incredible bravery in saving Menki's life. Maa had willingly placed herself in grave danger, a testament to the boundless love of mothers. Kuni, however, was deeply shaken by the incident and struggled to regain her usual composure.

In June 1945, Baba was transferred from Jeypore to Cuttack after his promotion to the position of Deputy Superintendent of Police. At the time, the Second World War was ongoing until Japan's surrender in September 1945. Kuni and the other children had the opportunity to witness British soldiers marching in front of our Mohamadia Bazar house. Their camp was situated in the Cantonment Road area. I remember how the children were initially apprehensive and reluctant to venture outside to watch the soldiers. Instead, they observed them cautiously through partially opened windows. Despite the initial fear, it provided daily entertainment, and Kuni found it particularly enjoyable.

During the brief eleven-month stay in Cuttack, Kuni assisted Maa in taking care of the baby Lakhi and her other siblings. While I attended school, the other four siblings stayed at home and received instruction from our home tutor, Kanhu Babu. Two orderly constables were assigned to help the family with various tasks outside the home. In the absence of domestic help, both Maa and Kuni took on the responsibility of managing all the household chores.

Kuni had a strong inclination toward religion, and she accompanied me every morning to gather flowers from nearby gardens for the home deity's puja. Each morning and evening, she would join Maa in the puja room for prayers. On Sundays, she would accompany our parents to the Cuttack Chandi temple to offer their prayers. I eagerly awaited their return, as it meant we would receive prasad from the Chandi temple, often in the form of delicious and sweet 'gulab jamuns'.

Upon moving with the family to Balasore, Kuni had the opportunity to reside in the spacious official quarters, as previously mentioned. It was in Balasore that Kuni developed her interest in gardening. She dedicated a small section of the compound, located adjacent to the children's bedroom, to creating her garden. In her garden, she cultivated beautiful flowers such as Anemone, Amaryllis, Hyacinth, Aster, Daffodil, Chrysanthemum, and more. I, along with Menki and Budha, eagerly joined in to assist her with her gardening activities, turning it into an engaging and enjoyable game for us.

Baba and Maa greatly appreciated Kuni's gardening efforts, as the flowers she grew proved to be very useful for the daily puja at home. Despite her responsibilities of helping Maa with household chores and tending to her garden, Kuni dedicated a significant amount of her time to studying various scriptures. She kept herself busy throughout the day and never missed an opportunity to assist Maa.

During one of the holidays around Dussehra in October 1947, the family visited Chandipur. The place was 16 kilometres from their house. It has a unique sea beach of Bay of Bengal. Here, during ebb tide, the sea water recedes up to five kilometres.

Due to this unique feature, the beach supports biodiversity. As one travels on the beach towards north nearer to the mouth of Budhabalanga River, one finds a beautiful picnic spot. Kuni and, all the children, loved to walk into the dried-up sea bed during ebb tide. There they caught extremely tiny red crabs and Sadabh Bohu insects (Red Velvet Mites). Kuni also collected the conch shells, beautiful pebbles and other items from the sea beach.

On this shoreline, one could encounter horseshoe crabs. Strictly speaking, they aren't classified as true crabs. Instead, they are referred to as marine creatures with an evolutionary history dating back four hundred fifty million years, earning them the title of 'living fossils'. Baba informed Kuni and the children that these creatures primarily inhabit shallow coastal waters with soft, sandy bottoms. They typically lay their eggs in the intertidal zone during spring high tides. Unfortunately, their population has been steadily declining due to heavy harvesting by some individuals. These particular species are more commonly found in the Atlantic Ocean region and typically measure around 24 inches in length and 12 inches in width. These revelations were quite fascinating for the young ones.

After a unique five-day family outing in Chandipur, they returned to Balasore. Upon their return, Baba received some exciting news: he had been summoned for an interview in Bhubaneswar by the Union Public Service

Commission (UPSC). The following period became very hectic. Following his selection into the IPS cadre, Baba began preparing to relocate to Keonjhar in February 1948. Kuni assisted Maa in packing up the household belongings for the move from Balasore to Keonjhar. It was a bittersweet moment for Kuni, as she felt saddened to leave her beautiful flower garden in Balasore, a creation that had solely resulted from her two years of hard work.

Despite her best efforts, Kuni couldn't recreate the same model of her flower garden in Keonjhar. This was due to the short duration of their stay in Keonjhar, which lasted only one year and four months, and the challenging rocky, dry, and tough soil in the area. This disappointment weighed heavily on her, even though the Keonjhar bungalow offered better living conditions compared to their previous home in Balasore. In Keonjhar, she did have the benefit of an exclusive, independent room.

Menki accompanied me on the way to our school, while Kuni stayed behind with our 7-year-old Budha and 4-year-old Lakhi. In addition to assisting our mother, Kuni took on the responsibility of looking after the two youngsters. She took it upon herself to begin teaching Budha in preparation for his future enrollment in Class IV. She also introduced Lakhi to the basics of alphabet learning in both Odia and English. Her remarkable patience in teaching these children had a significant impact, and as a result, both of her "students" performed well when they eventually entered schools in Bolangir.

During their stay in Keonjhar, the children frequently accompanied our mother to visit important tourist destinations. As mentioned earlier, the new family vehicle brought them immense joy, particularly to me and Kuni. Traveling in this vehicle, they were enthralled by trips to Telkoi Ghat to witness the waterfalls and visit Gonashika, the origin of the Baitarani River. When visiting the Ghatagaon Tarini temple, they often collected a generous supply of broken coconuts and kora (temple offerings) to satisfy their sweet cravings upon returning home.

Time passed quickly, and I successfully cleared my class IX examination while Menki completed her final exams for class IV. Shortly after, our family became engrossed in preparations for our move from Keonjhar to Bolangir due to Baba's transfer. He commenced his new posting in Bolangir in May 1949. As usual, Kuni was actively involved in assisting our mother with the packing, with the assistance of the household staff. Before heading to Bolangir, Baba had to meet with Mr. Clerici (the Inspector General and Head of State Police, equivalent to today's Director General) in Cuttack. We stayed in the Circuit House there for a week, from May 12th to May 18th, 1949. The Circuit House was situated very close to the Mahanadi River embankment. Kuni, along with me, Menki, Budha, Lakhi, and Maa, would often take walks along the embankment in the morning and evening.

During our stay at the Cuttack Circuit House, our maternal grandfather and our cousin sister Pari came to visit us. During this visit, it was decided by both Maa and Baba that cousin Pari would accompany our family to Bolangir to provide companionship to Kuni. Pari was the daughter of Jogi uncle, who was Maa's elder brother. Grandfather agreed to this arrangement, and that's how Pari became a part of our family for the move to Bolangir. We all arrived in Bolangir on May 20th, 1949, and Baba assumed his new position the following morning. After a few days, I enrolled in class X at PRHE School in Bolangir, and Budha began attending class IV at the same school. Menki and Lakhi were admitted to Maharani Girls School in classes V and I, respectively. During the weekdays, in the official bungalow in Bolangir, only Maa, Kuni, and Pari remained to manage their regular household responsibilities.

During this period, the friendship between Kuni and Pari grew stronger. However, both of them had to discontinue their studies after completing class VII due to their mothers' decisions. Kuni and Pari often assisted Maa with cooking and other household chores. Kuni gave up reading her books and abandoned her gardening hobby to spend more time with Pari. Pari, on the other hand, had no interest in English classics, Odia scriptures, or any other hobbies, which also influenced Kuni's reading habits.

After a few months, Kuni began to notice that Maa didn't reprimand Pari for similar mistakes as she did with her. This planted the seed of jealousy in Kuni, though no one else in the family seemed to notice. Gradually, Kuni lost interest in her work and surroundings, becoming unfocused and suffering from a form of insomnia. Consequently, she appeared drained even after getting sleep at night. This eventually led to the unfortunate accident of January 1950 that I have mentioned earlier.

On the second day of our parents' three-day visit to Cuttack for the Annual General Meeting of all SPs, Kuni experienced a traumatic episode. She believed that her parents had not taken her along because of Pari. This thought kept her awake the entire night and eventually led to the unfortunate incident that had a profound impact on her life. Following this accident, her behaviour became unpredictable. While she would be normal on some days, on others, she would have seizures. During these episodes, she also displayed violent and abusive tendencies. Only Maa and Baba were able to manage her during these challenging times. This was one of the reasons why we decided to hire Shankari. Her previous name was 'Sahebani' (madam of the house), which Maa appropriately changed for obvious reasons. Bringing Shankari into the household became necessary because seeking assistance from Pari to control Kuni would exacerbate the situation. Maa felt a significant relief from the burden of looking after Kuni once Shankari was employed. This maid essentially served as a constant presence to watch over Kuni.

Baba and Maa explored various avenues in their quest to cure Kuni. They attempted allopathy, homoeopathy, ayurvedic treatments, and even consulted psychiatrists over an extended period, all without achieving any positive results. As a last resort, when Baba was stationed in Cuttack, they arranged for her treatment at SCB Medical College. Baba had to wait until my eleventh-grade test results came in December 1950, and he had already requested a transfer from Mr. Clerici, which was approved, leading to his relocation to Cuttack in January 1951.

At SCB Medical College, Kuni received treatment from renowned brain specialists and the head of the psychology department in an effort to restore her to normalcy. While Kuni was cured of her seizures and violent behavior, complete normality remained elusive. After three months of treatment, the hospital prescribed medication for her to take regularly and discontinued the need for frequent hospital visits. Kuni's medical treatment concluded by the end of March 1951. However, she couldn't fully regain normalcy, and her recovery was never complete.

Many relatives and well-wishers of the family offered various suggestions to Maa regarding Kuni's well-being. Some of these suggestions were quite unusual, like seeking the help of a Tantric to dispel evil spirits or considering admission to a mental asylum until Kuni recovered her normalcy. Baba firmly rejected all these suggestions, including the idea of seeking help from a Tantric. However, he later remembered the advice given by the psychologist, which involved exploring the possibility of marriage for Kuni.

To assist in this endeavour, one day a well-known MLA from Anandpur in Keonjhar District, Mr. A. Patnaik (AP), paid a visit to their home in Cuttack. He had a close friendship with the family. After learning about Kuni's health condition and the psychologist's recommendation, AP suggested to Baba that they consider a marriage proposal for Kuni. He proposed his nephew, Jahar Patnaik (JP), as a potential match. JP was a graduate and worked as a manager at Rashiklal and Co. in Cuttack, where the owner happened to be his college classmate.

Upon receiving Baba's assurance that they would consider the proposal, AP mentioned that JP's father, Madhu Babu (MB), who had retired as the Estate Manager of the Maharaja of Keonjhar, would contact Baba soon, along with JP.

Within a week, both Madhu Babu and JP met with Baba, and the marriage was subsequently arranged for an early solemnization.

Following extensive preparations, Kuni's marriage to JP was held in Cuttack in November 1951. She then moved to her new home with JP in Naya Bazar, Cuttack, which was conveniently located near the OMP barracks. It was only half a kilometre away from Ravenshaw College, where I had enrolled in the 1st year of I.Sc. During this time, I visited Kuni and JP approximately twice a week, finding them happily settled. Baba and Maa also made monthly visits to see them. They enjoyed a content life together for nearly five years, and Kuni's behaviour seemed to return to normal. She even travelled to Keonjhar with her husband, JP, to meet her father-in-law and JP's elder brother, along with their respective families.

However, Kuni's happiness was short-lived. After five years of marriage, her fits and violent behaviour resurfaced. Despite the best efforts of her husband and his family over the course of six months to manage her condition, their attempts were in vain.

In 1956, Baba made the difficult decision to bring her back to our family home, where she would reside for the rest of her life. This marked the beginning of Kuni's long and tragic journey, which continued until her passing. She lived with this condition until 1983, outlasting even Baba. Her suffering continued for another fourteen years until she eventually succumbed to diarrhoea in her state of mental instability. During these years, Maa and Shankari, along with Budha and his wife, cared for her.

Urmila (Menki)

Urmila, the third child, was born on the 24th of October, 1938, in the Buxi Bazar house in Cuttack. Dada Maa had been present in the house since July to assist in managing the household and providing support to Maa during her pregnancy. Menki's birth coincided with the festive season in Cuttack, adding to the joyous atmosphere.

During this period of celebration, both Kuni and I were excited to welcome the new addition to the family. We eagerly watched as Maa and Dada Maa massaged Menki with turmeric paste every morning. We spent countless hours with Menki, only reluctantly returning to our beds when it was time to sleep. Menki was a robust and lively baby, inheriting sharp features from Maa and a light brown complexion from Baba. Dada Maa departed for the village when Menki was six months old. Approximately one year and three months later, the family bid a final farewell to the Buxi Bazar house, concluding their residence there after more than a decade.

Kashim Saheb, the owner of the house, bid a tearful farewell to our family. He and his wife regarded us as their own, showering us with valuable gifts during special occasions as a symbol of their deep affection and genuine love. Despite Baba's usual reluctance to accept expensive gifts, he couldn't bring himself to refuse their offerings, recognising that they were tokens of their pure affection. Kashim Saheb saw his own deceased son and family in Baba's family.

At that time, Kashim Saheb and his wife were quite elderly, both being over seventy-five years old. Following Baba's departure, they chose not to rent out the accommodation and instead moved into it themselves. Unfortunately, within three months of our departure, Begum Saheba passed away, and just a month later, Kashim Saheb also left this world.

As a gesture of respect, Baba travelled from Angul to attend their funeral rites. Kuni and I, who were deeply attached to Kashim Saheb and his wife, mourned their passing with great intensity. We would often open our boxes to gaze at the numerous gifts we had received from our beloved 'grandfather', Kashim Saheb. Even to this day, I can vividly imagine his always-smiling, chubby face with a bald head and white beard when I close my eyes.

During our stay in Angul, Menki began to grow into a strong child. Even at that age, she would get irritated if someone playfully touched her, which seemed to be an early sign of her quick temper—a characteristic that would stay with her throughout her life. When Menki was two years old, Bada Maa and Kuni took on the responsibility of caring for her. Bada Maa was married to one of Baba's cousin brothers and had been sent from the village to Angul in September 1940 to temporarily manage the household, as Maa was expecting her fourth child and was unable to handle household chores and the impending delivery.

Menki has very few memories of her time in Angul, as the family moved to Jeypore by March 1942, when she was about three and a half years old. At the Jeypore house, she began by crawling before attempting to stand while holding onto walls and doors. She would sometimes sneak out of her room and explore nearby areas.

On one occasion, Kuni had to bring her back into the room from the front verandah, where I would be receiving tutoring from a home tutor. In that area, there was a slope designed to make it easy for two-wheelers like bicycles and motorcycles to access. One day, without anyone's notice, including Kuni, me, and the teacher, Menki crawled to that slope and accidentally tumbled down. Fortunately, it was from a low height (2.5 feet), and she didn't sustain any injuries. However, her cries immediately brought Maa and Kuni running to the scene. That day, Maa let loose a verbal explosion on Kuni, myself, and the teacher. In response, Kuni and I ran away to hide while the poor teacher stood there like a statue, unsure of what he had done wrong!

During the turmoil of the 1942 independence movement, Kuni made sure that Menki stayed inside the house at all times, and nobody was allowed to leave their rooms. When the protesters gathered before the adjacent police station and shouted slogans, all three children would quietly peer through the partially closed windows to listen.

After a lathi charge on the protesters, during which some of them were apprehended near our house and reprimanded by the home orderlies, Kuni, Menki, and I rushed to the verandah and appeared to find the incident amusing. Later that evening, they excitedly recounted their amusement to Baba. However, they were surprised by Baba's reaction; he told them that the agitators were brave fighters for India's freedom and deserved respect from the children. Frankly, all three of us found Baba's sermon quite amusing.

When Menki was four and a half years old and Budha was three years and three months old, they welcomed their baby sister Lakhi into the family. Taking care of the young baby kept both Menki and Budha fully occupied, providing a welcome distraction from their mischievous antics.

Menki's formal education began in Class V when she enrolled at Gibson High School in Keonjhar in 1948. She continued her schooling in Bolangir (Classes VI and VII) and then in Cuttack (Classes VIII and IX). At Balasore, she completed her classes X and XI, earning her matriculation certificate from Utkal University in 1955.

Her college journey commenced in Baripada, where she completed her Intermediate Arts (IA) in 1957. She attended Saila Bala Women's College to pursue her Bachelor of Arts (BA) and received her degree in 1959. Subsequently, she enrolled in the Master of Arts programme in History. During this period, her marriage was arranged and took place before she could complete her post-graduation studies.

She was married in Cuttack in March 1961 to Natu, whose full name was Kumudanand. Her husband, Natu, happened to be my classmate during our time in class IX at Keonjhar's Gibson High School and later during our I.Sc. studies at Ravenshaw College in Cuttack. Following his completion of an engineering degree, Natu joined the Odisha government as an assistant engineer. Due to his posting in Mundali, located near Cuttack, Menki resided a few kilometres away from her parents. Eventually, they relocated to Bhubaneswar.

Menki's first child, Anita, came into the world at SCB Medical College on September 2, 1962. For almost six months surrounding the childbirth, Menki stayed with Maa and Baba in Cuttack. After Anita turned one year old, she continued to live with Baba and Maa. She received her primary education in Cuttack. Later on, she pursued a medical degree at Dibrugarh Medical College in Assam and completed her internship at SCB Medical College in Cuttack. During that period, she stayed with Baba and Maa.

Following Anita, Menki's second child, sadly, only survived for a few months after birth. Her subsequent child, and the last one, was also born in Cuttack on April 22, 1965. They named this daughter Benita, often referred to as Bini. In 1989, Bini completed her undergraduate studies in English literature at Miranda College, Delhi University.

Both daughters entered into marriage when the time was right. Unfortunately, Ani's marriage was short-lived, and she eventually separated from her husband. Later on, she adopted a son named Rocky, who pursued an engineering degree in Delhi. Ani currently works as a senior doctor in the MCD under the Delhi government. During Menki and Natu's visits to Delhi, she takes care of their well-being, provides them with specialised medical attention, and manages their flat in a West Delhi Co-operative Society. Recently, they sold the flat. She is an incredibly caring daughter.

Bini, who married in July 1972, has two daughters. The first, Chicky, is a doctor who got married on January 24, 2021, while pursuing her MS. The second daughter, Micky, holds an MBA from the USA and currently works for a well-known financial organisation in the United States. Bini's husband, Junu, received his education at BHU and later in the USA. He holds a high-ranking position in one of India's major corporate houses. Interestingly, he is the eldest son of one of my classmates from my time at Ravenshaw College in Cuttack.

After retiring from a senior position in a public sector undertaking (PSU), Natu continued to work in private companies until the age of seventy-five. They have settled in Bhubaneswar to enjoy their retirement years and frequently visit their two daughters each year.

During his active career, Natu had the opportunity to work abroad as well. He was stationed in Iran while working for Engineers India Limited (EIL). After retiring from EIL, he took on a private assignment in Malaysia. During Natu's assignment in Iran, Menki accompanied him.

Both Menki and Natu have had the chance to visit Egypt and the USA, while Bini and her family were living in those countries during Junu's postings. Similar to her elder sister Ani, Bini loves her parents and ensures they enjoy visits to scenic places in India and abroad.

I've maintained close contact with Menki's family and her children throughout the years. I cherish their company and wish them all the best in life. Recently, Menki faced several health issues, and Natu, due to his old age, has been dealing with joint pains and other ailments that have limited his ability to take morning and evening walks. While they primarily resided in Bhubaneswar, they often visited Delhi for treatment of major ailments and to seek assistance from Ani.

Sadly, Menki passed away in April 2021. Rest in peace, dear sister.

Durgadas (Budha)

Budha, the fourth child of our parents, was born in Angul on January 5th, 1941. When he was born, he had a fair complexion similar to that of Kuni and Maa. He retained his handsome and endearing appearance throughout his childhood and adolescence. He was exceptionally gentle, and everyone in the family cherished him.

He enjoyed good health during his childhood, and throughout our parents' lives, he never caused them any major worries due to illness. However, fate and the ways of God can be quite intricate, often beyond the comprehension of ordinary mortals. Later in life, after our parents had passed away, he faced significant kidney problems. Despite his suffering, he never voiced complaints and conducted himself with grace until the end. His remarkable composure was a rare quality not found in other members of our family. He has passed on this same calm demeanour to his brilliant son, Arun.

In 1950, Budha commenced his schooling in Bolangir, where he completed class IV. The following year, he joined class V at Ravenshaw Collegiate School in Cuttack. He remained at this school without any interruptions until he successfully passed his matriculation examination in 1958. During a significant part of his time at this school, spanning from 1953 to 1958, he resided in the school's hostel. Our family priest, Maheswara Pandit, who also served as a senior teacher at the school, became his guardian during this period. Maheswara Pandit was known for his strictness, and students generally held him in awe. His guardianship was a blessing for Budha, as it alleviated many worries for our mother.

Throughout his years at school, Budha formed close friendships with a few individuals. Some of them were his roommates at the hostel or fellow classmates. Several of these friends went on to achieve significant success in their careers and remained loyal to their friendship with Budha. In fact, a few of them even travelled from New Delhi during the early seventies to attend Budha's wedding in Nimapara, a rural area in Puri, Odisha.

In 1950, Budha commenced his schooling in Bolangir, where he completed class IV. The following year, he joined class V at Ravenshaw Collegiate School in Cuttack. He remained at this school without any interruptions until he successfully passed his matriculation examination in 1958. During a significant part of his time at this school, spanning from 1953 to 1958, he resided in the school's hostel. Our family priest, Maheswara Pandit, who also served as a senior teacher at the school, became his guardian during this period. Maheswara Pandit was known for his strictness, and students generally held him in awe. His guardianship was a blessing for Budha, as it alleviated many worries for our mother.

During his school years, Budha forged strong bonds of friendship with several individuals. Some of them were his hostel roommates or fellow classmates. Many of these friends went on to achieve remarkable success in their careers and remained steadfast in their friendship with Budha. In fact, a few of them even made the journey from New Delhi during the early 1970s to attend Budha's wedding in Nimapara.

Budha exhibited absolute neutrality and impartiality when facilitating mutually agreed-upon solutions between disputing parties. His reputation for impartiality quickly spread, and he was never swayed to make unjust decisions due to corrupt monetary incentives. This underscores the strong sense of honesty instilled by Baba in all his children, who wholeheartedly embraced Baba's unwavering commitment to integrity throughout their careers.

Long after the beginning of his service career, he got married in July 1972. The parents wanted him to marry only after the youngest sister got married in January 1971. Budha married Rama at Nimapara in Puri district. It being monsoon, there was incessant heavy rain during the period. All the 'baratis' (members of groom's party) had to face immense inconvenience during the time of the marriage. Due to unavoidable circumstances, I couldn't attend the marriage. However, other family members - Baba, Natu, Menki as well as Bibhu and Lakhi, had gone to Nimapara for solemnising the marriage.

On April 8, 1973, Budha and Rama welcomed their first child, Arun, into the world. Arun has proven to be an exceptionally bright young man. He achieved the distinction of becoming the top graduate of Utkal University and received a gold medal from the university for his M.Sc. degree in physics. His academic journey continued as he earned a doctorate in physics from the Institute of Physics in Bhubaneswar.

Following the completion of his PhD, Arun embarked on a career as a scientific officer at the Bhabha Atomic Energy Commission. Through his outstanding research efforts, he has ascended to great heights in the academic world. The government of India recognised his contributions by bestowing upon him the prestigious Best Scientist of the Year Award, also known as the S. Bhatnagar Award.

Currently, Arun serves as the Dean and Professor of Physics at NISER (National Institute of Science Education and Research) in Bhubaneswar. NISER, an institution affiliated with the Atomic Energy Commission, is an advanced educational institute dedicated to training scientists and educators in India, striving for excellence in their fields.

In 1982, Budha made the decision to leave EIMPA and take up a position at the Orissa Film Development Corporation (OFDC). At OFDC, he assumed the role of Deputy General Manager (DGM). This organisation was a government undertaking by the state of Odisha, with its leadership entrusted to a managing director (MD). Budha's extensive experience and dedication played a pivotal role in propelling OFDC to new heights, particularly after the acquisition of Kalinga Studio in Bhubaneswar. This development made OFDC a vital institution in the advancement of the Odia film industry.

However, Budha's exceptional performance garnered both recognition and envy, especially from his immediate boss, the MD, who attempted to create difficulties for him. Ultimately, justice prevailed, and Budha was able to reclaim his position and prestige with the intervention of the Industry Minister of Odisha. My assistance in this matter was significant.

Later on, Budha enjoyed a peaceful retirement, which took place in 1999 under the leadership of a new MD who happened to be my brother-in-law. During his retirement, he cherished time spent with family and friends, particularly in Cuttack, where he had formed strong and loyal friendships. These friends held a deep appreciation for his past kindness and assistance, which he had generously extended to them without any personal motives. During various family crises in the future, Budha could rely on their unwavering support and assistance.

Throughout his career, Budha was stationed in Cuttack. As usual, he and his family resided with Baba and Maa at the Tulsipur house in Cuttack. This arrangement was mutually beneficial, providing him with spacious and lovely accommodation while affording the parents the support of a son and his family in their old age. Unfortunately, this advantage was not available to me, as I was frequently posted outside the state, and Cuttack was not among my assigned locations during my entire service tenure.

Around the year 2001, Budha encountered a significant health challenge when both of his kidneys were damaged due to incorrect treatment and medication in Cuttack. Seeking a proper diagnosis and treatment, I arranged for him to undergo testing at the All India Institute of Medical Sciences (AIIMS) in New Delhi. The results confirmed that both of his kidneys had sustained complete damage, necessitating an urgent kidney transplant. However, AIIMS couldn't immediately facilitate the transplant due to a lack of suitable donors. Consequently, he had to return to Cuttack.

He underwent weekly dialysis at Kalinga Hospital in Bhubaneswar. I made sure that the proceeds from the sale of four acres of land in Choudwar, near Cuttack, provided him with significant financial assistance for his dialysis and related expenses. Apart from being expensive, the two weekly dialysis sessions at Kalinga Hospital in Bhubaneswar were also physically painful. His entire family, especially his wife Rama and son Arun, offered unwavering support throughout this challenging period.

In the year 2002, he had to travel to Chennai to undergo a kidney transplant, where suitable donor kidneys were obtained. Following the kidney transplant, he returned to Cuttack with detailed medical instructions on safety measures, dietary restrictions, and medication. These instructions were meticulously followed by him and his family. The kidney transplant significantly extended his life by nine years.

His last years were marked by a life filled with numerous restrictions and limitations. He had to maintain distance from all visitors, and even his own family members had to keep their distance to prevent any risk of infection. Public places and the homes of friends and relatives were strictly off-limits. His health and well-being relied heavily on a regimen of medications throughout the latter part of his life. For someone who relished food like he did, being confined to a diet of boiled vegetables day in and day out felt like a form of punishment. Every time I saw him, a profound sadness would wash over me, and I would curse myself for not being able to offer any physical relief. Despite all the hardships, Budha maintained a cheerful disposition as much as possible. He made a concerted effort to spread happiness to those around him, even while enduring physical discomfort.

A brief walk would leave him utterly exhausted, and he was highly susceptible to viral and other infections due to the deterioration of his immune system by post-transplant medications. It was truly heartbreaking for all his loved ones to witness the gradual fading of his once vibrant life. Such a vegetative existence was incredibly challenging for him and his family. At one point, he confided in me that he despised living his current life, which felt robotic and devoid of the joy he once knew.

During the final days of his life, he was hospitalised at the Cuttack Nursing Home. In the last stages, he slipped into unconsciousness. It was truly a pitiable sight for everyone to witness such a gentle soul in that state.

Ultimately, his journey came to an end on August 25, 2011.

May his virtuous soul find eternal peace in the divine abode of Lord Jagannath!

Lakshmi (Lakhi)

She was the youngest child of her parents, born in Jeypore, Odisha, on April 13, 1944. Like her siblings, her early education was primarily conducted at home. Her formal schooling began when she enrolled in St. Joseph Girls School in Cuttack in 1951.

At that time, the official residence of the Superintendent of Police (SP) in Cuttack was situated directly across from this school. In fact, the main entrance of the school was located on the opposite side of the road, nearly in front of the gate to Baba's official residence. Lakhi would simply walk to school, often accompanied by her relative and classmate, Pushpa. Interestingly, Pushpa happened to be Lakhi's "Mausi" (aunt), as she was the granddaughter of Maa's cousin. Lakhi continued her studies at this school for two years.

The remainder of her schooling took place in different locations. She attended classes VI and VII in Balasore and continued her education in Baripada for classes VIII and IX. Eventually, she completed her matriculation at Ravenshaw Girls School in Cuttack in 1960. Her higher education was pursued at Saila Bala Women's College, where she studied for her IA, BA, and MA (Odia) degrees.

During her educational journey, her cousin Pari, who had been a part of the family since their days in Bolangir (starting in 1949), also began her further education from class VIII onwards in Baripada. Pari became a constant companion for Lakhi throughout their school and college years.

Lakhi and Pari used the school and college buses in Cuttack for their daily commutes. These buses would stop at Tulsipur Matha Road near the Tulsipur house to pick them up. Before reaching their stop, the buses would also collect two of their friends from Sati Chaura Road. One of these friends was Rashmi, who would later become Lakhi's sister-in-law after marrying the me in 1963.

Lakhi had numerous college friends who resided near the Tulsipur house in Cuttack. She had witnessed the weddings of Kuni, Menki, mine, and Budha in Cuttack. Kuni's marriage took place at Baba's government quarter, while the other three weddings were held at our own Tulsipur house. Lakhi's own marriage followed suit, occurring in that very house on January 30, 1971.

Lakhi married Bibhu Kalyan Mohanty (Bibhu), who was then serving as a Lieutenant Commander in the Indian Navy. Bibhu was the son of one of Baba's former colleagues. In their family, he had five brothers and four sisters. Originally from Balasore district, they eventually settled in their newly constructed residence in Chauliaganj, Cuttack, after their father Basanta Mousa's retirement.

Upon his retirement, Basanta Mousa established a private security agency in partnership, specialising in providing security guards for offices, factories, and residences. The agency thrived during his lifetime. However, after his passing, one of the partners engaged in dishonest practices and took control of the agency. Despite legal actions pursued by his children, they were unable to recover their loss, resulting in a significant financial setback for the joint family.

During Bibhu's naval service, Lakhi lived in various naval establishments across India, including Cochin, Mumbai, Vizag, and others. As a naval officer,

Bibhu played a role in the Indo-Pak War of 1971, which resulted in the creation of Bangladesh. His final posting before retiring as a commander in the Indian Navy was in Kolkata, where he held the position of head of the Kolkata Naval Establishment. Their official residence, a beautiful bungalow located on the banks of the Hooghly River, served as a splendid venue for parties hosted for the Kolkata elite. I had the opportunity to visit this charming bungalow in Kolkata with Rashmi.

Lakhi and Bibhu have two children. Their son, Pintu, is an exceptionally bright student. After earning his engineering degree from BITS Pilani, he completed his MBA at the Xavier Institute of Management, Bhubaneswar. Currently, he holds a senior position at a prominent organisation in the USA. Despite being encouraged by his parents, Pintu seems to have reconsidered the idea of marriage after the breakup of his engagement to the daughter of a retired defense colleague of Bibhu.

Their daughter, Rupali, pursued a course in hotel management and briefly worked with the ITC group of hotels. Rupali is now married to an engineer who runs his own business in Delhi and Bhubaneswar. He hails from the family of a well-known political leader in Odisha, originally from Keonjhar.

Prior to his retirement, Bibhu built a house in CDA, Cuttack. After retiring, Lakhi and Bibhu relocated to this house. They organised Rupali's wedding after settling in Bhubaneswar, and it was attended by members of both their families. This event also served as a long-awaited family reunion.

Around this time, I had moved from Delhi to Bhubaneswar and I attended the wedding festivities at venues like Hotel Swasti Premium and Hotel Mayfair Lagoon. The wedding arrangements and the sumptuous feasts provided were delightful, featuring excellent cuisine.

Over time, Rupali and her family relocated to Delhi, where her husband had expanded his business operations. They purchased a flat in Delhi for their new home. With their son primarily residing in the USA and now their daughter moving to Delhi, Lakhi and Bibhu also decided to make the move to Delhi. Consequently, they acquired a flat in Delhi that was in close proximity to Rupali's residence. They find joy in spending time with their grandson, who is Rupali's son. Presently, the lives and lifestyles of many retired couples follow a similar pattern.

I extend my best wishes to Lakhi and her family for happiness and contentment in the future.

* * *

Childhood

For my birth, Dada Maa came to Cuttack to assist Maa in managing the household at Buxi Bazar. They located a "dai," a traditional house nurse who specialised in home childbirth, based on the recommendation of the district hospital doctor who was overseeing Maa's pregnancy. The dai was hired to look after Maa for the three months leading up to delivery, and she resided in the house, providing regular updates to Dada Maa.

During this time, Kashim Saheb's wife, Jahanara, who was the landlord's begum, visited frequently. She ensured Maa received nutritious meals for her well-being. After my birth, she showered immense love on the newborn, much like a grandmother would. Perhaps she saw in me a resemblance to her deceased grandchild. I still vividly recall the numerous gifts Jahanara grand maa bestowed upon me, ranging from unique toys to delectable chocolates and sweet "sevaiya," along with various homemade sweets. This early love for sweets may have contributed to my enduring fondness for them, even though I developed diabetes in my late forties.

Returning to the newborn, the baby was healthy and had a dusky complexion like his father. Baba was at home and fully awake at 11:20 p.m. when I was born on the night of February 26, 1935. Baba's joy knew no bounds when Dada Maa handed the newborn over to him late at night. He had been waiting in the room adjacent to where Maa was resting, which had been transformed into the "delivery room."

In those olden days, the delivery rooms were known as "antudi salaa." No males were permitted to enter the antudi salaa for twenty-one days! Consequently, only Kuni, Dada Maa, and the dai were allowed inside the room for the first three weeks. Even female visitors to the house could enter the room only after receiving clearance from Dada Maa, who ensured they were clean. This custom may seem outdated now, but at the time, it was deemed necessary for the safety of both the mother and child due to the high mortality rate.

After twenty-two days, everyone could visit Maa and baby Chandi (me) without any restrictions. I received daily massages with oil and turmeric paste from the dai twice a day. This continued for nearly four months, after which the dai's services were no longer required, and Dada Maa took over the massages for the following three months.

Kuni was always by the baby's side. To help take care of baby Chandi and manage the household, a new helper named Ramesh, who was 12 years old, was hired. This allowed Maa to attend to her household duties and Chandi's massages, among other things. When I was six months old, a shanti puja (peaceful ceremony) was held at Cuttack Chandi Mandir, and I was dedicated as a lifelong servant of the goddess. This fulfilled the promise my parents had made during their prayers to the goddess earlier, seeking a male child. To mark the occasion, a feast for one hundred Brahmins was organised at the temple. Maa and Dada Maa served the prasad (offerings) to them and sought their blessings for the child and the family. Later, the prasad was brought home for the family and others, and Dada Maa left for the village after the function.

I grew up in the warm and loving atmosphere of the house, where I was the apple of Maa, Baba, and Kuni's eyes. Kashim Saheb and Jahanara Begum were frequent visitors, playing with and doting on me as a baby. My maternal grandfather, Raju Babu, never missed a day without visiting after his working hours at the post office. He would hold me on his lap during these visits, and our domestic helper, Ramesh, was always nearby, with his sole duty being to keep a watchful eye on me when I was an infant.

The days and months passed swiftly. At the age of three, with the assistance of Kuni, Maa, Baba, and Ramesh, I began to stand on my own. I was a robust and energetic child, soon running all over the house with Ramesh closely following behind. At the age of five, during one of these playful escapades, I slipped on the stairs and had a close call. Fortunately, Ramesh was nearby and managed to prevent a serious accident. Following this incident, Maa scolded Ramesh severely, which made him extra cautious and attentive.

Much later in life, Ramesh started his own sweet business, specialising in son papdi. Whenever he visited our house with these sweets for me and the family, he would reminisce about the scolding incident. The son papdi he made and brought was incredibly delicious, melting in the mouth. Each time Ramesh visited, Maa would order five kilogrammes (at that time, five sers) of the sweet. However, this supply of sweets never lasted more than five days in our house, with the biggest consumers being Baba and me. Eventually, Son papdi became a favourite treat for Menki and Budha as well.

When I was three years and eight months old, newborn Menki became my little baby doll. Two years later, my younger brother Budha was born when I was six. It was around this time that Baba began teaching me the alphabet and numbers. Maa was an effective tutor and practitioner in this endeavour, as Baba's work often took him away from home for extended periods. For all practical purposes, my parents were my first and most important teachers.

When our family moved from Cuttack to Angul, we hired a private tutor for Kuni and me. This tutor would arrive at our home on a pony. With the tutor's permission, I had my first pony ride in Angul. I learned the fundamentals of writing and counting from this teacher.

I also learned the multiplication tables from this tutor, although I never forgot that Baba used to wake me up at the ungodly hour of 5 a.m. to review and recite what I had learned the previous day. He even made me recite the multiplication tables up to 25. I still consider it a form of childhood torture, as I would sit up in bed inside a mosquito net with half-closed eyes, undergoing this daily routine.

Kuni and Menki remained my closest friends during this time. The three of us would often explore the vast grounds of our residence, where we would catch various butterflies and dragonflies. We would also play chase with rabbits, squirrels, and various types of birds. During these adventures, we sometimes encountered snakes in pursuit of their prey. Luckily, we had household mongooses that protected us from these venomous predators. Our home had a pair of mongooses to ensure our family's safety.

While we were living in Angul, our family visited a nearby place called Satkosiagand, where the Mahanadi River flowed between two hills, creating a deep gorge. This area was home to many rare plants and animals, including large and ferocious crocodiles that could often be seen sunning themselves on the riverbank. It was the first time my sisters, Kuni and Menki, and I had seen crocodiles. During this visit, we also spotted a mother bear and her cub at dusk. Kuni and Menki pointed out how the baby bear resembled their toy teddy bear. I jokingly told them that when I grow up, I will own a real bear and not allow them to come near it. Both sisters responded with playful laughter and teasing.

I was happy to have a brother who was born at Angul during January, 1941. At that time Dada Maa had come to Angul to assist Maa. It was a difficult delivery and, that's the reason Dada Maa named the new born as 'Hairan Barik'. That term of Odia means a person who symbolises trouble. It was taken jocularly; the new born was subsequently named Durgadas (Budha).

I had a deep affection for Dada Maa, who used to share bedtime stories with me. She held a special place in her heart for me as well, always granting my requests for sweets and chocolates. Little did I know that Dada Maa was secretly providing these treats to Kuni and Menki as well. That's why she often advised me not to share these treats with my sisters. Looking back on it now, I can't help but laugh without any embarrassment!

Dada Maa left for the village at the end of June 1941, and that was the last time I saw her. Sadly, just a few months later, she succumbed to malaria fever at a hospital in Cuttack, where she was undergoing treatment after being brought from the village by Baba. Even during her final moments, she expressed a desire to see me. While Baba was making arrangements to bring me from Angul to Cuttack, Dada Maa passed away peacefully in her sleep that very night.

Her passing was a significant loss for the family. Her amiable, pleasant, and helpful nature had endeared her to everyone, including the children. She always wore a smile, even in the face of extreme provocation. Dada Maa was fair and good-looking, and Baba often remarked that she reminded him of his own mother, both in appearance and behaviour.

In March 1942, when the family relocated to Jeypore due to Baba's transfer, I couldn't help but shed tears at the memory of Dada Maa. I had cherished my bond with her and was deeply attached. However, with time, I began to heal amidst the new surroundings. After all, time has a way of easing the pain of loss.

At the age of seven, I had one more year to go before I could be admitted to a high school in Jeypore. To prepare for this, my parents arranged for a home tutor who would also teach the alphabet to Menki, who was around four and a half years old at the time. I found the tutor to be rough-mannered and quick-tempered. This was mainly because he burdened me with so much homework that it left very little time for play. Being mischievous, I decided to teach the tutor a lesson, but I had to bide my time until I had successfully completed my lessons for high school admission.

Our official residence in Jeypore was a spacious bungalow with a large compound. Here, I could play with my sisters and even give them rides on a small bicycle that my maternal grandfather had gifted me. However, I was not allowed to ride it on the busy road in front of our house. Maa had given strict instructions to the home orderly constable to ensure that the children never ventured beyond the compound and onto the road. This precaution was necessary at that time, as the Non-Cooperation Movement and the Quit India Movement were at their peak in 1942. Our house, being near the police station, was often a target for troublemakers.

On one occasion, I disregarded the constable's warning and rode my bicycle to the road. When this was reported to Maa, she came out, walked to the road, and dragged me back to the compound. The punishment I received that day was quite harsh, and I cried for at least two hours. My tears were not only due to the scolding but also because I was upset about losing the privilege of riding my bicycle. Maa confiscated the bicycle for a couple of months and stored it in the storeroom. After that incident, none of the children dared venture out of the gate or leave the compound without Maa's permission.

During this period, the tutor kept assigning more and more homework to me as the admission time for class IV at school was approaching. If I failed to complete my homework, the tutor promptly reported it to Maa, resulting in me being scolded and given additional work. This gradually became too much for me to bear, and my determination to teach the tutor a lesson intensified.

As my anger grew, I decided to give the tutor a memorable lesson. During our home tutorial sessions, where the tutor, Urmi, and I sat on a large mat in a remote corner of the front verandah, I hatched a mischievous plan. The seating arrangement was fixed, with the tutor positioned near the verandah wall. My devious idea led me to place several small pins under the mat so they protruded slightly on the surface where the tutor would sit. These tiny pinheads were almost invisible, particularly in the dim light of dusk when our classes took place.

As the tutor settled into his usual spot, he suddenly leaped up with a loud cry of pain. The back of his dhoti began to turn crimson from the blood, and he continued to howl in agony.

Maa rushed to the verandah upon hearing the tutor's cries of pain. The tutor, amidst his suffering, explained what had happened and declared that he would no longer teach me. The beating I received from Maa at that moment was so harsh that the tutor pleaded with her to stop. Maa instructed me to touch the tutor's feet, and I had to beg for his forgiveness, urging him not to leave. This theatrical scene marked the end of my pranks on the tutor, and he also seemed to forget the incident.

Thanks to this tuition, I successfully gained admission to class IV at the high school in 1943, while Menki entered class I at the primary school.

I completed my studies in classes IV and V at this school before Baba's promotion and transfer in June 1945. During my time there, the school had no complaints about my behaviour. Perhaps this was because of the values instilled in me regarding proper conduct at school by my home tutor. During school hours, the mischievous "Dr. Jekyl" in my nature temporarily overshadowed "Mr. Hyde." However, once school was out, I reverted to my old self and played pranks on both my sisters. I even pretended to be a "sadhu" (saintly person) in front of Baba. Maa never revealed my mischievous side to Baba or other visitors to the house.

In April 1944, a new member named Lakshmi, affectionately known as Lakhi, joined our family. Initially, Kuni and Menki were excited, but I began to spend more time with Budha. I observed that everyone else was paying more attention to the newly born Lakhi. However, a few years later, when she was around two years old, my attitude towards her completely changed. I developed a deep affection for her and often spent more time with her more than my other three siblings.

After we moved to Cuttack in June 1945, our family settled into a spacious two-story house. I was soon enrolled in the sixth grade at Practising Middle School (PMS), which was conveniently located near my father's office along the Kathjori River. This school was run by the government, and the classes were primarily taught by trainee teachers from the college of education, working towards their B.Ed. degrees. Consequently, the teaching methods at PMS differed from those at more established schools.

During this period, teh family also hired a private tutor for the children, as the educational environment in Cuttack was quite distinct from the places where we had previously studied. Finding an experienced and reputable teacher who also taught at a reputable school in Cuttack was essential. We were fortunate to find such a teacher, known by the name Kanhu Babu.

Kanhu Babu advised Baba to transfer me from Practising Middle School (PMS) to Pyare Mohan Academy (PMA) without delay. PMA was a renowned high school founded by the esteemed educator Pyare Mohan Acharya, who hailed from Baba's ancestral village. Baba accepted Kanhu Babu's suggestion, and within a month, I was enrolled in the sixth grade at PMA, marking the start of my education there, which continued through classes VI and VII.

During our two-year residence at Mohamadia Bazar house in Cuttack, I acquired the skill of riding a bicycle on the main road that connected Cantonment Road with the Chandni Chowk crossing. This road passed right in front of our house. The bicycle I used belonged to a boy named Abbas, who was the same age as me. Abbas assisted his father in their small shop, which sold pans, cigarettes, and condiments and was located in front of their house. Abbas and I became close friends, often playing football together in a nearby field. Additionally, Abbas taught me how to fly a kite.

One day, Baba caught sight of me sitting in Abbas' pan shop and was livid. He feared that I would be negatively influenced by my new friend and believed that this friendship might lead to my spoiling. At that point, Abbas had already discontinued his education and was assisting his father full-time in managing the shop. Following that incident, I was required to end this friendship. I was closely monitored at home by Maa, Kuni, and the orderly constable, preventing me from engaging in any covert mischievous activities. Abbas' father received appropriate instructions from the orderly constable, and Abbas himself was sternly reprimanded by his father. Abbas completely avoided me and wouldn't even acknowledge my presence from a distance.

In the company of my friends at my new school, Pyare Mohan Academy (PMA), I gradually forgot about Abbas. Some of my schoolmates also resided in the vicinity. One such friend was Sudama, who lived only about 100 yards away from my house. Sudama had a distant connection to the prominent zamindar Radha Prasanna Das (RPD) of Balasore, as his wife happened to be Sudama's cousin. Much later, under challenging circumstances, Sudama had come to Cuttack along with his cousin and her daughter to stay with his uncle.

Sudama's uncle held the position of Deputy Magistrate in the Orissa Administrative Service. His daughter was married to RPD. When Sudama's uncle was transferred out of Cuttack, Sudama had to relocate to Balasore and reside at RPD's house to continue his studies. It was during this time that Sudama and I became close friends while attending the school in Balasore.

Sudama was involved in a fascinating incident when he completed his matriculation at Balasore Zila School. This incident revolved around his assistance in the elopement of RPD's daughter with the eldest son of an IAS officer. The individual who assisted in this elopement later became a prominent owner of iron ore mines in the Keonjhar district. I will share the details of this incident later on.

Under Kanhu Babu's tutoring at home, I excelled as a student at Pyare Mohan Academy. I also began participating in various outdoor sports and activities. This interest in outdoor pursuits would become a significant aspect of my later life.

The school's headmaster was Basanta Kumar Das, known for his strict administration. His two lovely daughters also attended the same school, one in the fourth grade and the other in the seventh grade. The younger daughter was named Sumitra, and the older one was named Sucharita.

I was intrigued by both of these attractive girls and attempted to befriend them. However, they were quite arrogant and did not want to associate with other students, considering themselves superior because they were the headmaster's daughters. In response, I didn't care much for their haughtiness. In fact, I openly and loudly mocked both girls in front of my friends. Over time, this led to a change in their attitude as they realised their snobbish behaviour wasn't well received. Despite their efforts to mend their ways, I and my friends continued to ignore them.

It's no surprise that, for a considerable period during my entire school and college days in Odisha, I chose to avoid interacting with female students. To divert my attention effectively, I focused more on extracurricular activities during those crucial formative years. As a result, I also began to feign extreme shyness in the presence of girls in general and women in particular. This attitude was in harmony with the home environment that my mother had created around Baba.

In February 1946, when I was promoted to class VII, there was talk of Baba's transfer. class VII held significant importance in the school curriculum during those times. Baba didn't want me to change schools in that grade, so I remained in Cuttack while he and the family relocated to Balasore in April.

Arrangements were made for me to stay with my cousin, Gouranga Charan Mohanty, affectionately known as Benga Bhai. At that time, Benga Bhai worked as an assistant editor at the Odia daily Dainika Asha. Since Benga Bhai lived in a bachelor's mess, Baba arranged for both of us to reside there. Our accommodation was provided in the quarters of Bata Krushna Mohanty, an unmarried sub-inspector from the Lalbagh Police Station who lived with his elderly mother. He allocated a separate room for the two of us in his official quarters, located in the Lalbagh Police Station colony in the Chandni Chowk area of Cuttack. This was an entirely new environment for me, and I had to adapt with the assistance of Benga Bhai.

This house was situated adjacent to the one where Baba had previously resided, and it was also the place where Maa had stayed after their marriage. The "Jamu Rola" tree still stood beside it, serving as a reminder of an earlier story involving Maa's playful antics when she first arrived as a teenage bride to that house.

In front of these houses, positioned between the constable's barracks and the police station, there was a spacious area within the police station complex. I found great comfort in this house and appreciated the instructions I received from Benga Bhai. Bata Babu and his mother made me feel at ease. However, I still missed my family despite my monthly visits to Balasore, which I made by train. An orderly constable from Balasore, dispatched by Baba, would accompany me during these train journeys. The train ride typically lasted about three hours, with three stops between Cuttack and Balasore.

Every day, I walked to Pyare Mohan Academy school, taking a shortcut route that passed through a lane in front of the renowned temple of goddess Kali. This lane connected to the main road at Tinkonia Bagicha, adjacent to Ravenshaw Girls' School. Along the way, it also passed by Netaji Subhash Bose's ancestral home and birthplace in Odia Bazar.

Even to this day, I can clearly envision the path I took six days a week for nearly a year. The distance from my house to the school was roughly one and a half kilometres, a journey I could complete in about twenty minutes. This daily commute of three kilometres served as excellent exercise for me, helping me build a robust level of stamina, which was particularly beneficial for my involvement in football. My enhanced stamina and physical fitness proved to be valuable assets later on when I assumed the role of captain for the Allahabad University Football Team during my undergraduate and postgraduate studies.

On weekends, I dedicated my time to playing with kids who lived in the vicinity. Two of my special friends were Barada and Tarun. Barada's residence was located across the road from the police station, near the main entrance to the Governor's House. His father, Jai Krushna Das, was also a police officer who was stationed outside Cuttack at the time. His family rented a place in Cuttack to ensure their children received a proper education. In their home, they had several cows and approximately thirty or more chickens.

Tarun, who was the nephew of Inspector Gagan Babu at the police station, was one of the friends. Another friend, Charu, attended Ravenshaw Collegiate School with Barada. Charu used to visit his father's Ayurvedic medicine shop beneath Barada's house every afternoon. Interestingly, nearly seventeen years later, Barada's youngest sister, Rashmi, who was yet to be born at that time, would marry me.

One day, as the Durga Puja festival approached, all ten friends, including Barada, decided to organise a sports event for track and field competitions. They chose their playground for the event, and it was my idea. Everyone readily agreed, and they began preparing the ground and marking the tracks for the competitions. Tarun took charge of the ground preparation and enlisted the help of his uncle's constables for the job. Barada was responsible for arranging prizes to be awarded to the successful athletes. He put in great effort and successfully procured the prizes for the event.

The sports event lasted for two days, and at its conclusion, prizes were awarded. Inspector Gagan Babu, who served as the chief guest, had the honour of presenting all the prizes. I emerged as the top winner, securing the most prizes. Unfortunately, my friend Barada didn't win any prizes as he faced challenges due to his obesity, making it difficult for him to compete and succeed in athletic events during that time.

As the year passed swiftly, I found myself on the brink of leaving Cuttack after completing my final examinations for class VII in April 1947. Both my school friends and those near my residence organised a grand farewell for me, showering me with numerous gifts. I had gained a reputation for being well-liked among my friends. My departure left them feeling the void of my absence, and I too felt a sense of loss.

In the following years, as I moved to various places, I lost contact with most of my childhood friends. In fact, I can hardly remember many of my classmates from those early years at PMA. New places brought new friendships, gradually fading the memories of those cherished childhood bonds.

In the final days of our stay in Cuttack, Benga Bhai switched his job. He secured a government position in the postal department and began working as an assistant postmaster. After I departed for Balasore, he too left Bata Babu's residence and relocated to a new house near the post office. Bata Babu, on the other hand, received a transfer out of Cuttack in May 1947 and was assigned to the Badachana Police Station, which was closer to his native village.

These transitions worked out well for all of us involved. It appeared as though a divine plan had been waiting for the right moment to benefit me, Benga Bhai, and Bata Babu. Those two years spent in Cuttack are among the most cherished memories of my childhood. It was also a period when, as a child, I lived in a place without the constant presence of Baba, Maa, and my siblings for the first time.

Upon my arrival in Balasore in the second week of April 1947, I was enrolled in the eighth grade at Balasore Zila School. Baba accompanied me to the school for the admission process. There, I had my first encounter with the headmaster of the school, Mr. Phani Bhushan Mitra. Like most headmasters, he had a stern and serious appearance, which made him seem strict and formidable. It was widely believed that he had a fearsome disposition. I had a taste of his strictness a few months later when I received a loud reprimand from him due to a complaint made by a drawing teacher. This same teacher later faced severe consequences when he attempted to punish me without cause.

The school was located nearly a kilometre away from our residence. The road leading to the school, despite being an important arterial road of the town connecting the railway station, was not well maintained. It was riddled with potholes and had a rough surface with sharp black stone chips protruding, which caused discomfort for my feet. Like most children of that time, I walked to school barefoot. To avoid the discomfort, I was forced to walk on the softer surface of the sidewalks. I endured this inconvenience throughout the six school days each week, spending nearly an hour commuting each day.

The school itself was quite spacious and had a large playground. During the school's lunch break, students flocked to the playground in large numbers. The school day began with a collective prayer held on the same grounds. Students who arrived late for the prayer were subjected to punishment. If a student was late three times in a month, their parents were summoned to meet with the headmaster for guidance and potential action.

I made sure I was never late. I would arrive at the school grounds at 9:30 a.m., half an hour before the start of the school day. This early arrival gave me some extra time to play with a tennis ball that I brought with me to school every day. Some of my classmates adopted this practice as well, and the school grounds would be filled with a group of classmates before the morning prayer. This established me as a leader among the 'active gang'!

In my class, I also had my old friend Sudama from Cuttack. Alongside him, I forged friendships with Udaya Nath Mallick (UNM), who would later become an IAS officer, and Rabi Narayan Mohapatra (RNM), who would also become an IPS officer in the years to come. Another friend was Bhabani Shanker Das (BSD), the son of the District Magistrate of Balasore at the time. UNM, RNM, and Sudama chose to pursue the arts stream (IA) at Ravenshaw College in 1951, while BSD became my classmate in the science stream (ISc) at the same college. I mentioned an earlier unfortunate incident in Sudama's life, and to ensure it is not left out of this narrative, I'd like to recount it now.

This incident took place in 1951, when Sudama was in the final year of his matriculation at Balasore Zila School. During this time, he was residing in his aunt's magnificent house in Balasore. His aunt was the wife of Radha Prasanna Das, the most prominent zamindar in Balasore district. They had a lovely daughter who had fallen in love with the eldest son of the district collector. This young man had completed his post-graduation in economics at Allahabad University and had begun his mining business, initially located in Barbil, Keonjhar district, before eventually relocating his office to Cuttack.

However, there were significant obstacles to the marriage between the two lovebirds. The bride's father vehemently opposed it, so they decided to plan the wedding in secret. After Sudama completed his final matriculation examination, he was to accompany his cousin and her daughter to Cuttack. The three of them would discreetly depart from Balasore to reach the Cuttack residence of the bride's maternal grandfather.

The plan was a success, and the marriage was eventually held in Cuttack. The newlywed couple enjoyed a prosperous life, with the groom rising to become one of the leading mine owners in Odisha. Interestingly, he also became a distant relative of mine since his youngest sister married my wife Rashmi's elder brother, Barada (Badu).

However, Sudama soon faced a series of challenges. He had left Radha Prasanna Das's place and helped his wife and daughter escape, making him a persona non grata in the eyes of RPD. Unfortunately, his own uncle disapproved of his actions as well. Both considered him the central figure responsible for the escape and withdrew their support. Even the support promised by his cousin disappeared. He relocated to Tulsipur Matha for his residence in Cuttack, where he received free meals. From there, he commuted to Ravenshaw College for his studies.

In 1955, Sudama graduated. To support himself, he began offering tuition to children in the police colony nearby. Fortunately, he passed the examination for the State Secretariat Service and secured a position there. Subsequently, I lost contact with Sudama, and to this day, I have no knowledge of his later life.

Returning to the primary focus and activities at school, my time was fully occupied with both studies and extracurricular pursuits. I also made sure to allocate enough time for playing with my siblings at home. This marked the first time in Balasore when we didn't have a home tutor to assist Menki, Budha, and me with our school homework. All three of us had to put in extra effort to complete our assignments, which often took longer hours without any assistance. However, this experience helped us gain a deeper understanding of our lessons, and that clarity in our knowledge system has remained with us throughout our lives.

I struggled with sketching and received multiple warnings from the drawing teacher about my lack of improvement in this skill. On one occasion, the teacher became so frustrated that he struck my knuckles with a wooden duster typically used for the blackboard. The pain was intense, and I reacted by shouting, using harsh language, and even threatening the teacher.

The teacher forcefully escorted me to the headmaster's office. I received a stern warning, and the headmaster threatened to expel me from the school if I ever displayed such indiscipline again. The teacher was instructed to wait in the headmaster's office while I was asked to leave.

During my meeting with the Head Master, he scolded the teacher and informed him that his actions were unlawful, warning that my father could potentially have him arrested for his misconduct. I overheard these discussions while discreetly standing outside the headmaster's office door.

After the teacher came out of the office, I confronted him and threatened to break his head when he would go to the railway station on Saturday to catch his train to the village. Fearing for his safety, the teacher became extremely apprehensive and decided not to travel to his village that Saturday. Consequently, he overlooked my absence in his class, and I routinely skipped his class to spend time at a corner of the playground where there was a gym.

I was sociable at school and could easily connect with all my classmates. Since the school was exclusively for boys, I didn't experience any shyness that might have resulted from the presence of female students. Although I was an average student, I excelled in extracurricular activities. I had the honour of representing my school in the district sports competition held in November 1947 for children in my age group. In that event, I became the District Athletic Champion for my age category, marking the first time a student from Balasore Zila School had achieved this distinction. This accomplishment was announced to all the students during the morning prayer meeting the following day.

During that meeting, the headmaster made a special appearance and proudly displayed the trophy I had won for the school. From that day forward, I became a recognisable figure among the fifteen hundred students at the school. Additionally, I received a special commendation from the District Inspector of Schools, which was presented to me by the Head Master. My family was immensely proud of my sporting achievement, and they encouraged me to excel in my studies as well, ensuring a smoother path towards my life goals.

On that memorable day, Baba was so delighted that he gifted me a costly BSA bicycle. This generous gift is etched into my memory as one of my most cherished possessions. I willingly shared my bicycle with all my siblings, and they enjoyed going on "double riding" trips with me.

In January 1948, Baba received a promotion and was appointed to the Indian Police Service (IPS) cadre. He was assigned the position of Superintendent of Police (SP) for Keonjhar and was instructed to assume his new role by the end of the month. This meant that I would once again have to stay in Balasore for at least three more months, as my annual examination for promotion to class IX was scheduled for the second week of April. I could only join the family in Keonjhar by May.

Baba discussed my accommodations with the Head Master, and he readily agreed to let me stay in the school hostel. I moved to the hostel during the last week of January, when the family relocated. I was assigned to a double-bedded room, and my roommate was Suman Panigrahi, who was a year younger than me. Although the hostel provided food, I found it lacking compared to the delicious dishes prepared by Maa. To satisfy my hunger, I would eat the *pithas* that Maa had packed in my luggage for the hostel.

Suman's father owned numerous mango orchards, one of which was located approximately twenty-five kilometres away from Balasore. He also had another orchard near the hostel. These orchards boasted several tall, old trees that produced delicious local mango varieties. Tragically, a fatal accident occurred in one of these orchards, involving a resident of the hostel. This incident occurred after the final school examination in April 1948. The guards of the mango grove would permit many hostel students to enter and pick ripe mangoes since they were Suman's hostel mates.

One afternoon following the final examination, a hostel student ventured into the orchard alone. His purpose was to collect mangoes solely for himself to take home the next day as he was departing the hostel for the upcoming vacation. Unfortunately, while standing on a branch more than fifteen feet above the ground and attempting to shake the tree for ripe mangoes to fall, the branch suddenly snapped. He fell directly onto his head, resulting in instantaneous death.

Thankfully, Chandi and Suman were not involved in the incident. During that time, they had gone to watch a matinee movie. The police visited the hostel to question Suman. After verifying with me that Suman had indeed been with me at the cinema during the incident, the officer left. He was familiar with me due to my father, Baba, and decided it was best not to trouble the kids. Following that incident, the hostel residents were prohibited from leaving without written permission from the warden. This incident deeply affected me during my last days at the hostel, and I chose not to mention it to my parents.

In the first week of May, the exam results were released, and I was promoted to class IX. After obtaining my transfer certificate from the school, I left for Keonjhar. An orderly constable sent by Baba accompanied me. We boarded an express bus at eight in the morning for the approximately 180-kilometre journey, which took seven hours. The journey included three half-hour breaks at Bhadrakh, Jajpur, and Ghatagaon (Tarini).

The journey from Jajpur to Keonjhar was quite delightful as the bus passed through dense forests. We spotted various wild animals, like jungle fowl, foxes, rabbits, deer, and more, crossing the road. I enjoyed a delicious lunch at the Ghatagaon Tarini temple, relishing the tasty prasad. I also brought back a few coconuts offered at the temple for the family.

Finally, I arrived home around four in the afternoon. Meeting Maa, Baba, and my four siblings after more than three months filled me with immense happiness. I was greatly impressed by our well-designed bungalow, which served as our residence. Kuni and Menki gave me a tour of the house, and I was particularly thrilled to share a spacious room with Budha. Our room had a connecting door to the adjacent room where Kuni, Menki, and Lakhi stayed. Next to the sisters' room was our parents' room. I had never seen such large bedrooms with such high ceilings before.

When I arrived at Keonjhar, I was thrilled to discover that our house had a study room on the side where I could do my homework in peace. However, what really caught my attention was Baba's expansive home office. This office wasn't just a single chamber; it had two additional rooms attached to it. One was reserved for visitors, and the other was for his steno sub-inspector. Children like me were not allowed to enter this section when Baba was conducting official business. Public visitors who had appointments in advance could also meet with him in this home office. These experiences were entirely new and intriguing to me.

I also appreciated the spacious compound surrounding the house, which included a convenient portico for parking our car.

But the highlight of my time in Keonjhar was the family's recently acquired Ford V8 station wagon, proudly parked on the porch. It instantly captured my fascination. The powerful rumble of its engine sounded like sweet music to my ears, and its acceleration felt like the graceful leap of a Royal Bengal Tiger. Riding in this car was an exhilarating and comfortable experience, akin to the warmth and comfort of being in my mother's lap. I was ecstatic about the car and resolved to learn how to drive as quickly as possible, despite being too young to obtain a driving licence at the time. Most of my spare moments were spent on the front verandah, admiring the beauty of the station wagon parked in the portico.

My enrollment in the new school was just a couple of months away, as the next session always began in July. During these two months, I approached the office driver and asked him to start teaching me how to drive a police jeep. I managed to convince the Sikh driver, Gaja Singh, to provide me with lessons without my parents' knowledge.

On one occasion, while I was in the midst of my driving lessons, I accidentally collided with the police jeep with a large boulder. Fortunately, Gaja was able to regain control of the vehicle swiftly, preventing a major accident and any damage to the Jeep. Both the driver and my siblings were too frightened by my intimidating demeanour to report these incidents to Baba and Maa. Consequently, I continued my daily driving lessons almost six days a week, dedicating my full attention to learning how to drive quickly.

I later discovered that Gaja Singh's parents originally hailed from Patiala State in Punjab. Their relocation to Keonjhar occurred when the King of Keonjhar married the princess from Patiala State. As per the customs followed by princely states at the time, royal brides would transfer to their husband's palace accompanied by substantial dowries and a few families from their own states to serve as attendants.

Similar arrangements were observed in other princely states as well. For instance, the parents of an individual named Amar Singh, who were originally from Nabha in Punjab, settled in Bolangir State. They had accompanied the princess from Nabha State after she married the Maharaja of Bolangir. Subsequent to the mergers of states, Amar Singh, who was then in the service of the Bolangir king, became a part of the Odisha government and was later promoted to the IAS cadre in Odisha. These occurrences were quite common during that era, as many such marriages took place. Sons and daughters from various princely states across India, while studying in England, often fell in love and later formalised their unions. Such occurrences were not unique and transpired in different regions of the country as well.

Returning to my time in Keonjhar, our family frequently organised picnic outings during that period. My siblings and I thoroughly enjoyed these excursions, and our desire for more never seemed to wane, given the abundance of stunning scenic spots in and around the Keonjhar district. In hindsight, I now realise that if I had possessed a camera back then, it would have created a remarkable collection of memories.

Beyond the boundaries, at the rear of the official bungalow, stretched vast green fields that extended all the way to a distant hill. Every morning during those two months, I would take Menki and Budha for long jogs across these expansive green fields, from the rear of our bungalow to the forests on the hills beyond.

Once you reached a certain point along the forest's perimeter, you entered the terrain teeming with the hill's flora and fauna. Even during daylight hours, it was unsafe to venture further beyond a particular point. The forest was home to a variety of wild animals, including bears, hyenas, and other predators. Additionally, it served as a perilous habitat for numerous poisonous snakes. Late at night, wild bears would sometimes approach the boundary walls of the bungalow, adding to the sense of danger in the vicinity.

During these occasions, my mother kept a watchful eye on me, a necessity brought about by the fact that her other two children were often compelled to accompany the troublemaker, which was me. Over time, I became intimately familiar with the surroundings of this area, and I fondly referred to it as the "Wild West," a term I had picked up from some English fiction books. These visits to the area always felt rejuvenating, although we had to exercise extreme caution to avoid encountering snakes hidden in the bushes.

In July, my father took Menki and me to Gibson High School for our admissions. It was a coeducational institution, marking the first time both of us attended such a school. I was enrolled in Class IX, while Menki was placed in Class V. The school appeared to be as spacious as the one in Balasore, although it had fewer students—around 900 compared to Balasore's 1500. The school was located nearly a kilometre away from our residence, and Menki and I used my bicycle to commute to school.

The school did not have a canteen. There were no morning prayers. Its playground was small, and it neither had a gym nor a PT teacher. The language spoken by a sizable number of students had a mixed accent of Odia and tribal vocabulary. To adjust to these surroundings, I had to make enough efforts, which consumed considerable time. The school did not provide much scope for extracurricular activities. That was not good news for me. The children here appeared more introverted and seemed not to have the quality of fellow feeling. This was a novel experience for me.

I always revelled in the jolly outdoor spirit of the coastal populace. The fearful and antagonistic feelings of the Gadajat people were anathema to me. I assumed that the attitude of fear and lack of trust displayed by these people was probably induced by the perpetual tyranny of their earlier rulers! I had heard a lot of stories that indicated the brutality of their rulers.

I had to accept the school and all its characteristics as fait accompli. There was no other option, as this was the only high school there. I sincerely hoped for a change of place to happen soon. I hoped for Baba's transfer to a better place soon after I completed my class IX at that school.

This was the period when the transition from childhood to adolescence was taking place. The unfamiliar territory of the teenage years was slowly emerging. During this phase, some children tend to exhibit a rebellious attitude, especially in families where sarcasm outweighs love.

In families where discord is more prevalent than love, children can grow up without clear guidance, leading to potential psychological issues, extreme animosity, and imbalanced behaviour towards others. Such situations are more commonly observed in societies influenced by Western culture. However, the values and traditions instilled by Indian culture tend to mitigate these occurrences, fostering stronger family bonds despite the decline of the joint family system.

While some Indian families may adopt western cultural norms and experience such issues, my family was fortunate to be god-fearing, compassionate, and loving. All family members lived for each other, bound together by deep love and a strong connection. Our parents set ideal examples, and the siblings maintained harmonious relationships under the protective care of our parents.

The atmosphere at home was serene and filled with profound compassion. Consequently, regardless of external challenges, none of my family members ever lost their composure. They consistently sought to transform adverse circumstances into opportunities and possibilities. These qualities were inherited from our virtuous parents, with Baba deserving more credit for instilling them.

While I observed variations in the emotions, attitudes, and behaviours of my new classmates, it didn't lead me down a rebellious path. Instead, I quickly adapted and succeeded in doing so. I attribute this adaptability to my parents' upbringing and hold deep gratitude for the values they instilled in me, values that remain important to me to this day.

I noticed that many students in my class were not originally from Keonjhar Town. They either commuted daily from nearby villages, often covering the distance barefoot or by bicycle. The presence of such a diverse mix of students contributed to a more tolerant school atmosphere and encouraged adaptability among all. This also helped alleviate any reservations I initially had about my classmates.

My transition from childhood to adolescence occurred during my time in the Balasore Zila School hostel.

* * *

Ever Happy Family

Chandidas

Rashmi

Mona

Dimpy

Dev

Teenage

The pivotal period of my teenage years began to take shape upon my arrival in Keonjhar in May 1948.

My driving lessons with Gaja, the chauffeur, occupied my thoughts considerably. I made an effort to acquaint myself with the inner workings of motor vehicles, a subject that held immense fascination for me. This passion for cars and driving would remain a favourite pastime for over five decades. The family outings to nearby picturesque locations during the two months before school resumed provided enjoyable diversions and engaging activities.

Baba typically left for the office at 9:30 in the morning, with Gajapati driving him in a police jeep. After dropping off Baba, Gaja returned home with the jeep around 10 a.m. Then, three hours later, at 1 p.m., he would depart, carrying Baba's lunch in a tiffin carrier from home. These three hours, during which Gaja remained at the house with the police jeep, became my window for driving lessons.

I quickly grasped the driving lessons in just two months. Of course, I acquired these lessons after inadvertently colliding the vehicle with gate pillars, roadside mileposts, and trees multiple times. Fortunately, Gaja would intervene promptly, preventing significant visible damage to both the Jeep and the objects that got hit. Baba remained oblivious to these incidents, as he had no knowledge of my driving endeavours.

I began attending school in July. On the first day, I was dropped off and picked up by Gaja in Baba's car. Afterward, I would ride my bicycle to school. The school building had two stories, and my class was located on the first floor. The class consisted of forty students, including six girls.

The student desks were designed to accommodate two students each, with four desks in each row. All six girls sat in the front row, spanning three desks. The fourth desk in the front row was assigned to me, where I sat alongside another classmate, Rabi. I let Rabi sit to my left, which placed him closer to the girls' desks. I couldn't help but notice his happiness at being in such proximity to the girls!

One of Rabi's relatives, Natu, was also a classmate. He was a tall and lean boy, and coincidentally, his cousin was in the same class. Rabi also had a distant connection with her, and she sat at a nearby desk. During times when the teachers were not present, Natu and Rabi engaged in lively conversations with all the girls. This chit-chat would continue during lunch breaks as well. These interactions initially felt unusual to me. In my previous schools in Cuttack and Balasore, there were no female students in my class. For the first few days, I felt somewhat awkward until I formed my own group of friends.

Given my active involvement in sports and games, my circle of friends consisted of fellow enthusiasts of these activities. I was appointed as the captain of the school's football team, and under my leadership, the school secured the district football championship. This sudden success greatly boosted my popularity among the school's students. However, my older peers in classes X and XI were envious of me. Still, they hesitated to engage in any hazing or teasing since I was the son of the police superintendent of the district.

I recall a humorous incident that occurred at school. During one of the Sanskrit classes, the teacher asked me to engage in a conversation with a female student in Sanskrit. The task was to read aloud a scripted conversation between a girl and a boy, as provided in the textbook. Boldly, I informed the teacher that I wouldn't do it because the girl wasn't one of my friends. This surprised the teacher, but he tactfully chose not to insist on it.

In December 1948, the district-level sports competition for all schools in Keonjhar district was held. During this event, my group of friends and I achieved the highest number of prizes for our school. As a result, our school was declared the best school in the district by the Sports Committee. Personally, I excelled in multiple events, securing first place in the 100 metres and 200 metres races, as well as in the 400 metres relay race and the long jump event. The school recognised and honoured our achievements, marking a significant accomplishment for us.

During the Durga Puja festivities, my father was conducting his official duties at our residence one afternoon. I observed a gentleman who had come to meet my father at our home office. He had arrived in a brand-new Ford car and had parked it on the road near our front gate, leaving the car unlocked with the ignition key inside. I couldn't resist the temptation and got into the car, starting its engine. Assuming the gentleman would take at least twenty minutes, I drove the car for about twelve minutes and then returned it to the parking spot. To my shock, I saw the gentleman waiting for his car. The office attendants had informed him about my unauthorised use of the vehicle. When I exited the car, the gentleman inspected it to ensure there was no damage. Relieved that his car was unharmed, he praised my driving skills and advised me not to engage in such activities in the future. Thankfully, he chose not to report the incident to my father, and in hindsight, I am immensely grateful to him.

I later learned that the man in question was Sirajuddin, the largest owner of iron ore mines in Odisha. A few months later, I had the opportunity to meet him again when I accompanied my father on a tour to Barbil. Sirajuddin commended me as a smart young boy, and my father remained unaware of my misadventure with his car that had occurred a few months earlier.

Barbil, the place visited by me and Baba on that tour, was the hub of activities for the mining and allied companies. These companies were mining high-grade iron ores in vast areas of Keonjhar and adjoining Sundergarh districts. In these areas, the high-grade ore reserves were very high. The operations were earlier initiated with surface mining. Sirajuddin's company, being the biggest of the lot, employed a large number of mining laborers. It deployed a number of modern heavy mining machines. When I visited Sirajuddin's office with Baba, I was very impressed with that office's setup.

Before departing from Barbil, following lunch at the Dak Bungalow, I took a stroll through the expansive and bustling market of the town. The marketplace was teeming with people from various states, including a significant number of foreigners. It dwarfed the market in Keonjhar both in size and activity. The journey to Barbil took me through dense forests, where I had the opportunity to witness deer, nilgai, wild boars, hyenas, bears, and other wildlife crossing the road. It was a memorable visit, and upon my return to Keonjhar, I shared my experiences with my siblings.

In preparation for the final examinations in March 1949, my family and I explored several scenic destinations in Keonjhar. One of the highlights was driving through the Telkoi Ghat while visiting the Gonashika Temple, which was constructed at the source of the Baitarani River. Baitarani is one of the major rivers in Odisha, known for causing annual floods that inundate vast areas in Keonjhar, Balasore, and Mayurbhanj districts. These floods lead to significant damage to crops and habitats, exacerbating the poverty and suffering of a large rural population.

I had the opportunity to visit the Ghatagaon Tarini temple multiple times with Maa. These journeys took us through dense forests teeming with a variety of wild animals, including tigers and elephants. However, the visits I cherished the most were the ones with my parents and siblings to the numerous waterfalls nestled in the forested hills. These excursions immersed us in the untamed beauty of nature, offering glimpses of diverse flora and fauna. As time passed, I witnessed the gradual depletion of these once-dense forests, and the populations of wildlife dwindled significantly. The pristine beauty of nature now exists only in my cherished memories.

Reflecting on these experiences today brings me pure and delightful pleasure. Among the most grand and memorable visits was our trip to the Badaghagra Waterfall. Located nine kilometres from Keonjhar town and three kilometres downstream from the Sanaghagra Waterfall, this perennial waterfall is fed by the small Machhakandana river, cascading from a height of two hundred feet. The surrounding scenery is nothing short of breathtaking. My family and I spent half a day at this enchanting place, exploring nearby picnic spots and savouring a delicious packed lunch we had brought from home.

The results of my class IX final examination were released in the first week of April. I performed well and was promoted to class X. The school then closed for its summer vacation, which extended until the middle of June. In May, Baba received a transfer to Bolangir, and he was scheduled to assume his new position there in mid-May 1949. Consequently, during the summer break, I had to obtain my transfer certificate for admission to the school in Bolangir. Unfortunately, I couldn't bid farewell to my friends in Keonjhar, as they had already gone to their hometowns.

The packing of our household belongings was carried out by our family members, with assistance from four orderly constables and our driver, Gajapati. Towards the end of April, the family embarked on the journey to Bolangir via Cuttack. They made a one-week stop in Cuttack while the truck transporting our household goods continued straight to Bolangir. In the second week of May 1949, the family drove from Cuttack to Bolangir. Our cousin Pari also accompanied us.

In the middle of June, I was enrolled in class X at PRHE School in Bolangir. It didn't take long for me to notice that the spoken Odia dialect used by my classmates differed from what I was accustomed to. The way people spoke Odia in western Odisha, where Bolangir is located, had variations compared to the coastal Odia dialect I was familiar with.

The students in my class used to tease and make fun of me by calling me 'Kataki' behind my back. Because of this, I began skipping classes. I would return home after an hour, offering false excuses for my absence. After about a week, my deception was discovered, and I was reprimanded. When I explained the reason for my class-skipping behaviour to Baba, he sent his deputy to report the matter to the headmaster. That put an end to the mischief, and I happily resumed attending school regularly.

I made several friends among my classmates. One of my friends was the brother of my home tutor, whose name was Purna Chandra Rath. I affectionately referred to him as 'FMC,' which humorously stood for 'Full Moon Chariot,' translating his name Purna Chandra Rath into English. We remained good friends.

I completed my schooling, and after passing the test examination in class XI, I qualified to sit for the Matriculation Examination at Utkal University. I remember that the tuition I received from FMC's elder brother greatly helped me improve my command of the English language as well as my understanding of history and geography. I also received valuable guidance in mathematics from this home tutor, which strengthened my foundational knowledge. I felt grateful to him for helping me establish a strong educational base. Unfortunately, I lost all contact with him and his brother, and I can no longer recall the name of my dear tuition master.

For the final matriculation examination, which took place in January 1951, I had to change my examination centre due to Baba's transfer to Cuttack. My new examination centre was Cuttack Mission School, conveniently located on the same road as Stewart School and Sailabala Women's College. This centre was much closer to Baba's official residence, where we would be staying for the next three years. In fact, the house was within walking distance, so I walked to the exam centre for all the papers of the matriculation examination in February 1951.

After the examinations were over, it was a period of pure fun and enjoyment. From February until the second half of March, I had a great time. I spent these days with Menki, Budha, and Lakhi, my siblings. I entertained them with many stories, played football with them in the yard, and occasionally punished them for their supposed wrongdoings. One of their favourite punishments was to rub their noses on the wall, smudging the wall paint onto their noses, and then make them stand against the wall, assuming a "chair" position.

It was quite challenging for the children to stay in that position for even five minutes, and tears would start rolling down their faces in just two minutes. At that point, I would tell them that the punishment was over and take them to my room to narrate made-up stories about my encounters with ghosts, adding an element of excitement. Then I would give them lozenges as consolation. The sweets were purchased using their money from the "Gandhi Fund," which was another playful scheme I devised for my siblings. I initiated this fund and convinced them to contribute from their pocket money, telling them it would be used for any emergency needs of any one of them. However, this fund never served its intended purpose, and my three siblings were perpetually fooled by it. They never complained, as each of them was apprehensive of their overbearing older brother and his punishments.

During one of those days, Baba had an important duty for the state governor, and he needed to go in full uniform with his loaded service revolver. The Reader Babu, who was a Steno SI attached to the SP at his home office, took out the loaded revolver and placed it on a verandah chair. It was meant for Baba to pick it up after he had his breakfast. All four of us, as children, witnessed this. I grabbed the revolver and began to play with it, even threatening Lakhi with it and attempting to aim it at her. However, before I could aim, the revolver accidentally discharged with a loud bang. This happened because the Reader Babu had forgotten to engage the safety lock, and the trigger was inadvertently touched. Fortunately, no one was injured, but all of us children ran outside and hid. Furious, Baba reprimanded the Reader Babu for his carelessness.

There's an amusing anecdote about this Reader Babu, whose real name was Nalini Kant. However, I had given him a humorous nickname due to his unattractive face. I called him "Pati Muhan," as his face resembled that of a red monkey. To conceal the true meaning, we would refer to him as 'Paster Muster' behind his back. When he proposed to marry my cousin Pari, she rejected the proposal upon learning the hidden meaning of his nickname!

By the end of May 1951, the results of the matriculation examination were announced, and I passed in the second division. I was a bit disappointed as I missed achieving the first division by just 7 marks. In June 1951, I enrolled in the 1st year of Intermediate Science (ISc) at Ravenshaw College. However, during that time, the college was experiencing a student strike, and the police were stationed on campus. There was even a lathi charge, and some students were arrested by the police. Following Baba's advice, I decided to stay away from the college until the strike concluded in mid-July.

I was quite enamoured with the college campus, its hostels, and the library. The gym, badminton, and tennis courts were novel for me, as such facilities were not available in the schools I had previously attended. I also noticed that, unlike in schools, all the classes for I.Sc. students were conducted in English. Moreover, for different subjects like english, mathematics, physics, chemistry, botany, and zoology, students had to go to different lecture theaters. Another new experience was the freedom to wander around during the breaks between classes, which was greatly enjoyed by all the new college students.

I made the choice not to study botany and zoology, as I had no intention of pursuing a medical degree. Instead, I opted for general knowledge (GK) as an additional subject for examination, alongside physics, chemistry, and mathematics. In hindsight, this was a mistake, as GK contributed only 50% of the marks to one's total, while botany and zoology offered 100%. This decision led to me passing the I.Sc. examination in the second division, narrowly missing the first division by just 12 marks. I regretted this earlier choice.

I formed new friendships in college, some of which became very close and lasted into the later stages of my life. I had friends like Bimal, Bhabani, Prafulla, Prabhat, Basanta, Ashish, Raju, and Natu. There were also friends from the arts faculty (I.A.), including Barada, Rabi, Jagannath, Sudama, and Amaresh. College classes were interesting, and my friends were quite different from those I had in school. During my free periods, I often visited the South Indian Restaurant and the Gujarati Tiffin Centre, where my friends treated me, and I reciprocated their kindness with treats of my own from time to time.

There were six female students in my class, and the boys would identify them by their roll numbers: 4, 15, 57, 96, 99, and 102. Among these girls, three were particularly popular among the boys due to their beauty and fair complexions. One of them, with roll number 57, had a slightly snobbish attitude. This demeanour stemmed from the fact that her elder sister was an

English lecturer married to the English professor of the college. Interestingly, this English professor happened to be the elder brother of my friend Bhabani. Although classmates would playfully tease Bhabani as the brother-in-law of his sister-in-law's sister, he hardly reacted. Bhabani always maintained a cool and composed demeanour, much like Lord Shiva himself. Later in life, Bhabani became a marine engineer and married a Malayali girl, while the girl with roll number 57 became a doctor and married an Odisha government officer.

The other three girls with roll numbers 4, 99, and 102 also pursued careers in medicine. Unfortunately, little is remembered about the remaining two girls, Roll 15 and Roll 96. In a twist of fate, my friend Ashish later married the elder sister of Roll 99, who was also a doctor, despite a six-year age difference between them. Another intriguing love story involved our classmate Bijoy, who eventually became a doctor and joined the Indian Army Medical Corps. He was deeply in love with Roll 57 and would cycle to her neighbourhood every evening, serenading her with love songs from Hindi films as he passed her residence. Tragically, Bijoy became a martyr during the 1962 Chinese aggression in Arunachal Pradesh, and his body was never recovered.

The father of my friend Prafulla was a professor of physics, while Prabhat's father held the position of professor of economics. I used to visit their residences located within the college complex and fondly recall enjoying delicious Odia cakes during my visits. Similarly, I would also visit my friend Bimal's home in the SCB Medical Complex, where his father served as the Professor of Anatomy at the SCB Medical College. I visited Bimal's house more frequently than my other friends' places, and we often studied together at each other's homes. Both of us also attended private evening English classes conducted by the renowned teacher Amjad Ali, which took place near the famous Bilimoria petrol pump at Buxi Bazar.

Bimal was an exceptionally bright student. After completing his engineering degree at IIT Kharagpur, he pursued his MS (engineering) at the University at Buffalo, USA. He went on to serve as a vice president at IBM, overseeing their operations in Europe and Latin America. Later, after obtaining a green card and becoming an American citizen, he visited my place multiple times during his trips to India.

My daily commute to college involved a five-kilometre bicycle ride, which took approximately fifteen minutes. Weekday classes began at 11 a.m., so I typically left home around 10:30 a.m. after an early lunch, a common practice in those days. I returned home around five in the afternoon, and during my free periods, I enjoyed light refreshments either at the Gujarati or South Indian restaurant. To cover these expenses, I used my daily pocket money of two rupees. However, these costs were offset when a friend treated me. After receiving three to four such treats from friends in a month, I would reciprocate by treating them in return.

Most days, I made the journey back from college alone. However, on one occasion, my friend Amaresh, who studied in the arts faculty, rode back home alongside me on separate bicycles. As we were riding near Mangala Bagh crossing, we accidentally collided with a milkman carrying two large earthen vessels filled with curd on a shoulder yoke. Both vessels broke, and the entire load of curd spilled onto the road. Without waiting for the stunned milkman to react, Amaresh and I quickly pedalled away. After cycling rapidly for about ten minutes, we paused on Cantonment Road to check if anyone was following us. For several days afterward, I avoided using the road to the college, opting instead for the ring road along the Mahanadi River embankment. Similarly, Amaresh chose the ring road along the Kathjori River embankment.

During this time, I distinctly remember attending the teenage marriage ceremony of my friend and classmate, Basanta K. Sahu. He was the grandson of the renowned Odia MP Laxmi Narayan Sahu. The wedding took place in 1952, when we were in our second year of I.Sc. All his friends, including myself and Bhabani, were invited to the wedding. We decided to cycle together to join the groom's marriage procession. However, while riding a bicycle that Bhabani was propelling, the bicycle suddenly skidded, causing both of us to fall into a drain near 'sutahat,' completely covered in filth. We had to return to our homes to clean ourselves and change our clothes before joining the marriage procession, albeit a bit late. This incident became the subject of jokes for quite some time. Basanta went on to pursue further studies, earning his IIT Kharagpur degree and later completing his MS and PhD in geology. He eventually received the prestigious Shanti Swarup Bhatnagar Science Award in 1980 in the subject group of Earth, Oceans, etc.

During this period, my father purchased a brand new Ford Zephyr car, distinguished by its striking blue paint and unique appearance. Whenever my father was away on tour in a police vehicle, it was my opportunity to drive the Zephyr to college. It was, in a way, a bit of a show-off. On some occasions, my friend Bimal and I even drove it to Choudwar, where we climbed atop a damaged Dakota aircraft dating back to the Second World War.

During college holidays, I often went on picnics with my friends Prafulla, Prabhat, Bhabani, and Ashish to various nearby locations. One of our most frequented spots was Chandikhole, situated about 40 kilometres away from Cuttack. We typically travelled there by train, although sometimes we used our bicycles. Chandikhole had a hill with a temple dedicated to the goddess

Durga. This hill was part of the Eastern Ghat range and featured a diverse range of flora and fauna, some of which were quite rare. In later years, the government developed Chandikhole as a tourist destination, offering facilities for overnight stays and guides for trekking in the hills and forests. It also became a popular stop for transporters, who enjoyed meals at nearby dhabas while taking breaks from their journeys to places like Paradeep, Kolkata, or Chennai.

My bustling college life in Cuttack concluded with the final examinations in March 1953. The results were announced in the first week of May. Many of my classmates pursued studies in engineering and medicine, while a few of us, including myself, Prafulla, Prabhat, and Ashish, chose to pursue a B.Sc. degree. Prabhat and Ashish enrolled at Ravenshaw College for their B.Sc., while Prafulla and I decided to attend the University of Allahabad. We applied and were admitted to the university in 1953. At that time, the University of Allahabad held a prestigious reputation in India for the high quality of its teaching, boasting the best faculty and a track record of producing eminent administrators, academics, and scientists in the country.

Securing admission to the university's hostel proved to be a challenge. Fortunately, my uncle, Dr. P.K. Parija, had a personal connection with the Vice Chancellor of Allahabad University, Dr. Sri Ranjan. With his help, I was able to secure a hostel seat at the PCB hostel. However, Prafulla wasn't as lucky and had to arrange for private accommodation. He made arrangements with a research scholar named Dr. Tribikram Pati, who had rented a house very close to Nehru's Anand Bhawan. Since the hostel had to be occupied before the start of classes, I left for Allahabad earlier than Prafulla, who joined the university shortly after.

Classes commenced in July, and the science faculty was located in the Muir College block, approximately a kilometre away from the hostel. During that time, ragging of newcomers in hostels was quite severe. In my hostel, the ringleader of ragging was known to the freshmen as 'Kak Bhushandi' due to his rough and dark appearance. Thankfully, I managed to avoid severe ragging with the protection of a senior Odia student who had been residing in the hostel for over three years and was in his final year of M.A.

On the hostel campus, I had to adhere to the protocol established by the senior residents, which involved showing respect and obedience. This included giving the first right of passage to seniors when going to the washroom blocks and offering them precedence when going for lunch or dinner to areas where several cooks had set up their stalls to serve food to hostel residents.

The food served at the hostel stalls was delicious, and special dishes were available on Sundays and holidays. For tea and snacks, some residents arranged private deliveries to their hostel rooms, while others frequented nearby eating establishments along University Road. A popular joint in the area was known as the University Café, operated by a former student leader of the university.

After spending six months in the hostel, I was persuaded by my friend Prafulla to move out and join him and Dr. Pati in a nearby, newly constructed, spacious independent house with three bedrooms. This house was also located on Anand Bhawan-Sangam Road. They shared the house with their domestic help, Ram Avatar, who handled all the household chores, including cooking. I was pleased to have my own room and meals prepared according to my preferences. While both of my friends commuted to the teaching campus together, I often returned later because I had an optional english class that Prafulla did not attend. Besides, I engaged in sports like football, badminton, and table tennis at the University Arts Campus after our daily classes. I also participated in debates held on the same campus.

During this period, I became acquainted with Niranjan Panda (NP), who had joined the university to pursue his M.Sc. in soil science. I had a chance encounter with him in the chemistry department. He hailed from Sambalpur in Odisha, and his family had strong political connections in western Odisha. He was staying at a lodge that was located opposite Muir Hostel and near the entrance to the Science Faculty of the University. After my classes, I used to visit him before heading to the Arts Faculty Campus, and we became lifelong friends. Dr. Panda later earned his postgraduate degree in nuclear chemistry in agriculture and went on to complete his Ph.D. Later in his career, Dr. Panda served as the Vice-Chancellor of Sambalpur University and the Orissa University of Agriculture Technology (OUAT), Bhubaneswar.

During my badminton games, I got acquainted with a female player named Veena. She was the daughter of a professor of English who had a foreign wife. Veena was not only beautiful but also a skilled badminton player, excelling in tournaments at both the local and inter-university levels. We often teamed up for mixed doubles and won many tournaments together. I developed an infatuation for her but only confided in Niranjan Panda about it. Panda advised me to focus on my studies and let go of such an infatuation. At my insistence, Panda suggested that I first find out the girl's feelings on the matter and then proceed accordingly. However, I lacked the courage to openly express my feelings for her. Indirectly, through my friends in the badminton community, I learned that the girl had a boyfriend whose parents were family friends. She was deeply involved with her boyfriend and had little interest in anyone else.

My infatuation with Veena had a negative impact on my studies. I performed poorly in my annual examinations and ended up losing a year because I had to drop a subject in the final examination. However, after overcoming my infatuation, I managed to pass the B.Sc. examination, and I did so with distinction. I worked hard to regain my focus and concentration on my studies and life in general. This turnaround in my academic performance not only relieved the concerns of my parents but also marked the end of the stressful events in my life.

* * *

Adulthood

(Post-Graduation And My First Job)

After completing my undergraduate degree in science, I returned to Allahabad University in 1957 to pursue my Master's Degree in Economics. At that time, Professor J. K. Mehta was the head of the Economics Department and also the dean of the Commerce faculty. He was a renowned economist who had even turned down an offer from the government of India to lead the Planning Commission of India. Being aware of his stature, I was determined to study under his guidance, and I successfully became one of his students. During the admission process, I met Ashok, who was the son of Justice Bhargav (ICS) of the Allahabad High Court. Ashok and I quickly became close friends during our postgraduate studies.

Upon gaining admission to the M.A. programme in Economics, I also secured a place at the Madan Mohan Malavya Hindu Hostel within the university. By this time, I was already a senior student who had made a name for himself through participation in university debating competitions and excelling in sports like football and badminton. I was appointed as the hostel prefect and was assigned a single room. The hostel's warden was Mr. Sebastian, a devout Christian gentleman who had retired from his position as an English lecturer at Allahabad University following his wife's passing. Mr. Sebastian held me in high regard, and we developed a strong camaraderie during my two-year stay at the hostel.

In the Arts Faculty, I had the opportunity to meet several other Odia students, including J. P. Das and Gouranga Naik, among others. J. P. Das was pursuing his M.A. in Political Science, while Gouranga was studying Philosophy for his M.A. There were many amusing stories associated with Gouranga Naik, who resided in the Diamond Jubilee Hostel. One of the anecdotes revolved around his first year in the hostel. One summer night, while he was peacefully sleeping on the hostel's lawns, four senior students decided to play a prank on him. They lifted his cot, with him still fast asleep on it, and carried it to the main road in front of the hostel. They paraded around the hostel, cot and all, while loudly chanting "Ram Naam Satya Hai," a phrase often associated with Hindu funerals, suggesting that they were transporting a deceased person!

Gouranga was understandably shocked by this ragging incident, which later became a well-known joke at the university.

Despite the occasional antics, I remained focused on my studies to achieve good results. For my Master's degree in Economics, I chose a diverse range of subjects, including History of Economic Thoughts, Rural Economics, Theory and Practice of Statistics, Cooperation, Advanced Economic Theory, Mathematical Economics, International Trade, and Fiscal Policy. Additionally, I selected Trade and Tariff Policies in Underdeveloped Areas as my special paper. Throughout the two years of my M.A. degree, I had to submit research papers on significant contemporary economic issues, both in the M.A. previous and M.A. final years. These submissions were followed by Viva Voce examinations, and the marks obtained during these oral examinations were added to the overall result sheets.

I performed exceptionally well in the M.A. Economics (previous) examination and secured the second position on the university merit list. I had garnered the respect and admiration of both the faculty and fellow students in the Economics department. I was appointed as the Chief Editor of the Departmental Magazine, a prestigious role that came with the responsibility of overseeing its annual publication. During this period, I also achieved a series of victories in English debates organised by the university, further enhancing my reputation on the Arts Faculty campus.

In that same year, under my leadership, the university's football team emerged victorious in the inter-varsity football tournament. Additionally, I captained both the university's badminton and table tennis teams, both of which secured victories in the inter-varsity competitions. However, these extracurricular involvements did affect my preparation for the final examination, and as a result, my ranking in the university merit list for the M.A. final examination slipped from 2nd place to 9th.

During my M.A. (previous) studies, I can recall an incident involving two of my classmates that could have led to their expulsion from the university. One of them was a young man named Tyagi, a resident of Sunderlal Hostel, while the other was a female student and my classmate, Sonam, who resided in the women's hostel. One summer night, they were discovered in a compromising situation at the famous Albert Park in Allahabad by a patrolling police officer. The matter was promptly reported to the university proctor, and the consequences could have been severe, potentially resulting in their expulsion. However, my friend Ashok played a pivotal role in saving them. Thanks to his father's influence—his father held the position of Chief Justice of the Allahabad

High Court at that time—Ashok managed to shield both individuals from legal prosecution by the police.

My life in the Hindu Hostel was incredibly busy. I would wake up at six in the morning and start my day with biscuits and a cup of tea that I made in my room. After this light breakfast, I dedicated an hour to studying before heading to the university campus for my classes. Typically, classes would conclude around three in the afternoon. Once the academic day was over, I would engage in football practice, followed by badminton.

In addition to football and badminton, I also practiced table tennis in the hostel until eight in the evening. After dinner at nine, I would conduct my duties as the prefect of the hostel, which included making rounds to ensure everything was in order. Occasionally, I would visit the rooms of some of my Odia friends and playfully disrupt their studies late at night. After returning to my room around 9:30 PM, I would dedicate two more hours to studying before going to bed.

During the hot summer days, the hostel staff would move residents' beds to the front lawn or verandahs, and they would attach mosquito nets to the cots. Pedestal fans were strategically placed around these outdoor beds and connected through long extension cords to electrical outlets.

During holidays, I and my friends would visit cinema halls in Civil Lines and the Main Market areas of Motiganj. Our favourite theatres were the Palace Theatre in Civil Lines and Niranjan Cinema in Motiganj. The Palace Theatre usually screened English movies in the morning and had matinee shows on Sundays and holidays. For late-night shows, my group and I would either cycle together or ride the donkeys of washermen who lived in the nearby areas of our hostel. The memory of returning from the cinema hall after a late-night show, riding on donkeys, is one that I will never forget!

Students enjoyed a 50% concession on cinema tickets, which they could avail of by showing their university proctor-issued identity cards. The cost of tickets for the higher-class seats in the cinema halls was approximately one rupee. Students would typically watch three to four movies a month, and this expense was manageable within their monthly budgets. Their budgets primarily covered tuition fees, which were around nine rupees for the university, and about thirty-five rupees for hostel accommodation and food.

I received around one hundred twenty-five rupees every month from my parents, a princely sum in those days. Occasionally, I would lend money to some of my Odia friends upon their request, but unfortunately, many of these friends never repaid the loans. Later on, a few of them went on to qualify for the prestigious Indian Administrative Service (IAS) and Indian Police Service (IPS). Whenever I met these friends, I would playfully tease them about the loans they had never returned.

During my time in Allahabad, I had the opportunity to attend the 1954 Maha Kumbha festival. The festival grounds were vast, accommodating millions of devotees who came to take a holy dip at the confluence (Sangam) of the Ganga and Yamuna rivers. I, along with many other students, was selected by the university authorities to volunteer during the festival. We were stationed at the mela site and set up camp in a large tent along the riverfront, near a prominent fort. Our role was to assist the countless devotees who flocked to the site for the holy dip at Sangam during the festival. This experience of voluntary work was truly unique, and I felt fortunate to be able to help such a large number of devotees.

The Maha Kumbh festival takes place every 12 years and is a massive event compared to the annual Kumbh Mela. It is known for its sheer scale and the large number of attendees. However, with its enormous size, accidents are not uncommon. I remember one incident during our deployment when a pontoon bridge, set up at the confluence of the two rivers to facilitate pilgrims' bathing, suddenly collapsed due to the massive rush of devotees. The resulting stampede led to injuries, and many people had to be rescued from drowning. Fortunately, none of the student volunteers were injured. It was a unique and eye-opening experience for me and my fellow volunteers.

The Kumbh Mela attracts millions of visitors from all corners of India and around the world, showcasing the incredible diversity of our country. Sadhus of various orders and backgrounds set up camps and "Akharas" at the Mela, which covers vast areas of the dry riverbed spanning a few square kilometers. The Naga Sadhus, with their procession of horses, mules, and more, are a sight that few can ever forget.

During the last year of my stay in Allahabad, the first half was marked by numerous social events. However, in the last two months of the final quarter of that year, I shifted my focus entirely to my studies in preparation for the final examination. I significantly reduced my involvement in extracurricular activities and spent most of my time in the hostel. My only respite was a few games of table tennis each day in the hostel's common room. Even while taking leisurely strolls on the wide verandas and lawns of the hostel, I would go through my class notes and study materials. This period of intense preparation allowed me to moderately prepare for the final examination, which took place in March 1959.

After completing my final examination, I enjoyed my stay in Allahabad for over a month. I spent this time with friends and classmates, including Bhargava and a few others. We organised parties and outings to make the most of our remaining time before bidding farewell to Allahabad. The results were announced in the first week of May, and I was pleased to see that I had performed well, securing the 9th rank in the University Merit List. It felt like a redemption of my reputation as a good student, which had suffered during my undergraduate years in science.

As my departure date approached, I made final purchases of gifts for my parents and siblings using the money I had saved earlier. I attended several farewell parties hosted by classmates and faculty members in honour of the top ten students on the merit ist. Finally, on the 15th of May 1959, I bid my last farewell to Allahabad with tears in my eyes as the train left the city station at night. My several years of living in that historical city had transformed me into a responsible and well-rounded individual, and I will always be grateful for that experience.

Upon reaching Howrah station in Calcutta on the 16th morning, I waited for the 'Puri Express' train to Cuttack, scheduled for 9 p.m. I arrived in Cuttack around 6 a.m. on the 17th of May. After disembarking, I took a cycle rickshaw from the railway station to reach home, which took about twenty minutes. Baba, Maa, and four siblings were eagerly waiting for my arrival, as I had communicated my travel itinerary to them earlier. Upon reaching home, I touched my parents' feet as a sign of respect and affection and embraced my siblings, Kuni, Menki, Lakhi, and Budha. My family was delighted to receive the gifts I had brought for them.

I communicated my final examination results to whole of family. All were happy at my success. Baba informed that a call letter for my interview, to the post of a lecturer in Economics in Odisha Education Service, was received. I was scheduled to appear at that interview in August 1959. At the interview I was to present my I shared my final examination results with my entire family, and they were all overjoyed at my success. Baba informed me that I had received a call letter for an interview for the position of a lecturer in economics in the Odisha Education Service, scheduled for August 1959. I recalled that I had applied for this position with the Odisha Public Service Commission (OPSC) in February 1959, before my final M.A. examination.

I was hopeful that I would secure the job, but the interview was still about three months away. During this period, I contacted Ashok Bhargav and asked him to collect the required documents from the university office in July and send them to me. I provided Ashok with an authority letter to collect these documents, including the university proctor's character certificate. In the first week of July, Ashok collected these documents from the university office and promptly posted them to me.

The following days were spent in a leisurely manner. I enjoyed the affection and love of my doting parents and siblings. Baba and I went for long early morning walks together. Our usual route was along the ring road built on the embankment of the Mahanadi River, which ran along the rear boundary of our house. We walked on this road up to Chahata Ghat and then returned, passing by the Deer Park and Gora Kabar. These walks were truly invigorating and refreshing.

In the evenings, I would often take a stroll along the Mahanadi embankments with Menki, Budha, and Lakhi. After our walk, the four of us would collect evening snacks from Maa and head to the roof of the house to gossip while enjoying our treats. During these moments, I would share many stories from my time in Allahabad with Menki, Budha, and Lakhi. They were often surprised to hear about some of the incidents and experiences associated with their usually serious older brother.

I told them about how I used to attend late-night movie shows in Allahabad with a few friends, riding on donkeys that belonged to washermen living near our hostel. I explained that we would tie the donkeys at the cycle stand of the cinema hall, under the care of the cycle stand guard. They found it amusing that after the movie ended, we would ride back on these donkeys, singing loudly on the deserted streets in the middle of the night.

My siblings were also fascinated by my stories of late-night encounters with "ghosts" on the deserted roads of Allahabad's Civil Lines. These tales seemed never-ending. On one occasion, I shared a prank we played on an LLM student from Odisha who was staying at a lodge in Civil Lines. Little did we know that this gentleman would later become the Chief Justice of the Odisha High Court and eventually rise to the position of Chief Justice of the Supreme Court.

During his time in Allahabad, this future judge had the habit of drinking a lot of milk, both during breakfast and after dinner. He always kept a litre of milk in his room. My siblings were amused as I recounted how, in his absence, I and some of my Odia friends once placed a donkey inside his room. The donkey proceeded to drink all the milk and leave the room in a filthy state with its droppings. The gentleman's reaction to this incident caused quite a commotion, and it became a long-standing source of amusement among the student community in Allahabad.

I enjoyed my stay at the Tulsipur house. I found great pleasure in picking vegetables from the backyard garden. The house was surrounded by fruit trees, including bananas, mangoes, and jackfruits, which provided us with a healthy and delicious diet. Catching fish from the pond in the backyard also added to the enjoyment of my stay.

In July, I received all the necessary certificates from Allahabad University in preparation for my upcoming interview in August. I dedicated myself to preparing for the interview and reviewing various subjects. I also refreshed my memory on the topics of the research papers I had submitted at Allahabad University, as they might come up during the viva voce.

On the day of the interview, Maa lovingly served me curd and sugar before I left for the OPSC office at Cantonment Road. I arrived at the office around 10 a.m., as the interview was scheduled for 11 a.m. There, I encountered about fifteen other candidates from various disciplines who were also waiting for their interviews. While I tried to engage in friendly conversation with some of them to ease their nervousness, they appeared extremely tense and serious. Despite my efforts, it was challenging to put them at ease, so I eventually gave up trying.

The members of the OPSC board started arriving around 10:30 a.m. Many of them appeared to be retired government servants, and there were also experts for various categories of interviews present. The administrative staff took our original documents for verification and made photocopies, which was a time-consuming process. However, all the original documents were returned to the candidates after their interviews.

My interview lasted for more than half an hour, during which I answered the board's questions to the best of my abilities. They seemed impressed by my responses and were particularly interested in my extracurricular activities and achievements. They inquired about my transition from a science background to pursuing the arts, and I provided satisfactory answers to all their queries. Finally, the board hinted at my selection and wished me luck before bidding me farewell.

I received the appointment letter confirming my selection in the last week of September. The letter instructed me to join as a lecturer in economics at Fakir Mohan College, Balasore, by October 15, 1959. This college would later become an autonomous college and university, similar to Ravenshaw College in Cuttack.

In the second week of October, I travelled to Balasore and arranged accommodations for my stay. I reported for duty on the designated date, and the college principal warmly welcomed me and took my joining report. He mentioned that he, too, was an alumnus of Allahabad University with an M.A. in Political Science, establishing an amicable connection between us.

My first lecture was for the first-year B.A. Economics (Hons) students, and I chose to speak on 'The Evolution of the History of Economic Thought.' It seemed that the students enjoyed the lecture, and their positive feedback quickly spread among students in higher classes who also had economics as one of their subjects. In a typical week, I conducted fourteen classes for both B.A. (Hons) and B.A. (Pass) students, totaling nearly 120 students from the first and second years of both degree programs. Most of these students hailed from areas such as Balasore, Bhadrakh, Soro, and Niligiri and had completed their schooling in their respective hometowns. They were delighted to learn that I, too, had attended Balasore Zila School during my schooling days.

I became quite popular among my students. My lectures were known for their clarity, interesting content, and inclusion of facts and figures. Additionally, I would often join the students in playing football and badminton after classes, which was a pleasant surprise for them. This was quite different from the norm, as many other lecturers in colleges during that time tended to be aloof and distant. While my popularity grew, some of my colleagues at the college became jealous of my success and the innovative teaching methods I employed. However, their jealousy didn't bother me, as I had the full support of the college principal.

I wasn't entirely content with the remuneration structure and promotion policies in government jobs, which is why I chose not to appear for the UPSC examination to enter the IAS or IPS like many other Odia students who had studied in Allahabad. Instead, my plan was to pursue a doctorate degree through research under the guidance of Professor Mehta. Afterwards, I intended to join the teaching faculty at Allahabad University, where the pay and benefits were more attractive compared to Central services.

However, my original aspirations faced a hurdle. Central scholarships for research were only available from the second year onward, and my father had retired in 1958, making it difficult for him to finance another year of my education. Consequently, my initial dream had to be put on hold, and I returned home to take up the job in Balasore. Deep down, I knew that my ultimate goal would require me to move out of Odisha for better opportunities.

I kept my future plans to myself, not even sharing them with my parents. From the very first day of joining Balasore, I began searching for better prospects, aware that I would eventually need to leave Odisha to fulfil my dreams. However, I had to wait for another year.

In October 1960, I applied for a research job advertised by the Indian Chamber of Commerce and Industry (ICCI) in Calcutta. This position involved establishing a new department within ICCI dedicated to research and future planning for India's international trade. The goal was to develop practical schemes for ICCI's associates and members, helping them increase exports and optimise imports of raw materials for their production processes. It presented a highly challenging opportunity that aligned with my interests and promised to open up new career avenues both in India and abroad. I believed that working in this role would also enable me to pursue my doctorate (PhD).

I was also drawn to the job by the appealing remuneration it offered. The salary was nearly four times higher than what I was earning at the time, and it exceeded that of an IAS probationer by twofold. I had confidence that I would receive an interview invitation and ultimately be selected for the position. Beyond the financial aspect, I was genuinely interested in immersing myself in the dynamics of this new work environment.

The interview call arrived after the Durga Puja festival. I was scheduled to travel to Calcutta for the interview on November 25th. I appeared for the interview on the appointed day and was indeed selected for the position. I received the letter of appointment on the same day, along with instructions to join within three months, preferably by February 1, 1961.

I continued working at the college until the first week of January 1961. At that point, I submitted my resignation, collected my salary, and returned to Cuttack. I shared the details of my new opportunity with my parents, and while they were pleased with my decision, they had concerns about my accommodation and stay in Calcutta.

* * *

Zesty Life

(Between 26 and 58 years)

I was scheduled to begin my new job in Calcutta on February 1, 1961. I arrived in Calcutta on January 30th and went to the place my friend Amaresh had arranged for me to stay. It was a spacious house with eight bedrooms. The owner of the house rented out a portion of it, consisting of three bedrooms with an independent entrance, for six hundred rupees per month. This rent included breakfast and dinner service for three people. Amaresh was occupying one of the rooms in the rented portion, and another colleague of his was in the second room. Amaresh spoke to the landlord, and the third room was made available for me. This house was located on Rash Bihari Avenue in South Calcutta, near Desha Priya Park.

My office was in the ICCI Building at India Exchange Place, approximately seven kilometres away from my place of stay. Amaresh, who worked as a labour officer in a Birla shipping company, also had his office in the same building on the second floor. The ICCI Building had 14 floors, with the top 11 floors occupied by ICICI. The ground and first floors were rented out to the Bank of Baroda. The second floor was leased by companies of the Birla Group.

I had previously visited this building during my interview, which was conducted by Mr. Pandey, the Secretary-General of ICCI, in his office on the tenth floor. After my selection and receipt of the appointment letter, I met Mr. Ram Murty, the manager of administration. He instructed me to see him on February 1st when I came to join. Murty provided me with information about the newly established World Trade Department and mentioned that he would introduce me to the head of that department on my joining day. He also informed me that another member of the core team for the new department, G.S. Talauliker, had been selected a week earlier and would also start on February 1st. The department was slated to operate on the ninth floor of the ICCI building.

On February 1, 1961, I set out with Amaresh to reach India Exchange Place at around 9 a.m. We boarded a tram near our house bound for the Esplanade. At Esplanade, we transferred to another tram heading to Dalhousie Square. From Dalhousie Square, it was only a five-minute walk to the ICCI building. I took the lift to the twelfth floor and met Mr. Ram Murty's personal assistant. Murty arrived five minutes later, and both Amaresh and I were led to his office along with the other new recruit, Talauliker.

After a cup of tea with Murty, the three of us proceeded to the 9th floor to meet Mr. S. Guha Thakurta, the head of the newly established World Trade Department. Guha Thakurta warmly greeted and welcomed us. After a brief introduction, Murty left, and the two of us started discussing with Guha Thakurta the nature of our future work and the department's operational procedures.

In addition to the top three, Guha Thakurta, Guru (Talauliker), and myself, the department included another executive, Dutta Roy, as well as one personal assistant, two stenographers, and a peon. On our first day, I prepared my job chart and enthusiastically began my work. All team members were highly focused, and we made substantial contributions to the ICC's trading members in the realm of international trade.

Guru, Dutta Roy, and I developed a strong friendship, and we all had excellent rapport with our boss, Guha Thakurta. On one occasion, our boss invited Guru and me to sample a Calcutta delicacy known as "head of fish." The way he pronounced the dish in his characteristic fast-paced speech left both Guru and me thoroughly confused. Naturally, we didn't think he meant for us to eat the "head office"! However, when Guha Thakurta explained it slowly, we understood he was referring to a famous Calcutta dish: fish head curry. All three of us went to a renowned restaurant in North Calcutta to enjoy rice with this curry. While Guha Thakurta and Guru relished the meal, I didn't quite savour it. This difference in our enjoyment was understandable; the Bengali Guha Thakurta and the Goanese Guru had a deep appreciation for all types of fish dishes.

Guru had a close-knit group of Goanese friends in Calcutta, including Almeida, Wagle, Sardesai, Deshprabhu, Prabhu, Pais, Fondekers, and Kakodker. Almeida operated a soft drink factory, while Wagle served as the branch head of a finance company. Sardesai, Pai, and Prabhu worked for pharmaceutical companies like Abbott, Alembics, and Glaxo. Deshprabhu held the position of a scientific officer at the CSRI (Central Scientific Research Institute). Fondeker was a senior electrical engineer at Eastern Railways, and Kakodker held a senior position at the Reserve Bank of India. Guru introduced me to all of them, and they became my friends as well.

Over time, not only Guru's family but also the families of Fondekers, Prabhus, and Pais became close friends with my family. Even after our retirements, our families remained in close contact. Guru's family eventually settled in Pune, while the families of the other two settled in the United States with their children.

During our time in Calcutta, the days seemed to pass quickly. The newly established World Trade Department received accolades for its outstanding work, benefiting Indian Chamber of Commerce and Industry member exporters. Within six months, both Guru and I received significant raises in our monthly salaries. Our bond with Guha Thakurta, our boss, continued to strengthen.

I learned that Guha Thakurta had earned his M.A. degree from the London School of Economics. He had been married to a famous Bengali cinema actress but left her in a rather peculiar manner. One night, while his wife was sound asleep in their first-floor bedroom, he quietly descended from the balcony using bedsheets tied to the railings. From that moment on, he lived a solitary life. His outwardly jovial facade masked the underlying pain of his lonely existence.

Guru and I made a deliberate decision to devote some of our free time to Guha Thakurta, particularly after work hours and on holidays, in order to assist him in managing his depression more effectively. Our routine involved taking him on outings to areas like Chowringhee and Esplanade. The three of us would leisurely walk through these areas after the workday, which took about twenty minutes to reach. During these outings, we spent approximately half an hour casually strolling, engaging in window shopping, and engaging in light-hearted conversations. It was quite an amusing sight to see three professionals, dressed in office attire complete with neckties, briskly navigating the broad sidewalks of Chowringhee. After this routine, each of us would return to our respective residences. This approach had a significantly positive impact on Guha Thakurta, greatly aiding in alleviating his depression.

Six months later, I decided to relocate my place of residence, prompted by Amaresh's transfer out of Calcutta. Along with two of my acquaintances from the banking sector, namely Hegde from Canara Bank and Pai from Corporation Bank, I rented a flat near Lake Market, where the three of us established our new abode. Conveniently, there was a well-known South Indian restaurant in close proximity that fulfilled our main meal requirements. I continued to reside in this location until my tenure with ICCI in Calcutta persisted.

Given our hectic schedules, the three of us would depart from our residence at around 9 in the morning and typically return by 8 in the evening during the six working days of the week. On Sundays and holidays, we, as three bachelors, would take the opportunity to unwind in each other's company. Our excursions generally led us to explore scenic and entertaining destinations, primarily within the neighbourhoods of South Calcutta. It's worth mentioning that both Hegde and Pai hailed from Bengaluru, and Hegde remained a lifelong friend, eventually retiring as an executive director at Canara Bank and settling in Bengaluru with his family after retirement.

Baba paid me a visit and spent a week at our residence in Lake Market. He had purposely planned his visit for the weekend. During his stay, I took him on a tour of Calcutta using a car that I had borrowed from my friend, Almeida. Throughout Baba's visit, the car, along with the driver, remained at our disposal. Baba thoroughly enjoyed visiting various places in Calcutta, including the Kali temple, Dakshineswar temple, Outram Ghat near the Race Course, and the Victoria Memorial, among others. On multiple occasions, both Baba and I had our meals at restaurants such as Trinca and others located on Park Street. I immensely cherished the time spent with Baba in Calcutta.

Three months following Baba's return to Cuttack, my professional journey took a significant turn for the better. I secured a position at Burmah Shell, the largest multinational company (MNC) operating in the petroleum sector in India. In July 1961, the company issued a recruitment advertisement for five positions within their management staff cadre. This was a historic move, as it marked the first time the MNC in India had publicly advertised for such positions. These recruitments were specifically for the geographical area under the jurisdiction of their Calcutta Branch Office.

Historically, both before and after India's independence, executive positions within this company were highly regarded and often considered superior to recruitment into the ICS and IAS cadres of the Indian government. The MNC offered significantly better compensation, along with associated perks and pension benefits, compared to government positions. Previously, for these positions in India, the company independently scouted for educated and intelligent candidates from well-established aristocratic families. After collecting their curriculum vitae (CVs), the company would shortlist candidates for interviews and final selection, either in London or Bombay. The London interviews designated candidates as All India Assistants (officer/management cadre), while the Bombay interviews selected lower-ranking officers as Branch Assistants (officer/management cadre).

Subsequently, I discovered that in response to the advertisement for which I had submitted my application, there were thousands of applicants. To streamline the selection process, they initially shortlisted three hundred candidates for the written test. Following the written test, they further narrowed it down to twenty-five individuals based on the test results. The final selection of the final five candidates was carried out through a series of interviews with all twenty-five candidates. These interviews spanned a two-week period.

On August 1, 1961, I received a letter from Burmah Shell, which was a call letter instructing me to take a written test on August 16 at their Calcutta Branch Office located in Hongkong House, Dalhousie Square.

I participated in the written test and successfully qualified for the subsequent interview rounds, which commenced on September 1, 1961. Out of the initial twenty-five candidates, there were six interview sessions to choose the final five. These seven individuals, including me, were invited to meet with senior officials from the Bombay Main Office and Calcutta Branch Office over lunch. This meeting took place in the Officers' Lunch Room in Calcutta on September 10. During the pre-lunch gathering, six candidates enjoyed gin and tonic, while I opted for a Coke as I was a teetotaler at that time.

The session extended for more than two hours, during which the officials engaged in discussions with the seven candidates. It was announced that the selected five candidates would receive their appointment letters, while the remaining two would receive letters of regret by September 15. Among the chosen five were Chandidas, R. Banerjee, D. Sinha, A. Awasthi, and S. Chatterjee. While Banerjee and Chatterjee were from Calcutta, Sinha hailed from Patna, and Awasthi came from Lucknow. I, Chandidas, was the first Odia to be selected for Burmah Shell, a source of great pride for my parents.

The chosen candidates were required to commence their duties no later than October 1, 1961. The initial salary offered was nearly five times higher than my ICCI salary at the time. I approached Guha Thakurta and requested his assistance in facilitating my release by September 30. Thanks to Mr. Pandey, Secretary General of ICICI, my release was arranged on time. My selection in Burmah-Shell brought joy to my friends at ICCI, and my parents were overjoyed. On September 25, I received a farewell from the department, and on September 30, 1961, I bid farewell to everyone in the organisation.

My tenure at ICCI spanned nine months, during which I formed many new friendships. My closest friend was Guru. I considered myself fortunate to have established friendships with numerous individuals from Goa. Of course, my bond with Dutta Roy and Guha Thakurta held a special place in my heart. This phase of my career was filled with pleasant memories, and I developed a deep fondness for Calcutta. The significance of this city took on even greater meaning in my later life. It left a distinct impression and had a lasting impact on my future career and assignments in Calcutta.

Upon joining, I reported to the Calcutta branch office of Burmah Shell. I was informed that the first year would be a period of probation, training, and adjustment to actual field duties. I interacted with the branch personnel manager, who collected the joining reports from all five of us who were appointed. A two-week in-house classroom training programme was conducted. Subsequently, my four colleagues and I visited four divisional offices in Calcutta, Patna, Raipur, and Bhubaneswar as part of our training, which continued until the end of November 1961. Our branch personnel manager accompanied us during these visits and provided constant guidance and interaction.

Subsequently, the practical field training phase commenced. Each member of our group was assigned to different locations. I was stationed in Siliguri for a three-month period, starting from December 1, 1961, until the end of February 1962. This training focused on storage, logistics, and the delivery of the company's products at the Siliguri Depot. The depot superintendent in Siliguri made all the necessary arrangements for my accommodation and transportation. I thoroughly enjoyed the daily work routine during my training here. On weekends, I made the most of my free time by visiting the nearby town of Darjeeling and exploring the breathtaking beauty of the tea gardens, which I was seeing for the first time. On clear mornings, I had the privilege of witnessing the celestial sight of the Kanchenjunga peak in the Himalayas. These were unforgettable experiences that left a lasting impression in my memory.

Leaving Siliguri on February 28th to proceed to Raipur was a bittersweet moment. I was about to embark on the next phase of my training, which would last for three months. I flew from Siliguri to Calcutta on an Avro Turbojet. The aircraft had a cargo hold at the rear of the passenger cabin. The passenger cabin, which could accommodate 42 passengers, was separated from the rear cargo hold by a net partition. During this flight, I couldn't help but notice that the cargo area contained an iron-grilled container carrying approximately 10 mountain goats. Their continuous bleating was quite bothersome throughout the one-and-a-half-hour flight. Upon arriving at Dum Dum airport in Calcutta, I took a taxi to Howrah Station, where I boarded a train bound for Raipur on the same day.

The journey to Raipur was an overnight one. Upon my arrival, I met with the Divisional Manager (DM) at the office. I was assigned to work alongside a Divisional Officer (DO), who would be my mentor until the end of May 1962. He provided me with insights into the various intricacies of field operations at the depot, dealer, and distributor levels. These insights were gained during joint tours to various locations within the divisional office's jurisdiction.

It was the peak of summer, and the entire region was sweltering under scorching heat, making it feel like being inside an oven. It became evident to me that the training programme had been deliberately designed to prepare the trainees for field duties. In my case, the programme was structured in such a way that I experienced icy cold Himalayan winds in Siliguri during the winter and had to endure the searing hot summer winds, or 'loo', in Raipur, which was known as the hottest spot in India at that time. This experience proved to be immensely valuable and enduring, as it strengthened me to face the future challenges of my duties. During this period, I had the opportunity to visit several historical and tourist sites in the vicinity, including Khajuraho and other places of interest. It was my first visit to the areas of Madhya Pradesh, which are now part of Chhattisgarh state, with its capital in Raipur.

Upon completing the six-month field training on June 1, 1962, all five probationer trainees were summoned to the Calcutta Branch Office for a week, where our mid-term evaluation took place. The assessment of all five of us indicated excellent performance. The management was so pleased with our achievements that each of us was granted ten days of paid leave along with an ex-gratia vacation allowance of two thousand rupees. We were also informed that the final phase of our training would be conducted at a divisional headquarters near our respective homes.

For me, this meant reporting to Bhubaneswar, while Sinha and Awasthi were to go to Patna, and Banerjee and Chatterjee were to remain with the Calcutta Division. On June 8th, I returned to Cuttack, where I spent ten days of leave at my family home. My parents and siblings were delighted to have me back, and they appreciated the gifts I had brought for them, which I had purchased from the New Market in Calcutta before leaving.

The final phase of my training commenced when I reported to the Divisional Manager in Bhubaneswar. Mr. Sen, the DM, assigned me the responsibility of overseeing the territory of the Field Officer in charge of the Cuttack Oil District. This area encompassed three government administrative districts: Puri, Cuttack, and Balasore. The incumbent officer had gone on a three-month leave, and I was entrusted with the management of his territory for the concluding phase of my training. The company promptly provided me with an advance for the purchase of a car to facilitate my travels within the area. With Baba's assistance, I found a suitable Ambassador car in Cuttack. The car, bearing the registration number ORC 3545, marked my first ownership of a car and became the first family car to be parked on our Tulsipur residence's porch.

During my tenure, the sales proceeds for the territory under my purview recorded a remarkable increase of over 50% in the first month. This surge was in comparison to the sales proceeds for the same month in the previous year. Similar trends continued into the months of July and August. The DM was exceedingly pleased with these results and presented a letter of appreciation to the trainee officer, Chandi. This recognition was unprecedented in the history of Burmah Shell for a trainee officer.

The month of September brought a sweet turn of events. It was during this month that I selected my future bride, Rashmi. On the evening of September 5th, I visited her house with Maa. She happened to be a classmate of Lakhi in college and was the youngest sister of Barada (Badu), an old friend and acquaintance from my school and college days. Rashmi possessed exceptional beauty, and I fell in love with her at first sight when she elegantly entered the sitting room clad in a green silk saree. She remained my "Shy Dream Girl" forever, and even today, when I close my eyes and reminisce, that enchanting and graceful entrance of her, a celestial beauty, fills my heart with emotions.

Upon mutual agreement between our families, we decided to finalise the wedding date in six months. However, this timeline was later extended to one year due to my assignment away from Odisha. The formal marriage agreement, known as 'Nirbandh,' was conducted at the Goddess Chandi temple before I departed for my new posting in Gaya.

I received my letter of confirmation, along with the posting order for the Patna Division, on September 22, 1962. The specified place of posting was Gaya within the Patna Division, and I was instructed to assume charge by October 1, 1962. I took over the responsibilities from Mr. V.K. Purohit, who had been transferred to the Northern Branch. Before my departure for Gaya, the Divisional Manager in Bhubaneswar made a request to the Branch Office to retain me in his division. However, this request was not granted, and I was expected to report to Gaya as scheduled.

With the divisional manager's consent, I spent a few days with my parents in Cuttack before heading to Gaya. Baba and Maa were saddened by my posting in Gaya, and Baba arranged for a familiar driver to accompany me on my car journey from Cuttack on September 28.

The journey covered nearly six hundred kilometres, including an overnight stop in Ranchi after passing through Jaipur, Keonjhar, Chainebasha, and Chakradharpur. The route took us through forests and hilly roads. After having breakfast at the BNR Ranchi hotel, where I had spent the previous night, I continued my drive to Gaya, covering a distance of approximately 275 kilometers. The driver and I stopped for lunch at a roadside dhaba. We arrived in Gaya around 5:30 p.m. on October 1, passing through Dobhi and Bodh Gaya during our journey.

A Burmah Shell petrol station in Gaya provided directions to help me locate my colleague Purohit's residence. Prior to my arrival, I had a conversation with Purohit from the Bhubaneswar office to coordinate my schedule. Purohit informed me that he would need about a week to thoroughly brief me on all the work-related aspects and the operational setup in the area. He also mentioned that his family had already departed for his hometown, Jaipur in Rajasthan, and kindly offered for me to stay at his place. Purohit also confirmed that his current house in Gaya would be retained for my accommodation. This information eliminated many uncertainties and assured me of a smooth start.

Upon my arrival, Purohit and I had a formal discussion over a cup of tea. Subsequently, I freshened up and joined Purohit for dinner. Arrangements needed to be made for booking a return train ticket to Cuttack for my accompanying driver, who was scheduled to leave the next morning. Purohit contacted his dealer, the owner of Sarogi Petrol Pump, to handle the booking. Sarogi provided the ticket around 8:30 PM, and I had the opportunity to meet him when I paid for the cost of the reserved ticket.

The following day was a holiday in observance of Gandhi Jayanti. On that day, Purohit organised a meeting with the dealers, agents, and distributors from Gaya town and the surrounding areas at his home office. During this interaction, I was formally introduced to all of them.

In the evening, Purohit took me to the Gaya Club. The company had secured permanent membership for its local officials at this club. There, I had the chance to meet club members, including the District Magistrate,

Superintendent of Police, Executive Engineer PWD, Superintendent Excise, and Chief Medical Officer of Gaya district. I was also introduced to other important individuals, like retired Colonel Swami of AMC and retired Excise Commissioner Hafiz. This introduction was a customary procedure for all new members and served as a foundation for future public relations activities and acquaintances with influential local figures from higher social strata.

That evening, Purohit and I engaged in a game of bridge at the club. At my table, I had the pleasure of playing with the District Magistrate, Executive Engineer, and Colonel Swami. Colonel Swami became my bridge partner, and together, we emerged victorious against our two opponents. From that point on, Colonel Swami, who was nearing 70 years of age, became not only my patron but also a close family friend throughout my tenure in Gaya. In Gaya, he was widely recognised as 'Colonel Saheb.' He drove an imported open-top Red Rover and was a familiar face in Gaya's elite social circles. Purohit and I returned from the club around 10:00 p.m.

The following five days were exceptionally busy. Purohit took me to various locations, including Bodh Gaya, Sherghati, Aurangabad, Terigna, Dehri on Sone, Tilaya, Koderma, Nawadah, Nalanda, Rajgir, Bhaktiarpur, and Patna. Koderma was particularly noteworthy as it was India's largest mining area for the production of high-quality mica, an essential element for electronic equipment and a crucial raw material for the emerging IT industries. Koderma also hosted one of the major and bustling Burmah Shell Depots to meet the petroleum product needs of this industry. During our visits, I was introduced to influential individuals and heads of institutions. We also toured the company-operated depot and related facilities.

In Patna, we visited the divisional office located on Fraser Road near Gandhi Maidan. This office was situated on the fifth floor of Patna's only high-rise tower at the time. Interestingly, ITC's divisional office was also one floor below our office. After meeting with the Divisional Manager, D.P. Mukherjee, and the Divisional Officer, Kanwaljeet Singh, I had the opportunity to meet my colleague officer, Talwar. On the evening of October 8, 1962, Purohit and I returned to our residence in Gaya, marking the conclusion of the Handing Over and Taking Over phases. Purohit departed from Gaya on October 9, 1962.

On that day, I paid a visit to the owner of the bungalow that was to become my residence following Purohit's departure. The owner was a respected resident of Gaya, and his family had settled in the city nearly eighty years ago. He possessed a significant amount of property in Gaya and was commonly known as Dr. Khan. The title of Khan Saheb had been bestowed upon his ancestors by the Mughals, who ruled over Bengal before the British

Raj. Interestingly, he hailed from a traditional Bengali Brahmin family, and his actual name was Dr. Biswambhar Bhattacharjee.

Upon my arrival at Dr. Khan's house, I received a warm welcome from him. After some formal discussions, he graciously informed me that I could retain the bungalow for as long as I was stationed in Gaya. He also mentioned that the monthly rent would remain unchanged at Rs. 300, the same amount Purohit had been paying. Throughout my stay in Gaya, I maintained an excellent rapport with Dr. Khan's family, and their members, including relatives from Calcutta, frequently visited my residence. One such notable visitor I recall was the famous Bollywood actor Abhi Bhattacharya. Like most Bengalis, he inquired about my time in Calcutta and my impressions of the city.

The residence itself was an imposing bungalow with Gothic architectural features. Its front verandah was supported by four round pillars that held up the wooden beams of the high roof, standing at a towering fourteen feet. The lofty roof was designed to combat Gaya's scorching summer temperatures, which often soared above 45 degrees Celsius. The house boasted four bedrooms, a sitting room, and an office space. The kitchen and storage rooms were located at the rear verandah's end, followed by the servant's quarters and a car garage. The house was connected to the main road by a cemented driveway featuring an iron-grilled gate at the entrance. This main road linked Gaya with Bodh Gaya and was further extended to Dhobi, where it met the National Highway (NH) connecting Delhi and Calcutta.

My residence was situated in an upscale neighbourhood, in close proximity to Gaya Club and Colonel Swami's bungalow. In a matter of days, Colonel Swami assisted me in finding a reliable driver-cum-butler. This young 24-year-old Muslim man had previously worked for a doctor and was named Zaheer Ali. I retained his services for as long as I remained in Bihar. Several months later, when I bid farewell to Bihar, I facilitated his transition to a permanent driver's position in the Bihar Police. This was made possible through the efforts of one of my Gaya acquaintances, Executive Engineer Prasad, who happened to be the son-in-law of Bihar's Inspector General at the time. Prasad's request to his father-in-law led to Zaheer Ali's appointment.

My hectic routine began about two weeks after my arrival in Gaya. I diligently reviewed all the official documents and familiarised myself with the area's issues and the networks under my supervision. In order to devise a future action plan, I needed to conduct thorough tours of the region. I met with and provided guidance to all individuals within the distribution network of the area, ensuring they were well-informed for both their own growth and the company's operational success. One of my primary focuses was expanding the kerosene trade, which served as the primary revenue source for the company's operations in the Gaya area. Additionally, I emphasised the need for increased sales of petrol, diesel, lubricants, and grease in all retail outlets.

Bulk sales of lubricants and grease primarily catered to large industries in Dehri on Sone, Mica mining companies, and DVC (Damodar Valley Corporation) establishments in the Koderma area. I also identified potential locations for new retail outlets of the company, commonly known as petrol pumps. These tasks demanded intensive effort and consumed nearly sixteen to seventeen hours of my daily schedule for approximately six months.

This endeavour was successfully concluded by the end of March 1963, just before the onset of summer. The results were promising, and by the end of June, during the divisional review meeting, I received accolades from divisional manager Mukherjee for doubling the revenue turnover in my area. Consequently, I was rewarded with a double increment and a higher salary. I had become a favourite employee of the divisional manager.

In early July 1963, I received a phone call from Sri Mukherjee. He informed me about his scheduled visit to Gaya on July 10. He and his wife were planning to perform "Pritupaksha Pindadan," a religious ritual, in Gaya. Their plan was to arrive in Gaya around 10 a.m. on the tenth and, after the ritual, depart for Patna at approximately 3 p.m. on the same day. He also mentioned that neither of them would have lunch that day in observance of religious customs. Accordingly, I was tasked with making all the necessary arrangements in Gaya, including coordinating the programme and ensuring everything was prepared for the boss's visit.

Earlier, I had never made any arrangements for such pujas. I called my locally influential dealer, Saraogi. I requested that he help me make the arrangements. Accordingly, a priest of the Visnupad Mandir was engaged for this purpose. All other foolproof arrangements for the pindadan were also made. The pindadan was to be performed in the Visnupad Mandir Complex. The place was on the banks of the River Falgu at Gaya. The complex had many other Hindu deities besides the famous banyan tree, which was known as the "moksha tree". I had a detailed discussion with the main priest of the mandir concerning the pindadan. After finalisation of all arrangements, Mukherjee was appropriately informed on the 8th of July. I again rechecked all arrangements to be doubly sure that nothing went wrong on the scheduled day.

On July 10, I waited in my car near the entry point of Gaya on the Patna-Gaya Road from 8.30 a.m. onwards. Earlier that day, I had sent Saraogi at 7:30 a.m. to the mandir complex, where the pindadan was to be performed. At 9:45 a.m., Mukherjee and his wife's car arrived. I greeted them and drove my car ahead of theirs to make them reach the place of puja around 10 a.m. Immediately, the couple sat in the puja. The pindadan ceremony took around four and a half hours. After the successful puja, the Mukherjees were freed by 2.45 p.m.

They were extremely pleased and left for Patna on time at 3 p.m. That night, around 9:30 p.m., I received a call from the Mukherjees. Mrs. Mukherjee thanked me profusely for all the arrangements. She said that I would get the blessings of their ancestors. Later, I learned that Sri Mukherjee belonged to the famous aristocratic family of Sir Biren Mukherjee of Calcutta.

Apparently, the time used to fly due to my packed, busy schedule. I went on a tour of my area for almost twenty days in a month. Whenever I was at Gaya, I went to the club to play bridge. During the holidays, I played tennis at the club. For the doubles game in tennis, I partnered with Colonel Swami. The Colonel was an avid player, even at his advanced age. Our pair always won easily over the opponents. At the card table of the club, for the game of bridge, the four permanent members were Col. Swami, Prasad, Hafiz, and me. Our sessions used to extend late on Saturday nights.

I was often invited for lunch and dinner by Swami, Hafeez, and Prasad. I still remember the treat given by Mr. Hafeez during the Eid festival. I thoroughly enjoyed the days spent at Gaya. The club venue remained my favourite rendezvous even after my marriage in December 1963. Rashmi, too, enjoyed her club visits.

I vividly remember a very dangerous event that took place in September 1963 that I faced while returning from Patna to Gaya. After attending a meeting at the divisional office, I left Patna around 5:30 p.m. I drove to Gaya along with my driver, Zaheer. My colleagues advised me not to drive on highways late at night as there were frequent dacoities and holdups by criminal gangs. This was a common occurrence on the Patna-Gaya highway.

By 6:30 p.m., it was quite dark when I crossed Bhaktiarpur and headed for Rajgir, Nalanda, and Nawadah. I reached Nawadah by 9 p.m. and moved towards Gaya. Thirty kilometres before Gaya, I could see that a lot of broken tree branches were lying across the road around fifty metres ahead. It was meant to stop traffic. Fortunately, the branches were not too big. Zaheer, who was in the back seat of the car, told me that it seemed to be a holdup. He advised me to speed up and drive very fast over those obstructions. As I drove fast over the cut branches of trees, I could hear the loud metallic noise and feel the vibrations in the car from its bottom. At that time, Zaheer could see from the back seat that more than ten people were running behind the car and throwing stones. As the car drove fast over the obstacles, some more people came on to the road from both sides of the high embankments. The car was slowed down from its breakneck speed only after nearing Gaya. It was indeed a close save—a very nasty and traumatic experience! From that day until I left Bihar, I never undertook a night drive on the highways of that state.

On November 5th, 1963, Baba telephoned me. He said that my marriage had been fixed for December 9. He advised me to come to Cuttack by November 25th, taking a month's leave from my work. There was a meeting scheduled for Patna on November 15. I decided to personally request for leave from the divisional manager after that meeting. Mukherjee was happy to learn about my proposed marriage. He allowed me three weeks' leave beginning November 30. During my absence, Talwar was asked to temporarily look after my area for three weeks, from November 30 to December 20. I briefed Talwar about the important jobs that needed action during my absence. Talwar visited Gaya on Thursday, the 28th of November, before I proceeded on leave. Due to the new entry of Caltex in the area, Talwar was particularly told to safeguard the mica mining sector and the volatile kerosene market in the area.

After ensuring that driver Zaheer took care of the house during my absence, I left for Cuttack on the morning of the 30. I reached Cuttack in the late evening of December 1. After dinner and a chat with my parents, I retired for the night around 11 p.m. The next morning, the police driver, Majhi, took my car for servicing. Majhi was Baba's official driver at Baripada and had been called to Cuttack for 15 days from December 1st. Baba had requested SP Mayurbhanj to send driver Majhi. On the return of the car from servicing, Baba and Maa went to the market with me. All three of us went to shop for the forthcoming marriage.

The next few days were very hectic. Natu and Menki arrived to attend the marriage. The marriage invitation cards were distributed by Budha, his friends, and office staff. I personally gave the cards to my friends Ashish, Rabi, Prabhat, and others who were at that time available in Cuttack. Some of them were to accompany the barat on the 8th evening. Cousins from the ancestral village, along with Baba's childhood friend, Ghosal, arrived and stayed at the Tulsipur house. Some invitation cards were posted for relatives, friends, and close acquaintances of the family who were staying outside Cuttack.

For all the guests who were staying and the workers who were giving final touches to the decoration of the house, a special kitchen was set up in the courtyard. The kitchen was run by a bevy of hired cooks. The prepared food was also taken by all family members.

The barat was to start from the house to the bride's place at the auspicious hour of 6:30 p.m. on December 8. My friends, who were to be a part of the barat (the groom's marriage procession), arrived around 5 p.m. at the Tulsipur house.

Tea, cold drinks, and refreshments were given to them. They were also treated with Rasagulla from the famous Bikala Kar of Mahanga.

In the afternoon, my maternal cousin, Manika Apa, came to help me prepare for the barat. She applied sandalwood paste to my forehead and draped a white silk chaddar over my white silk kurta and dhoti. I also wore a makuta (headgear) that covered my head. Manika Apa was incredibly fair, beautiful, and intelligent. She was renowned for her exquisite and serene beauty. She had a love marriage with Nanda Das, a famous Odia sportsman and police officer. Both of them lived nearby in the grand Zamindar house that belonged to Manika Apa's late father.

The barat procession began promptly at 6 p.m., and in accordance with customs at the time, no ladies accompanied it. I sat in a decorated car with my father, while other cars in the procession were occupied by some members of the groom's party. A few others walked in front of the cars along with a band party that played popular tunes from Hindi and Odia film songs. Some individuals in the procession set off fireworks along the one-kilometre journey. We reached the bride's house around 6:45 p.m. My father, I, and my friends were escorted to the room where I would spend the night. The marriage ceremony was scheduled to commence at 9:30 a.m. the following morning. Consequently, my father departed for home and planned to return the next morning. Meanwhile, my accompanying friends went out to enjoy the reception feast hosted by the bride's parents for the guests.

The baratis were the first to be served dinner at the bride's reception party. All the guests from the bride's side also joined in for the feast on the night of the 8th. Meanwhile, I and a few of my friends were scheduled to spend the entire night in the designated room. The entire floor of that room was covered with thick mattresses. I chatted with my friends throughout most of the night, and before I knew it, I had drifted off to sleep.

Some of my friends, who had eaten at the reception feast, returned to my room to visit and bid farewell. However, both the groom and the bride were not permitted to have dinner. They were only given 'dahi sorbet' during the night and into the next morning until the marriage puja was completed. Ashish and Rabi stayed with me throughout the night, keeping the mood light with their playful and humorous yet slightly inappropriate jokes. Barada, Rashmi's elder brother, also came to my room to check if we needed anything.

Baba returned at approximately 9 a.m. on the 9th, and with his arrival, the marriage puja and havan commenced punctually at 9:30 a.m. The marriage pandal, or "bede," was set up in the courtyard, and Rashmi had been seated there from the beginning. I joined her at the bede around 10 a.m. The ceremony concluded around 12:45 PM, and Rashmi and I broke our fast. As per tradition, I first consumed 'dahi pakhal' from my mother-in-law's hands before having my lunch. Following this, Baba, Rashmi, and other members of her family enjoyed a meal together. Subsequently, Rashmi, Baba, and I departed for the Tulsipur house at 4:30 PM.

Upon our arrival at the house, Maa, accompanied by six other married ladies, welcomed Rashmi with 'Puja Thalis' as part of her 'griha pravesh' (house entry) ceremony. The ensuing ceremonies lasted for about an hour. Around 9 PM, the family and guests gathered for dinner, which was arranged on the front lawn beneath a decorated shamiana.

Following the dinner, Manika Apa adorned Rashmi with her most exquisite jewellery and dressed her in a new Banarasi saree. She then guided her into a beautifully decorated room filled with red rose petals and had her sit on the bed. Manika Apa then called me and gently pushed me into the elaborately decorated room. This night would forever remain sweetly etched in our memories. I discovered that Rashmi was naturally reserved and introverted, a characteristic she had possessed since her school and college days.

Over the next four days, Rashmi and I participated in numerous pujas and observed the formalities of post-marriage customs, all guided by our family priest, Maheswara Pandit. On the 13th of December, a Friday, the groom's side hosted a reception. This lavish event took place in an adorned enclosure under a Shamiana, set up on the front lawn adjacent to the Tulsipur house's portico. The reception spanned from 7:30 p.m. to 10 p.m. and was a splendid affair, with guests enjoying the delicious dishes served. This marked the grand conclusion of the entire marriage schedule.

Since my official leave extended until the 20th of December, Rashmi and I had plans to depart for Gaya on the 18th of December. On Monday, the 15th, my youngest sister, Lakhi, who was also Rashmi's classmate and best friend at Sailabala Women's College in Cuttack, took her sister-in-law to the college. Rashmi was adorned with her jewellery and was widely recognised as the 'college queen'. She looked exceptionally beautiful, and nearly all her friends in the college embraced her as she bid farewell, leaving the college for good.

During this time, I had my car serviced and prepared for the long journey to Gaya. Baba arranged for a cook and servant named Kashi to accompany Rashmi and me. On the 18th, we departed from Cuttack after an early lunch at 11 a.m. Maa had prepared plenty of *pitha* for us to take along. The departure was filled with emotion as Rashmi's parents, brothers, and sisters were there to bid us farewell.

Our first overnight stop was in Keonjhar. Barada (Badu) had advised me to have dinner at his uncle's house, who was the brother of his mother, during our first stop. This uncle held the position of sales tax officer in the Keonjhar district. After reaching Keonjhar at around 5:30 PM, we rested in a room reserved for us at the Dak Bungalow. Rashmi's uncle came to the Dak Bungalow at around 7:30 PM and took both of us to his home for dinner. There, Rashmi had the opportunity to meet her aunt and her cousin. Following dinner, we departed from their house at 9:30 PM, and Rashmi's uncle also sent food for Kashi in a tiffin carrier, which Kashi was waiting for at the Dak Bungalow.

On the morning of the 19th, at approximately 6 a.m., we set off for Ranchi after having a cup of tea and some biscuits, which we also provided to Kashi. As we drove through the thick forests along the Chaibaha ghats, Rashmi thoroughly enjoyed the journey. The experience was already having a transformative effect on her, causing her to shed her shyness and truly appreciate the beauty of nature. Consequently, Rashmi developed a deep passion for travel, eagerly desiring to explore new places. Travelling quickly became her new favourite pastime.

We reached Chakradharpur around lunchtime and stopped at a restaurant for a meal. The journey from Chakradharpur to Ranchi took four hours. In Ranchi, I had already booked a room at the renowned BNR hotel, which was owned by the Railways. Once our luggage was taken to the room by the hotel bellboy, I ordered some tea. We used the remaining two hours to recharge our energy. We had an early dinner at 8:30 p.m. in the hotel's restaurant and retired early since the next day's journey was anticipated to be long, spanning approximately seven hours with breaks for lunch and tea at roadside dhabas. The drive was challenging, as it included hilly tracks in Hazaribagh and was flanked by dense forests throughout the entire route.

On the morning of the twentieth, we had our breakfast and then checked out of the hotel. We started our drive for Gaya at nine o'clock. We had launched from a dhaba on the GT road near a Burmah Shell petrol pump. The dealer of the pump was well known to me. He had made the arrangements to bring the dhaba food to the nicely furnished guest room at the pump. After lunch, I thanked the dealer and started for Gaya. Around 5:30 p.m., we reached our Gaya residence. Zaheer greeted us. He touched Rashmi's feet and opened the house. He had kept the house sparkling clean. Kashi was introduced to Zaheer. He took him and his luggage to one of the rooms at the outhouse.

Rashmi and I were very tired after the long journey. I gave some money to Zaheer and instructed him to take the car in the evening and bring the food for our dinner. The food was brought from the nearby restaurant that earlier catered for me. The next morning was going to be a busy day. Me and Rashmi had our early dinner at eight p.m. and retired for the night.

On the 21st of December, 1963, both woke up around six in the morning. By that time, Zaheer had made Kashi familiar with the kitchen and the provisions in the storeroom. Kashi brought tea for both of us to the front verandah. Breakfast was taken around 9 a.m., after which I went to the office room. I telephoned Talwar and got details of events that happened in my absence.

Around 10.30 a.m., I talked to the divisional manager, who congratulated me on the marriage. He told me to bring my wife to Patna during my next visit. His wife, Mrs. Mukherjee, wanted to meet my wife to bless her. I thanked Mr. and Mrs. Mukherjee for their good wishes and promised to make the next visit to Patna along with Rashmi. I was happy to notice the smile of Rashmi as I mentioned the desire of Mrs. Mukherjee to meet her. This was scheduled for the next divisional meeting in January.

The day was a Saturday. I never carried out any of my official work after 2 p.m. on Saturdays or the whole of Sundays unless there was extreme urgency. This had been the acclaimed protocol of the management of Burmah Shell for all its employees. It was officially meant to increase the efficiency of all officers. A real off, for a day and a half, invigorated their spirit for better performance. They could also fruitfully spend their time with their families and take them to new places for picnics and outings.

That afternoon, I and Rashmi visited Colonel Swamis house. The Swamis treated Rashmi like their daughter. During this visit, Lady Doctor Padmavati was also introduced to Rashmi at Swamis place. She was the superintendent of Gaya's government hospital. This was later converted into a government medical college. The Swamis forced me and Rashmi to have an early dinner at their place. After that, we and the Swamis went to the Gaya Club.

At the club, Rashmi was introduced to families and other members of the club. These members wanted a party from me the next day. The party was duly given to all club members and their families. The day happened to be a Sunday, when all the members visited the club with their wives. The party became a grand affair. Rashmi won the hearts of all her guests. I was congratulated for my extremely pretty and cultured wife. It became a favourite topic on the social circuit in Gaya. Incidentally, Dr. Khan and his wife, who were the owners of the bungalow where we resided, were happy to interact with Rashmi. They also invited the newlywed couple to have lunch at their place next Sunday.

I took Rashmi on a tour of the Koderma area during the coming week. We stayed at the Tilaya Dam guesthouse of the DVC. It was on a hilltop overlooking the huge dam on the Barakar River. This river is the main tributary of the Damodar River. The place was extremely scenic. Boating on the lake was also available for residents of the guest house. The cook of the guest house used to make delicious dishes with fresh fish caught from the dam.

I was always treated as a VIP guest in the guest house. I had an official as well as friendly family connection with the Chief Engineer of DVC. The lubricants for all the DVC Power House machines were supplied only by Burmah Shell from their Koderma and other depots. In this guesthouse during one of my earlier visits, I had the enjoyable company of Bihar's Chief Minister Binodananda Jha. The quantity of fried fish the CM consumed during the stay was unbelievable. In one go, he used to eat almost five kilogrammes of fried fish!

Rashmi thoroughly enjoyed her stay at Tilaya, especially boating in the lake at the dam. We stayed there for four days. I used to do my official work for six hours by going to the depot and visiting the offices of Mica Mines Companies. I also met the Chief Engineer of DVC at his office in the Power House complex. I used to drive out early after breakfast at seven in the morning and return at one p.m. for lunch. Rashmi used to be alone in the guesthouse during this period. For her safety, Zaheer was kept at the guest house while I drove out in my car. On Friday, after lunch, I and Rashmi drove back to Gaya. We kept our lunch appointment at the house of Dr. Khan on Sunday.

Next Monday, the 30th of December, I took Rashmi on a tour to Sherghati, Aurangabad, and Dehri on Sone. It was for visiting the agency and dealership points along the route. While Rashmi stayed in the car, I got relevant documents and information from each point of visit. I spent seven to ten minutes at each point. Our night's stay on this trip was in one of the guesthouses of a company at Dehri on Sone. In December, we returned to Gaya to celebrate the new year at Gaya Club.

The entire first week of January was spent in Gaya. I was to prepare a comprehensive annual report for submission to the division. During this time, I had asked all other dealers to visit Gaya and meet me for a discussion. They were to provide relevant information about their sales plan for next year.

The Gaya Depot manager, Thomas, who worked under me, was a Keralite. He also attended the meeting to finalise the supply programme of products to the network during the next year. Thomas and his wife were a very sociable couple. Mrs. Thomas became a good friend of Rashmi. She used to give her company many times when Rashmi remained alone in the house. Sometimes,

I was compelled to have unavoidable outstation night halts during tours. At such times, I used to ring up Thomas so that his wife could be with Rashmi.

On Saturdays and Sundays, I played tennis in the afternoon at Gaya Club. In the evening, I and Rashmi went to the club. The next day, the seventeenth of January, was my scheduled visit to Patna. After lunch, I left for Patna along with Rashmi. We checked into my regular hotel, opposite Gandhi Maidan.

The divisional meeting was on the 18th. After attending the meeting, I returned to the hotel around 5 p.m. I and Rashmi had tea and cake. It was a complimentary treat given by hotel owner Fernandez to the newlywed couple. For that stay in the hotel, the couple was neither charged for the room nor for the food! Around 7 p.m., I and Rashmi drove to Mukherjee's residence at Boring Road.

Mrs. Mukherjee welcomed us and took us to their sitting room. Rashmi had her fruit juice along with Mrs. Mukherjee, while I gave company to the boss with his drink of Scotch. Mrs. Mukherjee had a long chat with Rashmi. I and the boss listened to the talks of the ladies over our drinks.

Mrs. Mukherjee congratulated me. She insisted that both of us have our dinner with them. Ultimately, even after our polite denial of the dinner, the boss ordered me to accede to Mrs. Mukherjee's request. Before our departure to the hotel, Rashmi requested that Mrs. Mukherjee come to Gaya some time in the future and have lunch prepared by her. Mrs. Mukherjee happily agreed and promised to taste her preparations.

After breakfast the next day, we left the hotel for our return journey to Gaya. On the way, we stopped at Rajgir and Nalanda. I showed her the ruins of Nalanda University. Then began a photo session of Rashmi by 'photographer me' with my Agfa camera. It became lovable future memorabilia. In the background of the surrounding hills, we ate our packed lunch, brought from the Patna hotel. After we drove and crossed Nawadah, I pointed out to Rashmi the spot where I had earlier faced a holdup at night during my return from Patna.

Time flew by, and my marital happiness didn't lead me to neglect my official duties and responsibilities. In the last week of January 1964, I initiated a project to establish a highly successful retail outlet for Burmah Shell in Bihar. It quickly rose to become the top retail outlet for the company in the entire Eastern India region. This outlet was located in Dobhi, approximately 30 kilometres from Gaya, at the intersection of the Gaya-Bodh Gaya Road and the Delhi-Calcutta GT Road. It featured all modern amenities, including a guest house for travellers, a well-equipped restaurant, and a sales show room for merchandise. In today's terms, it was what we would call an "IN & OUT" outlet, which was quite unheard of during that era, nearly six decades ago!

The dealer I selected for this venture was the wife of a gentleman named SP Singh, who held the position of Superintending Engineer in Bihar PWD. He came highly recommended by my club friend, Prasad, who was an executive engineer in PWD and also happened to be the son-in-law of the Bihar Police Chief. Mr. Singh, the husband of the dealer, was a remarkably enterprising individual. He facilitated all the necessary government approvals for the outlet at his own expense and managed to secure them in a record time of just three weeks. Despite being a government servant, he had to offer bribes to individuals, even up to the ministerial level, to expedite these approvals. This situation validated the common saying that circulated within the corridors of the Patna Secretariat: "There always existed a marginal cost for moving files from one desk to another in the process of obtaining any government approval!"

The outlet was ready for operation in three months. It was inaugurated by the divisional manager, Mr. Mukherjee, in the third week of April. Besides other achievements in the Gaya area, this was one of my biggest. I was placed at the top of the company's Achievers' Log for the year 1963.

While Mr. Mukherjee went to Dobhi for the inauguration of the mentioned outlet, he left his wife with Rashmi at my residence. It was to fulfil an earlier promise made by Mrs. Mukherjee. After returning from the inauguration, Mr. Mukherjee joined his wife to have their lunch prepared by Rashmi. The Mukherjees praised Rashmi for the preparations, blessed her, and left for Patna. Before leaving, Mrs. Mukherjee gifted a gold bangle to Rashmi. When she refused to accept the gift, Mrs. Mukherjee said that she was like a mother-in-law to her and that there was no reason for her to refuse the gift. Rashi touched her feet and accepted the bangle with humble gratitude. Mrs. Mukherjee hugged her. Soon they left for Patna. This was their last meeting with Rashmi.

During the next month, Mr. Mukherjee was promoted and transferred to the London office of the Shell Group. He handed over the charge to the next incumbent, KL Lamba on May 15, 1964. The Mukherjee family left Patna by the end of the month.

After the month of May, on the advice of Dr. Padmavati, I did not take Rashmi on tour due to her five-month pregnancy. The doctor indicated that she had a tendency for miscarriage. I avoided tours with night halts. If I was to stay for the night, as it was during divisional meetings at Patna, a nurse was provided by Dr. Padmavati to remain with Rashmi. Colonel Swami and his wife too came and met Rashmi at the house.

In early August, she was admitted to a nursing home under the care of Dr. Padmavati. On October 19, 1964, a baby girl was born. During her birth, the child got infected with jaundice. She expired on the fifth day.

Her body was taken by me and buried deep inside the bed of the Falgu River. Rashmi was totally heartbroken. Maa came to Gaya on October 26 to take care of and console her. She stayed for a month. When she wanted to return to Cuttack, I and Rashmi planned to accompany her to Cuttack during November. It was done on a road trip.

On November 25, 1964, all three, along with driver Zaheer, drove for Cuttack in the morning. En route, we first stayed at Ranchi. Our second night's stay was at Ghatagaon Dak bungalow, where the night was marred by mosquito bites.

The Dak Bungalow had no mosquito net. Without proper sleep, we left the place early, at 3.30 a.m. Reaching Haridaspur, we headed for the house of Menki and Natu and reached there around 5:30 a.m.

Natu was working at that place as the Chief of Construction of the Ferro-Chrome Plant. Maa, Rashmi, and I rested for three hours and recouped our lost energy due to the previous night's sleeplessness. We all had our morning breakfast. Natu left for the construction site until lunchtime. We all had our lunch after Natu returned. On Menki's request, we stayed for one more night at their place and left the next morning.

While at Haridaspur, we experienced an unbelievable supernatural event. This raised the perineal question of the existence of ghosts! In the evening, Natu, Menki, Maa, Rashmi, and I went to see the natural surroundings around Haridaspur. Natu drove all of us in his car to see and enjoy the hills and forests. In the midst of the natural surroundings, the river Baitarani was flowing parallel to the road. A very long bridge, almost 100 feet above the river bed, was built two years ago on that road. This was for the transportation of iron ore from Keonjhar mines to Paradeep Port. This road also connected Haridaspur with Cuttack as it joined the Calcutta-Madras National Highway.

By the time Natu drove his car over this bridge, it was already dark. Suddenly, I saw a moving, lighted kerosene lantern held by a person without a head! I thought it was a hallucination. But on hearing that Natu too was seeing the same, the car was moved towards the object. The vision was confirmed as we approached closer. They also saw that the feet of the person were not touching the surface of the road bridge. The image suddenly vanished. It was really scary.

Subsequently, it was learned from neighbourhood people that a ghost regularly walked on the bridge at night. It was the person who was stealthily sacrificed at the construction site of the bridge!

The next morning, I and Maa, Rashmi, and Zaheer left for Cuttack. It was two hours' drive. We crossed over the same bridge where the ghost was observed to walk! We all had our lunch at Tulsipur House. Baba consoled Rashmi for the loss of her child. After staying for a week, I and Rashmi drove back to Gaya and reached there on December 6, 1964. I immediately got busy completing some of the unfinished official work. There were some communications from the divisional office that were not only irritating but totally false and malicious.

Soon after, a trainee officer named Roy Choudhury (RC) came to Gaya and was attached to me. It was his last phase of training and probation. This was to end in mid-December. Since RC belonged to Cuttack, I put him in the guestroom of our house. I used to send Roy Chowdhury on tour for field work. I allowed RC to use my car and driver for these tours.

Later, I learned that this trainee officer, RC, was planted by DM Lamba to spy on me. RC was confidentially advised that, once I was transferred, he could take charge of the Gaya area after the completion of his probation. Lamba's dislike for me arose as I was the favourite of his predecessor. It seemed that when Lamba was earlier working under Mr. Mukherjee, he had a very tough time. At that time, Lamba's snobbish attitude was hated by his colleagues and the boss. Besides, Mukherjee also rated his efficiency below average. The adverse feeling of Lamba against me was further fuelled by the lies fed to him by colleague Talwar and his spy Roy Chowdhury.

The scheme of the conspirators succeeded. I was transferred to Chapra to take charge of my colleague Kalsi, who was leaving Burmah Shell. Kalsi was going to join the Indian Oil Corporation.

I never forgave RC for his betrayal and indulgence in activities prejudicial to a senior belonging to his own state. RC's shady activity against me continued despite all the help, facilities, and amenities that I provided. I had treated him like a younger brother. Later, RC got his ultimate punishment through divine intervention. He stayed at Gaya only for a few months. He resigned and left for Bombay to join Hindustan Lever. There, he was soon killed at a private party during a drinking brawl.

After dispatching my luggage to Chapra, I drove with Rashmi and Zaheer to Patna on February 2, 1965. I stayed for the night at my favourite Capital Hotel in front of Gandhi Maidan. This hotel, as mentioned earlier, was owned by my Goanese friend Fernandez.

The next morning, I drove to the jetty on the Ganga River in Bankipur, Patna. I got my car loaded on a big steamer. It had to cross the flooded river to reach Sonepur on the other side of the river bank. At that time, there was no road bridge to connect Patna to North Bihar. When the car was being loaded, it was raining heavily. I and Rashmi remained seated inside the car after it was placed on the parking platform of the steamer.

Throughout the journey, the rain continued till the steamer reached the jetty at Sonepur. It was a unique experience. During this journey, both of us felt that the steamer was going to sink in the middle of the river. The heavy flood made the river very turbulent. While moving ahead, the steamer rolled violently on the swollen Ganga. The river looked like a vast, disturbed sea. The breadth of the river at the crossing was nearly three and a half kilometres.

It was afternoon by the time the car was unloaded from the steamer on the jetty of Sonepur. I and Rashmi drove to the irrigation Dak Bungalow in Sonepur to spend the night. Kalsi had made the arrangements for our stay at the Dak Bungalow. After taking tea and some snacks, we rested for a while to get over the trauma of crossing the swollen Ganga. Afterwards, we went around the town and saw the place where, annually, the biggest cattle fair in Asia was held for several decades.

After returning to the Dak Bungalow, I made a telephone call to Kalsi. I was informed that the truck carrying my household goods had reached Chapra, and it was unloaded and kept in their house. Kalsi planned to leave Chapra in a week's time. He was to introduce me to the networks of the area and all the important people in government and industry. The area to be covered was Saran and Gopalganj, as well as parts of Muzaffarpur and Darbhanga districts. It was the sugar belt of Bihar, and many big sugar mills operated in that area.

We reached Chapra in the afternoon on February 3, 1965. Straight away, we drove to Kalsi's house. We were greeted by the couple. Mrs. Kalsi and Rashmi instantly became friends. I and Kalsi had a chat over tea. Kalsi was a simple and straight-forward Sardar Ji without any false pretensions. He belonged to the royal family of Patiala. Mrs. Kalsi belonged to a big zamindar family of Amritsar. Being very sociable, they had a big circle of friends in Chapra. He introduced many of them to me and Rashmi over lunch at his house that very day.

After the guests departed, the Kalsis offered to give me the cook Ramu and the domestic help Balu. He said that, since he would be leaving Bihar for good and joining his new post of IOC at Chandigarh, he couldn't take these two helpers away from their native place. He vouched for their sincerity, conduct, and good service. I accepted the offer and thanked Kalsi.

Kalsi confirmed that in the coming seven to ten days, he would take me around the area. He would inform me of the latest position concerning the field events. He had already learned about the dirty politics of Lamba, Talwar, and Roy Choudhury, which led to my transfer. He termed the three "cobras" whose heads needed to be crushed to end their evil conspiracies. He also narrated his bad experience with Lamba as well as Talwar. He cautioned me to be careful in my dealings with them.

In the afternoon, Zaheer, Kalsi's cook Ramu, and the house help Balu quickly set all the household items at their designated spots in the house. The entire next week became extremely busy. I and Kalsi toured the whole area and met all persons of importance in the networks, industries, and government departments of the area. After handing over the charge, Kalsis left Chapra on February 14, 1965.

I intensely delved into my official activities. I was earlier given the sales and revenue collection targets for the area for all the quarters ending March 1966. Lamba had set it at figures that were double the previous year for the same period. Besides, there was a large amount of money to be collected from the sugar mills in the area that accrued for products supplied over the last few years. Most of the sugar mills were sick, and their financial position was critical. In spite of huge amounts to be recovered, the state government used to pressurise the divisional office to release their supplies against the receipt of a small part of their old dues. This had further escalated the problem for Burmah Shell.

I successfully achieved the big quarterly targets of sales and revenue for each quarter from February 1965 until March 1966. It became a matter of utter dismay for Lamba and his coterie. They never anticipated my success in this endeavour. As far as the collection of old dues from Sugar Mills was concerned, I submitted in the first week of March 1966 a workable proposal for its quick resolution. I had prepared it after a detailed discussion with the owners of those sugar mills. I requested that Lamba give written approval to my proposal for implementation. Lamba did not respond. I was forced to temporarily suspend all supplies to these mills after informing the owners of the reason.

This was the beginning of more serious friction between Lamba and me. He could not restore supply to sugar mills under the pressure of the state government. That increased his friction with the state. While Lamba was planning his revengeful action, I continued with my excellent marketing performance. In the social circle of Chapra, I and Rashmi made our mark. In March 1965, I was elected as the Governor of the Lions Club of Chapra. The collectors and the police superintendents of my area became good friends.

Sugar mill owners also became friendly acquaintances in spite of my temporary suspension of supplies of diesel and lubricants to their factories.

Suddenly, in the first week of April 1966, I was transferred to the Patna divisional office as an OSD (Officer on Special Duty). I was asked to join by April 7, 1966. The intimation also mentioned the abolition of Chapra HQ. Its administered area was divided into two parts. One part was to merge with Muzaffarpur and the other with Darbhanga. The reason for the abolition and the split was mentioned as an exercise for rationalising the divisional set-up for cost cutting and administrative efficiency. But I could clearly see through the entire camouflage! It was part of a hidden vendetta by Lamba against me. It had nothing to do with the minimization of the operational cost, nor did it boost the company's trading revenue. It also had no customary approval from the branch office.

I initiated swift action to protect my own interests. I requested my friend, the Divisional Engineer Kuriakose, to immediately arrange a flat for me in the same building where he stayed at Pataliputra Colony. It was promptly arranged. I and Rashmi entered this flat on the 6th of April, 1966. Only driver Zaheer accompanied. The cook, Ramu, and the other helper, Balu, were released and left behind at Chapra after they were paid off.

My household goods reached my Patna flat from Chapra on the 7th forenoon and were properly placed in the flat. After purchasing provisions in the afternoon, I became tension-free. I was ready to join the office the next day. I showed absolutely no stress or tension.

On April 8, 1966, to the utter surprise of the Lamba coterie, I joined the Patna divisional office. Lamba told me that I was to only operate at the divisional office. I would have no external tour. Further, there would be curtailment in my car and travel allowances, and they would be replaced by a fixed allowance. This meant a monthly financial loss of over fifteen hundred rupees for me. However, I neither bothered nor made any request to Lamba for reconsideration of such a decision. This was quite a shock to Lamba.

Lamba imposed further limitations on my regular divisional office duties. I was informed that my role was now confined to providing advice to my colleagues in Muzaffarpur and Darbhanga. They could seek my guidance if they encountered any marketing or related issues in the previous Chapra area. I was explicitly instructed not to undertake any official trips for this purpose. If necessary, my colleagues could be summoned to Patna for discussions. However, such a situation never arose. It soon came to light that there was a confidential directive concerning this matter. Both my colleagues in those two locations were friends of mine and discreetly informed me about Lamba's covert instruction. They had been instructed confidentially not to reach out to me and instead share their issues with Talwar.

Despite the office environment, I remained unruffled and devoid of any tension. I made a concerted effort to shield Rashmi from all work-related problems and stress, ensuring she never felt burdened. In the evenings, we would continue with our normal routine, going out to watch movies and enjoying dinners at the renowned restaurant at ITC Mayura. We also visited our friends' homes and occasionally embarked on weekend trips to Fernandez's Capital Hotel. I strived to maintain Rashmi's life as normal as possible, which became my most effective strategy in dealing with my adversary. I continued to adhere to my office hours, engaging in my preferred pastimes of reading and writing. No official tasks were assigned to me that required my attention, and all of these developments were courtesy of Lamba.

Two weeks of my idling at the office passed without any major incidents. In the third week of April, the branch sales manager, Mr. Peter Jervis, was due to visit Patna for the performance review of the division. Before the scheduled visit by Jervis on April 22, 1966, Lamba called me to his chamber. He told me not to raise any of my personal problems with Jervis. He said that, in his opinion, there was no job left for me in the division, and I should better tender my resignation!

Such talk by Lamba stretched the limits of my patience. I immediately retorted. Filled with anger, I gave a bit of my mind to Lamba. I told him categorically and loudly that I was not going to resign. I also told him that he had no power to dismiss me. With all the excellent past performance attributed to me, even at my last posting at Chapra, the management of Burmah Shell won't take lightly the harassment that he perpetrated on me. I further charged and cautioned Lamba of his full liability for the harassment meted out to me. I made it clear that the higher management would surely ask Lamba for a satisfactory explanation of the whole issue. After that unpleasantness, I left Lamba's room in a huff and went back to my own cabin. I calmed myself and waited for the arrival of Jervis. The entire office was stunned at the loud exchange.

After arriving at the divisional office, Jervis wanted to first meet all the officers in their cabins. Lamba took him to each of the four cabins for an introduction. When Jervis entered the fourth cabin, he was surprised to see me sitting there with a newspaper. Jervis had known my abilities since the interview days. He used to keep track of my progress with the earlier divisional manager, Mr. Mukherjee. He had a very high opinion of my capability and efficiency. He had many times praised me and given my examples at training programmes held at the branch office. He told me to meet him separately after the divisional review meeting. Lamba became visibly upset and uncomfortable.

Jervis met me alone in the meeting room. I narrated all the incidents from the time Lamba transferred me from Gaya to Chapra. He was told how I was posted as an OSD at Patna without any work. I also narrated the events of the previous day when Lamba asked for my resignation. Jervis was aghast at the way Lamba had behaved on heresy. He assured me of giving full justice and restoring my honour and importance in consonance with my capabilities.

Lamba and the number two of the divisional office, Kanwaljeet Singh (popularly known as KS), were then called to the meeting room. In my presence, Jervis told both that he was upset at the below-par performance of the Patna division. He fumed at the loss of two vital customer groups in the Patna division to Caltex. He said that he was very concerned about the heavy outstanding dues that had been pending recovery for more than a few years from the sugar mills. He informed me that these mills were trying to patronise another major competitor, Stan Vac.

Jervis told Lamba that he was unhappy with the unfavourable developments in Patna Division. He further said that he would now personally monitor these issues from Calcutta. He informed me that he had already assigned this work to me, and I would directly report to him with immediate effect. He again repeated that I had been entrusted with the task of rectifying the adverse situation and providing the desired results in two months, beginning April 25, 1966.

The two tasks that I was entrusted with by Jervis were: to bring back the fuel and lubricant supplies of all Mica Mines and the DVC power houses in the Koderma area from Caltex; to collect two-year-old dues of five crores from seven sugar mills in Saran, Gopalganj, and Darbhanga; and to tie them up with Burmah Shell for future supplies.

Jervis again asked me if I would be able to carry out these tasks in time. I confirmed that I would try my best to achieve these goals in time.

I requested that Mr. Jervis accord his approval to three things:

I should get all assistance from the divisional office when asked for.

Permission of unrestricted movement in my own car for travelling to Koderma, Saran Gopalganj, and Darbhanga areas;

Approval of my earlier note of March submitted to Lamba in the context of the debt recovery.

Mr. Jervis approved the first two requirements immediately. He asked Lamba to show him my note that had yet to get approval. When Lamba produced the note, Jervis went through it and gave instant approval. He reprimanded Lamba for sitting on the note so long without approval. He restored the withdrawn car and tour allowance facility to me and told me to report directly to him. He directed me to concentrate only on the given two assignments. I was asked to provide the progress report directly to Jervis every tenth day over the telephone.

Subsequently, before leaving Patna, Jervis called and consoled me for all the wrongdoings of Lamba. He said that he specifically visited Patna to redress all the wrongdoings of Lamba. He wished me luck in my assignments. I expressed my gratitude to him. What surprised me was how Jervis came to know about my trouble. My best guess was that my previous boss, Mr. Mukherjee, must have told Jervis, who happened to be his batchmate. Mr. Mukherjee was still in contact with his previous PS at Patna, who must have routinely informed him of this.

The actions taken by Jervis terribly shook Lamba and his coterie. It was another matter that, subsequently, in 1968, all members of the entire coterie were thrown out of Burmah Shell on the voluntary retirement scheme of the company.

I started my work immediately. I made an advance programme for the work in such a manner that it could be successfully completed within a period of less than six weeks. On April 24, I planned to take Rashmi and Zaheer with me and drive to Koderma. I was programmed to stay there for two weeks at the Tilaya Dam guest house and successfully complete the first one of the two assigned tasks.

Earlier, I had called my old friend Srivastava. He was still continuing as the Chief Engineer of DVC at Koderma. I told him the purpose of my visit. I requested that he permit my stay for two weeks at their Tilaya guest house. Srivastava was very happy to agree to my request. The only condition he made was that I and Rashmi should agree to have our launch at their place on arrival. He said that Mrs. Srivastava, who was a dear friend of Rashmi, had made this request. I thanked Srivastava and promised to meet them over lunch.

At 6 a.m. on the twenty-fourth of April, I and Rashmi headed for Koderma. Rashmi was happy to go to Koderma and have her lunch with Mrs. Srivastava. The prospect of staying at the Tilaya Dam guest house for two weeks was very alluring for her. I, too, became a party to her happiness. After almost six months, both fully regained their jovial mood. Both of us soaked ourselves in the ecstasy of each other's happy company. For a moment, during their drive, I became emotional. I thanked God for giving us back our happiness. We arrived at Koderma around 12:30 p.m. Straight away, we drove to the hilltop DVC Guest House. After freshening ourselves, we drove to the house of Srivastava. Rashmi and Mrs. Srivastava hugged each other like long-lost friends.

After lunch, I and Srivastava had our official discussion. Srivastava said that he had already initiated action for the cancellation of Caltex supplies. He had also passed his orders to resume the DVC contract with Burmah Shell for supplies from the BS depot at Koderma. He promised to hand over the written order to me the next day. He would also simultaneously hand over next month's supply orders for all their units for the current month and the next month.

During the chat, Srivastava said that his cousin, Ashok Saxena, was the biggest mica mine owner at Koderma. He was the All-India President of the Association of Mica Mine Owners. This was God-sent news for me. Earlier, during my Gaya days, I had met Ashok several times. I remembered having made him happy by settling all his lingering old claims on Burmah Shell in one go. Srivastava had already talked with Saxena about my task. He informed me that Saxena had agreed to ensure that my objectives would be attained in two days. I decided to meet him the next day and confirmed the same over the telephone from Srivastava's house. I was asked to come to his main office in the mine area the next day at 11.30 a.m.

The next day, when I reached Saxena's office, I was surprised to see all the mine owners and their general managers present in his office. Saxena, as president of their association, had called all of them at 9:30 a.m. for a meeting. In the said meeting, they all had already decided to return to the fold of Burmah Shell for their petroleum product requirements. When I joined the meeting, Saxena and other mine owners welcomed me and apprised me of their decision. I was overwhelmed; I profusely thanked Saxena and others individually. Saxena said that, on the 26th evening, he had planned a dinner for the mine owners and their spouses. He requested that I and Srivastava join the dinner with our spouses. Saxena said that letters of confirmation of their decision to patronise Burmah Shell would be handed over to me after the dinner.

After this successful meeting, I drove to Srivastava's office and collected the letter from DVC regarding the switching back of their supplies to Burmah Shell. When I told him about next evening's dinner party, Srivastava smiled and mentioned that he had already gotten feedback from his cousin. He also mentioned that Mrs. Srivastava is already with Rashmi at the guest house, and they were expecting them to join for lunch.

The dinner on the evening of April 26 was a grand affair. Saxena and his wife arranged the party in the dining hall of their bungalow. The dining hall was well lit with prismatic Belgian chandeliers. The hall was big enough to accommodate twenty couples. A bevy of appropriately dressed bearers were present to serve the guests. I and Srivastava, with our better halves, joined the gathering around 7:30 in the evening. The party continued close to midnight amidst the musical 'Mushaira' by famous Ghazal singers brought from Lucknow and Patna. After dinner, I was handed over a bunch of letters from all the mine owners. Each of the letters confirmed the immediate switching back of their mines' supply requirements from Caltex to Burmah Shell.

During the next four days, I went to the Koderma depot and ensured that Burmah Shell supplies were promptly released to DVC and all the mica mines against their received orders. After the resumption of these supplies, I called Mr. Jervis and gave him this good news. The resumption of Burmah Shell supplies to DVC and Mica mines made Jervis happy. He highly commended my achievement. He again wished me well and asked me to similarly succeed in achieving the second target. He indicated that, after completion of the two assigned tasks, I would be placed at the Calcutta Branch office on another important assignment. Lamba was dismayed when the news of my success reached the Divisional HQ, courtesy of Mr. Jervis.

I left Koderma on April 30, 1966, after a final round of meetings and the farewell meeting with Srivastava and Saxena on the previous day. I informed them that I was going to leave Bihar for my next posting at the Calcutta branch office by the end of May, and after reaching Calcutta, I would contact them and give them my details. Both were also invited for a future Calcutta visit. I gave them the telephone numbers of Mr. Jervis and told them to contact Mr. Jervis for any future problems who was already aware of the assistance they extended to me.

After driving back to Patna, I stayed there for three days. During these days, I met Mr. Naveen Mishra, who was the principal secretary in the cooperative department of the Bihar government. I knew him well as the elder cousin of my old classmate and friend Ashok Bhargav. I asked Mr. Mishra about the problem of outstanding dues that these seven sugar mills owed to my company for almost two years. I said that the government was withholding around Rs. 11 crore of these seven mills' subsidies for a long period. I requested that Mr. Mishra release at least fifty percent of the withheld subsidy directly to the seven sugar mills. The balance amount of five crores needed to be given to Burmah Shell for adjustment against the pending dues of these mills with the company.

Mr. Mishra agreed to help in this matter. However, he asked me to obtain, from each of those sugar mills, details of their subsidy claim in writing. He also asked to obtain the authorization letter of each mill for the adjustment of part of the released subsidy amount by the government against their outstanding Burmah Shell (BS) dues. Mishra informed me that the owner of each of these mills had direct links with the Chief Minister (CM) of Bihar. The owners should also talk to the CM to approve Mishra's proposal instantly. He assured that, after positive action on the mentioned issues, it wouldn't take him more than a week to release five crores for adjustment against BS dues. After this assurance, I felt that my goal would be achieved in a week or ten days' time. I immediately drew up my schedule for the plan of action during the next seven days.

I was confident about the timing. Earlier, while preparing my note for the collection of these outstanding amounts, I had already gathered the relevant documents related to each mill's claim for the subsidy owed by the Bihar government. These documents had been properly endorsed and signed by each of the seven mill owners and were already in my possession.

The only thing left for me to collect from the mill owners were letters from each of them authorising the adjustment of their full BS dues against the government-released subsidy. The total outstanding amount, according to the latest bills from Burmah Shell, was approximately seven crores, which included two crores in interest. I had secured Jervis's approval for the note, which allowed for the waiver of the imposed penal interest of two crores. This was a significant advantage for the mill owners and confirmed my earlier commitment to them. They were all willing to comply with my request.

I had decided to embark on a ten-day trip to the Saran, Gopalganj, and Darbhanga areas starting on May 5. This was essential for the success of my second assignment, and my schedule was quite hectic. I chose to leave Rashmi in Patna during this time. Her stay was secure as Kuriakose's family lived below our flat. Rashmi and I went shopping together to purchase all the provisions needed for the month of May. I assured Rashmi that I would talk to her on the phone every night, and she shouldn't worry. I informed Kuriakose and his family about my planned itinerary and requested that they offer assistance to Rashmi if necessary. Mrs. Kuriakose assured me that they would provide any help needed and promised to send her elder daughter to stay with Rashmi every night in my absence.

I took driver Zaheer and left for Chapra in the morning of May 5. The previous day, from the Patna office, I had contacted all seven owners of sugar mills. I had requested each of them to be present on my given dates (between the sixth and the twelfth of May) for the resolution of their outstanding debt. I had briefly indicated how I intended to get their long-pending subsidy released. I said that it would boost their finances and help them finally settle their Burmah Shell dues.

Each one of the seven owners agreed to meet, discuss, and resolve the problem on the given dates. It perfectly suited my plan. During that week, the

Bihar assembly was also in session. That ensured Bihar's CM's availability at Patna for the mill owners to contact him as proposed by the Secretary, Mishra. I had already found that, in three out of the seven mills, the CM had nearly 25 percent. Another four among the seven belonged jointly to his son and elder brother. These facts made my task easier to achieve.

I met, discussed and finalised all actions with the seven sugar mill owners. Their authorisation letters were also obtained on scheduled days beginning 6th May, 1966. Each one also talked over phone in my presence to the CM to ensure speedy release of the subsidy. I triumphantly returned to Patna on 13th of May.

On the 14th, I met Principal Secretary Narendra Mishra. I handed over the required documents. Mishra went through all the documents and called the joint secretary, Sinha, and the PA to his chamber. In my presence, he dictated the note. The joint secretary signed the note. Mishra then put his remarks on that note to get the approval of the CM. Sinha immediately carried the note, along with all the documents given by me, to the CM's secretary. Sinha followed up and obtained the approval of the CM on May 15th. Mishra called me to meet him on May 19th and collect the five crore rupee cheque favouring Burmah Shell.

I met the secretary on the 19th, as advised. Secretary Mishra said that he got the CM's approval on the 15th itself. The entire subsidy of Rs 11 crore was approved for release to the seven mills that very day. After adjustment of Burmah Shell dues, he has already sent to all mills the balance of six crores. I profusely thanked the secretary.

With the collected cheque of five crores, I went straight to the main branch of the State Bank, where the Patna account of Burmah Shell was operated. I entered the manager's cabin, gave the said check, and asked him to credit instantly the amount to Burmah Shell. It was done immediately, as this branch also operated the accounts of the state government. I requested the manager issue the credit note and hand it to me for records. After getting it, I made a call to Jervis from the manager's cabin and informed him about the payment.

Jervis congratulated me and said that he was confident in my success. He mentioned his confidence in me to accomplish the assigned tasks within a month's time, against a given target of two months. Jervis was happy to announce five increments in my salary and my promotion to the next higher grade after superseding twenty-five of my senior colleagues! I was also told about my transfer order to Calcutta and placement at the branch office. By June 8, 1966, I could be in Calcutta. Jervis also mentioned that the letters for these orders were being carried by a person from the branch office to Patna the same evening. It would be handed over to him personally at Patna the next day. I expressed my gratitude and thanked Jervis from the bottom of my heart. I sincerely conveyed my obligation and gratitude to him. Jervis's only reply was, "Arrive soon at Calcutta and have a drink with me."

From the bank I drove straight home to give the good news to Rashmi. On receiving the information, she tightly hugged me. Tears of joy rolled down the cheeks of both. We stood there in ecstasy for a long time until the doorbell rang. It was Kuriakose at the door. He had already heard the good news about me at the divisional office. He had come home for lunch and wanted to congratulate me first. I thanked him and asked him to come inside. Kuriakose said that he would come in the evening to have a detailed chat.

Around 5 p.m., Mrs. Kuriakose came and congratulated me and Rashmi. She invited us to their house for the celebration dinner. She said that Kuriakose had told her to arrange the dinner on his way back to the office after lunch. It became a celebration dinner party that evening at Kuriakose's house. Me and Rashmi thanked the Kuriakose's for all their help during my days of stress. Later, I helped Kuriakose secure his desired posting at the Trivandrum divisional office with the help of Jervis.

The next day, I planned to visit the Patna divisional office to collect my letters sent by Jervis. I also wanted to take my personal belongings out of my cabin. After receiving the letters from the Calcutta branch office around 3 p.m., I went around to bid good-bye to my friends at the Patna office. I met all except Lamba and Talwar. These two were already ashamed of their wrongdoings against me and were conveniently absent at the divisional office for the majority of that day. Everyone in the office knew the uncouth nature of both. All except these two were happy about my achievements and my promotion.

On hearing that I had declined to accept the farewell of the divisional officers and staff the next day at the office, Lamba came out of his room and personally conveyed his regrets for all his wrong actions against me. He requested that I forgive, forget, and accept the farewell. I then agreed to say farewell. But, in spite of my forgiveness, I could not ever forget the stress that I and Rashmi had undergone over the past few months due to Lamba's vindictiveness.

In the first week of May, Rashmi began experiencing symptoms of morning sickness. I took her to a well-known female gynaecologist, who confirmed her pregnancy. I informed the doctor of my plan to drive with Rashmi to Calcutta by the end of the month and inquired about the safety of a road trip given her condition. The doctor's opinion was that, since the pregnancy was less than two months along, it would be safe for her to make the journey to Calcutta by car. However, we needed to ensure that each day's travel did not exceed 300 kilometres, and she should have adequate rest with breaks every three hours during the journey. We planned the trip with Rashmi's consent. She didn't want to travel by flight or train because she enjoyed experiencing new places up close rather than from a distance, and I, as always, respected her preferences.

Before leaving Patna, I managed to secure a permanent driver position for Zaheer in the Bihar police force with the assistance of my friend Prasad from Gaya. Before officially joining the police department, Zaheer accompanied us on our road journey to Calcutta. On the morning of May 31, 1966, Rashmi, our unborn child, and I set off from Patna for Calcutta in my Ambassador car. The evening before our departure, I had arranged for our household goods to be transferred to a truck, and I had also secured company accommodation in Calcutta starting on June 1, 1966. It was a lovely apartment on the second floor of a new four-story building on Ekdalia Road near Gariahat, Ballygunge.

After covering a distance of 300 kilometres, Rashmi and I spent the night at a Dak Bungalow located on the National Highway. This bungalow had been reserved by a nearby Burmah Shell dealer, who had also arranged for our dinner and breakfast the following morning. Our stay was comfortable, and after having breakfast, we resumed our journey towards Calcutta. Around 2 p.m., we stopped at a roadside dhaba for lunch and eventually arrived at our accommodation in Calcutta at 6:30 p.m. on June 2nd, which happened to be a Thursday. I had a total of five days before I was scheduled to start my new position on Wednesday, June 8th, 1966.

Upon our arrival in Calcutta, I drove to the nearest Burmah Shell petrol pump on Gariahat Road, where Bose, the dealer of that outlet, had the key to our rented apartment. He handed over the key to me and sent one of his attendants to assist in transferring our luggage from our car to the flat. After opening the flat and moving our belongings inside, the attendant took my car to the petrol pump for parking and servicing the next day. Rashmi and I had our packed dinner, which we had purchased earlier from the dhaba on the highway where we had stopped for tea. After dinner, we slept on the bedroom floor, as our household goods were expected to arrive by truck the following day.

At 5:30 the next morning, the house bell rang. I opened the door and found an old lady standing. On inquiry, she said that Bose Babu, owner of the BS pump, had sent her to serve as a cook and maid in our house. Her name was Bela, and she stayed near Ballygunge railway station. Her place was a 15-minute walk from our Ekdalia flat.

She was told to come every day at 5:30 a.m., do all the cooking and household work in the house, and leave around 9 p.m. She would have her meals during the day at our place, and her monthly salary would be fifty rupees. Bela appeared to be over fifty years old. Rashmi was happy to engage her. She told her that the truck carrying our luggage was expected to arrive around 8:30 a.m. and, after arrangement of all the effects and cleaning of the rooms, she could cook their lunch around 2 p.m. Rashmi explained to her about her daily, regular household work.

The next day, the truck with our luggage reached us at 8 a.m. All the things were brought up and arranged by the packers and movers' personnel. By 11 a.m., everything was properly arranged and set. In the meantime, Rashmi had taken Bela and gone to Gariahat market for the purchase of a monthly ration and two days of fish, vegetables, eggs, etc. Bela prepared the lunch after cleaning the house and served food to us at 1 p.m.

The flat had two bed rooms with attached washrooms, one sitting-cum-dining room, and an anteroom with the third washroom. The anteroom was used by Bela for rest during the day. The flat had a kitchen and a storage room. There were two balconies, one in front overlooking Ekdalia Road and the other at the rear. The rear balcony faced the Gariahat Road that was fifty metres beyond. Gariahat Market was visible between the twenty-foot-wide gap of two buildings at the rear of our building. Across Ekdalia Road, there was an old Zamindar's red haveli with a big compound.

On the ground floor of our building lived the Kashmiri Ganju family. They had four daughters. The first floor was under the occupation of a businessman (the Agarwal family) with old parents and a daughter. On the top floor, above our flat, stayed the Banerjee couple. Banerjee was a judicial magistrate, and the couple had no children. It was a good locality near Mande Ville Gardens. Rashmi loved the place.

I utilized the nearby Burmah Shell petrol pump owned by Bose Babu to park my car overnight. This marked Rashmi's first visit to Calcutta. Over the next four days, I took her on a tour of the city to explore various attractions such as the Maidan, Victoria Memorial, Race Course, Outram Ghat along the Hooghly River, Fort Williams, Red Road, Dalhousie Square, Esplanade, Chowringhee Road, Park Street, and other points of interest. The city was entirely new and fascinating to her, and I also took her to the Kali Maa temple at Kalighat.

For the initial five days, Rashmi and I instructed Bela not to prepare our dinner. During the afternoons of these days, I chauffeured Rashmi around Calcutta, and we enjoyed early dinners at renowned restaurants in the Park Street and Chowringhee areas. During this time, Rashmi and I paid visits to the homes of my friends in Calcutta, including Felix Almeida (an entrepreneur), the Prabhu family of Alembics, the Prabhu family of Glaxo, the Fondeker family associated with the railways, the Hegde family from Canara Bank, the Deshprabhu family of NSL, and a few others. Rashmi was introduced to these families, which brought them great joy and delight.

At 9 a.m. on June 8, 1966, I reached the BS Branch office in Hong Kong House at Dalhousie Square. I went to the second-floor office of Mr. Jervis. He was yet to come. I waited for him at his PA, Ms. Sylvia's, cabin adjoining the room of the boss. Sylvia was a smart Anglo-Indian girl. I was instantly at ease with her; earlier on many occasions, I had met her while meeting Mr. Jervis. I did not have to wait there for long.

As Jervis came, he called me to his chamber. He told me that I had been posted under his group at the branch office. My immediate job was to upgrade major BS outlets in Calcutta. These have to be similar to the new outlet set up by me a year ago at Dobhi. His estimate was that it might take nearly six months for me to remodel around twenty of the major outlets in Calcutta. The buildings, their canopies, and the facilities of these outlets need to be remodelled and rebuilt before they are recommissioned as merchandising outlets. There was no financial constraint for the massive remodelling job.

Jervis told me to complete the assignment by coordinating with Mr. Bir, the divisional manager of Calcutta. For any problem in the execution of the project, I could always contact him for advice and direction. I came back to my cabin, which was nearest to the boss's room. All members of the Group of Branch Sales Managers (GBSM) met and welcomed me. I discussed the new assignment with the Engineer of Retail Outlets (ERO) attached to GBSM. I formulated ideas for the next discussion with Mr. Bir.

Mr. Bir was a foreign-educated young engineer. He was a very amiable Sikh gentleman—almost the opposite of Lamba. My vibes perfectly matched those of Bir right after our first meeting. In two hours' time, both gave shape to the remodelling work of selected outlets. It had a time frame for implementation and completion. The completion was scheduled for the end of November, 1966. Bir selected the twenty major outlets spread all over Calcutta's south, central, north, east, and west zones. The first five, where work was to start immediately, were at Alipore, Park Circus, Esplanade, Chittaranjan Avenue, and Ballygunge.

For a week, I, along with N.K. Roy, the Chief Retail Outlet Engineer (CRE), and Sambhit Chatterjee, a Calcutta Division Officer (CDO), visited these five outlets for a survey. The blueprints for the remodelling were prepared. After the CRE made the drawings and calculated the cost for each, I and the CRE discussed the proposal with Bir. The cost of remodelling the five outlets was estimated at one and a half crore rupees. Bir and I met Jervis and got his nod to go ahead and complete this part of the project in one and a half months, i.e., by August 15th, 1966.

I requested that Bir temporarily attach the CDO Sambhit with me until the assigned project was completed. This CDO had earlier accompanied me and the CRE for the survey. To help me full-time for the completion of the scheduled task, Bir agreed, and Sambhit Chatterjee was attached to me. Incidentally, Sambhit was the elder brother of the famous Bengali actor Soumitra Chatterjee. Much later, I learned that Sambhit, after his retirement, developed Alzheimer's disease and passed away in 2014.

Coming back to the completion of the assigned project, I earmarked August 12, 1966, as the day when it would be completed. I and Bir requested Jervis inaugurate the remodelled outlets on the 15th of August, synchronising with the 19th Independence Day of India.

Peter Jervis had other ideas. He planned the inauguration of the biggest company-operated and remodelled outlet at Park Circus, to be done by West Bengal CM Prafulla Sen. Accordingly, the inauguration of the five remodelled outlets was done by five personalities. The Chief Minister inaugurated the Park Circus outlet. Alipore was opened by the branch manager, Chopra. The one at Esplanade was inaugurated by BSM Jervis. DMC Bir opened the Chittaranjan Avenue outlet, while the one at Ballygunge was opened by me and Sambhit together.

After the Independence Day flag hoisting ceremony, the CM, Prafulla Sen, drove to the Park Circus remodelled merchandising outlet at 11 a.m. He was highly impressed with the facilities, the look, and the variety of different daily-use items stocked in the merchandising section. He applauded Chopra and Jervis for this unique effort. When I and Sambhit were introduced to him as the main architects for this venture, the CM congratulated us. He knew Sambhit well and greeted him in Bengali. As scheduled earlier, the other four outlets were also inaugurated one by one during that day by 5 p.m. Bose, the owner of the Ballygunge outlet, took my good wishes after its inauguration.

Newspapers of next morning headlined the Chief Minister's Independence Day inauguration of the novel project of BS. The aspect of merchandising in a petrol pump was unique as highlighted by the press. *Today, what one sees at an "IN & OUT" petrol pump was actually initiated by me more than fifty years ago, in 1964! I had created this facility at the new Dhobi Outlet during my Gaya posting.*

The remodelling of the other 15 outlets was also completed much before time, at an expenditure of around six and a half crores. Thus, my workload eased by mid-December 1966. I could give more time to Rashmi, who was expecting our child, any time after the third week of December. Earlier, I saw to it that Bela took enough care of her in my absence.

I wanted to be with her all the time to minimise the discomfort of her advanced stage of pregnancy. Rashmi, with her ever-lovable and amiable disposition, never had any complaints about me. She was always tolerant and accommodating in her attitude and demeanour. She was slim and strong. Seeing her belly bump, no one could believe that she was nine months pregnant. In her pregnancy, she looked exclusively regal and excitingly beautiful. I continued to enjoy her tantalising looks, her captivating smiles, and her graceful gaiety. For me, like my first days with her before marriage, she looked like a heavenly fairy in the form of a dream girl! Anyone would have been jealous of my luck for having this lady as a wife!

To look after her, I applied for three weeks of leave starting on December 22. It was duly approved. Earlier, every month, I used to take Rashmi for her routine check-up by Dr. Sarita Sen, the famous gynaecologist. She was attached to the Presidency Nursing Home (PNH), where she was examined each month. This nursing home was nearer to our residence and was on Ashutosh Chowdhury Avenue, Dover Terrace, Ballygunge. It hardly took ten minutes' drive to reach there. As a precautionary measure, Dr. Sen advised me to reserve a cabin for December 22 so that Rashmi could be moved there at any time on or after December 22. The reservation was done as advised, and I paid the charges in advance for a week.

Rashmi was happy that I would be with her all the time for the next three weeks. Sitting on the front balcony for hours, we used to listen to music, play Ludo and card games, and talk about the baby yet to grace our lives. In between, mostly in the evenings, families of our friends used to drop in to assure Rashmi that everything was going to be fine.

Prabhu's wife, Reema, a dear friend of Rashmi, came to our house in the evening of December 23, 1966. She presented her with a big boutique painting of Goddess Durga. She was a good painter who was trained at Bombay's famous J.J. School of Art. She had created the painting on a Tussar silk cloth. She had specifically made it for Rashmi. She hung the painting on the wall of Rashmi's bedroom and told her that she and her child would always have the protection of "Maa Durga".

Her words still echo in my subconscious. This painting remained with the family for quite some time. It was even hung on the staircase of our Bhubaneswar Bungalow as a good omen from 2007 onwards until I left the place in September 2017. The painting wasn't affected a bit over a period of fifty years! I felt sorry that it could not be brought to Noida when I shifted. This might have continued to provide the family with good, divine vibes!

On the 24th evening, Dutta Roy dropped by our house. Bela had made Paratha and mutton dopiaza for our dinner. Rashmi had told her to make a few more parathas for the guest too. Bela left for her house around 9 p.m. Rashmi served the dinner to all three. Dutta Roy left for his house around 10.30 p.m.

After half an hour, Rashmi started feeling the labour pain. I immediately rang up the dealer, Bose Babu, to urgently send his driver along with my parked car to his petrol pump. The car was brought at 11.15 p.m., and I took Rashmi to the nursing home. Straightaway, she was wheeled to the delivery room upon arrival. After an hour and a half, at 0100 hours on December 25, 1966, we got our first "Bundle of Joy" in the City of Joy!

Dr. Sarita, who conducted the delivery, reported that both the mother and the baby girl were in excellent health. She permitted them to be transferred to their designated cabin at the nursing home for immediate rest and postnatal care around 6 a.m. My heart swelled with immense joy, and I drifted off to sleep in the reclining chair placed inside the cabin. The following morning, Dr. Sarita visited to examine Rashmi and the child, confirming their well-being. She suggested that I go home for an hour or two so that the nurses could tidy up the room, attend to Rashmi, and make arrangements for the mother and child's feedings.

I returned to our flat and shared the wonderful news with Bela. I called my parents and close relatives to share the news. My mother asked about Rashmi and the newborn's health and inquired about the baby's appearance. I described the child as very beautiful, with plump cheeks, bright eyes, a round face, and a fair complexion, much like her mother. My mother immediately proposed the name "Moonie" due to the baby's moon-like face and complexion. So, the baby was affectionately called that until Rashmi eventually changed it to a more modern and widely accepted name, Mona. My father asked for the baby's time of birth to prepare her horoscope.

My in-law's household was filled with happiness, and Rashmi's elder sister (Sanju Apa) and elder brother (Badu Bhai, also known as Majhi Bhai) conveyed their best wishes and blessings. Both houses, Tulsipur and Sati Chaura, were adorned with a festive atmosphere. That evening, my father and mother went to Chandi Mandir to offer prayers and distribute prasad as part of the celebration.

I asked Bela to make puri, halwa, and kheer for lunch and pack them in a tiffin carrier for me and Rashmi. I was not too sure whether the nursing home would allow Rashmi to eat home food. Around 12.30 p.m., I reached Rashmi's cabin. Both the mother and the child were in deep sleep.

The attending nurse told me that Rashmi had already taken her lunch provided by the nursing home as per the menu given by Dr. Sarita. Rashmi had also breastfed the baby. The nurse told me to quietly eat the lunch that I had brought. After eating, I took a nap on the cushioned bench meant for the rest of the attending family members. The nurse visited the room often for the regular check-ups of the mother and the child.

Rashmi woke up around 4 p.m. She was happy to learn that I had brought her favourites, halwa and kheer. She spoke to Dr. Sarita and was told that she could take small portions of Halwa and Kheer along with her night's diet.

I narrated to Rashmi about the information that I had already given about the newborn to all our friends and relatives. I also informed her about Maa naming the child Moonie and Baba's preparation of Moonie's horoscope. We shared many other pieces of information. I told her that I would stay with them at the nursing home during all the days and nights until their discharge from the nursing home. Every morning, around 7.45am, I left them for three hours and went to the house to allow Bela entry for cleaning the flat and cooking lunch and dinner. I usually return to Rashmi's cabin around 11 a.m.

Rashmi and baby Mona were discharged from the nursing home in the afternoon of December 31, 1966. The family celebrated their new year (1967) at their Ekdalia Road residence. It was a quiet affair, as Dr. Sarita had advised him not to allow any outside visitors for three months. Her advice was scrupulously followed. Even Bela remained in the house for 24 hours without going to her home during that period. Every fifteen days, I drove Rashmi and baby Mona for check-ups to Dr. Sharita's chamber. After six such visits, Rashmi and Mona were declared absolutely fit and required no more check-ups. Soon after that period, Natu visited Calcutta for official work. He also came to Ekdalia House to see Mona. He was the first among our relatives to hold Mona.

I joined duty on Monday, the 9th of January, 1967. I had carried a few boxes of Sandesh for distribution among colleagues in my group. This was to mark the happy occasion of the birth of Mona. A box each was given to Mr. Bir, Sylvia, and Mr. Jervis. All of them conveyed their best wishes for Mona, Rashmi, and me. Jervis told me to take it easy at work for the next three months so that I can take care of the family. Although I used to go to work at 7:30 a.m., I used to return home by 5:30 p.m. I never neglected my work and kept to the deadlines for all assignments.

As per Jervis's instructions, I was only to make daily inspections of the twenty newly remodelled merchandising outlets in Calcutta. They were to be advised to optimise their performance. This became necessary due to Bir's request. This arrangement was agreed upon by Jervis, subject to the condition that I would undertake such duty only at noon. In the afternoon, I would work for GBSM. Jervis had also ordered me to leave the office sharp by 5 p.m. and take full days off on Saturdays and Sundays. To ensure desired results, every working day I left home early, at 7.30 a.m., after breakfast. I also coordinated my inspection with Sambhit of the Calcutta divisional office. Mr. Bir had made Sambhit in charge of the twenty new merchandising outlets.

By the month of April 1968, there was a move in the Indian government for the nationalisation of foreign petroleum companies operating in India. It was the beginning of turmoil in the operations of the three major MNCs: Burmah Shell, Stan Vac (Esso), and Caltex. A lot of reshufflings at all levels of operations in these companies were being done at senior levels for the expatriate officers in India. These changes began in June 1968. In this context, Peter Jervis was promoted and posted at Burmah Shell HQ in London. His order was received on July 1st, and he was asked to report to the London office by August 15th, 1968. I was saddened by these developments. I was happy at the promotion of Jervis but could not assess my own future position after the departure of Jervis. In fact, I was really worried; I did not want to leave Calcutta before another year. This was a necessity due to my family situation.

When I met Jervis to congratulate him on July 2, 1968, he made me sit in his chamber. He explained to me various probabilities due to the nationalisation plan of the government. According to him, many of the company personnel over the age of 45 may expect sudden adverse changes in their careers and need to be prepared for them.

Jervis assured me that I need not be perturbed by any immediate change, not at least for the next two years. My age at that time was around thirty-three years, and the company would like to retain me even after nationalisation. However, I would most likely be posted outside India in any one of the southeast Asian countries where the company operated. In case I wouldn't like any such posting outside India, it was advisable for me to look for a change and join any Indian company. Later, I acted on this advice.

The branch manager, Mr. Chopra, retired in July 1968. In his place came Mr. B.U. Rana, who was the Head of Indonesian Operations of the Shell Group. He was designated as CEO of the Calcutta branch and was expected to operate as the head of the combined portfolio of BM (Chopra) and BSM (Jervis).

Rana happened to be a batchmate of Jervis from the days of their selection in London. They remained good friends and had excellent rapport with each other. That's the reason Rana immediately developed a liking for me. Jervis might have briefed Rana earlier about me. Rana posted me in his own secretariat on August 16, 1968, after the departure of Jervis.

My post assumed importance at the beginning of the difficult period of nationalisation for Burmah Shell. Rana fully depended on me for all feedback information from the four divisions as well as the branch office in Calcutta. All the staff, irrespective of their place of posting, were very jittery about the prospect of nationalising the company. They used to be hesitant to provide the required data on their personnel to me. Rana had to intervene. He warned all the divisional managers and department heads. He ordered them to provide all the information to me, as I was only acting on his instructions. I was also made to decipher, analyse, and condense all government as well as BS Head Office directives on nationalisation aspects. Later, I was appraising Rana on all these issues. I used to get his approval for future implementation on various service-related issues among the company's staff and officers at all levels.

Constantly, Divisional Offices (DOs) and Departmental Heads (DHs) used to contact me to confirm the latest directives. However, I did not pass them any information without the consent of my boss, Rana.

Beginning in October 1968, a directive was received from Bombay HQ to start the process for the Voluntary Retirement Scheme (VRS) of the company. This was applicable to all categories of its employees in the age group of 45 years and older. The scheme was open with immediate effect and was to continue till it was officially withdrawn. This was a bombshell for all the employees in that age group.

The VRS was a death warrant for many serving in the management cadre. Some at the level of divisional managers were also going to be affected. Rana asked the personnel head of the BO to prepare a list of management-level personnel who had three or more poor ratings in their recent Annual Assessment Report (AAR). As per confidential guidelines, such people were to be terminated if they did not opt for the VRS. This information, though known to me through Rana, was a top secret.

Upon receiving the list along with the AARs, Rana instructed me to meticulously review each name on the list along with their accompanying AARs and their service files. My task was to compile the initial list of twelve individuals from the provided list of thirty, each of whom would be summoned to the branch office for further discussions.

It was a laborious, ungrateful, and unpleasant assignment, but I recognised its inevitability due to Rana's trust in me. I created the list, which included two divisional manager-level officers, namely Lamba and Mittal. Among the remaining twenty-eight, there was also the name of my colleague Talwar from the Patna division. Although I felt sympathy for the three who had previously caused trouble and conspired against me, I had no compassion for them. I viewed it as a form of 'Poetic Justice of the Divinity' being served upon these three schemers.

Starting on Monday, October 16, 1968, two individuals were called to the branch office each day. The first two were Lamba and Mittal. Both of them came on their designated days and waited in my office before being summoned by Rana. They inquired about the purpose of the summons, of which I pretended to be unaware. Later, it was discovered that all thirty individuals mentioned on the earlier list had opted for the Voluntary Retirement Scheme (VRS) by the end of November 1968. During this period, nearly 60 percent of the unionised staff and 55 percent of the management staff in the Calcutta Branch chose VRS and departed from Burmah Shell before nationalisation took place.

The process of nationalisation of the three foreign oil marketing companies had its final culmination in 1974 for Stan Vac (ESSO), in 1976 for Burmah Shell, and in 1977 for Caltex. The retail outlets of Burmah Shell became outlets of Bharat Petroleum (BP), and those of Stan Vac and Caltex went under a single operative, PSU Hindustan Petroleum (HP). Without forgetting my past loyalty to BS, I subsequently patronised the Bharat Petroleum outlets for my personal car as well as for the vehicles of subsequent companies that I served. There was also a third very big PSU in the oil sector. It was the Indian Oil Corporation (IOC). This company has become one of the largest petroleum companies in the world for oil refining and marketing.

In spite of my extremely busy schedule, my first priority always remained the love and care of Rashmi and Mona. I left for the office at 9 a.m. but ensured my return at 6 p.m. on every weekday. Saturdays and Sundays were exclusively for the family. With little Mona's varied mischievous antics, we were fascinated all the time. Our time was passing rapidly, along with the child's healthy growth.

Soon, it was Mona's second birthday. A big party was organised by me at the prestigious Bengal Club of Calcutta on Wednesday, the 25th of December, 1968. Being the day of Christmas, the club, as per its regular practice, was decorated with Christmas trees and associated extravaganza. Me and Rashmi invited our friends' families along with their children to the birthday party. We had also invited the Ganju and Banerjee families, who were residents of our building. It was quite an enjoyable affair. In the midst of the real enjoyment of kids, Rashmi held Mona. She made Mona cut her birthday cake. Finally, all left for their houses at around 11 p.m.

Rashmi purchased a pram for Mona. It came in handy for Bela to take Mona out every afternoon to nearby Singhi Park. The child used to enjoy such visits. After her afternoon nap and meal, she used to make noise if there was a delay by Bela to take her out to the park. As long as we remained in Calcutta, this was a regular activity for Mona. As she began to crawl and then stand around the age of two and a half years, she used to go to the front balcony. Standing there, she made noise, danced while holding the railings, and played pranks with the three grownup big girls of the next building. They also loved to tease her from their balcony on the top floor of the adjacent building.

Earlier, when Mona was ten months old, on every second and fourth Saturday of the month, I took Rashmi and the kid Mona to Peking Restaurant at Park Street for dinner. It was an exclusive Chinese restaurant at the entrance of Park Street. We always used to put the baby between us on the sofa of the restaurant cabin while relishing our Chinese dishes.

This practice continued as long as we stayed in Calcutta. Of course, Mona started partaking and enjoying the dishes once she was two years old or older. The child was like a rainbow in our lives. She filled our lives with varied hues of happiness. She made us so happy and vibrant that neither Rashmi nor I could ever imagine that such delight in life ever existed! The 'Bundle of Joy' was bringing tonnes of happiness to our daily existence. She was the twinkle of our eyes, the throb of our hearts, and the nucleus of our happiness!

At the office front, the whole of 1968 kept me busy with varied work relating to the pre-nationalisation period. Rana had asked me to prepare a rationalisation plan for all four divisions with respect to the minimum requirement of personnel as well as supply points (depots). For this, I had to extensively travel in each division along with the divisional manager. This report was prepared by me by the end of February 1968. Rana approved the submitted report and ordered reorganisation with immediate effect beginning in the second week of March 1968.

In the meantime, I told Rana about my search for jobs in Public Sector Undertakings (PSU). At that time, Rana also confirmed that Jervis had talked about this aspect with him earlier. He asked me to think once again about this matter. He said that he would like to take me to Jakarta in a higher position when he goes back there to head Indonesia's Shell Head Office. He also told me that, in the meantime, he wouldn't stand in my way of applying for new assignments and would also allow me to appear at future interviews.

I did not confide in Rana that I and Rashmi had already made up our minds not to leave India due to our family obligations.

Against my applications, I got interview calls in the month of May, 1969. The first interview call was from the IOC, and the second was from the Fertiliser Corporation of India (FCI). The interview of the IOC was at their

HO in Bombay on June 21, 1969, on a Friday. The second was also scheduled for Friday, June 28th, 1969, in New Delhi.

In both PSUs, the post was that of area manager. I showed the call letters to Rana, who congratulated me and also told me that I would definitely get selected in both. He approved my leave for fifteen days from 15.06.1969 to 30.06.1969. Immediately, I booked my tickets for flights from Calcutta to Bombay on June 18, Bombay to New Delhi on June 23, and New Delhi to Calcutta on July 1, 1969.

Rashmi was happy to learn about the interviews. She inquired about the arrangements for my proposed stay in Bombay and New Delhi. I told her that in Bombay I was to stay at friend Talauliker's flat, and in New Delhi it would be the house of friend Ashok Bhargav. I also told her that on arrival at those places, I would ring her up and inform her. I had already talked to Talauliker and Ashok. They were very happy about my scheduled visits for the interviews and were eager to meet me.

I reached Bombay on June 18 and was received by Guru (Talauliker) at the airport. At that time, he was the branch manager of the Bank of India in Bombay. He took me to his house in central Bombay. I was introduced to his wife, Nalini, and his two sons. I loved my stay at Guru's place. On the day of the interview, Guru dropped me off at the IOC office at 9.30 a.m. The interview went off well. The interview board wished me well and indicated that I would be informed about the result by July 7, 1969. I returned to Guru's office and told him about my interview. We both returned together to his flat.

On the 23rd, I left Bombay for New Delhi. Ashok had come to receive me at the Delhi airport. We both travelled to his flat in Vasant Vihar. Ashok's wife, Neetu, was expecting her first child sometime in late August. She had gone to Allahabad to be at her parents' place for the delivery. Ashok was all alone at his flat. He had a cook, a housekeeper, and a driver. He was a senior executive at Sri Ram Group of Industries and was with them for the last eight years. I and Ashok chatted over our drinks and had dinner at 9.30 p.m. Before the dinner, I called up Rashmi and told her about all the developments up until that time. Ashok also talked to her and invited her to his place after Neetu's return.

On June 28th, around 9 a.m., Ashok dropped me off at the HO of the Fertiliser Corporation of India in South Extension, New Delhi. My interview at 11 a.m. went off well. I was told that the results would be communicated to me by July 10. Before I left the FCI office, I was called by B.L. Wadhera, Industrial Relation Advisor (IRA) of FCI. Wadhera asked me about the time that I would take to join if selected. I said that I had to give at least three months' notice to

Burmah Shell after my resignation. Wadhera, much later, became the Chairman and MD of Coal India.

I returned to the Vasant Vihar residence of Ashok, who had sent his car for my pickup. We had our lunch at the house. I requested Ashok to arrange the preparation of my flight ticket to Calcutta for the 8.30 p.m. flight that day. It was arranged by Ashok's office, and I returned home around midnight. As Rashmi was informed about the changed programme of arrival, she was awake to receive me. She was very happy to see me three days before the earlier schedule of return.

After joining the office on Tuesday, the first of July 1969, I met Rana and told him about my interviews at the offices of the IOC and FCI. Rana was sure about my selection. His assessment proved true when my selection letters were received from the IOC on Friday, July 5th, and from FCI on Tuesday, July 9th, 1969. In both letters, it was mentioned to immediately send my acceptance and join by Wednesday, the 1st of October, 1969. I weighed both offers. Both offered the identical post of Area Manager and had similar pay scales, along with ten increments in the initial basic of the scale. Even then, it did not come close to the remuneration that I was receiving from BS at that time. It still fell short by more than fifteen hundred rupees per month. This was the best that any PSU could offer those days.

After weighing the pros and cons of both offers, I decided to join FCI since its marketing division was in the formative stage, whereas in IOC, I would have become junior to my former BS colleagues who had joined IOC a year before. Accordingly, I sent my consent letter to FCI on July 11, 1969, and affirmed my joining on or before October 1, 1969.

I showed Rana my consent letter to FCI before its dispatch. He agreed with my assessment and congratulated me. He told me to give my letter of resignation immediately to ensure my release by September 23rd. After thanking Rana, I submitted my resignation and requested release on or before September 23, 1969.

In the interim period, before my release in two and a half months' time, I ensured the due completion of all tasks entrusted to me. On my own, I submitted to Rana a weekly report of pending work that I had completed. Rana highly appreciated this. He also told me that in the future, if I ever wanted to join Shell outside India, he would ensure that it was definitely offered to me. Finally, I was released from BS on September 23, 1969, in Calcutta.

Our departure from Calcutta was perfectly timed. West Bengal had been in political turmoil since the beginning of 1968. President's Rule was promulgated in the state as the Naxalbari Movement had disturbed its peace. The terror of the Naxalite movement had reached Calcutta. The once peaceful city was witnessing the naked dance of terror. Killings became almost a daily feature in the state. Extortions and ransom demands were received daily by the business community and industrialists. The situation was moving from bad to worse almost on a daily basis.

On the 27th of September, the household goods and my car were dispatched to Delhi through the transport agency of BS Ballygunge dealer, Bose. It was estimated that the car and the goods were likely to take six to seven days and reach Delhi by the 3rd or 4th of October. I planned to fly to Delhi on the afternoon flight on September 27th and reach Delhi by 4.30 p.m. Prior to my departure, I had talked with personnel of the FCI head office and reserved a room for me and my family for three days at their Delhi guest house.

Arriving in Delhi, we took a cab from the airport. We reached the FCI Guest House around 6 p.m. on September 27. After freshening up, we three went for a stroll in the South Extension Market. Mona enjoyed the window shopping that her parents were doing. I and Rashmi had some delicious chaat in one of the restaurants. Rashmi fed a bit of that to Mona. All three had kulfi with falooda. We skipped dinner at the guest house and went to bed early.

Next morning, after having my breakfast with Rashmi at 9 a.m., I walked down to the head office of FCI. I met B.L. Wadhera, the Industrial Relation Advisor, to submit my joining report. Wadhera then took me to meet Dr. S. Mukherjee. He was FCI's Director for Production and Commerce. Dr. Mukherjee called Mr. Vachharajani, who was then looking after corporate marketing. He was a senior officer on deputation to FCI from the Defence Audit and Account Service of the GOI. He was introduced as the future zonal manager of FCI's marketing division, which was under formation. After Dr. Mukherjee's inquiry about my family and work experience, he told Wadhera that he had found the right marketing man for FCI. He told me to discuss with Vachharajani and follow his advice for starting my innings at FCI. He also told me that, any time I feel the necessity, I can always contact him directly.

Vachharajani had a long discussion with me. He told me that there were only two fertiliser plants (units) of FCI in the northern zone—one at Nangal and the other at Gorakhpur. Besides, in the eastern zone, it had Sindhri, Barauni, and Namrup units. In the western zone, it had the Trombay Unit. Each unit was independently marketing its products through sales staff attached to the unit. The marketing of each unit's products was controlled by a sales manager, who reported to the general manager of the unit. With the formation of the marketing division, in less than three weeks' time, the marketing staff of all the units were to be automatically transferred to the marketing division. These staff would be posted under various zonal, regional, and area offices in different areas of the country.

Vachharajani asked me as to whether I would like to operate in the present coordination section of the corporate HO in Delhi or would like to take up the task of active field operation. I opted for the later. Vachharajani told me that, in that case, I would have to go to Nangal for two to three weeks. During that time, I had to establish the area office in Chandigarh. After its establishment, I could move to the Chandigarh area office and control the marketing areas of Chandigarh UT, along with those of the states of Punjab, Himachal Pradesh, and J&K. I was also informed that, for the time being and until another manager was recruited, I was also to look after the marketing activities of Haryana state. All these areas were prime areas of the Green Revolution in India and used very high doses of chemical fertilisers.

I told Vachharajani that my household goods and car were reaching Delhi in the next five to six days. He assured me that the administrative department of FCI would arrange the unloading and storage of the goods in the Delhi guest house. It would also immediately arrange to send me my car on its arrival. My family and I could comfortably stay at the guest house of Nangal Unit until we moved to Chandigarh. My household goods, stored in Delhi, would be sent by the FCI administration to Chandigarh when I moved there from Nangal. This was okay with me. I told Vachharajani that in a couple of days, My family and I would move to Nangal. He told me to take a company car from Delhi to Nangal. The driver who would bring me my car on its arrival would bring back the company's Delhi car from me.

On Sunday, the 5th of October, I, along with Rashmi and Mona, left Delhi for Nangal after breakfast at the guest house. The drive was for six hours. En route, at Ambala, the family and the driver had their lunch at 1 p.m. The driver took us to the famous 'Purna Singh Dhaba'. The food, particularly the mutton roganjosh, was delicious. Near Chandigarh, the journey headed towards Nangal. The place was sixty kilometres away from Chandigarh via Ropar, which was the district headquarters for Nangal.

We reached Nangal around 5 p.m. and went straight to the guest house. I had already received an intimation from Delhi about my stay. The guest house manager, Chowdhury, welcomed us and took us to our suite. He was an extremely courteous middle-aged gentleman. He was a popular person among all the officers of the unit. He used to act as the master of ceremonies in all functions at the Officer's Club of Nangal Unit. He later became a good friend of mine.

The guesthouse of the Nangal Unit was a two-story, spacious building. It showcased an artistic structure with five-star hotel facilities. It had twelve bedrooms and four suites. The guest house was on the bank of the Sutlej. From the windows of its suites and rooms, one could see and enjoy the scenic beauty of the Aravalli hills and the blue waters of the Sutlej River. The flower beds and the well-laid guesthouse lawn, extending to the river bank, reminded me of one of the eye-catching natural beauties of Gulmarg in Kashmir. A short distance from the guest house was the residential colony of the unit. The guest house was a kilometre away from the office of the unit. The main gate of the fertiliser plant was almost three hundred metres away from the office.

After having dinner, Rashmi, Mona, and I had a little stroll on the lawns. They enjoyed the sight of the lighted embankments of the river. From there, in the distance, we could see the bright lights of Bhakra Dam. The day being a Sunday, Chowdhury invited me and my family to the Officer's Club to meet the attending families. I politely refused the invitation and told her that we were extremely tired and would like to retire early to bed. In any case, we would be in Nangal for three weeks and would have enough opportunities to meet resident families. Besides, according to protocol, I should first meet T.V. Reddy, the sales manager, and Antony, the general manager of the unit, before any meeting with others.

The next morning, I went first to Reddy's office. After some time, Reddy took me to Antony's office for an introduction. Antony was aware of the ensuing developments in the establishment and operation of the marketing division. He asked me about my views and the immediate course of action that was intended to follow. I said that all marketing staff of the unit would be treated as part of the Marketing Division. I said him for the discussions that I had with Dr. Mukherjee and Vachharajani. Antony said that, after my due familiarisation with the unit's marketing and allied activities and discussions with Reddy, I should undertake the next course of action as advised in Delhi.

After a cup of coffee with Antony, both returned to Reddy's office. Reddy was a senior to me. But Reddy's basic salary was lower than mine due to the ten increments that I got in my basic salary at the time of appointment. Reddy was well aware of it and gave me due weight and respect. I learned that the officers in the sales wing, including Reddy, were graduates of Agriculture Science (B.Sc. Ag.). I felt that a few more sales officers with marketing experience needed to be inducted soon by open advertisement.

I and Reddy planned to increase the dealer network and induct more sales officers and agronomists. This was required in view of the introduction of new products like urea and NPK fertilisers. These products were to be made available for marketing in the near future. I also planned to develop and introduce a new format for invoices and other marketing documents to facilitate operation in a computerised system like that of Burmah Shell. All the marketing personnel needed acclimatisation to the new system of documentation for better productivity.

During my first day at Nangal, I met all the marketing officers and staff who were working at the marketing office. Some of the staff were earlier recruited for plant operations and were unfit for the sales department. I kept in mind that these people should be sent back to their parent departments.

CAN, or calcium ammonium nitrate fertiliser, produced at the Nangal Unit was a favourite product of the farmers. It required no fresh effort for marketing. The crux of the problem was the introduction of new products in that area. I and Reddy decided that the recruitment process should start immediately for new dealers and officers under the chairmanship of Reddy. Besides being a part of this selection process, I was also to select a building in Chandigarh for the opening and operation of the area office.

During the selection of officers between the 6th and 11th of October, G.R. Kaura, a Deputy Director of Agriculture of Himachal Pradesh posted at Mandi, was selected for the post of Senior Agronomist. He was attached to SM and T.V. Reddy. A subsequent week was earmarked for the selection of new dealers. Nearly forty-five new dealers were selected. For the next lot, it was decided to leave a gap of two months. Only after evaluation of the performance of the inducted new ones was a final decision about the required number of additional inductions to be taken.

On October 7, I talked to Madhusudan Sharma, the FCI sales officer posted in Chandigarh. He was advised to scout for a suitable building in Sector 18 for the Chandigarh Area Office. I specified to Sharma that the building should be an independent bungalow. It should be big enough to accommodate the area office, the area manager's residence, and two official guest rooms. Besides, it should have two adjoining independent portions—one to accommodate the office with two guest rooms and the other for the area manager's residence.

Sharma rang up on 11th afternoon and informed me about the identification of five such buildings. He requested their early inspection by the next day, i.e., on Sunday, the 12th. I took Rashmi and Mona and went to Chandigarh to inspect all five houses. The one selected was a bungalow located in Sector 18. It was Kothi No. 27 in the main area of that sector.

The house was very close to Sector 17, which had government offices, a market complex, a MARKFED office, cinema halls, and the main bus terminal. The owner of the proposed office building was present during the inspection.

I asked him to make certain modifications in a week's time. The owner agreed to do the modification. I said that, on Sunday, the 19th of October, I would finally see the modifications and then lease the Kothi from the 20th of October. Accordingly, it was inspected and hired on October 20, 1969.

I gave this information to Reddy, Antony, and Vachharajani. Vachharajani told me to make the office functional on November 1, 1969. He also told me that my household effects would be dispatched from Delhi and would reach my residence-cum-office on Sunday, the 26th of October. This enabled me to complete the first phase of my own set target.

I had only five days left to move from Nangal to Chandigarh. Immediately, I made arrangements to transfer a steno, a sales officer, an assistant, and a vehicle with a driver from the Sales Department of Nangal to Chandigarh. I also intimated Madhusudan Sharma (MS) to place orders for the furniture in the area office and the guest rooms. I specifically told him to place this order at the showroom of Godrej in Chandigarh. It was to be positively delivered by the afternoon of October 26.

I selected Steno Chopra, Sales Officer Sobti, Assistant Rana, and Driver Ram Raksha for immediate postings in Chandigarh. It was ensured that a new Ambassador car for the area office was immediately allotted. From the Godrej furniture catalogue, all items serial numbers were given to MS to place the order. I told Sharma that, as instructed earlier, all items have to be positively delivered at Chandigarh office premises on the 26th afternoon.

I and Rashmi were given an official farewell by the officers and their families on the 25th evening at a dinner at the club. GM Antony, along with Mrs. Antony, Mr. and Mrs. Reddy, and other senior officers with their spouses, were present. I left Nangal on the 27th morning and reached Chandigarh at 11:30 a.m. By that time, my household effects were unloaded and placed in the residential portion of the building. Sales officers Madhusudan and Sobti were also present. They had with them the PA Chopra and Assistant Rana. Driver Ram Raksha, who drove me and my family to Chandigarh in the newly allotted car, was a part of the Chandigarh office staff. He had ensured the presence of his son, Rajan, at the office. I had agreed to appoint Rajan as a temporary attendant for the office and guest rooms.

Rajan and Ram Raksha were asked to help Rashmi put household items in place in the residence. A maid (Dolly) was already arranged by MS for household work. She also assisted in the arrangement and cleaned the residence. After the office and guest room furniture were received in the afternoon, they were also put in their places.

The office consisted of a big room for the area manager and a big hall for accommodating the sales officer, Steno, and the assistant. A wide verandah in the front connected it with the two guest rooms. The identical portion at the rear had three bedrooms and a hall that served as the drawing room and dining space. A kitchen and a store were across the rear verandah, adjacent to the master bedroom. Similar to the front lawn, there was a lawn at the rear. By its side were the outhouse and a garage. The house is connected to the road through the main driveway. There was also a staircase at the rear for going to the roof terrace.

The adjacent Kothi belonged to a Sikh family. It belonged to Harbans Singh, a retired Punjab Civil Service Officer (PCS). He lived with his son, Harbhajan, his daughter-in-law, Balwinder Kaur, and their school-going daughter, Rita. Harbhajan, like his father, was serving as a PCS officer in the Punjab government.

As per the plan, the area office became totally functional by November 1, 1969. It had three telephone connections: two for the office and one for the residence. Out of two office lines, the one connected to a fax machine was put in the area manager's room and the other one in the office hall. The office also had a refrigerator. While the hall had fans and coolers, AM's room and the guest rooms had air conditioners. I and Rashmi were now fully settled. I could enjoy the homely and tasty food prepared by Rashmi. Mona also liked the new environment.

The formal opening of the office was done by Dr. Mukherjee in the presence of Vachharajani, Antony, and Reddy on November 3, 1969. It was the first area office of the marketing division of FCI. In the evening, a party was thrown by Dr. Mukherjee at the Mount View Hotel in Chandigarh. Chief Secretaries, Secretaries of Agriculture, and Directors of Agriculture of the Punjab and Haryana governments attended the party. All appreciated FCI for opening their first field office in Chandigarh. They assured me they would extend their help and cooperation to me as the area manager. I was introduced to them by Dr. Mukherjee.

After the visiting officials left, I got into the act of planning and organising the area office activities for the month. I called a meeting of all sales officers from Punjab, Haryana, Himachal Pradesh, and J&K on November 5, 1969. The meeting was at the area office. In the meeting, I outlined their responsibilities for reporting developments in their operative areas every week by phone call. I also assigned the sales targets for their areas for November. After a two-hour meeting, followed by an official packed lunch, they left for their headquarters in the afternoon.

During the lunch, I told the Shimla sales officer, Kewal Kishen (KK), that I intended to make a call to the Secretary of Agriculture and Director of Agriculture of Himachal at Shimla. I scheduled it for Monday, the 10th of November. After attending the office, I left for Shimla in the afternoon of Saturday with Rashmi and Mona. Earlier, KK was told to book a government guest house from the afternoon of Saturday until Tuesday afternoon. He was asked to confirm both the appointments and the reservation by the 7th. KK confirmed the meeting with the Director of Agriculture at 10 a.m. and with the Secretary at 3 p.m. on Monday. He also confirmed the reservation of a suite at the Wild Flower guest house, two kilometres away from Shimla Secretariat. This guest house was specifically built for the stay of Jawaharlal Nehru during a Congress session that was earlier held at Shimla. Much later, it was sold to the Oberai Hotel Group to operate for rich tourists.

Rashmi was happy about the proposed visit to Shimla. She duly packed two bags containing dresses for her, Mona, and mine. After lunch, at 2 p.m., we three left for Shimla in the official car with driver Ram Rekha. The hill drive lasted for nearly five and a half hours. It was my first visit to Shimla. Driver RR was asked whether he had earlier driven to Shimla. It was a totally hilly drive going up to an elevation of 7,467 feet. RR told me that it would probably be his thirtieth drive to Shimla!

The journey covered a distance of 112 kilometres. It was scenic and enjoyable. We crossed Panchkula, the beautiful Pinjore gardens, Kalkaji railway station, and the cantonment area. Up and up, we drove. The road ran by the side of the light railway track that connects Kalkaji with Shimla. In many places, the road used to cross the railway track. For the most part, the road ran parallel to the track. Around 4.30 p.m., we crossed the toy train standing near a station. It was a sight that made Mona jump with joy.

Finally, we reached Shimla around 6 p.m. It took us another forty minutes to cover the distance of 11 km and reach the Wild Flower Guest House (WFGH). KK and his wife, Smita, were waiting to receive us. Both belonged to Patiala in Punjab and were married only six months ago. Smita touched Rashmi's feet. She said that she would again come to give her company on the day her husband goes with the boss for meetings with government officials. Rashmi told her that she would love to have her company, and they could have their lunch together during that day. Soon after, the couple left, and I and Rashmi had coffee on the lawn amidst the surrounding flower beds.

All of us were extremely tired after five and a half hours of hill driving. We had our dinner at 9 p.m. and retired for the night. Waking up fresh in the morning, all three went out for a walk after tea and changed into warm clothes.

During the night, there was light snowfall. The snowflakes on the leaves and branches of innumerable pine trees gave off the look of Christmas!

The guest house was at a height of 8,100 feet, almost 1,100 feet higher than the MSL height of Shimla. The sun's rays through the pine trees cascaded the colours of prismatic rainbows due to the snowflakes. It was a wonderful celestial sight. I and Rashmi enjoyed the scenic extravaganza. Little Mona was running around the gardens of Wild Flower Guest House. Rashmi had to run after her for her safety. I thoroughly enjoyed the playful act between mother and daughter.

After breakfast, driver RR, who was acquainted with all the scenic spots around, drove us to those places. At one place, we saw, for the first time, the huge Chamri cow and the big mountain goat. It was near an adjacent market. Mona had the ride on the Chamri. Photographs were taken of a mother-and-daughter duo with the Chamri and the Mountain Goat. Alas, these photographs, along with other photos of Chandigarh days, were lost during shifting to other places on transfer.

By lunchtime, we had moved to see Shimla town. Our car was parked on Mall Road. I told the driver, RR, to have his lunch and wait. We then walked on the mall road. After window shopping, we proceeded to the ridge. There, we enjoyed the wonderful spectacle of habitats around the hills. We had our lunch in the 'Open-Air Restaurant' on the ridge. In spite of our desire to spend more time, we had to walk back to our parked car to visit some other interesting tourist spots.

In our day's schedule, only the visit to Kufri remained. It was 15 kilometres away from Shimla and was famous for ice skating. It was as enchanting as many other places around Shimla. We finally returned to the guest house at 7 p.m. The next day was a busy day for me. I was to have several meetings at the Himachal Secretariat. After dinner, I went through some related official documents and finally went to sleep around 11 p.m.

The next morning, after breakfast, I was ready to go to the Shimla secretariat for the morning meeting. At 9 a.m., KK reached the guest house with his wife, Smita. Smita was left at the guest house to give company to Rashmi. I and KK left for the meeting at 9:15 a.m. We first met the Director of Agriculture (DA). It was very cordial and fruitful. The DA requested that I increase the fertiliser supply by an additional 3000 MT every month. He also requested consideration of the supply of specific insecticides for apple orchards. I said that, after my return to Chandigarh, I would review the position and inform him about the future position in a week's time. Before leaving the DA's chamber, I was informed that the timing of the meeting with the Secretary of Agriculture (SA) had been changed. It would be at 1 p.m. over lunch at the Oberoi Hotel. I invited the DA for lunch, but the DA excused himself, citing some personal work.

I and KK drove to the Oberoi Hotel and waited for the arrival of Mr. Mohapatra, the Secretary of Agriculture. He was an Odia IAS officer in the HP cadre. After his arrival, me and Mohapatra went to the reserved table for our luncheon meeting. We discussed the request that the DA had earlier made. It was agreed that a favourable decision by FCI would be communicated to the state government. Both of us then exchanged some personal information about ourselves and our families. We also talked about mutually known people at Cuttack. It was found that Mohapatra also studied at Ravenshaw College with B.C. Das (Badu), the elder brother of Rashmi. Mohapatra said that his wife Bandana was a classmate and good friend of Rashmi. Thus, a personal bond was established. Both agreed that during their next visits to Shimla and Chandigarh, the families would meet.

On my return to the guest house, I informed Rashmi about the meeting with her friend Bandana's husband. She was also informed that, during our next meeting, both families would also meet. Rashmi said that Bandana was her friend at school and college. Her house was near Kafla Police Outpost, nearer to their Cuttack house at Sati Chaura Road. Her elder sister was also the college friend of Rashmi's middle sister, Mini. Bandana was equally anxious to meet Rashmi.

The next day, we headed for Chandigarh. I intended to stop for some time at a few important and scenic places during our return journey. The places we visited were Solan, Timber Trail (TT), and Dagsahi. Solan and TT were both 47 kilometres away from Shimla, whereas Dagshai was another 11 kilometres down towards Chandigarh. As a matter of fact, after crossing Solan and moving further 18 kilometres, one reaches the spot on the National Highway to go to Timber Trail by cable car.

Timber Trail was located 65 kilometres away from Shimla, i.e., only 47 kilometres away from Chandigarh. It was a place where two hills appeared to merge. At this place, there are resorts for visitors. Resorts are accessible by ropeway cable cars, which, in itself, is exhilarating. The length of the ropeway is 1.8 km. It is laid from the highway to a further height of 2000 feet to reach the resorts. These resorts are at a height of 5000 feet above MSL. This place is a must-visit for tourists.

Solan is the district headquarters and is at a height of 5100 feet. It was the capital of the erstwhile princely state of Baghat. It is also called the Mushroom City of India. The temple of the goddess Shoolini Devi is situated here. In June every year, a fair venerating the goddess is held, featuring a three-day mela at the central Thodo grounds. Rashmi enjoyed the temple visit and offered bhoga to the goddess.

From Solan, my family and I moved to Dagshai. It is one of the oldest towns in Solan District. It seems that long ago, in 1847, it began as a British cantonment town. Buildings in the town have Gothic architecture. It is located at a height of over 5100 feet on a picturesque hillock—a soothing and pleasing sight to nature lovers. My family and I visited the museum and St. Patrick's RC Church. This happens to be one of the oldest churches in North India, having been completed in 1852.

By the time we left the place and reached Timber Trail, it was almost 2.30 p.m. We were all hungry, as it was past our lunchtime. We went straight to the restaurant at the resort. While having lunch, we could see the mystifying Shivalik Range. The lush pine woods and the meandering rivers were spectacular sites. The environment was invigorating. Timber Trail is located near the town of Parwanoo. The resort is based on two opposite hills separated by the Kaushalya River. It is joined together by a cable car system. The family had decided to have that cable car ride during their next visit. By the time we left TT, it was almost 5.30 p.m. We reached Chandigarh around 7 p.m. on Tuesday, the 11th of November, 1969.

During my three-year stay in Chandigarh, from October 26th, 1969, to October 30th, 1972, my family and I used to visit Shimla at least once every two months. We also visited many other scenic areas of Himachal during that period. Some of the important places that were visited by me and my family were Chail, Kasauli, and Kullu Manali. But Chail was our favourite place.

Chail, which is 45 kilometres from Shimla and 45 kilometres from Solan, is at an elevation of 7380 feet. It is known for its salubrious beauty and virgin forests. Excellent accommodation, with wide lawns and parks, made it a favourite spot with the family. We visited the place many times and enjoyed its beauty and serenity.

At the southern edge of Chail town is another good resort near Monkey Point. From the resort's lawns and parks, one could see the beautiful sight of the forest with horse chestnuts and Himalayan oak. Nearby, the Gilbert Nature Trail winds through lush green countryside rich in birdlife. I, Rashmi, and Mona stayed many times in this resort, which was often our favourite rendezvous away from Chandigarh. We took care that Mona never went out alone to the lawns and parks of the resort. There were a lot of red-faced monkeys around the trees on the slopes.

Visits to Kullu and Manali were the perfect medicine for tired minds and fatigued souls. Nestled in the lap of the Himalayas, offering a perfect blend of tranquilly and adventure, they were very popular tourist destinations. Both places were flooded with visitors during the summer months. People of the northern plains escaped the burning heat of summer by visiting these cool places where the temperature used to be between 6 and 16 degrees Celsius. During the rainy season, it was best to avoid any visits to this area; landslides and damaged roads became common problems during rains.

We visited Kullu and Manali only once during our Chandigarh stay. Much later, the family, with all three children, visited these places in 1987 from Delhi. The scenic beauty of these places was unforgettable. Even now, at the ripe old age of eighty-six, when Rashmi has departed to God's abode two years ago, the remembrances provide contentment and providential bliss to me.

After the Shimla visit from November 9th to November 11th, 1969, my busy official schedule continued. I rang up Vachharajani and got his permission to make FCI's supply of insecticides to apple orchards in Himachal through the agriculture department of HP. For that, I tied up the supply plan with a famous insecticide manufacturer. Supplies of insecticides were made in packages marked as those of FCI. It became FCI's first endeavour to supply allied products as supplements to their fertiliser supplies! FCI also got a handsome commission from the manufacturer.

After a review of the order and sales position of all areas of Punjab, J&K, and HP, figures were collected for Haryana and the Ganganagar district of Rajasthan. I planned to make a whirlwind tour of Punjab for three days starting Tuesday, the 18th. On the first day, I covered Sangrur, Patiala, and Ludhiana districts with sales officers (SOs) Suman, Surinder, and Raghubir. We touched on all dealership points. After meeting Dean Dr. Randhawa of Ludhiana Agriculture University, I made the night halt at the Irrigation Guest House near Ludhiana. At the request of sales officer Raghubir, I had my dinner at his place. The dishes included lip-smacking *makki di roti and sarso da saag*. The Punjab tour was interesting, and the farmers' attitude assured me of their acceptance of urea and balanced fertilisation. I was greatly relieved by this revelation.

On the next day, I toured Gurdaspur and Bhatinda districts with SO Akshaya Kumar and discussed the problems with the network of dealers. He had arranged for the lunch at the Irrigation Dak Bungalow (IB) of Pathankot. The said IB was on an elevated platform on a hill on the bank of the river Ravi. Nearby, on this river, Ranjit Sagar Dam was built for a hydroelectric project.

The drive to the IB was scenic and eye-catching. On the opposite bank of the river Ravi, a little distance away, was the border of Pakistan.

After lunch and some rest, I left for Amritsar. SO Karnail Singh received me at Amritsar around 5 p.m. He took me to Hotel Singh International, owned by his friend Surinder Singh Kairon. Surinder was the son of Punjab Chief Minister Pratap Singh Kairon. When asked about the hotel's tariff, Karnail told me that I needed to pay only as per my official daily allowance. The hotel was very good and not far from the Golden Temple. After freshening up, I visited the Golden Temple.

On the 20th, after visiting dealership points, Karnail and I visited Jallianwala Bagh. Then we went to the Wagah border and saw the spectacular ceremony of the lowering of flags in the evening. After my return to Amritsar, I stayed in the hotel for another night. I checked out the next morning after breakfast and drove straight to Chandigarh, a distance of 226 kilometres. I reached home at lunchtime. After lunch, I rested for half an hour and then attended the office and went through the mail. PA Chopra was called, and I dictated a note on various marketing issues. It concerned the issues in the areas I had toured. One of the issues pertained to the introduction of urea and NPK in the farming sector. It was meant to lower farmers' dependence on CAN and ensure balanced fertilisation of the soil.

On December 1, 1969, I convened a meeting with all the sales officers (SOs). During this meeting, we reviewed all the marketing activities for the month of November. Sales targets and related marketing objectives were assigned to each SO for the upcoming month of December. Following this discussion, we served a packed lunch in the office, and we also deliberated on the annual sales targets for the year 1970. We outlined tentative targets for all three products, CAN, Urea, and NPK, within the areas of responsibility for each SO. Furthermore, we advised each SO to communicate their marketing activities from the previous week via telephone every Monday to either me or Sobti (SO, coordination) at the Area Office. This practice allowed for effective monitoring and control in achieving the marketing objectives for the area.

On December 8, I took Rashmi and Mona on a trip to Shimla. Although it was officially a meeting with the Secretary of Agriculture, Mohapatra, it primarily involved an invitation from Mohapatra to his home for lunch. The main purpose was to facilitate Rashmi's meeting with her friend Bandana. It turned out to be a delightful gathering of both families, with Mona becoming the centre of attention, especially for Bandana and her four-year-old daughter Megha, during lunch.

During coffee after lunch, Rashmi extended an invitation to Bandana and her family to join us for our sixth marriage anniversary, which was the following day. We were planning to travel to Kasauli after leaving Shimla, where we intended to spend the night at a resort. Our anniversary was scheduled for the next day in Kasauli, and the Mohapatra family joined us for the anniversary lunch. The celebration was splendid and left lasting memories for me, Rashmi, Mona, and the Mohapatra family. After tea, the Mohapatra family returned to their residence in Shimla.

The next two weeks passed by following our usual routine. After office hours, in the evenings, Rashmi, Mona, and I would often take a stroll to the lovely shopping arcade in Sector 17. It featured excellent restaurants and two cinema halls. One of these theatres was owned by Surinder Singh Kairon, who had instructed his cinema hall manager to extend invitations for free viewings of each new film release to me and my family. I tactfully avoided taking advantage of this free offer by citing various pretexts. Almost every weekend, we preferred to watch movies at the other new cinema hall, which consistently screened the latest releases.

Christmas was just around the corner, and the market complex was beautifully adorned with decorations. On Christmas day, which also happened to be Mona's third birthday, we had planned a special celebration for her. Throughout the day, we visited the renowned Rock Garden and enjoyed a boat ride on Sukhna Lake. We marked the occasion by cutting the birthday cake during lunch at the Oberoi Mount View Hotel. Mona, dressed in her new branded attire, had a joyful day with her affectionate parents.

In January 1970, we enrolled Mona in the nursery classes at Carmel Convent School in Chandigarh. Every day, she was taken to school on a bicycle by Rajan, the office peon, who also brought her back home in the afternoon. Mona had a positive experience at the school, and her class teacher effectively engaged all the children in various educational and play activities.

I chose the Area Office Building for Haryana, located in Karnal. This building provided the same amenities, combining an office space, a guest room, and a residence. We appointed the new Area Manager, Bawa, in March 1970, and he officially assumed his role in charge of the Haryana Area in May 1970. Before transferring the responsibility to Bawa, I provided him with two months of induction training.

I continued my extensive tours of Punjab and J&K with great enthusiasm. The marketing activities in these regions had been fully operational for the previous two years. However, during one of my tours, I encountered a delay on my return trip to Chandigarh. Consequently, I had no choice but to stay overnight in Ludhiana. It was already 11 p.m., and there were no available reservations for accommodation. I had to settle for staying at a roadside PWD Dak Bungalow in Ludhiana. The bungalow had three rooms, and two of them were already occupied. I requested the chowkidar open the third room for my stay.

Initially, the chowkidar seemed hesitant to open that room, and when I insisted, he reluctantly complied. He warned me that touring officers typically avoided staying in that particular room because it was rumoured to be haunted. I dismissed his superstitions and went to sleep in the room without much thought. Meanwhile, Ram Rekha, the driver, chose to sleep in the office car since we were scheduled to depart for Chandigarh at 6 a.m. the next morning.

During deep sleep, I had a vivid sensation of a baby crawling all over my body. At the same time, I felt the presence of a shadowy, ominous figure advancing towards me. Shaken and drenched in sweat, I woke up abruptly. I was trembling, and my skin was covered in goosebumps. After turning on the bedside table lamp, I took a glass of water to calm myself. I glanced at the clock and noticed it was 1 a.m. The room had an eerie atmosphere, and I decided to step outside onto the portico where Ram Rekha was sitting inside the car.

I noticed that RR was fully awake. When asked why he had not slept, RR narrated the detailed version of the chowkidar's story. It was an incident that happened in Dak Bungalow a long time ago. It was bone-chilling. This was the reason why RR strolled on the verandah in front of my room. He became concerned for my safety. It seemed that in that room, years ago, the wife of a previous chowkidar had committed suicide after killing her two-year-old son. Since then, the room became a haunted place. Through this experience, I came to believe in the existence of a supernatural world. According to Hindu mythology and tantric scriptures, unliberated souls haunt their last spot of existence. Spirits don't like to have any living company after midnight.

Without any further delay, I decided to leave. We drove back to Chandigarh and reached there around 5 a.m. While narrating my experience to Rashmi, I again got goosebumps! I could see that Rashmi's face had a scared look. This incident has been etched in my memory for a long time. Since then, Rashmi started insisting on putting a blue-tinged night lamp at the bottom of the wall in our Chandigarh bedroom. For some time, I noticed her getting up in the middle of the night and touching and looking at me. This habit persisted for a few months and then vanished, much to my relief.

In August 1970, Sanju Apa, Rashmi's eldest sister, visited Chandigarh. She was ten years older than her and treated her like a daughter. Due to a broken affair during college days, she did not marry and became a lecturer in

English at a Bhubaneswar college. She had come on a 10-day holiday. Rashmi was extremely happy, and little Mona never left her side after returning from school.

During her stay, we took her to all the scenic places. She enjoyed her visit to Shimla, Chail, Kasauli, Amritsar, and Pathankot. During her stay in Chandigarh, we strolled in the evening and went to Sector 17 Marketing Arcade. We mostly had our dinner there in popular restaurants. Apa immensely liked Chandigarh. She was happy to see her little sister's family—a loving husband and an adorable kid. After her departure, we felt an unmitigable void.

In September 1970, I made some transfers of SOs. Patiala SO Surinder was posted at Jalandhar, and Sobti from the area office was given additional charge of Patiala District. Madhusudan, besides his liaison with officials of Punjab, Haryana, and the UT of Chandigarh, was given part of the coordination work of the area office. A newly recruited SO, Sandhu, was posted at Jammu.

During this time, the Chairman of FCI, Ramesh Chandra (ICS), visited the area office. He was impressed by the office and commended my excellent contacts with the officials of Punjab and Haryana. He had gotten feedback from his earlier subordinates. Earlier, he had held the post of Chief Secretary of Punjab. After his return to Delhi, he sent a letter of appreciation to me. Dr. Mukherjee and Vachharajani rang up and conveyed their appreciation too. I was extremely happy with my achievements. My effectiveness was credited to my ever-caring and loving wife, Rashmi.

The year 1970 passed off well for FCI, with spectacular marketing achievements. During the year, the Marketing Division became stable and fully functional. Three general managers (GMs) started functioning in Delhi, Calcutta, and Bombay. The northern zone, comprising the states of Punjab, Haryana, HP, J&K, Rajasthan, Madhya Pradesh, and Western Uttar Pradesh, was controlled by Delhi GM. Western and southern states were controlled by Bombay GM. The north-eastern states, along with Sikkim, West Bengal, Bihar, Odisha, and eastern and central Uttar Pradesh, were controlled by the Calcutta GM. In April 1970, I was nominated to attend a two-week FAI marketing course in Delhi.

In December 1970, Baba telephoned me to inform me about the marriage of Lakhi. It was fixed for the 30th of January, 1971. I was asked to come with my family at least seven days before. He also told me to bring my car to help with the local movement. I decided to take leave from January 19 to February 4, 1971. I also arranged for a Nangal unit driver for that period to drive me to Cuttack. It was a distance of 1967 kilometres that took a minimum of three days by driving almost 650 kilometres each day.

I made the plans for official work for January 1971 in an SOs meeting held on January 4. Since I was to be away for nearly a fortnight from the 17th, I asked Sobti and Madhusudan to constantly monitor the progress and keep an appropriate record. I took sanction for my leave and ensured that Nangal driver, Satnam, reported to Chandigarh on the 16th night. In the meantime, Rashmi had packed our luggage for nearly three weeks. Although the journey was long and the cars of those days did not have AC, it became tolerable due to the winter.

On the 19th morning, which was a Tuesday, our journey to Cuttack began. I had planned three-night halts at Agra, Varanasi, and Ranchi. My FCI colleagues at Lucknow and Patna arranged reservations for my night halts at those places. The arrangements were for onward as well as return journeys. I had decided to break the journey only for tea, breakfast, and lunch. These were taken at proper roadside Dhabas having washroom facilities. Without any incident, we reached our Tulsipur house at Cuttack on Friday, January 22nd, at 5 p.m. Parents were happy to see, for the first time, their granddaughter, Mona. She also took a liking to Baba and was initially apprehensive of Maa. The driver, Satnam, was given a corner room on the front verandah for his stay.

I sent Satnam with the car for servicing to a Burmah Shell pump whose dealer was known to me. In the afternoon, I drove the car with Baba, Maa, Lakhi, and Rashmi to the main market. Rashmi purchased jewellery and a Banarasi saree for Lakhi according to the would-be bride's choice. When Maa wanted to pay, Rashmi did not allow her. She said that these were presents for Lakhi from her side. I had earlier handed over Rs. 30k in cash to Baba as my contribution towards marriage costs. Rashmi and I had budgeted Rs. 60k for this marriage. This was exceeded by Rs. 17k. Rashi's gifts cost an additional 35k, and the overrun cost of the marriage feast for invitees and baratis cost another Rs. 12k to me. The marriage went off well. After the marriage and departure of Lakhi on the 31st of January, I and my family drove back to Chandigarh on the 1st of February, 1971. We reached Chandigarh on the evening of February 4, 1971.

The year 1971 was quite an eventful year. I perfected the marketing setup in the states of Punjab, Himachal Pradesh, and J&K. The sales volume of newly introduced urea and NPK fertilisers touched new heights. This ensured a bumper Rabi harvest, for which the state governments lauded FCI. Dr. Mukherjee and Vachharajani appreciated my efforts.

Towards the end of the year, two incidents were vividly recapitulated by me. On December 2, 1971, I took Rashmi and Mona to Pathankot. I had booked the scenic Dak Bungalow on the hill over the bank of the Ravi. We reached there in the evening. It being a Thursday, we intended to stay there for four days and leave on Monday morning. However, on Sunday morning, during breakfast, the attendant of the bungalow told me that the entire Dak Bungalow had been reserved for the military, and all the guests were to leave by 2 p.m. after lunch. The attendant could not give any reason for this action.

Around 2.30 p.m., we left for Chandigarh. The reason for clearing out all guests from the Dak bungalow could soon be guessed. I could see military conveys moving towards Pathankot, but the reason for such heavy movement was not clear. It was only known when, on the third night, Pakistan bombarded Amritsar and other areas of Punjab. India declared a full-fledged war against Pakistan on December 3. In this war, Pakistan was totally defeated. Ninety thousand of its troops in East Pakistan were taken as prisoners of war by India. East Pakistan was liberated to become the independent country of Bangladesh.

In the beginning of the 13-day war, a few bombs fell near Chandigarh. One had fallen near the cinema hall in Sector 17. Civil Defence Personnel (CDP) of Chandigarh advised all, during the first week of the war, not to switch on their lights at home after sunset. All were advised to draw heavy curtains on doors and windows before putting any candle lights in any room. Mona did not like these conditions. Whenever Rashmi used to put candle lights in the room at night, Mona used to stealthily go to the windows, open the curtains, and look at the outside darkness. In spite of Rashmi's reprimand, she did not stop. One evening, the civil defence personnel patrolling nearby loudly shouted, and seeing the candle lights, they ordered us to draw the curtains. This ended Mona's pranks.

During this time, Suni, the younger sister of Natu, and her doctor husband, Balabhadra, had come to stay with us for safety. Balabhadra was in Chandigarh doing his MS (paediatrics) in PGI. Whenever the siren was heard during the days of the war, Suni and Balabhadra used to rush to the spot under the staircase and lie flat on the floor to avoid any falling bombs! These hilarious antics of both continued till the end of the war, when sirens were no longer heard.

In October 1971, T.V. Reddy was promoted and transferred to Hyderabad as the regional manager. Taking his place, A.N. Kashyap assumed the role of regional manager. Around the same time, Antony, who was the general manager at Nangal, was relocated to the FCI Ramagundam Plant as the GM. His replacement at Nangal was R. Hassan, a senior IAS officer from the UP cadre who was on deputation to FCI. Later, he was absorbed into FCI and eventually became the Director (Personnel) of FCI in 1973.

I had a good rapport with Hassan, but I wasn't pleased with the interference of Kashyap in my work. I brought this matter to the attention of Vachharajani. Subsequently, Kashyap stopped interfering, possibly after receiving instructions from Vachharajani.

In August 1972, I was summoned to Delhi for a meeting. During my visit, Vachharajani introduced me to Dr. Mukherjee, who discussed an important assignment with me. Dr. Mukherjee outlined the marketing issues that FCI was facing in the Assam region. This region, comprising seven northeastern states, was crucial for FCI. The Namrup Plant in Dibrugarh district produced urea for supply to all seven northeastern states and its tea gardens. Additionally, North Bengal and its tea estates also received urea from this plant.

At the time, the regional incharge was a person named Choudhry, who was on deputation from the Assam government's department of agriculture. He had struggled to recover outstanding dues of nearly ten crore from the tea gardens in Assam and had lost control over the region.

I was told to take charge of the region in a month's time and recover the outstanding at the earliest. I was to improve the region's operation and make the existing three area managers more functional and effective. I was told that I would be promoted as sales manager and incharge of the region with effect from 1.9.1972, the day I was to take charge of the Assam region at Guwahati. I was glad to comply.

I planned my return to Chandigarh on the same day. There was less than a month's time to leave for Guwahati. Before leaving Delhi, I gave Rashmi information about the impending transfer. Her voice sounded concerned at the change. I assured her that it was good for all of us. When I arrived back in Chandigarh that evening, I explained everything in detail. When she learned about promotion and independent charge of a region, she shed her concern and became happy. Rashmi then celebrated the good news with a hug and a kiss.

We decided to send our personal vehicle and household goods to Delhi by August 17th. From there, the FCI administration department would arrange its dispatch to Guwahati. These were to be moved by a metre-gauge goods train from Delhi to Bongaigaon in Assam. The transit time for the items was around ten days from Delhi to Bongaigaon, the last railway station for the Assam rail route during those days.

Besides the air and road connections for Assam, this was the only rail connection. From Bongaigaon, the booked items were to be carried by the consignee's representative by road to Guwahati. I gave advance information to our Guwahati office about the booked material around August 28th. I also told the area manager of Guwahati to hire a residence for me. The received material could then be moved to that residence. The house was to be hired on September 1, 1972.

On August 5, I called the meeting of all officers in my area in Chandigarh. In the meeting, I informed them about my transfer to Guwahati by the end of the month. It was quite a shock to all of them. But, at the same time, they were also happy to learn that I was being promoted to take charge of an important region.

They insisted on hosting a farewell dinner for me and my family at the Oberoi Mount View Hotel during the meeting. I agreed, and my family attended the dinner. During the event, the officers praised both me and Rashmi. They expressed that Madam Rashmi had always shown concern for their families, and they would miss her compassionate presence. Rashmi became emotional and informed them that there were still more than three weeks left before our departure. She suggested that they could visit Chandigarh with their wives, and she would be delighted to meet them. These meetings did take place, and the officers' families visited Chandigarh to meet Rashmi. She warmly hosted them with excellent refreshments on the office lawn.

We had a series of farewell gatherings, including those from government officials of agriculture departments in all three states, the FCI distribution network, and various colleagues from the Nangal Unit. Finally, on August 25, 1972, we departed from Chandigarh for Delhi. My family and I stayed at the FCI guest house. The next day, I met with Dr. Mukherji and Vachharajani, informing them of my flight to Guwahati scheduled for Sunday, August 27.

I collected my air tickets from the admin department along with the goods and car booking railway receipts (RRs). On Sunday morning, Ram Rekha dropped me off at the airport for the Guwahati flight. Before my departure, Ram Rekha became emotional. He touched my and Rashmi's feet with his eyes filled with tears and thanked us for giving a permanent job to his son, Rajan. We were extremely moved by the amount of love and respect that all the staff members had for us.

The flight left Delhi at 7 a.m. It took three hours for the direct flight. At Guwahati airport, two area managers, P.U. Ahmed and D. Gohain, received us. The office car with driver Sharma took us to the IOC guest house. Ahmed and Gohain, who followed in another office vehicle, had tea with us at the guest house. Ahmed said that the household goods had already reached Bongaigaon along with his personal car. These can be delivered the next day by presenting the RRs. I gave him the RRs. Both Ahmed and Gohain also talked about the finalisation of a house for my residence. I said that Rashmi and I would like to see the house in the afternoon.

We visited our future residential house with Ahmed and Gohain. The house was a pucca building constructed on a plot created by blasting part of a hillock. Its rear boundary touched the steep, rising side of the hill. The house had two bedrooms, a sitting room, a store, and a kitchen. The car garage stood on one side. It had direct access to the road leading to the house.

The house was very near Holy Child School. It was at a distance of around 300 metres from our house on an adjacent hill. Mona could easily walk down to the school. While going, she was easily visible from the house. Rashmi thanked both the AMs for finding such a nice house.

From Bongaigaon, the household effects and my personal car were brought to our newly hired residence in the afternoon of the 28th. Gogoi drove the car. The truck with household effects followed the car. Ahmed helped Gogoi put the things in the house, and the car was parked in the garage. Ahmed had also arranged for one office security guard to be posted there. After the arrangements, Ahmed took Gogoi to the IOC guest house to meet me around 7:30 p.m. I thanked both and asked Ahmed about any agency that could unpack and arrange the items in the room on the 29th in our presence.

Ahmed promised to do the needful and said that he will be present with the agency people at the residence at 10 a.m. on the 29th. Accordingly, driver Sharma was asked to come with the office car to the guesthouse at 9:30 a.m. the next day to take us to the residence for unpacking.

All household goods were unpacked and placed in their proper positions by the agency workers as per the directives of Rashmi. The entire task took almost seven hours, with a one-hour lunch break. I, Rashmi, Mona, and Ahmed went for an hour to the IOC guest house for lunch.

We also got the packed lunch for the newly engaged housemaid cum cook, Anu. She was a middle-aged Bengali woman from Cachar who had lost her family. Earlier, she had moved to Guwahati for employment. A few days ago, she was working in the house of a friend of AM Gohain. On the recommendation of Gohain, she was engaged by us. She stayed at the house as a domestic helper and cook for the family.

After the house was properly laid out with furniture, we moved into the house by Monday morning. I advised Ahmed to call AM Karan Saikia from Tinsukia to Guwahati on September 1. The first official meeting of all three AMs with me took place in my chamber at the Guwahati office.

The family moved to the house, along with the domestic helper Anu, after their breakfast at the IOC guesthouse. Rashmi became busy making the lunch and teaching Anu how to cook dishes according to the tastes of the family.

Along with Rashmi and Mona, I walked down to the office of Sister Nivedita. She was the principal of Holy Child School. From our house, we walked down to the school in seven minutes. Earlier, I had talked with Sister

Nivedita about Mona's admission. She had seen the transfer certificate for Mona issued by Carmel Convent School of Chandigarh. Mona was admitted to class I, and, after a few months, she got a double promotion to class III due to her knowledge and performance. Even in later life, her brilliance in studies continued. There was never any need for a tuition master for her or for any of the other two children who were subsequently added to the family. However, help was always available for them from their loving parents. For any help in teaching, they were more comfortable with their mom than their dad.

In the afternoon, the family walked around the nearby areas of their house and enjoyed the beauty and serenity of the whole area. The compound of the school had a magnificent green lawn, a playground, and beds of beautiful flowers. This was quite a change from the surroundings of their Chandigarh residence. The next day was going to be a busy day for me. The family had their dinner early. The dinner was prepared by Anu under the supervision of Rashmi.

On September 1, 1972, I took charge of the FCI Regional Office at Guwahati. After a formal introduction to all officers and staff of the regional office, I conducted my first meeting with the three area managers. I reallocated the new operational duties and activities of the three managers. The new duties of the three were:

Ahmed: He continued with his posting at Guwahati. He was assigned coordination work at the regional office. He was also told to coordinate the marketing affairs of the state of Meghalaya (directly under RM). He was responsible for the marketing in the two districts of Kamrup and Bongaigaon. He controlled three SOs posted at Guwahati, Bongaigaon, and Shillong.

Gohain: He was also posted at Guwahati. He looked after the districts of Darang, Naogaon, Sonitpur (Tezpur), Goalpara, and Cachhar, with five SOs posted at the headquarters of those districts. He was also to help RM recover ten *crores outstanding* from the tea gardens with the help of his other two colleagues. He was also given the charge of initiating the developmental work for fertiliser use in Arunachal Pradesh.

Saikia: His posting continued to be at Namrup. Besides coordinating the dispatches from the Namrup factory, he retained control of marketing activities in the districts of Dibrugarh (Tinsukia), Jorhat, and Shivsagar. He also coordinated the marketing affairs of the four states of Nagaland, Manipur, Mizoram, and Tripura. Under him worked six sales officers—one for dispatch coordination at Namrup, three in district headquarters, one at Imphal, and the other at Agartala. His major task was to collect almost seven crores outstanding from four major tea estates in his area.

After appraising them for the major tasks that are to be tackled in the region, I said that I believed in the decentralisation of power. The three AMs were free to make vital marketing decisions in their areas and were fully responsible for the end results. They could inform the regional manager about such decisions in their monthly DO letters to him. In turn, they could also ask their SOs to submit monthly reports of their marketing activities to them. After reviewing the reasons for the region's below-par performance in the past, I agreed to their five suggestions and their immediate implementation. One of the suggestions was regarding the transfer and posting of field officers. The performance of each SO was evaluated after an in-depth discussion with the AMs.

Only two SOs—Gogoi at Bongaigaon and Barogohain at Namrup Coordination—were not transferred. Both were posted there only six months ago. The remaining twelve were transferred with immediate effect to their new places of posting. *In the area of Ahmed* were posted Gogoi at Bongaigaon, Bharali at Guwahati (Kamrup), and Hazarika at Shillong. *In the area of Gohain*, Dutta at Naogaon, Das at Darang, Chakrabarti at Tezpur (Sonitpur), Sharma at Goalpara, and Goswami at Silchar (Cachhar) were posted. *In the area of Saikia*, Barogohain at Namrup, Barua at Dibrugarh, Bora at Shivsagar, Bardoloi at Jorhat Kakoti at Imphal, and Bhattacharya at Agartala were posted. The transfer orders were issued on the same day, and they were advised to join their new posts in seven days' time.

After the meeting, for two months I stayed in Guwahati. I monitored the achievements of each area vis-à-vis their targets. Satisfied that all AMs and their SOs were completely in tune with my directives and were achieving much more than the assigned tasks, I planned to tour the entire region for on-the-spot evaluation.

My first tour took me to Namrup. I met the Namrup Fertiliser factory manager, GM Phukan. After that, I toured the tea garden areas with AM Saikia. I discussed with the managers of the tea gardens their supply plans and the outstanding dues. All agreed to clear their past outstanding dues in four equal monthly instalments. All of them indicated that the outstanding payment would be synchronised with the payment of each of the coming four months of their fertiliser supplies. This was a good beginning. I told Saikia to immediately inform his other two counterparts to apply the same modality for liquidating the dues of the old tea gardens in their areas.

My next tour covered the states of Nagaland, Manipur, and Mizoram. I visited Kohima and Imphal but did not go to Aizawl. This visit was with Saikia, who went alone to Aizawl. My visit to Shillong, the capital of Meghalaya, was with Ahmed. During these visits, the state governments of Nagaland, Manipur, and Meghalaya treated me as a state guest! It happened all the while, even later when I toured these states. During my stay in Guwahati, I never visited Mizoram, Tripura, or Arunachal Pradesh. This was due to the very little requirement for fertiliser in these areas, the limited scope of agriculture, and many logistical problems. Being thinly populated over vast hilly areas, it had very limited scope for the development of agriculture.

Most of my tours with Rashmi and Mona were to Shillong, which she liked the most. The place was nearer to Guwahati. During such visits with family, I stayed at the Pinewood Hotel in Shillong. During one such visit, we also went to see Cherrapunjee, reputed to be the wettest place in the world. The heavy rains here often swell the waters of Nohsngithiang waterfall. En route, we crossed Colonel Hunts Brewery. We purchased a few bottles of the famous red sweet wine from the brewery. This wine was liked by both Rashmi and me.

Shillong, 104 kilometres away from Guwahati, was the favourite town of Rashmi, Mona, and me. It is a beautiful plateau at an elevation of 4990 feet above sea level. Surrounded by gorges, waterfalls, hills, and lakes, it provided unbridled happiness to all visitors. We visited Shillong Peak, which lies five kilometres away from the town. On a clear day, the snow-clad peaks of the eastern Himalayas present a tantalisingly unforgettable sight!

By the end of the year 1972, the entire outstanding amount of rupees ten crores was collected from the tea gardens. The sales in the region saw a phenomenal rise. Fertiliser supplies for all the tea gardens in Assam were properly planned on a monthly basis. This distribution plan was so effective that the Tea Board of India (TBI) took my help and advice. A permanent tie-up system between the Tea Board and FCI for the fertiliser supply plan for all 1200 tea estates in Assam and North Bengal was made by me. It was accepted by TBI and FCI. My achievements made Dr. Mukherjee and Vachharajani extremely happy. I did not misplace their faith and confidence in me. They issued me appreciation letters and agreed to my suggestion of giving double increments to all staff in the region. Giving a double increment to all staff in a region was an unheard and unprecedented thing in any public sector undertaking!

More laurels were received on the official front during the year 1973 too. Day by day, the political and social climate in Assam was becoming hot. It started with the agitation to oust all non-Assamese from Assam. Subsequently, on April 7, 1979, the ugly head of the ULFA agitation began to separate Assam from India. Of course, it never succeeded.

In early 1973, I used to get threatening ghost telephone calls. The callers used to ask me to leave Assam or face the annihilation of me and my family. Initially, I thought it was a prank by unsound minds. But when it persisted and I could tell that non-Assamese officials of other government undertakings were also receiving such calls, I took the matter seriously. I also reported the matter to the Delhi Head Office.

In January 1973, when Rashmi showed signs of morning sickness, I took her for a check-up by Dr. Chang Kakoti. She was the best gynaecologist in Guwahati and had her own nursing home. Her examination gave the good news of a new addition to the family in the coming nine months. Both parents rejoiced at the news. Due to the earlier history of miscarriage at Chandigarh, I wanted Rashmi to have the least movement and to use the house to help Anu fully with all household chores and cooking.

Fortunately, nothing untoward happened, and a healthy baby girl was born at Dr. Chang Kakoti Nursing Home on September 22, 1973. The baby was named Dimpy. This was the happiest occasion for the family during the year 1973. This happy news was passed on to Baba and Maa, who too blessed her with their best wishes.

The first birthday of Dimpy was celebrated in Bhutan. The best season to visit Bhutan was between late September and January. This plan was synchronised with that of Mona and Rashmi. All of us visited Bhutan from Guwahati by road on September 21, 1974. The family started their visit in the office car driven by driver Sharma around 7:30 a.m. We drove to Bhutan via Rangia town in Kamrup district. It was a scenic drive of 55 kilometres and took an hour and a half to reach. It was another 138-kilometre journey to Bhutan, nearer the Phuetsoling Post of Bhutan. After entering Bhutan and going towards the said post, I asked driver Sharma to take us to the Guest House of the Border Road Organisation. It was another 20 kilometres away and was located on a hillock 1500 feet above sea level. We reached there around lunchtime. The first birthday celebration for Dimpy was enjoyed by the family in those scenic surroundings.

Due to the old age of my parents, I had requested Vachharajani for my next posting at Bhubaneswar some time in 1974. By that time, the Assam Region of FCI had become the best-managed region of the country. For my request to fructify, I had to wait until December 1974. The delay was primarily due to the delay in finding the right person for the Guwahati posting. At last, in November 1974, the recruitment of a regional manager was possible. The person selected was R. N. Prasad, a senior manager of Sri Ram Chemical & Fertiliser Company,

New Delhi. Finally, on December 6, 1974, my transfer order was issued. I was to take charge of the Bhubaneswar Region as Regional Manager by December 1974. Handing over charge of the Assam region to R. N. Prasad was completed by December 18, 1974, at the regional office, as Prasad desired to do the touring of all areas later.

After the receipt of the transfer order, I made arrangements to send my car and household effects from Guwahati to Bhubaneswar by road. The movement was via Siliguri and Calcutta. The time that it took was around four days. Accordingly, I planned to hand over the regional charge on December 18. My car and household effects (HHE) were dispatched on the 19th, and we left Guwahati on the 20th of December 1974.

A meeting of all three area managers was scheduled for the 17th of December. I told them my plan of charge handover to incoming RM Prasad. After this, I executed my movement plan from Guwahati to Bhubaneswar.

My family and I flew to Bhubaneswar via Calcutta on December 20, 1974. My personal car and the household effects were dispatched one day earlier. I had already informed the Bhubaneswar office to send an office car to the airport to receive me and my family and take us to Cuttack.

At the airport, we were received by PA Ghosh and SO HQ, Parija. I told Parija that I would stay for a week with my parents at Cuttack, till my car and the household effects reach Bhubaneswar by the 24th or 25th of December. However, I would come to the office the next day to take charge of the region from the temporary incumbent U.K. Mohanty (UKM), who had retired a week earlier. UKM was officially asked to temporarily continue until the charge was handed over to me.

My family and I reached Tulsipur house at Cuttack on the 20th afternoon. Baba Maa, Budha, Rama, and Arun were happy to see us. Dimpy, the plump child, immediately became the favourite of Baba and Budha. Baba and Maa were happy that my family and I would stay at least a week with them before finally moving to Bhubaneswar.

The next morning, I went to the Bhubaneswar office and took charge of the region. I was introduced to all the officers and staff. I was appraised of CBI cases under investigation against Dr. Ganguli, who was the RM when the cases were registered in 1971. After that, UKM was given charge of the region. I asked SO Parija to call a meeting of all SOs in the region on December 23. I saw a couple of houses for my residence and selected one at Saheed Nagar. The house owner, a police officer, was staying at Cuttack. I finalised the deal with him and took the house on rent with effect from the fourth week, i.e., from

December 23rd, 1974. For the next few years, this was to be my residence in Bhubaneswar.

On the 23rd, when I was having my SOs meeting in my office chamber, suddenly a person entered the meeting venue. When I asked him his identity, the person (Niranjan Das) told me that he was a CBI Inspector. He had come to question one of my officers. I did not allow him to take a chair and asked him to provide the name and telephone numbers of his Superintendent of Police (S.P.CBI). After getting the number, I rang up B. B. Panda (SP, CBI) in the presence of Inspector Das. I told Panda that I joined the office only a couple of days ago. During my meeting with the officers, Inspector Das gate crashed into the meeting and disturbed my official meeting. Such an act amounts to harassment of a senior officer of a central government PSU. Panda asked me to give the phone to Das. Panda's loud reprimand could be heard by all in the meeting. Immediately, Das apologised to me and left the venue. That was the end of the CBI harassment of my officers who were not involved.

This was a new experience for the officers present at the meeting. They had observed earlier how the previous RMs were scared of CBI. This had ended CBI interference in the present RM's official work. Subsequently, I and CBI SP Panda became good friends. Much later, B.B. Panda became the police chief (DGP) of Odisha before his retirement.

Household goods and the car reached Bhubaneswar on the 24th and were offloaded and arranged in the newly hired house at Shaheed Nagar in the presence of Rashmi. She had come from Cuttack to Bhubaneswar by office car driven by driver Manu. Budha volunteered to accompany and assist her. The house was locked after the unloading and arrangements for the household effects. One of the private office guards was posted at the house for a week. In the evening, Rashmi, me, and Budha returned to Cuttack.

The next day, December 25, 1974, was Mona's 8th birthday. It was the first time she was celebrating her birthday at Cuttack House. Maa made a lot of *pithas* on the occasion, and it was served with a regular birthday chocolate cream cake during lunchtime. I treated Baba, Maa, Budha, and his family to a lavish dinner at the famous Asian Hotel near Jobra.

The Bhubaneswar region was controlled by the Calcutta Zonal Office. Mr. Shyamal Banerjee was the zonal manager. He was a colleague of Vachharajani in the Defence Accounts Service. Like him, he had come on deputation to FCI. After my joining in Bhubaneswar, I talked to him over the phone. I had scheduled my visit to Calcutta to meet him on the 27th of December, 1974. I left Cuttack for Calcutta by train (Puri Express) at 9:30 p.m. on the 26th. The meeting on the 27th with Banerjee was cordial, and both had an immediate bond. I returned to Cuttack in the evening by Puri Express and reached there at 6 a.m. the next morning. I shared my experience with the new boss with Rashmi. She was happy to visualise a smooth period of my official functioning.

On January 1, 1975, my family and I shifted to our residence in Bhubaneswar. Mona was admitted to class IV at St. Joseph's Convent School. The school was in nearby Satya Nagar. It was at a distance of two furlongs from our residence. It hardly took 15 minutes to reach there with a cycle rickshaw hired on a monthly basis.

The next few months were very busy and hectic for me. Three newly available officers were posted as area managers. The three managers new postings were at Cuttack for Kapoor, at Sambalpur for Rao Tipperneni, and at Berhampur for Kakkar. I recruited some new SOs too. In other words, the entire establishment and the networks were completely overhauled to run smoothly during my posting at Bhubaneswar between December 21, 1974, and June 15, 1982.

Before my posting at Bhubaneswar, FCI had started construction of a coal-based big urea fertiliser plant at Talcher. It started production for a short period, beginning in 1980. It had adopted an obsolete, failed technology, and this plant was finally closed and dismantled. The general manager of the plant, Mr. Biswas, used to visit my office when he had work at the secretariat. We became good acquaintances.

Once, Biswas visited Bhubaneswar with Mr. R. Hassan, who had become the Director (Personnel) of FCI. I knew him well from my Chandigarh days when Hassan was G.M. of Nangal Plant. He used to treat Rashmi as his daughter and, many times, had appreciated her tasty cooked dishes at the lunch table of our residence. He, along with Biswas, had their lunch at my place. Both appreciated and praised the culinary art and ability of Rashmi.

In January 1975, I received imported urea at Paradeep Port. It was allotted for the seeding programme and marketing of future produce from the Talcher Plant. At that time, I engaged a young lawyer under retainership to take care of legal matters relating to imported fertilisers. This lawyer (AP) subsequently became CJ of the Odisha High Court and, subsequently, Justice of the SCI. Dealing in imported fertilisers exposed the officers of my region to different aspects of port operations. Port operations for marketing continued during my Bhubaneswar stay at HFC too.

On July 1, 1975, FCI was split into five independent companies. These were the *new* FCI, which retained Sindhri, Barauni, Talcher, and Gorakhpur plants; HFC, which had Namrup, Durgapur, and Haldia plants; NFL, which had Nangal, Panipat, and Gunna plants; RCF, which had Trombay plant; and PDIL, which became a separate company for planning and development work for the fertiliser industry.

The marketing staff posted in the NE and eastern zones became part of HFC. The staff posted in the north zone became a part of the NFL, whereas the staff in the west-southwest zone became a part of the RCF. The zonal managers became the general managers of the marketing divisions of the concerned companies. Thus, the establishments of mine and my boss, Shyamal Banerjee, became part of HFC.

In 1976, a delegation of agriculture officers and officers of the state-run fertiliser company of the Bangladesh government came for training at Calcutta. Their programme was sponsored by the government of India. The venue of the training was the Calcutta Zonal office. Shyamal Banerjee was made the chairman of the committee for the training. He was given the responsibility to arrange for the speakers for the training programme. I was called to Calcutta to speak to these trainees. The narration of my experience in fertiliser marketing in the eastern states of Assam and Odisha was quite interesting for the trainees from Bangladesh. The leader of the trainee team in Bangladesh said that he would definitely implement the salient features of my lecture on fertiliser marketing in Bangladesh. Shyamal Banerjee congratulated me.

In 1978, I was promoted to the post of marketing manager (MM). For the first time, Odisha got a regional charge of the rank of MM. In the meantime, I had made some changes to my official setup. At the request of Kapoor, I got him posted to the marketing wing of HFC HQ in New Delhi. In his place, I got from the New Delhi office S. Bhatia of AM's rank. I made changes in the postings of three AMs. Tipperneni was posted as AM at Berhampur. Earlier, incumbent Kakkar was brought to the Bhubaneswar regional office as AM coordination and chief incharge of Cuttack. S. Bhatia was posted as AM Sambalpur in place of Tipperneni.

In 1977, Rashmi was carrying her third child. On November 30, 1977, a son (Dev) was born at a Cuttack nursing home. At the time of delivery, I and Baba were waiting at the nursing home. After a week, Rashmi went to Tulsipur house. She and both of her daughters stayed there until December 15, 1977. Mona, who was in class VII, and Dimpy, who was in KG, had to miss their classes for a fortnight.

As long as I was posted at Bhubaneswar, my family and I regularly left on Friday evenings every week to Cuttack. We stayed there for the weekends and used to return on Monday mornings to Bhubaneswar. This practice continued without any exception. In late 1978, we moved to a more spacious residence in Shaheed Nagar. This was our second house on rent. We stayed here for two years. The third residence was taken after two years, in 1980. This house was also in Saheed Nagar, near its market. In this house, we stayed until June 1982. From here, we left for Lucknow on transfer. During the stay at the third house, Dev was admitted to the nursery at St. Joseph School. He accompanied both sisters to the school in their Rickshaw.

Dev's schoolgoing had a lot of comical aspects. After admission, he refused to go to school and resorted to all kinds of tantrums. Rashmi never gave in to such drama and used to force him to sit in the rickshaw between both sisters for school. After reaching school, once or twice, he refused to get down from the Rickshaw. The Rickshaw driver had to bring him back to the house. But Rashmi never tolerated such antics by the child. She used to immediately sit on the rickshaw and take him back to his class. This stopped such mischief by Dev. For a few days, he used to run away from his class. He used to run crying to the class of Mona. After a few reprimands, he had to drop this mischief too.

In the month of September 1981, I, as an alumnus of the Administrative Staff College of India (ASCI) in 1976, was invited to deliver a lecture during one of the courses for its trainees. It was on the eve of its silver jubilee celebrations. I accepted the invitation and visited ASCI in Hyderabad. My lecture to the trainees received appreciation from them as well as from the institute.

In late 1981, GM Shyamal Banerjee retired. In his place, the charge was given to Dr. S.P. Dua. He was earlier the Chief Agronomist of HFC. I did not have a good rapport with Dua. I complied with the order for my transfer from Bhubaneswar to Lucknow. My decision was primarily to make an attempt to go to Delhi and join another public sector undertaking (PSU). It was necessary for advancement in my career. I had already experienced that unless I left Bhubaneswar, such a change was not possible. Thus, much against the wishes of my parents, I finally left for Lucknow on transfer. I joined Lucknow on June 15, 1982, as marketing manager of HFC for Uttar Pradesh.

At Lucknow, it was an office cum residence at Gomti Nagar. The residence was on the first floor, and the office was on the ground floor of a large building. Mona, Dimpy, and Dev were admitted to classes XI, IV, and KG, respectively. While Mona was admitted to La Martiniere School, Dimpy and Dev were admitted to St. Fidelis School. They used to be dropped off at their schools in my car by the office driver. They were also picked up by him after school. The driver's name was Naseem, and he belonged to Lucknow. The office vehicle was a Jeep Station Wagon.

After an eight-month stay in Lucknow, I got an interview call from the Cement Corporation of India (CCI). The interview was scheduled for

February 7, 1983, at their corporate office in New Delhi. The post was that of a senior manager or chief manager (SM or CM).

After receiving the call letter on January 25, 1983, I got a telephone call from my previous AM, Tipperneni (Rao). He said that he has already joined CCI as a manager at their Delhi head office. He requested that I come for the interview. He wanted me to be his boss at CCI. In fact, he said that P.K. Tikku, who was a director at CCI, was looking after its marketing. Tikku wanted an experienced person to head the marketing. Till then, it was being looked after by a manager, S. Dewan, a colleague of Tipperneni.

I appeared for the interview on the scheduled date at CCI HQ at Nehru Place, New Delhi. The interview was in the chamber of Chairman and Managing Director (CMD) Maheshwari. Other members of the interview committed were P.K. Tikku, Director, and A.K. Srivastava, Chief Manager, HQ. After learning from me about my past career, Maheshwari told me that I would be offered the post of Senior Manager (SM) and, after three months' probation, I would be confirmed for the post of Chief Manager (CM).

I said that the SM of CCI and his present post in HFC are of the same rank, and I would not like to join as SM. The CMD said that his offer of salary for the post would match the initial salary of the CM. After three months, I would be made the CM. Tikku said that I should accept CMD's offer. I finally agreed to CMD's suggestion. I also told them that, in view of the three-month mandatory notice period to be given to HFC, I could only join CCI on July 1, 1983. I could resign from HFC only after I received the offer letter from CCI. The offer letter was given that day.

After the interview, I went to Rao's cabin and told him about the interview. I requested that Rao search for and hire a two-bedroom flat in areas nearby Nehru Place in Delhi by June 30, 1983. I intended to move with the family by July 1, 1983. It was a matter of great appreciation that Tipperneni could arrange such accommodation at Tara Apartments in the Alaknanda area. The apartment was only five kilometres away from the Nehru Place office.

After returning to Lucknow, I rang up Dua and talked about my intention to resign from HFC. I also said that I would like to be relieved by June 30th. Dua agreed to my proposal, and I sent my resignation letter on 1.4.1983. I started to complete all the pending official work. After getting Rao's confirmation in May 1983 about the finalisation of the hiring of my residence at Tara Apartments, I applied for the transfer certificates of all three children from their Lucknow schools. Rashmi and the children were happy to go to Delhi.

As per plan, my family and I left Lucknow on the 2nd of July. Our HHE was transported by Agarwal Packers and Movers (APM). I drove my car with the family. Naseem, the driver, was followed in the official Jeep Station Wagon along with the HFC Sales Officer (Goswami). He drove behind as the family's safe escort to Delhi. On the third of July, 1983, my family and I entered our flat at Tara Apartment. The truck that was following us reached us in the afternoon, and the HHE was unloaded and arranged in our flat by evening. Rao had come with his wife, and after the arrangements were done, he took me and my family to his residence for dinner.

On July 4, 1983, I arrived at the CCI office around 9 a.m. Rao took me to Tikku's chamber, where I gave the joining report. Tikku wished me well and then took me to meet CMD Maheshwari. After that, I went to meet the director (personnel) of CCI. I was surprised to see R.C. Gupta as the director. Earlier, Gupta was a senior personnel officer under Wadhwa at the FCI head office. He recognised me, and we were both happy to again come together.

Next week, Mona was admitted to class XII of Frank Anthony School. At that time, it was the only school in Delhi affiliated with the Board of Indian School Certificate (ISC) examination for class XII. After seeing the results of Mona for class X (ICSC) and the results of class XI in La Martiniere School at Lucknow, the principal admitted her to class XII. However, Dimpy and Dev could not succeed in getting admission to that school. Both were admitted to nearby Tagore International School in classes V and I, respectively. They were finally admitted to Frank Anthony School next year, in classes VI and II, when Mona topped the school's board results.

My first month at CCI was very hectic. I had to aquatint myself with the production facilities of CCI, which had 10 factories. The factories were: Charkhi Dadri in Haryana; Mandhar, Nayagaon, and Akaltara in Madhya Pradesh; Bokajan in Assam; Adilabad and Tandoor in Telangana; Yeraguntula in Andhra; Rajban in Himachal Pradesh; and Kurkunta in Karnataka. Besides, it had a grinding unit in Delhi too.

CCI had handling agents, who were mostly its big dealers besides being storage agents. The three big dealers, handling contractors, and storage agents in Bombay, Hyderabad, and Calcutta were, respectively, Waju Bhai Enterprises, Singh Brothers, and Chowdhury Enterprises.

Waju Bhai was a Gujarati and the owner of the Bombay establishment. Hardeep Singh, a Sardar, owned the Hyderabad establishment. Anil Chowdhury, a Bengali, owned the Calcutta establishment. These three were very powerful agents of the CCI network. The Bombay and Calcutta agents were under the patronage of CMD Maheshwari, and the Hyderabad agent had the blessings of Director Tikku. These three agents were handled with extreme caution by all marketing personnel.

I soon learned that CMD was the recipient of one rupee per bag of cement sold and handled by the CCI agents. The total amount ran into hundreds of crores of rupees every month. Knowledge of this came when I went to Bombay and visited Waju Bhai. While I was leaving, Waju Bhai handed me a bag for CMD Maheshwari. On inquiry, Waju Bhai talked about the bag containing a few crores of rupees of regular commission money (bribe) for Maheshwari. I politely refused to carry the bag, as I did not want to be a part of the racket. I told him to make some other arrangements for the future.

On my return from Bombay, I was called by the CMD to his office. Maheshwari inquired about my visit to plants and the distribution network, particularly my Bombay trip. I gave him all the reports but did not mention the Waju Bhai incident, even on prodding! As I learned later, Maheshwari had gotten information from Waju Bhai about my refusal to carry the bag containing the bribe money for him. From that moment of three months of service in CCI, began my official problems. These were created on CMD Maheshwari's advice.

On October 7, 1983, I learned that Baba had died on October 5. The message was received late by me as my home telephone was out of order for a week and Budha did not have my office number. I applied for leave for a fortnight and flew to Bhubaneswar along with Rashmi on the 7th. Rashmi explained to Mona how she should manage the house and the siblings for a fortnight. She ensured that all provisions were available in the house. She also requested the neighbour and her friend, Mrs. Kamlesh Gupta, to help the children if there were any necessities. Kamlesh's husband, N.P. Gupta, was a senior executive at BHEL.

As the cremation was already done, other religious formalities until the 11th day were performed by me at Cuttack. Maa was inconsolable. Rashmi spent all her time with Maa. She consoled Maa and provided her solace to partially overcome the grief. We flew back to Delhi on the 19th of October after failing in our persuasion to bring Maa with us to Delhi. I joined the office after my leave on Monday, the 24th. Rashmi was relieved to see all her three children safe and sound under the supervision of her best friend, Mrs. Gupta, of flat Q-11 of Tara Apartment. Her flat was below our P-33 flat.

When we returned, Mona told us that in the adjacent P-32 flat, a young couple with their three-year-old son had moved in. The young couple were Jollys, who then owned a small detergent (*fena*) factory in the nearby Okhla Industrial Area. Much later, this product became very popular and competed with the Surf of Hindustan Lever. Jolly's father had retired from Hindustan Lever. Jollys has subsequently become a medium-category industrialist! Another famous neighbour nearby was Sushma Swaraj. She was the youngest CM in Delhi and Haryana. Later, she became a central cabinet minister in the

Bajpayee and Modi governments. Her husband had also become governor of an NE state during A. B. Bajpayee's regime. The husband and wife were both lawyers who became politicians.

Tara Apartment used to be a famous landmark in Lutyens' Delhi. Its architecture was designed by the famous architect Charles Correa. It started as a Cooperative Housing Society of Senior Politicians and Bureaucrats. Its beginning is attributed to a famous group of 21 members headed by Dr. Sushila Nayar. She was the first Minister of Health in Pandit Nehru's cabinet. The decision for the apartment's construction was taken on November 12th, 1960, with the formation of Tara Cooperative Group Housing Society. Tara was the name of the mother of Dr. Sushila Nayar. The residents of Tara were famous politicians and bureaucrats. During my stay at the Tara apartment, Md. Safi Qureshi, the railways minister, was the president of the society. Besides, many other famous political leaders from different states owned their residences in this apartment.

Coming back to happenings at CCI, I joined duties on October 24, 1983. Since it had already been three months of my service at CCI, I wanted to upgrade to the promised post of chief manager. I met CMD Maheshwari and requested the release of the promised post. To my utter surprise, Maheshwari told me that, mandatorily, I had to wait for one year and nine months more. When reminded of his promise at the interview, he had the cheek to say that the promises given during the interview are broken once the candidate joins! At that moment, I took the decision to teach Maheshwari a lesson since he was a liar besides being highly corrupt. More surprises awaited me. The scheming CMD resorted to his plan of harassment due to my refusal to bring the bribe money from Waju Bhai to him.

After the end of my probation on July 4, 1984, I was confirmed for the post of senior manager. On August 8, 1984, I was designated as the zonal manager of the South West Zone and transferred to Hyderabad. The order indicated that I should be in Hyderabad by August 16th. I immediately wrote that I could only join in Hyderabad by keeping my family in Delhi since all my children were studying at Delhi schools. I had to pay my house rent allowance in Delhi. Although CMD Maheshwari was averse to allowing this facility, Director Personnel R.C. Gupta advised him to agree. He said that I, with links in the Ministry, can bring a charge of harassment against CMD and the company. Being a dishonest coward, Maheshwari was forced to accede to my request.

Rashmi was very unhappy about the transfer. I assured her that this difficulty would be of short duration. I also assured that I would return to Delhi on transfer in one year's time. Besides, every month I would visit Delhi twice for meetings with Tikku. Finally, on August 8, 1984, I left Delhi and went to Hyderabad. In Hyderabad, I stayed at the CCI Guesthouse in Ameerpet. With official sanction, I converted a portion of that guesthouse into the zonal office of the South West Zone to save on additional expenses for the company.

In setting up the office, Rao Tipperneni was of great help. This office for the South West Zone controlled the logistics of the cement movement of the five factories in Adilabad, Kurkunta, Yeraguntula, Akaltara, and Mandhar. Besides, it was also preparing the ground for marketing the future production of a million tonnes of cement at the under-construction Tandoor factory of CCI.

I also established a regional office of CCI in Bombay. Space was hired for this office in the RCF Office Complex, situated on the Bombay Express Highway. I also got three flats purchased for CCI from BMC at Vashi. These flats were meant for the residence of the regional manager and two officers. The newly recruited manager, Dhawan, was posted as regional manager of Bombay.

All six general managers of the plants (equivalent to the ranks of the chief manager) were highly dependent on me for quick transportation of their products, whether by road or rail. Most of the movements were by road, for which I appointed good transporters through an open tender. One of the transporters appointed for Yeraguntula and Tandoor factories subsequently became a Minister of State in the Fertilisers Ministry of the Narsimha Rao government in 1991. Later, this minister faced an awkward situation and lost face when he tried to boss over me when I had become the managing director of a fertiliser company that was a big joint venture of the governments of India and Nauru.

As promised, I visited my family twice every month. I used to plan my official trips in such a way that I spent almost one week every month in Delhi. From Hyderabad, I often toured to Bombay, Bangalore, Cochin, Trivandrum, Madras, Bhopal, and Calcutta. The Calcutta visits were mostly to the offices of the eastern and south-eastern railways for coordinating the rail movements for the dispatch of cement from the factories. The GMs of the factories also used to call on me in Hyderabad. Their visits were mostly for sorting out problems for quick movement of the produced cement. They also took my help in discussing the problems of their factory labour unions with the state governments of Andhra Pradesh and Madhya Pradesh. I remained extremely busy as a zonal manager. I never could gauge how quickly the weeks and months passed in Hyderabad.

My eldest daughter, Mona, passed her I.Sc. examination in 1985 with flying colours. She topped the class XII batch at Frank Anthony Public School. In the meantime, the other two children, Dimpy and Dev, were also admitted to Frank Anthony School after changing over from Tagore International School.

During the monthly visits to Delhi, I took Rashmi and the children out on a drive. Then I used to visit the places of our relatives, watch movies, and eat out at restaurants. The family used to eagerly wait for my visits. I used to talk almost daily over the phone with Rashmi and the children from Hyderabad.

During one of my return flights from Delhi to Hyderabad in May 1985, I met a close friend in the aircraft. He was a senior IPS officer on deputation to the Central Government (CBI) in Delhi. We were meeting after almost twenty years. This friend was mostly posted at Bhubaneswar and Cuttack, being an IPS of the Orissa cadre. During that period, I was posted to Patna, Calcutta, Chandigarh, Guwahati, Lucknow, and Delhi. This friend had attended Rashmi's wedding with me. The most intimate school friend of Rashmi was his cousin.

During the flight, we talked about incidents that had happened in our lives. He then came to know about difficulties that were created by my boss (CMD), as I did not toe his dishonest line. That boss wanted me to be a conduit for collecting bribes for him. My friend was shocked. He also showed concern about Rashmi's forced, lonely stay in Delhi for the sake of children's education. He told me that God never forgives such people, and they are punished through divine dispensation. I noted that he was furious and seemed to plan something!

After a few days, I almost forgot about my chat with that old friend. As usual, I had gone on tour out of Hyderabad for fifteen days in a month. The dealership network was already streamlined. The handling agent network and fine-tuning of the logistics of all six factories were in place. I also made a few friends among the circle of my acquaintances in Hyderabad. Most prominent, among others, were two of Odia's friends: i) Mohanty, the police commissioner of Hyderabad, who was a confidant of the CM (NTR) of Andhra Pradesh; and ii) Mishra, the zonal head of the State Bank of India at Hyderabad. Already, a year has passed since I was posted to Hyderabad.

On October 1, 1985, I had a meeting in Delhi with Tikku to finalise a transport contract for cement movement to Kerala from the Yeraguntula factory. Reaching the office in the morning, I learned that a CBI raid had taken place suddenly in the afternoon of the previous day. The raid was at the residence and the office of CMD Maheshwari.

It was learned that the CBI had seized many files and documents from his office. They had seized crores of cash from his residence. It included a few sacks filled with currency notes thrown out of his residence on the rear service road before the raiding team entered his house. One of the government directors on the CCI board, Sisodia, the additional secretary (finance) of the industry's ministry, had temporarily taken charge as CMD. Maheshwari had been removed and suspended. Tikku was busy with the new incumbent CMD. He asked me to wait in Delhi for a few days since Sisodia was individually meeting all senior officials.

I met Sisodia along with Tikku in the afternoon of October 3. Tikku explained the good work that I had done in stabilising the marketing activities of CCI during the last year. On Sisodia's query, I narrated all my grievances. I told about the way I was duped by Maheshwari when the promises he made during the interview were not kept after my appointment. I also narrated his harassment by forcible separation from my family due to his posting in Hyderabad. Sisodia listened calmly and told me to wait until Monday, the 5th. He assured me that he would try to assist me with some of my personal issues by issuing appropriate orders.

On the fifth morning, Tikku had a meeting with me. At the meeting, Rao Tipperneni, a confidant of mine and Tikku, was also called. In said meeting, it was decided that I would be transferred back to the Delhi corporate office by November 1, 1985. I would hand over the Zonal charge to Rao Tipperneni by October 30, 1985, after the transfer of Rao to Hyderabad. The minutes of the meeting were duly signed by all three, and they were put before acting CMD Sisodia for his approval. The approval was given the same day. The official order was then issued by Tikku and handed over to me and Rao. It was confirmed by Rao that, after winding up his Delhi residence, he and his family would move to Hyderabad by October 22.

I was finally back in Delhi on October 30. I took charge of my Delhi assignment on November 1, 1985. By that date, Maheshwari had already been dismissed from CCI service and had faced the hearings at the CBI court. I had my last laugh! Poetic justice was meted out to my tormentor of two years! The family rejoiced at my return. Rashmi celebrated the occasion by throwing a big party for the family at their favourite restaurant, 'Moti Mahal Deluxe' at Greater Kailash-I.

Tikku had a good relationship with me as well as with Sisodia. The marketing operations of CCI were strengthened, and the entire network performed with vigour. A part of their earnings was no longer milked out like in the earlier days of the Maheshwari regime. The consolidation took some time until the new CMD, C.N. Garg, was appointed on December 1, 1985. Earlier, Garg was the executive director of BHEL in Hyderabad.

I had met Garg in Hyderabad along with R.C. Gupta. We also had our lunch at his place during my first meeting. Gupta had earlier mentioned to Garg my trouble with Maheshwari and his subsequent harassment and denial of the post of Chief Manager as promised. Garg had already been appraised of my excellent performance at CCI by Sisodia. On the first day of his charge, he ordered an interview with me for promotion to the post of chief manager (CM). After the interview, I got my order of promotion after a fortnight. I became Chief Manager with effect from December 26, 1986, and held the charge of Marketing Head at the corporate office.

Garg was a very sincere and honest chief executive. He was a hard taskmaster, too. He had developed a format for the daily report of production, sales, warehouse stocks, etc. at CCI. Every morning, at 10 a.m. on each working day, I used to provide him with this report along with proposed action for the coming week. Garg appreciated my work. He used to encourage me by saying that I was meant to be a part of a bigger organisation and could be its CEO. His observation was accurate. It was proved later when I actually headed an organisation bigger than CCI. I always remembered and felt that Garg was my true friend, philosopher, and guide.

In March 1987, I saw an advertisement for recruitment for the post of general manager (GM) of marketing at Paradeep Phosphates Limited (PPL). It was a big joint venture between the governments of India and Nauru. Its plant was in Paradeep, Odisha. It was the biggest producer of DAP fertiliser in Asia. The company was a 'B' Schedule PSU, whereas CCI was in Schedule 'C'. Thus, a director of CCI was on the same scale as a GM of PPL. My current position as CM at CCI was equivalent to the post of deputy general manager (DGM) at PPL. I applied for the post and was called for an interview at PPL's Nehru Place Office on May 25, 1987.

I had kept CMD Garg informed about my application for GM's post in Paradeep Phosphates. All information, beginning with the application for PPL post, the scheduled interview, and my final selection and issue of the appointment letter, was personally intimated to Garg. The CMD was happy with the progress in my career. Garg immediately issued instructions to me to prepare a marketing manual for CCI in two months' time. This was duly done. It was highly appreciated and was immediately implemented in CCI by his order.

Returning to the process of my induction to PPL, I learned that Bhagwan Singh, ICS and retired Ambassador of the GOI at Fiji, was a personal friend of Garg. Both belonged to Agra. At that time, Singh was a director on the PPL Board. That's the reason there were no impediments from CCI to allowing me to join PPL. I was relieved by CCI in the afternoon of June 17, 1987, and joined PPL in the afternoon of June 18, 1987, as general manager, marketing. I gave the joining report to A. K. Bhattacharjee. At that time, Bhattacharjee was the Chief of Finance of PPL. He was temporarily acting as managing director before the appointment of the permanent incumbent, P. Arunachalam.

PPL head office was on the 2nd floor of Mansarovar Tower at 90 Nehru Place, New Delhi. PPL had earlier also hired accommodation on the first floor of Hemkunt Tower at 101 Nehru Place. A few marketing personnel, like Sr. Manager A.P. Srivastava, Assistant Manager Aravind Panigrahi, etc., were sitting at a portion of that accommodation. A big room with an attached PA cabin also formed part of that accommodation. Mr. Jacob, the first Managing Director of PPL, was occupying this space. Subsequently, he moved to Mansarovar Tower when the facility for the MD's chamber and his secretariat were ready for occupation. I, as the first general manager (marketing) of PPL, was given the room earlier used by Jacob. An official AC car with a company driver was allotted to me. The administration department of PPL provided AC, sofa sets, etc. at my home as per my residential entitlement. The free use of an office car by my family was also one of the entitlements.

The family was delighted at my new post and its facilities. By this time, the eldest daughter, Mona, was doing her B.A. (Hons.) in history at Lady Shriram College (LSR). The college was adjacent to Frank Anthony School, where the other two children were studying in classes X and VI, respectively. The school-going children used the school bus, and Mona used to go to the college on the DTC bus. Some days, Mona was accompanied by her friend Neerja, the daughter of Mr. and Mrs. Gupta, their neighbours at Tara Apartment. Neerja was doing her B.A. (Hons.) in Economics at LSR.

In September 1987, P.N. Arunachalam joined as the managing director of PPL. He was selected by the Public Enterprises Selection Board (PESB) in July 1986, and the notification of his appointment was issued in August 1986 after the Cabinet approval of the GOI. It was as per the standing guidelines for appointments of CMD\MD\Directors of Central government PSUs.

Normally, chairmen cum managing directors (CMDs) head the central PSUs. Besides being MDs, they also chair the board meetings. PPL was a joint venture of the governments of India and Nauru. Its board had an equal number of three directors from each government. The president of Nauru was a board member from Nauru. Nauru President desired that the Fertiliser Minister of India be the Chairman of the PPL Board. The Indian Constitution did not have any provision to allow a cabinet minister to be the Chairman of the Board of any PSU. The Nauru President had to agree for the Secretary of the Fertiliser Ministry to chair the board meetings of PPL. That is the reason why PPL CEO was termed Managing Director (MD) and not Chairman & Managing Director

(CMD) as long as it remained a joint venture. PPL MD enjoyed all the perks and powers of a CMD. The managing director effectively controlled the PPL organisation, whereas the chairman (secretary of the ministry) only chaired its board meetings.

Jacob was the first managing director of PPL. Before the completion of the first phase of the PPL project, Jacob suddenly decided to leave PPL and settle in the USA. This created a vacuum in that post for a few months. The company's administration was temporarily held by Financial Adviser Bhattacharjee.

As mentioned earlier, P.N. Arunachalam (PNA) joined as the second managing director of PPL on September 1, 1986. By October 1986, he had reviewed the status of Phase I of the PPL project. After review, he declared the first phase of the project commissioned. Work for Phase II was then initiated. This plan was a fully restructured one and was different from what Jacob had proposed earlier. The second phase of work was stated with new zeal.

On September 2, 1986, Arunachalam had a long meeting with me. He discussed the marketing setup of Madras Fertilisers Ltd. (MFL), where he was previously serving as the general manager of technical and production. Like me, he had also started his career in the fertiliser industry at FCI Nangal. Both PNA and I jelled well in PPL. Our relationship over the years was more like friends than a boss and subordinate. I apprised PNA of the then-marketing setup of PPL that I had reshaped over the last three months. I showed him the note of my future plan for PPL marketing. This I had earlier prepared for the PPL Board and was awaiting inclusion in its meeting agenda.

The note suggested that an effective marketing strategy was needed for the biggest producer of DAP in India. PNA agreed with my note. He said that in the coming fortnight, he would call his first board meeting to vet my proposal.

As per the suggestion of the PNA, I discussed the note with Nauru's two board members, Bhagwan Singh (BS) and Kartar Singh Bhalla (KSB). PNA had a prior discussion on this note with the Secretary of the Fertiliser Ministry, P.B. Krishnaswami. The board meeting was fixed for the afternoon of September 18, 1986. For all board meetings, Arunachalam had selected me (GM, Marketing) and A K Bhattacharjee (Financial Adviser, or FA) as permanent invitees to the board after consent from other members. From the GOI side, there were two board members besides PNA. They were the Joint Secretary (Administration) K.A. Shivaram Krishnan (KASK) and Joint Secretary (Finance) R. Srinivasan (RS) of the Fertiliser Ministry.

In the BM of the 18th, there was only one agenda item: approval of the marketing setup of PPL. The paper for the meeting was circulated to all board members seven days before. However, with the permission of the PNA, I had already met both the Nauru directors before the meeting for the smooth passage of the agenda. I met BS and KSB at the Vasant Vihar house of BS on September 12. I explained in detail my proposal for the marketing setup. They agreed to support the proposal. Thus, the proposal was put on the board's agenda without any modification. PNA was happy to receive this news.

The board meeting started sharply at 10 a.m. PNA asked the chairman and board members for permission to allow me to explain important aspects of the agenda item. Permission was granted. I explained to the members of the board the salient features. The explanations were made through a Microsoft PowerPoint presentation. The explanation and description of the agenda, item by item, took more than an hour. For the queries made by the chairman and the board members, I effectively answered and cleared their doubts. The board passed the agenda item unanimously without any modification.

Some of the highlights of the board's sanction were as follows:

1. Strength of marketing personnel pegged at 200 with a grade-wise breakup;
2. iCreation and setup of 10 regional offices in its all-India marketing area;
3. Dealing in imported fertilisers;
4. Hiring and setting up of godowns and handling agents;
5. Administrative and financial powers of the GM (Marketing) along with the power to delegate; and, finally,
6. Power to independently prepare the annual marketing budget.

After getting the approval of the board on September 18, 1986, I formulated the plan of immediate action for the next two months.

The recruitment of the minimum number of required staff at all levels was completed by the end of October 1986. Formalities for hiring buildings for regional offices in Chandigarh, Agra, Lucknow, Patna, Calcutta, Bhubaneswar, Bhopal, Bombay, and Hyderabad were also completed by November 10, 1986. Rao Tipperneni, who was recruited as a senior manager in PPL by me, took charge of the Hyderabad regional office. Similar postings were made for all the other regional offices. All the actions for the smooth operation of the marketing department were completed within three months of board sanction on December 18, 1986. On that date, I completed six months of my service at PPL and also successfully completed the probationary period as general manager.

My confirmation as the general manager called for a celebration by the family. I took Rashmi and the three children to a celebration dinner at the Taj Man Singh hotel in New Delhi. In a week's time, on December 25, the family came to the same hotel for Mona's 20th birthday and Christmas dinner. The latter half of December was a time of celebration for me and my family. During this time, I and Rashmi flew to Hyderabad and then to Tirupati to have the 'Darshan' of Lord Venkateshwara. Rao, RM Hyderabad, accompanied us to Tirupati.

On the work front, the regional offices and the sales officers posted in the field became fully operational. Expanded dealer networks, new field godowns, and handling agents completed the marketing infrastructure in all the regions. The entire DAP production of the PPL plant up until December 1986 was completely sold out. It generated healthy cash flow for PPL for the first time. The board recorded its appreciation for my work. A letter of appreciation was issued by the managing director. Even the chairman, Krishnaswami (Secretary of the Ministry), personally congratulated me at the board meeting. The entire marketing wing celebrated the occasion.

I was not satisfied with these laurels. The PPL factory was producing only 30% of its capacity of 7,20,000 MT of DAP, and the annual production was around 2.4 lakh MT. I requested that PNA get sanction from the ministry to handle and sell imported fertilisers (DAP and urea). Accordingly, he moved the ministry. In my subsequent follow-up, approval from the Ministry was obtained.

During this time, I developed a friendship with U.S. Jha, a railway traffic official on deputation to the Fertiliser Ministry. He was in the post of Director (Movement). Jha and his family became our family friends. On many occasions, both families had their dinner together at famous restaurants in seven-star hotels in New Delhi. Jha controlled fertiliser movements in the country and was also the nodal officer who made the allotment of imported fertilisers by assigning ports for their imports.

Sometime in the early part of 1987, PPL's first shipment of imported DAP was assigned for discharge at Paradeep Port. PPL Plant had its own exclusive mechanised berth. The berth was connected by a two-and-a-half-kilometre-long covered automatic conveyor belt system. It connected with huge silos of the plant. The discharges from the allotted ship were extremely easy and economical. The cargo of 10,000 MT of imported DAP was dispatched from PPL silo through five jumbo rakes to field godowns. The field staff were already tuned for the operation. All the material was sold in a month's time, with a net profit of Rs. 15 lakhs for PPL. This also raised the confidence of the dealer network for continuous future supplies.

With the above success, PPL was allowed to operate in the ports of Gujrat, Andhra Pradesh, and West Bengal (Haldia). Port operation and handling of imported fertilisers became a permanent and important activity of the marketing department of PPL. To some extent, this mitigated the financial problems of PPL that arose due to its factory production not reaching the expected level of capacity utilisation. PNA congratulated me on this achievement and hinted that I was surely going to take over PPL from him after his retirement in 1989. This statement of MD became prophetic; none were happier than boss Arunachalam when it actually happened later.

PNA was a widower when he joined PPL in 1986. In the beginning of 1987, he married a Bengali lady who was the widow of a senior IAF officer. Theirs was a registered marriage. The lady had a beautiful and pleasing personality. She became a good friend of Rashmi. Once, both families visited Khajuraho together. This had happened after me and Arunachalam addressed a meeting of PPL dealers in Bhopal. The meeting was arranged by the regional manager of Bhopal in late 1987. The visit of both families to Khajuraho developed a strong personal bond between PNA and me. Together, we ensured an enhanced rate of growth for PPL in all spheres of the economic activities of the company. We made it an important fertiliser company in the country.

The year 1988 was a period of consolidation for PPL's marketing activities. Its own products as well as the imported products were marketed all over India, except in the states of Karnataka, Tamil Nadu, Kerala, and the Union territories of Pondicherry and Goa. All products were packed in HDPE 50-kg bags with the PPL logo.

During the financial year 1986–87, after my joining PPL in late June 1986, the company attained sales of over 2.4 lakh MT of its own DAP and 0.6 lakh MT of imported fertilisers. The sales were of urea (1.5 lakh MT) and DAP (3 lakh MT). The total sales turnover was around Rs. 477 crore. It provided a net income of around Rs. 40 crore to neutralise the loss due to the low capacity utilisation of its plant. Similarly, during the financial year 1987–1988, I budgeted a sale of around 3 lakh metric tonnes of my own factory's estimated production besides the handling and sale of imported DAP of 1 lakh MT. This sale was supplemented with an additional 1.7 lakh MT of imported urea. The projected cash flow was Rs. 690 crore. Thus, the marketing division budgeted a net contribution of Rs. 65 crore to PPL's kitty. It required some control over the marketing costs with a better logistical model. It also envisaged a cut in storage charges with better turnover of field godowns. These estimates were fully realised. The marketing division of PPL exceeded the projected net contribution of rupees sixty crores by five crores more. It minimised PPLs over all losses due to a dip in the achievement of the factory production target.

On the home front, in 1988, the eldest daughter Mona graduated from LSR (Delhi University) and was selected for admission to M.A. (History) at JNU.

The second daughter, Dimpy, was going to pass her examination in class IX, and our son, Dev, was in class V at Frank Anthony School. During November of 1989, I took my entire family on a holiday outing to Jaipur.

The family made Jaipur their base and visited nearby tourist attractions like famous old forts like Amer Fort, Nahagarh Fort, and Jaigarh Fort. The family also enjoyed the visit to Pink Palace. Beautiful water bodies like Man Sagar Lake, Chandlai Lake, Ramgarh Lake, and Sagar Lake were wonderful sights. It was a thoroughly enjoyable holiday after a long time. The best part was that the children had the presence of both parents all the time. The children knew that it was well and truly impossible when their dad joined the office.

That year, I also became a member of the prestigious India Habitat Centre in New Delhi. Besides, I continued my membership in the Bhubaneswar Club, which enabled me to use the facilities of more than 140 affiliated clubs spread all over important cities across the country. Later, I enjoyed these privileges at Jeypore and Agra Clubs when my family and that of my brother-in-law visited these places together.

To lighten my burden of official work, I recruited, during 1988, a Deputy General Manager in the Marketing Division. The recruitment was done by a duly constituted selection committee approved by MD. I was the chairman of the selection committee. The other members of the committee were Joint Secretary Srinivasan, Dr. Mukaria of FCI, and PPL's FA Bhattacharjee.

Three people from PPL—Srivastava, Rao Tipperneni, and Raza—and three from outside applicants were called for interviews. I wanted Rao to be selected, but Dr. Mukaria (under the influence of Srivastava) opposed it, citing the reason that Rao needed to wait for one more year as per the specification of the appointment. He further said that it was better to take one from another organisation.

That's how Gurdial Singh (GS) of IFFCO was selected as the DGM. I never forgot the politics played by Srivastava, and I transferred him to Chandigarh. For Raza, who was a colleague of GS in IFFCO, I recommended his promotion to DGM scale under the plant's quota. MD approved my recommendation. D. Panigrahi, the GM of the PPL plant at Paradeep, had just retired. Raza, on my recommendation to PNA, was transferred from marketing in Delhi to Paradeep. He headed the establishment of the plant as DGM in charge.

During the year 1988, a general manager for personnel and administration (GM, P&A) was recruited. The person selected was A.I. Bunnet (AB). He came from another PSU in the power sector. AB became a good friend of mine. Bunnet was a happy-go-lucky person. He was capable of handling the complex personnel and union problems of PPL. PNA was fully dependent on his advice, particularly that of the PPL's Labour Union. The President of the Union was Prabhat Samantray (PS). He was a member of the Rajya Sabha from the ruling Biju Janata Dal (BJD) of Orissa. He belonged to Paradeep and was a very shrewd, soft-spoken politician. He was also considered a favourite of Chief Minister Biju Patnaik.

The year 1989 was a drought year in India. It threw up a lot of challenges for all fertiliser marketers due to dips in sales and offtakes. I had experience with the difficulties faced in marketing fertilisers during the previous drought year of 1976 in India. At that time, I was the regional manager of HFC in Bhubaneswar.

That experience came in handy for me to tackle the situation in 1989. I provided a lot of attractive packages for the dealership network, including an extended credit period that was to be passed on to the client farmers. I also asked my field officers to focus more on the irrigated areas to boost their sales efforts. Such planning produced the desired results. I was delighted to note that my previous experience could successfully tackle the prevailing situation of drought.

The volume of sales of PPL for the drought year 1989–90 equaled that of the previous normal year for indigenous as well as imported fertilisers. It indicated the sale of 3.5 lakh MT of the factory's own DAP along with 1.5 lakh MT of imported DAP plus 1.0 lakh MT of imported urea. During the majority of the year, I had to extensively tour all the states to encourage the regional staff as well as the port operation staff. This had given the desired result of a sales turnover of Rs. 729 crore.

During the year 1989, Mona creditably passed her M.A. examination from JNU. She had enrolled for her M.Phil. there. She appeared at the Civil Services Examination next year. Dimpy had passed her ICSC Board exam for class X creditably. She topped the list of her school batchmates. She had joined the arts stream in class XI at the same Frank Anthony School. Dev had gone to class VII at that school. Dimpy demanded and got a walkman from me for passing the board examination with a good percentage of marks.

That year, I was nominated to attend a six-week management course in the USA. It was conducted by the International Fertiliser Development Centre (IFDC) at Muscle Sholas. The place was in Alabama, USA. I was to attend the course from August 14th, 1989. Accordingly, I drew up the work schedule for DGM Gurdial Singh for three months to effectively control and supervise the marketing activity. Since he was new to the organisation, I advised him to consult Raza if a necessity arose.

I left for the USA on August 4. My flight, both onward and return, was booked in such a way that while going, I could stop in Bangkok for two days, in Tokyo for two days, and in Hawaii for four days. While returning, I could spend one day in New York and three days in London. The idea was to avail the best benefits from the airlines for free stays in five-star hotels at the selected places at airline cost.

I arrived in Bangkok from Delhi on August 5 with Lufthansa Airlines. After visiting all its tourist spots in two days, I left for Tokyo on the seventh morning with Japan Airlines. Most of my two-day stay there was spent visiting tourist locations in and around Tokyo. In the evening of August 9, I left Tokyo for Hawaii with Delta Airlines and reached there on August 10. My emigration check-up for the US was done in Hawaii. The stay in Hawaii was really exhilarating due to its scenic beauty and many enchanting spots on the island.

After enjoying a two-day stay there, I finally flew down to Muscle Sholas in Alabama. I arrived there a day in advance for the beginning of the course. The course director was Dr. Gulati. He was an American Indian. He received me, and I was put in the IFDC guesthouse on the campus of the institution. The guesthouse also had thirty other coursemates from different countries. They were all senior executives of fertiliser companies, belonging to twenty different companies in Asia, Africa, and Europe. All had their introductions at the first night's dinner, arranged by IFDC. The course started on August 14 at the IFDC Training Centre. At the opening session, the Managing Director of IFDC addressed the participants. After the address, Dr. Gulati briefly described the programme schedule.

The training was very interesting. Besides the classroom lectures, there were field visits to different fertiliser factories and establishments in the U.S.A. The logistical arrangements for the movement of fertilisers through riverine and sea ports were a unique experience. For this experience, a number of tours were arranged. The tours were mostly on Saturdays and Sundays. Luxury buses that carried all course participants and Dr. Gulati for these trips were arranged by IFDC.

The city of Muscle Sholas (MS), a part of Alabama, is also an interesting tourist destination. It is on the bank of the Tennessee River, close to the Wilson Dam on that river. The dam has large wharves to navigate big cargo boats across the river to industrial cities. The place has a world-class fishing centre, hiking and biking tracks, beautiful golf courses, picnic spots, and the famous River Heritage Park. It is the place of birth for many famous Americans, including Helen Keller.

I remembered three trips during the training period, which were very interesting. One was to the beautiful city of Mandeville, Louisiana. It is a lovable tourist spot that is around 600 kilometres away from MS. It took the team six hours to reach there. Starting from MS at 6:30 a.m. after breakfast on a Saturday, we had our lunch at Mandeville and visited all the local tourist spots. We returned to MS for dinner. The second visit was to Houston. The place was around 1100 kilometres from Muscle Sholas. For that visit, we left after an early breakfast around 6:30 a.m. A packed lunch was carried for everyone. We reached the hotel around 5:30 p.m. The next morning, we visited the famous Museum of Natural Sciences and other important spots. After that, the team returned to the IFDC guesthouse. The third trip was to Florida for three days. The journey was by flight, and the accommodation was booked by IFDC at the Florida Disney Land hotel. It was a remarkable visit, and I immensely liked the Disney Land panorama.

Another very interesting thing happened during my stay at Muscle Sholas. I was invited to address the business management students at Alabama University. I accepted the invitation and addressed the students for an hour and a half. Many interesting questions regarding the running and management of Indian companies were raised by the students during the interactive session. I enlightened them on all aspects of the management of Indian companies. They were also informed about the way the industries functioned under the licence raj of the Indian administration. The visit to Alabama University was memorable. The Dean of the Faculty of Management thanked me for the lecture and interaction with the students. He said that my whole programme has been recorded for their faculty's news magazine. Before I left the campus, I was introduced again to the whole faculty before sharing the refreshment. I was very impressed by the curiosity of the American students and their uninhibited cross-examination during the lecture.

After the end of the training, certificates were given by IFDC on September 22, 1989. The participants departed for their home countries. I first flew to New York by Delta Airlines and stayed for a day there to purchase gift items for Rashmi, Mona, Dimpy, and Dev. The next day, i.e., on the 28th, I boarded the BOAC flight for Gatwick. As scheduled, I stayed in London for three days to visit some friends and acquaintances at Cambridge and Oxford. I flew back on a BOAC flight to New Delhi from Heathrow Airport on September 28, 1989. After reaching Delhi, my immigration and customs clearance was done quickly. It was prearranged by the administration manager of PPL. I reached home around 9 a.m. on September 29, 1989. The family warmly received me.

I rested the whole day and shared the pleasure of distributing the gifts to my family members. The gifts were liked by each of them. I shared the delicious launch, prepared by Rashmi. In the evening, we went out to the India Habitat Centre at Lodhi Road. The family had dinner there. On the 30th, we visited the families of Rashmi's brother and that of my sister. Both families were handed their gifts.

On October 1, 1989, I attended the office and met PNA. I handed him his gift, brought from the USA. I narrated my experience of almost a month in the USA. The letter that Jacob Engineers of California sent through me was handed over to PNA. This letter was given during my visit to their plant. PNA read the letter and said that it was an invitation for him to go to their main office in the USA with Bhattacharjee (FA of PPL). Both were needed for finalising the work order for retrofitting the phosphoric acid plant at PPL. This plant was set up earlier by them. Bhattacharjee was called, and, after due discussion, the PNA decided to go to the US with the FA for ten days on October 12. PNA said that, during his and the FA's absence, I was to hold the charge of MD, PPL, for regular day-to-day tasks. If needed, I could seek his advice over the phone or by fax on any major issues.

Returning to my chamber in Hemkunt Tower, I called DGM Gurdial Singh. I wanted to review the situation regarding marketing-related issues that occurred during my absence for a month. After carefully analysing the facts given by Gurdial, I pointed out the negative trends in sales in some of the regions. I immediately faxed advisories to concerned RMs for the remedial measures that were to be taken immediately. The date for the next monthly review meeting of RMs was set for October 10, and I advised Gurdial to send an intimation to all the RMs. After talking with S.O. (Coordination) Raperla, I contacted Raza at the factory and told him to prepare a note that can set the modalities for finding ways and means to market gypsum. This was a by-product of the phosphoric acid plant that was discharged into the gypsum pond. Since the product was highly coercive for the soil and water, it had to be emptied from the pond and disposed of or sold to make space for the day-to-day operation of the phosphoric acid plant.

I learned that during my absence, Gurdial could not collect over Rs. 50 crore of government subsidy for PPL. This had already set the cash crunch for the operation of PPL. Gurdial told me that, in spite of his several visits to the Subsidy Disbursement Section of the Fertiliser Ministry, they had not entertained his pleas to release the subsidy. I immediately telephoned the Joint Secretary (JS), who controlled the subsidy section. I requested that he release this subsidy in full as the company was facing a severe cash crunch. The JS had to take immediate action for the release of subsidies. He knew well that any delay would make me complain to the secretary of the ministry. He knew that the secretary would pull him up. The subsidy check for Rs. 150 crore was released the next day.

At the RM's meeting on October 10, I reviewed each region's performance. I set targets for sales in each region during the quarter ending December 1989. Separate targets were set for PPL's own production as well as the estimated volume of imported urea and DAP that was likely to be made available. While fixing these targets, I kept in mind the targeted volume of sales during the financial year 1989–90. The value of total sales was estimated to be over Rs. 725 crore for the set target.

I appreciated the performance of the Hyderabad, Bhubaneswar, and Chandigarh regions. The RMs of the Calcutta, Bhopal, Lucknow, and Agra regions were advised to pull up their socks and be more active and effective. At the meeting, I declared that the Bombay regional office would start functioning in October and Bhubaneswar RM, P. Rautray, would head that region. I also mentioned that Rao (RM of Hyderabad) had resigned to join as DGM (Marketing) of Godavari Fertilisers, whose plant was in Kakinada. Surya Kumar was named as Rao's successor. He was to take over the charge from Rao by the end of October. Hyderabad was an important region where marketing faced tough competition from Coromandel fertilisers as well as Godavari fertilizers. Surya Kumar, a capable local officer, was a good find. He was also recommended to me by Rao.

As per the earlier schedule, PNA and AB left for the USA for a fortnight on the 12th of October. From that day on, I also looked after the function of MD. The secretary to the MD used to bring all mail to my office during the PNA's absence. On each of the communications of a routine nature, I used to pass orders immediately, and the secretary was told to keep these orders separately in a new folder for PNA's information. On urgent issues, I used to talk with the PNA and carry out his instructions. PNA returned on the 28th of October. On Monday, October 30, 1989, he came to the office, and I apprised him fully of all events that took place during his absence. He was happy to note that there was no pending action that required his immediate attention. He was pleased with my good handling of PPL during his absence for a fortnight.

The production target of 3,50,000 MT of DAP at the plant, with a capacity utilisation of 49%, was achieved during that year. In the last quarter, a list of probable customers and users of gypsum was prepared. The marketing wing could make the beginning of the first dispatch and sale of some quantity of gypsum. But the diluted phosphoric acid residuals in the product posed new challenges for its wider use in agriculture, industry (cement), and the making of gypsum boards. It was decided to form an R&D wing in PPL to provide solutions. The formation was planned after the commissioning of the second phase of the PPL plant and before the retrofitting of the phosphoric acid plant.

The estimated time was in the year 1991 or in a subsequent period. Thus, marketing efforts for the sale of gypsum were kept in abeyance for a long period of time. Later, I learned that, after the privatisation of PPL, this objective was pursued with success.

In November 1989, I was praised by the Dean of JNU for my inspiring lecture. On invitation, I spoke at the UNESCO-JNU training workshop for live science.

In the month of February 1990, the ministry selected me to carry out a short-term assignment for a World Bank (WB) project. It was regarding the assessment of funds required for modernising the phosphate mines in Jordan. At that time, PPL was also importing rock phosphate from Jordan for the production of phosphoric acid. Rock phosphate was used as one of the raw materials in the production of DAP.

I was required to visit all such mines in Jordan. The collection and compilation of relevant data were needed for the project report for WB. The issue was also to be discussed with the holding company of the Jordan government, Jordan Phosphates Ltd. (JPL). The visit and discussions were to be completed in ten days' time. An initial report for financing the project was prepared after returning from Jordan. This report was submitted on March 10, 1990. Before leaving for Jordan, I collected relevant information about the loan and the related mines from the Delhi office of the World Bank.

My journey to Jordan was undertaken on February 5. A manager of JPL, who was sent from Amman to Delhi, accompanied me. We flew to Aman on a Jordan Airways flight from New Delhi. In the afternoon of the 6th, I met the CEO of JPL. The chief explained to me the details of the task and said that arrangements for my visit to the selected seven mines had been made. I started in the afternoon with the JPL manager, who had accompanied me from Delhi. The journey was undertaken by road in a luxurious Mercedes Sedan.

After the visit to the seven mines, details of each mine's required inventory of modern machinery were collected, along with various other data and operational facts about the mines. The final discussion at JPL headquarters was done by me on February 16, 1990. After collecting further relevant data from the CEO of JPL, I left Amman in the evening for New Delhi. I reached home around 2 a.m. I already had dinner on the flight. Being extremely tired, I went to bed to rest and sleep.

Since it was a Saturday, I could have a proper rest for two days before joining the office on February 19, 1990. My visit to Jordan exposed me to many tourist places like Wadi Rum, the Black Sea, Ajiona Castle, Karuk Castle, Dana Nature Reserve, etc. I narrated all about these places to Rashmi and the children. A Jordanian robe and fancy sandals that JPL had gifted for Rashmi were liked by her.

A.P. Srivastava, RM of Chandigarh, was contacted on Monday morning. He was told to come to Delhi on a five-day trip. After his arrival on the 20th morning, I provided him with the data and information that had been collected during my Jordan visit. Srivastava was asked to analyse these data and information and prepare a draft report for my perusal. I asked him to sit with DGM Gurdial and prepare the draft report by February 23, 1990. After that, I met PNA and gave him information about my Jordan visit.

The submitted draft report of Gurdial and Srivastava was discussed by me with both. The final report was prepared and submitted by me to the Ministry on March 10, 1990, five days before the deadline. I forgot about this work until the next contact by the World Bank in July 1990. The World Bank informed me at that time that they had enrolled me as a consultant on their active roster. Subsequent action on this topic was scripted later in July 1991.

In 1990, the All India Management Association (AIMA) made me a member. After three years, AIMA conferred on me the life membership with the tagged title of LMIMA. This was a rare privilege. Only a few Indian managers were awarded this title for exemplary work in the field of management.

In late 1989, I purchased my own flat at Tara Group Housing Society. The flat belonged to a South Indian gentleman. He got this flat from his father-in-law. The FIL was a previous cabinet minister in the Petroleum Ministry of the GOI. The flat required modification. This was completed in three months' time. My family and I moved to our own flat by the end of March 1990.

The working results of the marketing division for the financial year 1989–90 were excellent. It motivated the marketing staff at all levels. Many were rewarded with promotions to the next grade. This followed the PPL Board's unanimous recorded praise for me and all my staff for the good results for the period 1989–90.

The beginning of the financial year 1990–91 had many challenges. The sales and cash flow growth rate of 10% per year were targeted for achievement. Improvements in the logistical model for indigenous as well as imported products were conceptualised for better cost control in movement and storage. More responsibility and authority were given to all the RMs as well as other field officers.

Much of my time during January 1990 was spent preparing a marketing manual. This manual was meant to guide the field officers of PPL at all levels. It covered officers at base level, RMs, DGMs, and the officers and managers of the finance wing in the marketing division. This manual got the approval of the PPL Board in its February 1990 meeting. With this approval, the road to meeting all the challenges of 1990 became smooth. The set sales and financial targets of 1990 were fully met.

During the period of 1990–91, the sales volume achieved a growth of around five percent. The actual volume of sales was 4 lakh MT of own DAP, 1 lakh MT of imported DAP, and 48 thousand MT of imported urea. It registered a cash flow of over Rs. 788 crore and a net contribution of over Rs. 78 crore. It could lower the losses of PPL that arose out of the delayed commissioning of phase II and the dip in its capacity utilisation. Although the capacity utilisation of the plant had increased during the subject financial year, it still stood at only 55% of the rated capacity. Repeating the fact, it was noted that the financial losses of PPL were due to poor capacity utilisation and delayed commissioning of its phase II operation.

To spend full time with my near and dear ones, I took a fortnight's leave along with LTC in early June 1990. We had planned to spend the holidays in Bombay, Goa, Bangalore, and Mysore. The family mostly took flights to major cities and enjoyed five-star hotel hospitality at those places of stay. Our visit to all the tourist and historical spots around those places gave immense joy to Rashmi and her children. The boat ride in the Arabian Sea from the Gateway of India to visit the Elephanta caves was a new experience. Breaking waves on the sea at Goa was an experience par excellence for the children. The drive from Bangalore to Mysore, enriched with the relics and monuments of Tipu Sultan, became a true treasure in remembrance of that visit. In Mysore, we stayed a night in a hotel. However, we also visited the house of Bini, whose husband Junu was employed by an IT company.

In July 1990, the World Bank assigned me a visit to Amman for five days. It was to discuss certain more issues with JPL for their applied loan for modernization of the rock phosphate mines. WB intended the visit on the basis of my earlier submitted report. After the visit and due discussion with the CEO of JPL, I submitted the final report to WB by July 25, 1990. By December 1990, only the World Bank had released a significant portion of the funds to JPL. Simultaneously, the WB warned that all the machinery for mine modernization would have to be in place by the end of August 1991. For the release of the last installment of their loan funds, I was to examine the actual position of previous fund utilisation and then recommend the right steps. I again visited Jordan in July 1991 as the World Bank's consultant and inspected the installation and placement of new machinery before certifying the fund release.

Daughter Mona cleared the UPSC Civil Service Examination in 1990. She qualified for the preliminary and final examinations. She was called for the final interview. She was selected for the Indian Revenue Service (income tax) and was at the top of that list of IRS recruits for that year. Her joining, training, and posting were to begin in the year 1991. During that time, her younger sister Dimpy passed her I.Sc. board examination (class XII) with a high percentage of marks. She joined Lady Shriram College (LSR) for her graduation in psychology (Hons.). Their brother Dev had been promoted to class IX at Frank Anthony School. Both daughters remained alumni of LSR. All three children had also completed their schooling at the Frank Anthony School of New Delhi.

The performance of PPL's Marketing Division continued to be excellent. It surpassed the previous year's performance and again received the board's appreciation for the result of 1990–91. The year 1990 saw the removal of Financial Advisor Bhattacharjee by the board due to his indulgence in unfair practices. He had to face legal prosecution for his act.

During the last part of 1990, action had already been initiated to move PPL's head office to Bhubaneswar. It was done under the pressure of the Chief Minister of Odisha. The hired building took almost three months' time to get ready for final occupancy in January 1991. The building was owned by Orissa State Handloom Warehousing Corporation (OSHWC). It had a basement plus four floors. The building was in a prominent area. It was closer to the Secretariat of the Odisha government and other important offices of the state and central governments. PPL hired the top three floors at a monthly rental of Rs. 6 lakh.

Earlier, Nauru members of the PPL Board were opposed to the purchase of the said building. It was a wrong decision by them. In less than seven years, the total rent payment for the hired space could neutralise the demanded purchase price of seven crores for the entire building! The current value of that building stands at almost seventy-five crores!

The hired spaces at Nehru Place in New Delhi were retained as PPL's New Delhi office. This status continued as long as the company remained in the domain of a PSU of the central government.

The majority of PPL personnel serving in the Delhi office were transferred to Bhubaneswar at the beginning of 1991. A building was hired at Forest Park in Bhubaneswar for the MD's residence. The other two big buildings at Shaheed Nagar were hired as PPL guest houses for senior and junior personnel. I and Bunnet used the senior guest house for our stay during our Bhubaneswar operation.

Both did not move to Bhubaneswar due to family obligations. Their families stayed at their own flats at Tara Apartments in Alaknanda, New Delhi, and at an apartment of the Patparganj Housing Society of Delhi. During our stay at the Bhubaneswar guest house, me and Bunnet used to play table tennis in the evenings before going for our dinner at the Swasti Hotel. I often wondered at the capacity of Bunnet to take three or more Patiala pegs of whisky during dinner; he still retained his normal behaviour.

In September 1991, Mona was to join her initial training with some IPS batchmates at the Hyderabad Police Academy. Me and Rashmi took her to Hyderabad from Delhi by morning flight. It was a day earlier than the beginning of her training. All three stayed for the night at the Krishna Oberoi Hotel in Banjara Hills, Hyderabad. The next morning, Mona was dropped off at the academy, and the parents left for Tirupati to have the darshan of Lord Venkateshwara.

We stayed at a cottage in Tirumala, arranged by Cadappa MP Jhansi Laxmi. She had arrived there by earlier arrangement. She had known me since my days in Hyderabad at the Cement Corporation of India. Her son was a transporter of CCI cement from the Yeraguntula plant. Courtesy of this MP, who was also a trustee of the Tirumala Board, Rashmi and I had the darshan of the Lord at the inner sanctum of the temple. It was good of Jhansi Laxmi to accompany us for this darshan. The next day, we flew out from Tirupati to New Delhi via Hyderabad. The darshan of Lord Venkateshwara brought solace; both felt relieved of all their tension.

The first quarter of 1991 passed amidst the chaos of the Delhi-Bhubaneswar movement of PPL staff of all categories. The magnitude of the shifting upset lagged many development plans of the company by a few months. Some of these also couldn't be initiated.

The first board meeting of PPL at Bhubaneswar was held on January 25, 1991, in the board room of the new office. All board members, except the President of Nauru, attended the meeting. The list of attendee directors of the PPL Board indicated: P.B. Krishnaswami, Secretary Fertiliser Ministry; Bhagwan Singh, Retd. ICS and Former Ambassador to Fiji; K.S. Bhalla, Consul General of Nauru; P.N. Arunachalam, MD PPL; K.A. Shivramkrisnan, Jt. Secretary of Fertiliser Ministry; and R Srinivasan, Jt. Secretary of Fertiliser Ministry.

The board room was adjacent to the Chamber of MD on the third floor. This floor also had the chambers of GM Marketing, GM P&A, and GM Project. The floor also accommodated PAs of three GMs as well as the cabin for PS to MD and MD's secretariat. The second floor had officers and staff of corporate finance, P&A officers, and project engineers. Marketing officers of GMM also operated from this floor. The first floor was partitioned into two sections. One section had the office and staff of the Bhubaneswar regional manager, and the other accommodated other corporate staff. After the board meeting, all board members left for Delhi. PNA, along with his wife, left for Delhi the next day.

On January 28, 1991, I conducted the monthly RM's meeting—the first in Odisha. The meeting was actually held at a famous resort on Puri Beach. For this meeting, I had obtained permission from the PNA to call all field RMs with their family members. This was a very novel idea. For no other PSU, such a thing ever happened earlier. It was meant as an incentive for managers of the marketing division.

All, including the marketing finance manager and his family, were booked for their stay at Puri in a good resort. The stay was for three days at the company's expense. My family and that of Gurdial also arrived from New Delhi. It was an excellent get-together for the families of the marketing fraternity. In the evenings of the first and second nights, an open-air programme of music and dance was arranged for the entertainment of the families. Children enjoyed the sea, the sand, and the entertainment. The food was excellent, and the stay was comfortable. It was a modest courtesy that the company extended to the families of its senior marketing personnel. The families and all the attending personnel remembered the occasion for a long time. All of them thanked their boss and his family from the core of their hearts.

PNA's tenure as MD was till the end of May 1991. Before his tenure ended, he planned a visit to the US for a month, from April 13th to May 12th, 1991. He and his wife were to meet his daughters and their families settled in the US. Before his departure, he had obtained permission from the board and the chairman to issue an office order. This order allowed me to act as MD of PPL during his absence. This order was issued on April 12, 1991.

On March 7, 1991, the Public Enterprises Selection Board (PESB) notified the public about the interview of three candidates for the post of PPL's Managing Director. These three were: i) I, General Manager of PPL; ii) R. Gupta, CMD of Fertiliser Corporation; and iii) U.S. Awasthi, CMD of Pyrites & Phosphates Ltd. This event indicated that PNA was not getting any extensions and was to retire by May 31, 1991. It meant that 17 days after returning from leave, he was to finally retire.

On March 13, 1991, I received a letter from PESB asking me to appear for an interview for the post of PPL MD on March 18 at 10 a.m. The interview was in the chamber of PESB Chairman Mr. P.H. Vaishnava. I was selected for this interview. Although PESB and the Department of Personnel of the GOI did not take much time to get Cabinet approval for this selection, the file got stuck in the office of Devi Lal. At that time, he was the Deputy PM as well as the fertiliser minister in the Cabinet of Prime Minister Chandra Shekhar.

When I made an inquiry at Dy. PM Devi Lal's office, I was directed to meet his private secretary, who happened to be his grandson. When I met this PS, I was asked to pay a substantial amount of cash for the release of the appointment file. It surely meant illegal gratification or payment of a bribe for the release of said file. I flatly refused to yield to this pressure. My well-wishers carried this message to the Odia MP of Kalahandi, Shree Bhakta Charan Das. At that time, Shree Das was also the Minister of State for Railways in Chandrasekhar's Cabinet. He was close to the PM. He ensured that the file was immediately released from Devi Lal's office for notification. No further approval was necessary for notification, as it already had the approval of the Cabinet Committee for the appointment. The biggest political hurdle had to be tackled with greater political acumen.

Finally, the order was issued on May 6, 1991. I was to take over the charge as Managing Director of PPL on June 1, 1991. The incumbent PNA was superannuating on 31.5.1991. When PNA joined the office on May 1, he called me to his chamber and congratulated me. He told me that, since he was retiring at the end of the month, I needed to be with him till that date. I would be apprised of all earlier confidential and important decisions. Also, the decisions taken by PNA for the remaining period of the fortnight should be made with my knowledge and consent. I thanked Arunachalam. I told him that it was a real pleasure to work under him. Further, his association with me I will always cherish more as a friend and guide than as a boss.

Over the ensuing week, grand farewell parties were arranged for Arunachalam. At the Bhubaneswar corporate office, it was on May 21st, and at the PPL plant site, it was on May 23rd. The final one was in New Delhi on May 30 at the Taj Mansingh Banquet Hall. At the New Delhi farewell, the chairman and all the board members participated. The board members also welcomed me as the new MD. In all the farewell parties, Rashmi was present to give company to Mrs. Arunachalam. Mrs. and Mr. Arunachalam bade goodbye to PPL on May 31, 1991. They left for their residence in Chennai.

A new era of PPL began with my taking up its reign on June 1, 1991. According to the recommendations of PESB and the Department of Personnel, my period of appointment was to be from June 1, 1991, to March 31, 1995, coinciding with the completion of age 60 as per norms for CEOs of central PSUs. The retirement date was subsequently changed to March 31, 1993. The new date coincided with the day when I turned 58. However, this was clearly a violation of the norms applicable to the retirement age of the board members, which was the completion of age 60 for Central PSUs. The retirement age of 58, as was applicable for PPL employees, was not legally applicable for a member of the PPL Board.

This was unfortunately done due to the review of the new Prime Minister, Narsimha Rao. He reviewed the appointments of all chief executives of Central PSUs who were positioned during the period of his predecessor, Chandrasekhar. The new PM did this review after taking office in June 1991. His decision was wrong. The new PM overlooked the previous Cabinet approval that could not be changed by his personal whim or bias. A fresh Cabinet approval was needed, which he had not taken. On the advice of Secretary P.B. Krishnaswamy, I did not contest the decision of the new PM. I thought it prudent not to contest the decision as the fertiliser portfolio was also with the PM. The contest could have created problems for me as well as for the company I headed.

As the managing director, I had already set my priorities for improving the financial health of PPL. I found that the company made huge payments in foreign exchange. It was towards the cost of the imported raw materials for the production of DAP. Its annual requirement for the import of liquid ammonia, phosphoric acid, and rock phosphates was almost 1.5 million tons. Liquid ammonia imports were around 3 lakh MT, while those of phosphoric acid and rock phosphates were 5 lakh MT and 7 lakh MT, respectively. I had also learned that the exporters of these materials from the US, Africa, and Middle East countries used to jack up the material cost by 15 US dollars per MT. This increase formed part of the commission of 22.5 million US dollars per year. It was paid into the foreign accounts of the previous chiefs of PPL, who were comfortably settled in the USA.

Being an incorruptible, straight-forward man, I wanted to get rid of this unethical practice immediately. I called the representatives of the exporting companies. I firmly told them to stop the unethical practice and reduce immediately the price of their exports by 15 US dollars per MT. This single act saved PPL $22.5 million in its annual import bill. Thus, my first act saved PPL the annual recurring cost of 22.5 million dollars. In terms of rupees, the annual saving was nearly Rs. 79 crore, as the then rate of exchange was 35 rupees to 1 US dollar. I did not officially report this matter either to the Chairman or to the PPL Board. It would have been one of the biggest corporate scandals for PPL without any gain to the company from the past event. The matter would have also taken on a political tinge and, internationally, been adverse financial news for the country. Nauru certainly would not have remained quiet.

My next task was to make a list of items that required board approval. I consulted the chairman and called a board meeting in New Delhi on June 22, 1991. Many of the items on the agenda relate to the repair, modification, or replacement of some equipment at the plant. One of the agenda items related to the promotion of Gurdial as GM (Marketing) and Raza as GM (Operation).

The board accorded its approval to all the agenda items. The promotion orders for Gurdial and Raza were issued on June 23, 1991. Gurdial was posted at the Bhubaneswar corporate office, and Raza was posted at Paradeep Plant. After receiving their orders, they met and thanked me. I congratulated them and advised them to fulfil all tasks under their domain as targeted for the balance of the year. Specifically, Raza was told to enhance the pace of completing all pending work in the plant for the commissioning of Phase II. Gurdial was told to achieve a turnover of Rs 810 crore for the financial year 1991–92.

In July 1991, PMO advised me through the ministry to visit Jordan in early August. It was for the completion of my balance of the World Bank assignment from the previous year. I was to check the placement and operation of all new mining machinery purchased from the loan funds provided by the World Bank for the modernization of seven selected phosphate mines. The report was to be given to WB at the latest by August 15, 1991. I planned my three-day visit for August 3. I talked to the CEO of JPL, who confirmed that his officer would come to New Delhi and accompany me to Amman for a proposed visit.

When I was all set to leave by flight for Jordan on August 3, I received a telephone call from the Minister of State for Fertilisers (MOS) on August 1. The MOS told me to accompany him from New Delhi to Paradeep for his visit to the plant. I said that the GM operation at the Paradeep plant would accompany him from New Delhi for the proposed visit. The minister got annoyed and insisted on cancelling my foreign visit.

The MOS was not aware of the directive from the PMO for my visit to Jordan. This minister, as stated earlier, was a transport contractor for CCI during my Hyderabad days. He had previously taken favours from me. That was the reason his ego got hurt when I remained firm in my decision. On continued insistence from the Minister, I told him that my going to Jordan was as per the directives of the PMO. For the cancellation of my Jordan visit, the MOS should talk to the PMO. On hearing this, the MOS came to his senses. He told me to keep to my schedule. He agreed to go to Paradeep accompanied by the GM (operation). After that, the MOS never tampered with my work and remained cordial in his dealings with me in the days ahead. This incident became a wildly discussed topic in Shastri Bhavan, the office of the Fertiliser Ministry.

On the scheduled date, I reached Amman. Immediately, I took off for a visit to the seven mines of JPL. Accompanied by a JPL manager, I visited all concerned sites and verified the installations as well as the purchase orders for the new machines. I took copies of all related documents. Returning to New Delhi on the 7th of August 1991, I prepared the final report and submitted it by the 12th of August 1991. Later, I learned that WB accepted my report. It released the funds from the last installment to JPL. I received a letter from the CEO of Jordan Phosphates thanking me for the help. He also intimated me that, for supplies of rock phosphate from Jordan to PPL, there would always be a ten percent discount in their ruling price!

In August 1991, in a function of the Delhi Management Association (DMA), I was given the DMA-PEPSI award of 'Manager of the Year'. In the same month, I also became the Chairman of the Fertiliser Association of India, Eastern Zone. I was already a director on the board of FAI in New Delhi as of June 1991.

During the whole month of September, I concentrated on improving the plant operation at Paradeep. I made several visits to the plant. I discussed the rectification of the main boiler after personal verification of its recurring problems affecting production. The target set for its modification and repair was completed in ten days' time. Plant production has considerably increased.

With GM Raza, I discussed other issues affecting plant production. The problems of sulfuric acid, phosphoric acid, and granulation plants were discussed in detail with the senior managers who were heading the operation of these plants. I shared my ideas with them for improved operation of all these plants for better capacity utilisation. The engineers of the plant were astonished at my technical knowledge. In the future, I commanded their full respect, and they did their job according to my advice. I also discussed proper maintenance of all machines with the maintenance head. There was also discussion with the transportation manager and the loading contractor (Mahima Mishra) to improve the road and rail dispatches. I advised them to ensure a minimum stock in the silo at the end of each month. Every month, the position of stock in all inventories of the plant, including the raw materials and finished stock, was meticulously monitored by me.

Raza was told that, from next month onwards, the Review Meeting of Plant Operation would be taken by me on the first Tuesday of each month. The meeting would be held alternatively at the Bhubaneswar Corporate Office and the plant. The meeting will be attended by the GM (P&A), GM (Project), GM (M), GM (O), and all senior managers of various plants and departments of the PPL factory.

Such meetings started on a regular basis in September 1991. This continued without any break till the end of my term as MD. There were, in all, nineteen such monthly meetings. Proper minutes were recorded for each meeting. The minutes were circulated among all participants. They formed the basis for actions that were to be taken during the month. Actions taken were reviewed during the next meeting. This was extremely helpful for the better running and administration of the company during my stewardship. Such actions also expedited the efforts to complete the Phase II work. This had become one of my important priorities during the stewardship of PPL.

In September of 1991, I accepted the deputation of an IPS officer of IG's rank to join PPL. He became the first Chief Vigilance Officer of PPL. He was posted at the Bhubaneswar corporate office and reported directly to me. Although his position, as per deputation terms, matched that of a DGM, I granted him all the facilities and perks applicable to general managers. He was quite helpful to me in preventing any illegal activities by staff and officers of PPL. He belonged to Odisha, although he was an IPS officer in the J&K cadre. His father-in-law, Mr. Mathews, was the earlier chief secretary of Odisha. Mathews had married an Odia lady from Berhampur, Ganjam district.

I stayed at the official MD's bungalow in Bhubaneswar. However, my family stayed in New Delhi at our own flat at E-33, Tara Apartment. This was necessary as my daughter Dimpy and son Dev were studying in Delhi. However, I ensured that for almost ten days a month, I operated from my New Delhi office and also enjoyed the company of my family.

In October 1991, I had a four-day tour to Chandigarh and Himachal. On this tour, I took Rashmi, Dimpy, and Dev with me. At that time, Mona was away in Hyderabad, undergoing her training as a probationary IRS officer. Our outings in Chandigarh and Shimla covered visits to many scenic spots around Chandigarh and Shimla.

In the month of November 1991, I appointed, purely on an ad hoc basis, Mr. C.N. Garg, the retired CMD of Cement Corporation, as a consultant. He was retained to suggest, from time to time, ways and means for the better operation of all the plants. His first task was to prepare and recommend the staff strength of each plant for efficient and better operation. It was to encompass technical and non-technical personnel.

For the above work, I advised Garg to take into account two factors. Factor one was the approved manpower of the plant, and factor two was the actual men in position. His report was also to indicate the category-wise deployment of all staff and the sections of their plant postings. Garg's consultancy lasted for nearly two years. He used to visit the Bhubaneswar corporate office and the plant at Paradeep. Mr. Garg was renowned for his technical knowledge and efficient implementation of project work. He got his engineering degree from Roorkee. He had gained administrative competence during his long service in top positions at BHEL and CCI. His suggestions were implemented by me at PPL. It was helpful for the completion of the long-pending commissioning of PPL's Phase II during the subsequent period.

Mr. Garg, after his retirement as CMD of CCI, stayed in his own DDA flat at Alaknanda, very near Tara Apartment. We had become family friends and used to visit each other's residences often in Delhi.

Garg and I have been members of the Strategic Management Group (SMG) since October 1991. After 1993, both became very active contributors to the functioning and effective operation of SMG. We regularly attended its important meetings together. Both of us were also members of the Indian Council of Arbitration (ICA). We were nominated as its members after our retirement from active service. Together, we had earlier acted as arbitrators in many cases of central PSUs. Both were prominent speakers at many management institutes and conventions all over the country. Our lectures were always interesting, as we laced our talks with typical examples of our experiences in solving varied industrial problems.

I addressed the students of AIMA during 1990 and 1991 as a member of the institute. Subsequently, as an honour, AIMA conferred on me its Life Membership and allowed the use of the word LMIMA. During this time, I was also made a life member of the ICA. I used to be a member of many ICA tribunals for arbitration cases. The disputes were mostly over the terms of the agreement between private parties and central PSUs. These disputes mostly related to violations of contractual terms that resulted in big financial losses for one party.

At home, during the third and fourth quarters of 1991, Mona was undergoing IRS training at their academy in Nagpur. The parents were getting a lot of proposals for her marriage. These were from families in Odisha. The sons of these families were either undergoing training in Class 1 All India Civil Services or were in active service after training.

Due to the above reason, Mona was called to Bhubaneswar from her training academy in Nagpur. Rashmi and I wanted to gauge the mind of Mona on this subject. It was necessary before arranging any meetings for such proposals in mid-1992. Subsequently, Mona, Rashmi, and I had several meetings with the interested parties. However, nothing substantial could be achieved.

After some time, Mona told her mother about a Delhi boy. This person belonged to the previous batch of IRS. He was undergoing his training late at the academy with her batch. He had already indicated his intention to marry her and had sent fillers through mutual friends. She suggested that her parents could meet his parents in Delhi. At that time, the boy (Vimalendu) could also be present. After that, they could evaluate and make their decision. Soon, such a meeting was held between the two families, and the marriage of Mona and Vimalendu was finalised. The marriage ceremony took place in January 1993.

The rituals of the marriage ceremony were held during the day in the Jagannath Temple at Hauz Khas, New Delhi. The Baratis and my relatives had their Maha Prasad Seva at the Jagannath temple. The evening reception for the marriage was given by me to invitees of both sides at the prestigious Samrat Hotel in Chanakyapuri, New Delhi.

My pursuit to improve the performance of PPL on all fronts continued unabated during the financial year 1990–91. Gradually, signs of positive results were visible. The defects in the sulfuric acid plant could be identified, and the rectification process was initiated. It was necessary to make it ready for the subsequent commissioning of Phase II of PPL.

The monitoring system for plant operation and the schedule for proper maintenance of the plant were successfully implemented during the first quarter of 1992. The cost control measures at each profit-generating centre in the plant were identified. Measures were taken to fully implement the modalities of all improvements in each quarter. Staff at all levels were fully involved in all these activities. They had understood the importance of the daily monitoring systems.

My first-year stewardship generated unbelievable results at PPL. A few months ago, any investment in PPL was considered bad. This perception was totally changed by the results obtained at PPL during 1991–92. The annual capacity utilisation of the plant during 1991–92 jumped to 89.1% from the previous three-year average of 55.6%. Production of indigenous DAP reached a figure of more than 6,40,000 MT. The higher volume of sales of indigenous production along with imported products recorded an all-time higher volume of sales of over 9 lakh MT. It generated a higher cash flow of over Rs. 810 crore. During 1990–91, the balance sheet of PPL proudly showed a net profit of Rs. 16.38 crore. It included a net contribution of over Rs. 4 crore from the marketing operation.

The achievement of 1990–91 was commended by the Board in its review meeting in Delhi in the second week of April 1992. The board recorded its appreciation for me (MD). It also congratulated all the officers and workers of the company. After the board meeting, the president of Nauru presented a 2-litre big bottle of Johnny Walker Blue Label Scootch to me in appreciation.

Personnel of the company at all levels rejoiced at the company's achievement. But, for me, a few unsolved challenges remain for early resolution.

During April and May 1992, to completely rectify the problem associated with the sulfuric acid plant, a full-proof plan was formulated. The German company, which had erected the plant in Phase I, agreed to do it in time. I also wanted the retrofitting work on the phosphoric acid plant to be completed simultaneously. The job undertaker, Jacob International of the USA, agreed to complete their work by the end of July 1992. With these two major things tied up, I became confident enough to commission the delayed Phase II of PPL by the end of November 1992.

Gurdial Singh, GM, Marketing, requested that I allow him to hold the annual marketing meeting at Puri in the last week of May. He wanted to hold it in a similar manner as it was held earlier by me. RMs and other senior officers of the marketing division were to be at Puri for three days with their families at the company's expense. He also requested that I join them with my family on May 28, 1992. I accorded the approval and also attended it with the family for a day. Then, on May 29, 1992, I left Puri with Rashmi, Dimpy, and Dev. We travelled to Gopalpur for a three-day holiday. The stay was at the Oberoi Grand Hotel in Gopalpur. The lawn of the hotel, laid on the seafront, extended right up to the beach. Dimpy and Dev used to spend a lot of time on the lawn, enjoying the sight of the rising and ebbing sea waves. The family thoroughly enjoyed this holiday. We returned to Bhubaneswar on the 31st evening.

The family stayed with me at the official residence in Forest Park until May 5. During their five-night stay, the family was called for dinner by the family of Chitta Ranjan Patnaik (CR) at least on two occasions. Chitta was the resident representative of HSL Rourkela in Bhubaneswar. His own house was just on the other side of the road from our official residence. He was a nice gentleman. He was also related to me through the family connection of the brother-in-law who had married my second sister. CR was the elder brother of the then-industry minister of Odisha. His wife was the principal of the Government Women's College (Rama Devi College) in Bhubaneswar. A serving senior professor at this college was a dear friend of Rashmi from her school and college days. She was Padmalaya Garabadu. Rashmi enjoyed the gossip with Chitta's wife.

My family and I went to Delhi on the 6th of May. After attending the work in Delhi for a few days, I returned to Bhubaneswar on the 12th. I worked out the agenda for a major in-house meeting. It was scheduled for the month of June. On June 2, 1992, I held the monthly meeting related to plant and allied departments. I was satisfied with the progress of the operation and the work in all sections of the plant. I appreciated the achievements of all officers and workers at the plant.

In the above meeting, I outlined the most important task that was to be carried out on priority during June 1992. This was necessary for achieving the targeted objective of PPL phase II commissioning by the set date. This date was earlier communicated to the GM (Operation) and his team. At the same meeting, Gurdial was again reminded of the target of 1992–93 sales volume and the cash flow expected from the Marketing Division. B.K. Tana was advised to continue his vigil and pressurise the foreign consultants and contractors to complete all pending jobs at sulfuric acid and phosphoric acid plants. He was asked to monitor, on a daily basis, the job that was carried out by the two foreign companies in Germany and the USA. Tanna was advised to report the progress every day to me and ensure completion by the end of June 1992.

In the evening of June 5, I took a flight from Bhubaneswar to New Delhi. After attending the Delhi office and the Ministry from June 8th to June 11th, I went on a five-day tour to Chandigarh and Himachal Pradesh with the family. The Himachal visit was to Kullu, Manali, and other sites near Rohtang Pass. It was an enjoyable outing for the family. We enjoyed the charming, cool surroundings and the magnificent scenic visuals of the Himalayan extravaganza. Our enjoyment was limitless. Pleasant zephyr, passing over the ice-cold waters of the brooks originating from the Himalayan hills, was a pleasant experience. Photographs were taken amidst the snowy surroundings in typical Ladakhi attire worn by all. The idea to visit Rohtang Pass was dropped due to IMD's warning of a snowstorm. The visit couldn't be extended due to my work in Delhi.

All of us returned to Delhi on June 12. I spent another two days with the family and, on the 15th morning flight, returned to Bhubaneswar. The remaining fifteen days of the month I spent shuttling between the Bhubaneswar corporate office and Paradeep Plant almost every second or third day. This was necessary to speed up the plant's new modification work for my earlier self-set target.

My efforts had an electrifying effect on all officers and workers at the plant site. On June 30, 1992, the problematic main boiler of the plant became normal in its operation. The sulfuric acid plant, too, started running at full capacity by June 30th. The phosphoric acid plant, after its retrofitting, achieved a higher production capacity on June 29, 1292. I told GM Operation to cautiously watch the behaviour of these plants for the next ten days and report the status to me every morning. In a few days, another much-awaited milestone of PPL plant operation was achieved.

On the 10th of July, I had collected all the operating data of the preceding week concerning the matrixes related to capacity utilisation in each of the allied plants. These data I sent to the technical and financial experts in the fertiliser industry for their evaluation before a final decision was made on an important issue of PPL. After I received positive feedback from these experts, I conveyed my final decision during the plant review meeting on July 15, 1992.

That day, I declared the commissioning of phase II of PPL. Messages were sent, along with the minutes of the 15th meeting and experts' opinions, regarding the commissioning of phase II to the chairman and all members of the board. At the board meeting of July 21, 1992, the commissioning of Phase II was duly ratified, and the ministry was officially informed about the successful commissioning of Phase II of PPL. It was an extraordinary success for me in such a short time. It laid the foundation for the future progress and growth of the company. The ministry commended the function of the company and gave an example for other loss-making fertiliser companies in the public sector.

At that time, the Odisha state government had formed a high-power committee for the reorganisation of its PSUs. This committee was to suggest and implement various new measures to improve the workings of the state PSUs and reduce their losses. I was inducted as a member of that committee. This was done after I agreed to the request of the State Development Commissioner, Sri Sundararajan. This committee submitted its report in the record time of three months. Its recommendation was implemented in Toto. Later, it was found that many of the sick units could be successfully revived. However, some other units were either closed totally or sold to the private sector. The Chief Minister, Biju Patnaik, personally congratulated all committee members in a meeting held later in his chamber.

At the beginning of October 1992, labour unrest started at the plant. It was at the instigation of Union President Prabhat Samantray, who was a Rajya Sabha member from the state ruling party (BJD). He was a resident of Paradeep and was in good standing with the CM. It started with go-slow work and dharanas by the members of the Plant Workers Union. The demands pertained mainly to pay scale revision, an annual bonus equivalent to four months' pay, a costly uniform, and 45 days of paid leave in a year. Despite several discussions by the management and agreeing to reasonable pay and bonuses, the union remained adamant in its demand. Due to worker indiscipline in all the plant's operational areas, production started to suffer. When the agitation took a turn to violence and some of the supervisors were assaulted, I hardened my attitude.

I met the Chief Minister and apprised him of the situation. The CM told me to be very firm and to get rid of the disruptive union leaders. I then had meetings with the Chief Secretary and the Director General of Police. The Commandant of CISF, deployed at the plant site, provided me with an intelligence report for today. The report indicated that large-scale violence and destruction would occur at the plant site if any actions were taken against the union leaders. These facts were duly reported to the state government and the Ministry of GOI.

When the union tried to completely shut down the factory, I dismissed from service all the union office-bearers. The CISF Commandant was instructed not to allow entry for dismissed employees and the Union President inside the plant. The dismissed employees were also asked to surrender their official quarters at the plant township. The dismissed employees, along with some more workers, continued their 24 hours of dharna outside the plant's main gate under an erected shamiana. When they started obstructing entry to the plant, police removed them forcibly to a place two furlongs away from the gate.

In the meantime, Prabhat Samantray instigated the BJD MLAs to create a ruckus in the Odisha Assembly. That made the CM announce, on the floor of the house, that PPL management was not listening to the state government and that it would withdraw police protection from the plant and the management. After this statement, I met the CM and reminded him that I had earlier apprised him of the situation at Paradeep Plant. Only after his advice and consent to taking stern actions did I decide to be firm in protecting the interests of PPL. At that time, PPL was one of the top five industries in Odisha. Its contribution was enormous to the prosperity of the state. Future big investors in Odisha were critically watching the situation faced by PPL.

Due to the stiffening attitude of the state government during the strike period, the prime minister, who had the fertiliser portfolio, talked to the CM about extending all help to PPL. The cabinet secretary also suitably advised the Chief Secretary of Odisha. I initiated a blitzkrieg in all local newspapers and media. B.K. Panda, the PR manager of PPL, was advised to ensure that media pressure continued on the government. Citing the dangerous situation at the PPL plant in Paradeep, the media questioned the disinformation and stepmotherly attitude of the state government towards an upcoming large industry. The media also highlighted the danger that lurked for lakhs of people residing in places within a hundred-kilometre radius of the plant. They enumerated several dangerous impacts on thousands of people. They mentioned that prolongation of the strike might cause mishaps at the plant site. It might result in the leakage of several thousand metric tonnes of dangerous liquid ammonia, leading to an unimaginable disaster and the loss of life. The death toll might run to several lakhs!

Even after ten days, there was no appreciable decrease in tension. The plant maintenance operation was in jeopardy. PPL management informed the state government that if the deteriorating situation continued for a few more days, it would be difficult to maintain the low temperature of minus 32 degrees for the huge quantity of stored liquid ammonia meant for DAP production. The government was informed in writing that if any of the storage tanks burst due to maintenance failure and ammonia gas leaks out, then there will be total devastation in areas under a hundred-mile radius of Paradeep. There was a likelihood of the deaths of lakhs of people living in Paradeep and nearby villages, towns, and cities, including Cuttack and Bhubaneswar. The local press and media became very vocal about the imminent danger and the negligence of the state government.

Ultimately, the state relented. A committee was constituted by the central government to solve the issue in a week's time. The members of the committee were the central government's Jt. Secretary of Fertiliser Ministry, the Jt. Secretary of Labour Ministry, Odisha State's Secretary of Agriculture, Labour Secretary, and Secretary of Home. The managing director of PPL and his general manager (P&A) were also members of the said committee.

The settlement arrived after three days of consultation. As per the committee's recommendation, PPL management agreed to take back the dismissed employees, but, as per PPL management's insistence, the committee agreed that they would not be posted in the plant. Their posting was to be outside Odisha in the marketing and logistics field jobs of PPL. The annual bonus for the year was fixed at fifteen days of salary. There was to be no revision in the pay scales of workers, but a procedure was laid out for their advancement in careers. With these implementations, the strike ended, and the period of the strike of fifteen days was adjusted as paid leave for the absentee staff. These decisions of the committee were binding on the union and the management of PPL.

The state government representatives of the committee insisted on the immediate transfer of the general manager (operation) from Paradeep. They said that he had a role in labour unrest. They further mentioned that, if he was not transferred, he would be arrested by the state government for his part in the instigation of unrest. Thus, there was no way left for PPL management but to transfer Raza and give charge of the plant operation to the Deputy General Manager, Samantray.

On November 3, 1992, the monthly review meeting was held in Bhubaneswar. I made an assessment of the loss of plant production due to the 15-day strike in October. Plans were drawn to recoup the loss during the month as well as add 5% more production to the original target set on the basis of 90% capacity utilisation of the plant. I discussed the manpower requirement of the plant as per the submitted report of C.N. Garg. The plant's senior officials, present in the meeting, agreed with the submitted report. I decided to put this report for approval at the next board meeting set for December 3, 1992.

After the review of the plant operation, the targets for sales and cash flow during November were set. It was in accordance with the annual target set for the financial year 1992–93. This envisaged a sales volume of a million MT of fertiliser. It indicated the sale of 6.3 lakh MT of own DAP, 1.5 lakh MT of imported DAP, and 2.2 lakh MT of imported urea. The cash flow was estimated at Rs. 1,300 crore, with a gross contribution of Rs. 8 crore towards profit. This aim synchronised with the overall financial objective for PPL, set at over Rs. 20 crore (net) during 1992–93.

On December 3, 1992, an important board meeting of PPL was held in Delhi. The main items on its agenda were: i) review of the labour strike at the plant; II) approval of the plant's manpower strength; and iii) review of production at the plant during the period subsequent to the commissioning of phase II. I presented relevant information to the board. The board recorded its appreciation for the manner in which the strike was handled. It gave its approval to the manpower strength for the plant. It also appreciated the way plant capacity utilisation had risen from 50% to over 80% and was moving forward towards a target of 90%.

After returning to Bhubaneswar on December 7th, on the basis of board approval of plant manpower, I promoted Samantray to the post of GM (operation) and many other plant officials to posts one grade higher. A similar upgrade was also done for eligible workers. This encouragement spirited all the employees of the plant, and they worked with new vigour and forgot the trauma of the recent strike. For the personnel of the Marketing Division, similar promotions were also made. All in all, the company's activities became more vibrant in all fields of its operation. The only point of sorrow was the resignation of Raza, who could not tolerate his ordeal that started due to the illogical attitude of the state government. I was very unhappy about this incident. I could not understand the state government's vindictive attitude towards Raza. Earlier, Raza had toiled hard for the success of the PPL project and was popular in the state administration.

Like every year, in 1992, the Fertiliser Association of India (FAI) held its annual seminar in December for three days. Nearly 1500 delegates from fertiliser and allied industries from different countries all over the world attended the seminar. The seminar was inaugurated by the Fertiliser Minister of India. Many research papers covering varied aspects of the fertiliser industry were presented by prominent personalities in the world belonging to the fertiliser industry. After each paper's presentation, the subject was thrown open for discussion by the delegates during the six sessions of the three-day seminar.

During the 1992 seminar, I presented a technical paper on "Control of Environmental Hazards from Products of Phosphoric Acid Plants." My presentation of the paper and the subsequent question-and-answer session by the delegates were interesting and lively.

Daughter Mona's marriage was set for January 1993. I took ten days of leave, but for an hour every day, I went to the Delhi office. I used to take stock of the happenings in the company on a day-to-day basis. This kept all senior officials on their toes. After the marriage ceremony was over, I returned to Bhubaneswar.

During this month, the chairman of the Indian Oil Corporation (IOC) called on me at the Bhubaneswar office. He discussed with me the use of PPL's captive berth by the IOC at Paradeep Port. It was for materials to be brought to Paradeep for their proposed big oil refinery. The discussion was fruitful. IOC was allowed the use of the facility on payment of leviable charges to PPL. During this time, the chairman of Oswal Fertilisers also called on me. He took my advice about the import of technology, plants, and machinery for its DAP plant that was being set up at Paradeep.

Earlier, the Essar Group was refused permission to use the PPL facility. They had asked to use the facilities of the PPL plant during the construction of their proposed iron ore pelletization plant. I refused to give my consent due to Essar's ulterior motive. They were secretly proposing to take over the share of the Nauru government in PPL. I learned that they had tapped the Nauru government and influential politicians of the GOI to achieve their objective! I never desired the privatisation of PPL. I always considered PPL a 'gold mine' for the country's economy and an important asset of the government. On this, I also aired my views in an interview with Doordarshan that was telecast.

The results of the monthly review meeting on February 2, 1993, indicated that we would certainly achieve our objectives for the financial year 1992–93. I wanted to achieve this goal on the eve of my superannuation. I never wanted to continue in the service after superannuation. I had already decided not to accept any official extension on an ad hoc basis. Krishnamurthy, Secretary of the Ministry, who also acted as PPL Chairman, had given me enough hints that my services were required for another two years.

PESB had not advertised for PPL MD's post in January 1993, as per usual practice. This used to be normally done three months prior to the retirement of any existing incumbent at the level of director or above in any Central PSU. The reason as to why the PESB did not advertise was that the Fertiliser Ministry did not inform them about the vacancy at PPL since it was planned for my continuance. I had kept, as a top secret, my decision to quit PPL on the due date of superannuation!

I fixed the first quarterly review meeting of 1993 on the 27th of March at Bhubaneswar. I had asked GM (Operation) and GM (Marketing) to come to the meeting with actual figures of production and sales up to March 26th. I had also told them to project these figures up to the end of March 31, 1993. The reason was to assess the production as well as sales of the company for the financial year 1992-93 vis-à-vis the target set earlier. This was to be the last meeting that I chaired in PPL. Keeping in mind the farewell that the officers were likely to give me, I had brought Rashmi to Bhubaneswar when I returned from New Delhi on March 20th. She attended all the farewell parties at Paradeep Plant and at the Bhubaneswar corporate office. Both the GMs presented the production and sales figures of PPL for the financial year 1992-93 up to the end of March 26th. It indicated the achievement of earlier set targets at 99.56% for each. When the projected figures for the next five days were added, the achievement figures were estimated to cross the 100% mark.

The published balance sheet of PPL for 1992-93 vindicated these estimates. The DAP production of the plant during 1992-93 stood at 6,55,250 MT, which was 91% of capacity utilization. The volume of sales indicated the sale of 6.4 lakh MT of own DAP, 1.5 lakh MT of imported DAP, and 2.3 lakh MT of imported urea. Thus, the total sales volume indicated 10.2 lakh MT of product with a sales turnover of Rs. 1,309 crore. This achievement gave me extreme happiness on the eve of retirement. The net profit in the balance sheet indicated rupees 23.22 crores. The tide had turned! I had succeeded in restoring the health of the company.

Keeping in mind my earlier decision, after the meeting on March 27, 1993, I dictated two letters. One letter was meant for PPL employees at all levels and also for PPL board members. The second letter was given to the Minister and the officers of the Fertiliser Ministry, DOPT, and a host of important suppliers of PPL. In the first letter, I thanked and congratulated all PPLers for their cooperation and excellent performance. In the other letter, I thanked all concerned for their cooperation and their goodwill in achieving my goal of taking forward PPL.

In both letters, I indicated that my services wouldn't be available for PPL with effect from April 1, 1993. I humbly thanked my well-wishers in the ministry who wanted me to continue with an official extension after superannuation. *Thus ended* Chandi's era at *PPL*. The morning of "Odisha Day" in April 1993 found me and Rashmi leaving the official MD's bungalow of PPL at Bhubaneswar. We went to Bhubaneswar Airport to take our first flight to New Delhi. We reached our residence at E-33 Tara Apartments around 1145 a.m. Though it was a Thursday and the college and schools were open, both Dimpy and Dev did not attend their classes and waited for the arrival of their mom and dad.

For our lunch, we four drove to the India Habitat Centre (IHC) at Lodhi Road. We had our buffet lunch at Dilli O Dilli restaurant, which allowed only IHC members. From that restaurant, we also got packed items for the dinner of the night. Rashmi was too exhausted due to hectic farewell parties at Paradeep and Bhubaneswar during the last week. I did not want her to prepare our dinner. This was the first day of my post-retirement period.

After a week of my retirement, I got a call from PBK, Secretary, Ministry of Fertilizer. He was very cordial and told me that he had advised the CMD of HFC to temporarily take over the charge of PPL from me. HFC-CMD would contact me in this regard. Mr. Singh, a Madhya Pradesh cadre IAS on deputation to HFC as its CMD, immediately contacted me. Singh was told by me to come to my residence in Tara Apartments with a handing-over note dated March 31, 1993. Singh came, and the note was duly signed by me and Singh. That is how I handed over my charge of PPL to its provisional occupant.

Later, after Nauru's disinvestment, PPL temporarily became a 100% GOI company. The board of directors of this new PPL, in its meeting held on July 2, 1993, placed on record their gratitude for the contribution made by me during my tenure as its managing director. The resolution passed by the board in this regard mentioned:

"That the Board places on record its sense of appreciation for the services rendered by Mr. C. Mohanty during his tenure as Managing Director of the company."

PPL Factory at Paradeep

Pseudo Retirement

I was not a person to sit idle at home after my retirement. After staying at home for a week and evaluating the options available, I had to decide my future course of action. I had many offers to join the boards of private fertiliser and cement companies on the eve of my retirement. I had also gotten an offer from a big private fertiliser company to head it as its CEO.

A month after my retirement, I, along with Garg as a partner, registered a company for the import and distribution of fertilisers. It was registered as GMP Overseas Private Limited. Its registered office had an address in Kalkaji, New Delhi. The office provided enough accommodation for its partners and space for three office staff. It had the facilities of two cabins for the partners, a big hall for the office staff, a lobby, a reception, and a meeting room. It had fax, xerox, and printing facilities attached to the office computer. These were operated by a PA who had joined after his retirement from BHEL.

The company distributed a lakh MT of rock phosphate and muriate of potash among three fertiliser companies. The supplies were made between May and October 1993. The income from this operation, for GMP Overseas, just broke even after meeting the fixed costs. It did not provide any surplus to service the investments made by me and Garg. Similar income also accrued in the coming three months. Both I and Garg decided to close the company after the end of the three-month notice period for the staff and the owner of the office premises. This decision could be easily taken by us. The earnings that both Garg and I generated from our consultancy and arbitration work were quite significant for each of us.

As stated earlier, I had already decided not to join any private company, either as a board member or as a CEO. I had made up my mind to take up independent management consulting work for companies that aimed at restructuring. This activity was suggested by AIMA. I was an important life member of it. Many of the AIMA-associated large industries had already contacted me for consulting.

The Arbitration Council of India (ICA) and the Standing Conference of Public Enterprises (SCOPE) offered me many assignments for arbitration on disputes related to the member companies. It was an ongoing process that lasted too long. The work was enjoyable. The incomes were attractive and kept me extremely busy. My earnings during the period as a consultant and arbitrator were much more than what I used to earn as the MD of PPL.

In early 1993, after completion of training and probation, Mona and her husband were posted to Calcutta as Assistant Commissioners of Income Tax. They had their official quarters in the IT colony. I and Rashmi visited them twice in Calcutta. Their period of posting in Calcutta was almost four years. Subsequently, both were transferred to New Delhi in 1997.

The first outing for me and Rashmi was to Calcutta in 1993, after I retired from PPL. We stayed with Mona for four to five days. During that time, we also visited the residence of Lakhi, whose husband, CDR Bibhu, headed the naval establishment at Calcutta. This visit brought back many sweet memories for Rashmi of her earlier stay in Calcutta when I served in Burmah Shell. During this visit, we also visited the families of Fondeker, Prabhu, Pai, and Almeida, our old Calcutta friends. We also visited the Ganju family, who were residents of the Ekdalia Road building where I and Rashmi had earlier stayed.

During that visit to Calcutta, we had to rush back to Delhi. The reason was the hearing of the first arbitration case by me. The arbitration was for the dispute between the RSP of the Steel Authority of India (SAIL) and their stockyard contractor in Bhubaneswar. The tribunal of arbitration had three members, including me. The other two were retired Chief Justices of the Odisha and Patna High Courts. The first hearing was in Delhi. I was in Delhi, while the other two members were to travel to Delhi from Patna and Chennai. The hearing was at the SAIL headquarters at Lodhi Road, New Delhi.

Subsequent hearings of this arbitration were held in Bhubaneswar, Patna, Puri, and New Delhi. After six sittings over six months, the award was given in favour of RSP in September 1993. The fees of arbitration received by each arbitrator were more than one and a half lakh rupees.

The consultancy work during this period also covered two cooperative federations. They were MARKFED of Punjab and HAFED of Haryana. The consultancy was to suggest better management of their inventory and a better system of cash generation and management. At that time, during 1993–94, I also became an adviser for the National Textile Corporation, restructuring its production and distribution system. I completed the assignment in three months. For this, I made several visits to the office of its chairman, Solanki, who happened to be my friend.

In 1993, Dev passed his ICSC (class X) examination and joined the science stream of I.Sc. (class XII) at Frank Anthony School. In the year 1994, Dimpy did her graduation (B.A. (Hons.) in Psychology) from LSR College at Delhi University. This year I purchased a new Maruti Zen (Vxi) in lieu of a year-old Maruti 800. Like most of the time earlier, I made it a point to keep my weekends free for the family. Saturdays and Sundays were exclusively earmarked for Rashmi and children. Never did I carry out any work of consulting or arbitration on the weekend unless out on tour. I wanted to make up for the lost time that I could not share with my family during my service career. Every Sunday, it almost became mandatory for me to take the family out for lunch to famous Delhi restaurants, including the India Habitat Centre.

In the last quarter of 1994, Mona was expecting her first child. Me and Rashmi asked her to come and stay with us in Delhi in mid-August 1994. After she came to Delhi, we took her for a checkup at the clinic of Dr. Sheela Mehrotra. She was a renowned gynaecologist in Delhi. She was also attached as a specialist at the Moolchand Hospital in South Delhi. Dr. Sheila's private clinic was at Defence Colony and was very near Moolchand Hospital. The doctor, after the check-up, mentioned that everything was normal. She advised coming for the next examinations in the first weeks of September and October. After the checkup on October 2, 1994, the doctor advised booking a room at Moolchand Hospital from August 14 onward. To facilitate the booking, she wrote a letter for hospital admission.

After moving Mona to Moolchand Hospital on the 14th of October, Dr. Sheela examined her there. She was kept in the reserved cottage. By rotation, Rashmi, Dimpy, Dev, and I used to spend the nights at Mona's cottage. On the night of October 18, at 22:52 hours, a healthy baby boy was born. Both mother and son were transferred to the cottage in the afternoon of October 19. I and Rashmi spent the whole night of the 18th in Mona's room. We left the hospital the next morning after Mona and the newborn were shifted to the cottage. We left only after the arrival of Dimpy at the cottage.

Mona and the baby were brought back to our residence at Tara Apartment on the 20th of October. After consultation with Mona, it was decided that she could leave for Calcutta only by the 28th. Her husband and his parents visited

Tara Apartment to meet Mona and see the newborn on the twenty-first. It was decided that the baby's *'namkaran'* (naming ceremony) would be held in the fourth week of October—precisely on October 23rd. It was also decided that it would be held at the paternal grandparent's DDA flat in Janakpuri, West Delhi. For this ceremony, Mona, her husband, and the baby would have to be present from October 21st until October 24th at the mentioned West Delhi flat. I and Rashmi dropped Mona and the baby at that flat on Monday morning. We returned to our residence after promising that we would attend the pooja and Namkaran on the 23rd of October.

During the pooja, the priest selected the alphabet 'T' from the almanac. The baby was named Tanmay. After four days, on October 28, 1994, Mona, Tanmay, and Vimalendu returned to Calcutta.

Dimpy graduated in 1994. After her graduation, she appeared for the law entrance examination at Delhi University. She qualified for admission to the Law Faculty of Delhi University (DU). The classes were conducted on the north campus of DU, which was quite a distance from the residence at Tara Apartments. In order to avoid daily commutes, she took her admission in the DU hostel. She was in the hostel for almost three years. She got her law degree in 1999.

In the meantime, Dev had also passed the I.Sc. (class XII) examination in 1995. After that, he appeared for the UPSC examination for admission to the National Defence Academy (NDA). Simultaneously, he had taken the entrance test for admission to the hotel management course at the Institute of Hotel Management (IHM). The result of IHM came first. He was selected for admission to IHM's Calcutta institute, although his preference was for IHM's main institute at Pusha, New Delhi. I took him to Calcutta and got him admitted there. After two months of his stay in Calcutta, his UPSC result for NDA admission was declared. He had cleared this test too. On learning about this success, he desired to switch over to NDA and discontinue the IHM course. Rashmi persuaded me to accede to the new wish of Dev.

Before joining the NDA at Khadakwasla, near Pune, he was to clear the Medical Board test for defence services. His medical examination was set in Bangalore at the Air Force's Medical Test Centre. I flew with him to Bangalore and got him tested there. Dev was asked to appear again at the New Delhi Army Command Hospital for two further tests. After the clearance of the Delhi test, he was permitted to join the NDA in a week's time.

I flew with Dev to Pune. After my arrival in Pune, I was picked up by my friend Guru (Talauliker). At that time, Guru was the managing director of Finolex Cables in Pune. All three drove in Guru's car to his bungalow for our stay. The next morning, Dev was taken to the NDA. He was allowed to join his batchmates in 1995. All official formalities for joining the NDA were completed. I named Guru as his local guardian. During his NDA stay, Guru used to visit Dev almost twice every month. When allowed, Guru also took Dev to his house on a few occasions. He also ensured that Dev faced no major problems during his stay at Khadakwasla.

I spent two days with Guru, his wife Nalini, and his middle son, who was a chartered accountant. Guru had three sons; the eldest was an FRCS doctor in London, and the youngest was an engineer serving in the USA. After spending quality time with Guru, I returned to New Delhi.

Dev did well at the NDA during his first year of training. After the successful completion of the first year, he, along with his batchmates, returned home on a month-long holiday break. He, with his batchmates from northern India, returned on an Army Special Train to New Delhi. Dev looked very smart in his Army uniform. This he showed off to his friends in Delhi. Rashmi, Dimpy, and I were overjoyed for a month when he stayed at home. I drove all of them in my new Maruti Zen car several times for lunch and dinner at good restaurants in New Delhi as well as at the IHC restaurants. The time passed off quickly, and, after the month-long home holiday, Dev left with other NDA Cadets to Khdakwasala by an Army Special Train from New Delhi. Rashmi and Dimpy accompanied me to see him off at the New Delhi Railway Station.

After a couple of months, one early morning, I and Rashmi were surprised to hear the ring of the doorbell in our apartment. Rashmi opened the door to find Dev back at home with his baggage. That morning, around 0930 hours, I received a call from the commandant of the NDA. He inquired as to whether Dev had returned home. He said that Dev had stealthily left NDA without official permission. That constituted a serious offence under the Army Act. The NDA commandant also said that he was going to inform the Delhi Police Commissioner to immediately find him and send him back to NDA under custody! I assured him that, in a couple of days, I would personally present Dev before him. Both parents were shocked but kept their cool.

After breakfast, I counselled Dev and explained the repercussions that he would face for his act. I shared with him the NDA Commandant's morning telephone conversation with me. In two days, he was to be taken back to the NDA. I booked the next morning flight and took Dev to Pune. From the airport, Guru's vehicle picked us up. Me and Dev drove straight to the NDA campus at Khadakwasla.

We went to the office of the commandant. After giving a dressing down to Cadet Dev, the commandant asked him to wait outside. I then had a detailed discussion with the commandant on the whole issue. I told him that Dev did not want to pursue his further training, even after persuasion by me and his mother. I also told how Dev had told me that, if compelled to continue, he might even commit suicide! I requested the commandant to assist so that I could get his release from the NDA after obtaining the Defence Ministry's permission. I assured the commandant that, during the mentioned process, Dev wouldn't make any attempt to run away from NDA. He would only leave with me when I got the Defence Ministry's clearance.

It almost took 45 days to get clearance from the ministry after the confiscation of the bond money. Finally, I brought Dev back to New Delhi in May 1996. The reason for his quitting NDA, even after one year's stay and good performance throughout that period, remained a mystery for the family. The only guess was that, after a period of peaceful stay during the 1st year in NDA, he could not bear the severe ragging by the senior cadets that usually happens in the 2nd year. This could be just a presumption due to the absence of any other cognisable reason.

I was worried for Dev's future. I used my contacts and succeeded in admitting him to the B.Com., first-year class at Aravind College at Saket in New Delhi. During his first month at the college, he again appeared in the admissions test at IHM. He qualified and got his admission at IHM Pusa, New Delhi. He finally passed the hotel management course in 1999. Immediately, he was selected to join the 5-star Hotel Bristol in Gurgaon that year. In the year 1999, Dimpy also got her law degree from Delhi University and joined a law firm in Delhi. Dev commuted daily to Gurgaon, whereas Dimpy travelled only a few kilometres to her office at Greater Kailash II. Subsequently, Dimpy purchased a new Hyundai Santro car for her commute to her office.

After Mona and her husband were transferred from Calcutta to Delhi in the late nineties, they got their official quarters allotted at Laxmi Bai Nagar. The area was near the INA Market. It was almost seven kilometres from Tara Apartment, where we resided. Thus, once again, I and Rashmi got the company of our three children in New Delhi in 1999. On almost all weekends, the family get-together used to take place along with grandson Tanmay. The venue used to be either the Tara Apartment or the India Habitat Centre. Tanmay was very fond of eating tandoori chicken; his granddad always ensured that he was never disappointed.

During the first six years of my retirement, i.e., between 1993 and 1999, I had undertaken seven consultancy assignments. Two of them were for private industries, three were for PSUs, and two covered cooperative federations. Besides, I had undertaken three arbitration cases—one concerning a big engineering company in the private sector and two PSUs in the trading sector. This enabled me to generate sufficient additional income. It came in handy to pay off all liabilities of burrowed bank finance for the two purchased properties, one in New Delhi and the other in Bhubaneswar. I was never comfortable having any financial liability for long. At the same time, I scrupulously guarded my hard-earned money that was put in various safe instruments of savings and investments.

In the meantime, I became the advisor of the Belarus Potash Company and two other Belarusian government-linked companies. I signed MOUs with these companies. This operation continued for three years. The annual retainer fee was substantial. It had the separate perks of a journey by flight and a stay at five-star hotels in Bombay and the capital of Belarus (Minsk). This assignment was organised by the younger brother of a politician and previous Youth Congress President (INC in 1978–80). This politician belonged to Odisha. He was elected three times as a member of the Parliament of the 6th, 7th, and 10th Lok Sabhas from Aska, Ganjam. He was also a minister of state for chemicals and fertiliser. That's how he became aware of my capabilities. He wanted his own investments in the three companies to be safe. He was famously known in the elite circle of Delhi as the Babu from Odisha.

During late 1999, Rashmi conveyed to me that the second grandchild was expected sometime around the second quarter of the year 2000. As responsible and loving parents, we ensured to take Mona once again under our care. The famous gynaecologist Dr. Sheila, who had earlier looked after Mona during her first pregnancy, was consulted for the second. From January 2000, every fortnight, I and Rashmi took Mona to her clinic at the Defence Colony. Similar to her earlier advice during the birth of Tanmay, I booked Mona's admission at Moolchand Hospital for the delivery. The booking was done for the third week of April. On April 20, 2020, we admitted Mona to the hospital. On the afternoon of the 23rd, a healthy son was born to her. Later, the child was named Aman.

The period between 2000 and 2007 was very trying for me. Of course, there was no problem with my consulting, arbitration, and advisory work. However, I could not devote quality time exclusively to those works due to various incidents on the family front. That was the reason for my refusal to undertake new assignments beyond the year 2003. I wanted to finish all my pending consultancy work in three private industries: one in a cement company, another in a pharmaceutical company, and the third in a phosphate fertiliser company. There were four pending arbitration cases related to the steel, fertiliser, and cement industries. Of course, I was bound to be an advisor to three Belarusian companies until the end of 2003.

The year 2003 appeared to be a very bad year for the family. Rashmi lost one of her intimate friends at Tara Apartments. She was Rashmi's dearest friend. Her eldest daughter was also a friend and classmate of Mona at LSR. Her loss made Rashmi quite depressed after she attended her cremation at the Lodhi Road crematorium. During this time, the differences between Mona and her husband also surfaced. That ultimately ended in their mutually agreed-upon separation. Mona took custody of both her children and successfully raised them.

During this time, Dimpy and her three senior colleagues from the law firm left their jobs to start their own law firm. This enraged the owner of a previous law firm. This led to severe harassment of the four. They valiantly faced the ordeal and proceeded to establish, activate, and expand their own law firm. Their strong will, with the support of their families and the legal fraternity of Delhi, gave them enough strength to overcome this ordeal in one year's time. They became the proud owners of a successful law firm in Delhi. Their previous boss had to finally concede. He now has excellent rapport with all of them.

In 2003, Dev left his job at Bristol Hotel after being selected as an executive trainee in the ITC group for their hotel wing. The training was for one year. He had to stay at the trainee hostel of the institute in Gurgaon. After the training, he was posted as an assistant manager in one of the ITC hotels in Aurangabad, Maharashtra. Dev had been staying away from his parents since 2003. Of course, on and off, the parents either used to visit him at his place of posting or he used to come and visit them.

From the beginning of 2003, I became more concerned about my wife's sad and depressive demeanour. I attributed it to the loss of her best friend and to various, seemingly adverse, happenings in the lives of her three children. I thought it to be a passing phase and was hopeful that soon she would revert back to her loving, caring, and pleasant self. I spent more time with her and made her accompany me on visits to the residences of our relatives and friends in Delhi. It was done with the purpose of diverting her attention to different happenings. Every week I took her out to enjoy dramas, music festivals, cinemas, etc. at the India Habitat Centre. This provided varied and entertaining engagements for her. All my efforts were hardly making any difference. It did not bring back the cheer that used to ooze out of her ever-jovial and magnetic personality. Nothing seemed to work.

The entire two years from 2003 to 2004 continued to be gloomy for the family. Rashmi seemed to be lost in herself and became forgetful. I thought of taking her away for a few days from Delhi so that the change of place might trigger the required change. I planned a trip of ten days away from Delhi in February 2005.

Since Dev was in Aurangabad, I talked to him about my plan to take Rashmi to his place. I told him that she could visit nearby scenic spots so that her mind would move away from her depressive thoughts. Dev agreed. He planned a magnificent programme of ten days for both. He indicated that both would stay with him at the five-star hotel of ITC at Aurangabad, where he was a manager. The issue being settled, I booked a first-class AC Coupe on the Hazor Sahib Nanded-Amritsar Superfast Express train. The train plied weekly between Amritsar and Nanded via New Delhi. The journey was to begin during the second week of February, 2005.

Both I and Rashmi boarded the train in New Delhi on February 13, 2005. The train arrived at Aurangabad on the 14th. Dev received the parents and drove them to his place at the ITC. The hotel was known by the name of Rama International. We were taken to our suite, which was by the side of Dev's room in the hotel.

After rest and tea in the room, Dev took both of us out for a visit around the hotel. We saw its beautifully manicured lawns, exotic flower beds, tantalising swimming pools, and other attractive facilities. It was a prestigious hotel in Aurangabad. Dev introduced us to his boss, the general manager of the hotel. He was a pleasant person. He insisted on having many photo sessions with us amidst the scenic surroundings of the hotel. Rashmi seemed to enjoy this change. She seemed to be back to her normal self. She began her chat with her son. I was happy to notice the return of her smile. I hoped that she would not go back into a depressive cell again.

Dev had already prepared a detailed ten-day enjoyable programme for us. The first four days we were to spend at Aurangabad and visit all the historical sites around Aurangabad, Ajanta, and Ellora. The next two days, we were to visit Pune and spend time with Guru. From there, we were to travel to Shirdi and visit the Sai Baba temple for a day. After returning from Pune and Shirdi visits, we were to spend two days in Aurangabad in Dev's company. As per my earlier booking, we were to board the train at Aurangabad for our return journey to Delhi on February 25, 2005. Dev made arrangements for a car for our travels in Aurangabad and to other places. I and Rashmi were delighted when Dev told us the details of the programme.

Dev assigned a hotel's employee to accompany us for visits to historical monuments in Aurangabad and also for visits to Ajanta and Ellora. On the 15th and 16th, we visited the important spots in and around Aurangabad. The prominent ones that we visited were Bibi Ka Maqbara, the Tomb of Aurangzeb, Daulatabad Fort, and Aurangabad Caves.

The Bibi Ka Maqbara has a strong resemblance to the Taj Mahal. It is a beautiful mausoleum of Dilrus Banu Begum, wife of Mughal Emperor Aurangzeb. The Daulatabad Fort is located 15 kilometres away from the main city of Aurangabad. It is an ancient fortification that formidably rises in the midst of verdant greenery. Built in the 12th century, this is often hailed as the seventh wonder of Maharashtra. Aurangabad caves are the twelve rock-cut Buddhist shrines. They belong to the 7th century.

On the 17th and 18th of February, we visited the Ajanta and Ellora caves. Ajanta Caves, located 99 kilometres away from Aurangabad, is a UNESCO-designated World Heritage Site. The caves depict Buddhist culture and their stories through various sculptures and paintings. They take one to the world of Jatakas! The Ellora Caves are also World Heritage Sites. The sculptures here represent elements of three religions and do so grandly and beautifully! This visit was wonderful and reminded us of the richness of Indian heritage and culture. The visit was highly tiring. During our cave visit, we had to walk for long distances as the caves spread over vast areas. It was so interesting that, in spite of being tired, we both covered almost all the important caves. The depictions in all the caves were unique and demonstrated the continuity of the saga of the concerned period.

Rashmi and I were driven to Pune on the 19th morning after breakfast at the hotel's restaurant in the company of Dev. The distance was nearly 240 kilometres. Part of the drive was on hills. At around 1230 hours, we broke our journey for lunch in a nice roadside restaurant. The journey was resumed after an hour. We reached the residence of Guru at around 1600 hours. Guru and Nalini welcomed us. After tea and snacks, we took a rest for two hours. They had earlier told us that all of us would have dinner at home around 2100 hours.

After rest, Rashmi and I sat for some time with Nalini and Guru in the lobby. This was in front of the big lawn of their bungalow and had a swing. Rashmi was meeting Nalini for the second time after almost seven years. Their first meeting was at Tara Apartment when Nalini and Guru visited Delhi in 1998. Both the ladies had an engrossing conversation to catch up on the events of the gap period. Sitting on the swings of the lobby, we both chatted while I and Guru went for the evening walk within the colony. I and Rashmi were tired because of the long road journey of the day; we retired early to bed after dinner.

Guru was an early riser like me. We went for a walk around five in the morning. After an hour's morning walk, we joined the ladies for the morning tea. At the breakfast table, Guru and I took the decision, after consulting both ladies, to have the lunch and dinner of that day outside Guru's residence. I insisted on hosting the Chinese lunch at the famous restaurant 'Ban Tao Hyatt'. Guru hosted the dinner at the Pune Club. At both places, we were joined by Guru's eldest son and his family.

The next morning, we were to leave for Shirdi. It was around 210 kilometres from Pune. Guru had told us that we should stay the night in Shirdi. He said that engagements at Shirdi may take more than ten hours. He booked for us at Hotel Yogiraj for the 21st. After our breakfast, we bade adieu to Nalini and Guru. We drove to Shirdi and checked into the hotel around 1100 hours. We reached the Shirdi Temple at 1130 hours. Dev had arranged a VIP pass from the MP, who was also a trustee of the temple. Thus, we could enjoy a good darshan and perform the puja at the temple. After returning to the hotel, we had our lunch and rested for an hour. We then visited other important spots in Shirdi associated with Sai Baba. The most prominent among these places were Sai Theme Park, Gurusthan, and the Sai Heritage Village.

The visit was very interesting. It shed much light on the anecdotes revolving around the halo of Sai Baba. The Sai's devotees were millions and millions in India and abroad. After these visits, we spent time in the Shirdi Market and purchased a few souvenirs related to the epics of the Sai. We returned to the hotel around 2030 hours. The room service was ordered to serve dinner in our room. We checked out of the hotel the next day after lunch. The return journey to Aurangabad took around two and a half hours for a distance of 110 kilometres. We reached Aurangabad in the afternoon.

We had tea with Dev in his room. Rashmi narrated her experience of the last four days to him. Her narration was perfect. She did not miss any important events on the trip. I was delighted to note the transformation in the bearings and attitude of Rashmi. The next two days we spent nicely with Dev. On the 25th, he accompanied us to the railway station and made us board the train for the return journey to Delhi. On February 26, 2005, we reached Delhi in the late afternoon. The train journey had exhausted both, and we decided to have a light dinner of cheese sandwiches. We were so deep in our sleep that we did not even know when Dimpy returned home from her office late at night.

The next morning, at the breakfast table, we shared the details of our Aurangabad trip with Dimpy. After she left for work, both of us went to the Alaknanda Market. She went to the Alaknanda Store and ordered grocery items for the month of March. She told them to send groceries ordered in a couple of hours to our apartment. We then went to the SBI ATM at the market. I drew money that was to be handed over to her for the expenses during the next month. At the Mother Diary shop in the Alaknanda Market, we purchased milk, curd, vegetables, and fruits. We returned to our apartment by entering the complex from the rear gate. The Alaknanda Store delivery boy brought the groceries.

Rashmi seemed to be out of depression. Afterwards, it was noticed that she was developing forgetfulness. It could be gauged as she was preserving empty cartons and pouches of biscuits, Bournvita, tea, coffee, masala, etc. in the kitchen cupboard for future orders of her groceries and related items. This was found almost a year later when, for the painting of the kitchen, the cupboards were being emptied.

I got busy with my work to complete pending issues of consulting with five corporate bodies. I also had to join and conduct several pending arbitration proceedings. Earlier, arrangements were made with fellow members of the arbitration panel to conduct all hearings in New Delhi. In spite of these engagements, I and Rashmi never missed our weekend sojourns to the India Habitat Centre.

My first book, a book of English poetry, was awaiting publication after I finished editing it in late 2005. It was titled "A Bouquet of Wild Flowers". Its publication was arranged by Mona with Delhi's publisher, S. Chand & Co. The book was dedicated to my lifetime-loving companion, Rashmi. She had been my source of strength and inspiration throughout my life.

One day, I received a call from my niece, Dr. Anita. She asked me to conduct the MRI test on Rashmi as soon as possible. When I asked the reason, what she said was quite disturbing. She said that, since June 2006, Rashmi had completely stopped talking to her over the phone. Earlier, she used to ring her up almost every day and talk for ten to fifteen minutes. I was told that, for a correct diagnosis of her sudden aloofness, an MRI test is a must. Anita advised me to do the test immediately and suggested a lab near Hauz Khas. Without losing much time, I took Rashmi to that lab on November 26, 2006. It took them almost forty-five minutes to complete the test. I was asked to come the next day and collect the report.

The MRI report confirmed that the initial stages of the dreaded Alzheimer's disease had started. To have further confirmation and be doubly sure, Anita arranged for a check-up at VIMANS, New Delhi. I took her to VIMANS on November 28, 2006. After conducting several tests, VIMANS confirmed that she was already affected by Alzheimer's. They prescribed certain medications. I was advised that the medication was to be continued regularly throughout life. The disease has no permanent cure. It affects the brain cells of the patient, and these cells gradually die. Its effect also damages vital organs as well as the nervous system. As a result, the normal functioning of the brain and body is completely disrupted. With proper medication and care, the rate of advancement of the ailment can only be slowed down. No permanent cure for Alzheimer's disease yet exists. Even one of the presidents of the U.S.A. could not be saved! An advisory from VIMANS suggested coming after a year to check the progress of the disease.

With this development, I took the decision to move to Bhubaneswar in early 2007. This was of utmost necessity. With the progress of the disease and the gradual increase in amnesia, the patient would require twenty-four hours of nursing. Under the influence of the disease at the interim stage, the patients develop the tendency to go out of the residence unobserved and can get lost. The residence at Tara was not at all suitable for Rashmi's long stay. I decided to sell my flat at Tara Apartment to generate financing. A lot of money was required to upgrade my Bhubaneswar bungalow and to keep substantial amounts in the form of secured financial instruments for her future treatment.

By some intuition, I had earlier prioritised my future action plan for the year 2006. I had to complete all my official assignments in Delhi, sell my apartment at Tara, and prepare my Bhubaneswar bungalow for my stay early in 2007. All three actions were carried out simultaneously.

All my consulting assignments were completed by November 2006. Except for one arbitration case pertaining to Vishakhapatnam Steel, all other arbitration cases were over by December 2006. I had also initiated the repair and remodelling of the Bhubaneswar Bungalow; it was over by mid-January 2007. I initiated action for freehold of my apartment in the month of March 2006. The permission of the Delhi Development Authority (DDA) was obtained in August 2006. After negotiation with the buyer, registration of the sale deed was completed in the month of November 2006. The buyer was well known to me; he had agreed that I could stay in the apartment as long as I wished.

The only problem that yet remained was finding a residence for Dimpy after I and Rashmi permanently left Delhi. In a month's time, she fixed up a rented first-floor flat in the posh GK II colony. The owner of the three-story building was a retired government employee who stayed on the ground floor with his wife. The second floor was hired by a working girl journalist. Dimpy entered into a rent agreement with this landlord to rent the first-floor flat in January 2007.

After reviewing the position in mid-January 2007, I engaged Agarwal Packers and Movers (APM) to arrange the transportation of household goods and the car from Delhi to Bhubaneswar. The packing was completed by the evening of January 26, 2007. They loaded the packed items in the truck and took charge of my car on the 27th. The loaded truck and the car left Tara Apartments around 1100 hours for Bhubaneswar. Dimpy took us to her flat, where we stayed until the morning of January 31, 2007. She dropped both me and Rashmi at Delhi airport for the morning Bhubaneswar flight. *Thus ended the twenty-four-year eventful stay of Chandi and Rashmi in New Delhi.*

Before leaving Delhi, I had booked a suite and a car at the Bhubaneswar Club, whose membership I had had since 1975. The suite and the car were booked for four days, from January 31st to February 3rd, 2007. The club had 10 suites for its members or their guests. The suites were comparable to similar accommodations in five-star hotels at a fraction of their costs. After reaching the Biju Patnaik Airport in Bhubaneswar on January 31, 2007, we boarded the car sent by the club. We reached the club around noon and settled in our reserved suites.

I contacted the Bhubaneswar office of APM to inquire about the arrival of the truck and its household effects. They informed me that the truck had arrived at Bhubaneswar in the morning. The HHE stuff would be delivered the next day (1st February) at my bungalow in Sailashree Vihar. They said that the unpacking and setting up of the material in the rooms of the bungalow were likely to start around 8 a.m. It would be completed by the afternoon.

I asked the RM of PPL Bhubaneswar to send the bungalow duplicate keys through one of his officers to me at the club. I also rang up Rashmi's elder brother (Badu) at Cuttack and requested him to come to my Sailashree Vihar house around 4 PM. He was also to bring Krishna, whom I had engaged primarily as a cook cum housekeeper since October 2006. Krishna was the elder brother of Badu's cook cum housekeeper (Ramesh). Krishna left similar employment in Delhi to work for my household in Bhubaneswar. Before his real work started in February 2007, Krishna was sent to Bhubaneswar in October 2006 to supervise the remodelling work at my Bhubaneswar house. He was also to guard the house till I moved to Bhubaneswar. A gas connection as well as a few utensils were provided earlier so that he could cook his meals while staying in the house to supervise the work and guard the house.

Around 4 p.m., Badu arrived along with Krishna. I was quite impressed with the look and the new facilities provided in the renovated bungalow. Krishna was informed about the arrival of the household items the next morning. He was told to find a priest to do Pooja and 'havan' on the second February forenoon. Me and Rashmi were to finally shift to the bungalow after the pooja. In the evening, we, along with Badu, returned to the club. All of us had a long discussion about the future course of action for our long stay in Bhubaneswar. We also discussed the availability of home care services for Rashmi. After dinner at the club, Badu left for his residence at Cuttack.

The next day was an extremely busy and exhausting day for both of us. After having breakfast in our club suite, we reached the house at Sailashree Vihar. APM's truck had already arrived, and the packed items were being unloaded on the driveway of the bungalow. The unloading, unpacking, and setting up of the items were completed around late afternoon. It was observed that all furniture, etc., were not damaged. Even the crockeries and fancy items were not damaged. I tipped the supervisor and the worker team of APM before they departed. The supervisor said that the car was expected for delivery in another seven days. It was coming from the carrier of Maruti vehicles. Both Rashmi and I returned to our suite in the club by evening. After ordering tea and some snacks from the room service, we relaxed in the room. We even had our dinner in the room before retiring early for the day.

The pooja and 'havan' were done at noon the next day. It was performed in the dining space near the kitchen. Krishna had arranged all pooja material as desired by the priest. After the pooja, the priest went to all the rooms and put vermilion swastika marks on their doors of entrance. He went around the building three times, reciting shlokas in Sanskrit and splashing holy water from the Ganges. After the pooja was over, Rashmi served lunch for the priest. The items served were the sweets of prasad and the poori, bhaji, and kheer prepared by Krishna. The priest left after receiving a hefty 'dakshina'. Rashmi and I had our lunch of puri, bhaji, kheer, and sweets before we left for the club. The 3rd of February was a Saturday, and APM was delivering my car only during the afternoon of the 4th. We finally moved into the house in the morning of the fourth and also received our car that day.

Our Bhubaneswar bungalow displayed the marble name plate *'Charm'*. The name on the plate meant *'Cha'* for *Chandi* and *'rm'* for *Rashmi Mohanty*. It was a two-story building on a plot with sixty feet of frontage and one hundred feet of depth. The plinth area of the main building was 1350 square feet, and the porch was 144 square feet. The covered area of the two-story main building was over 2800 square feet. It had a tiled path around it with a wide front lawn, a rear kitchen garden, a car garage, and an adjacent outhouse with a washroom. A pump house adjacent to the UG water tank completed the setup. The first floor of the house had three bedrooms, an anteroom, and a wide covered balcony in front of two bedrooms. The ground floor had a lobby at the entrance, one sitting room, one bed room, a large stair-case cum entry room, a kitchen, and an adjacent spacious dining area. The roof of the second floor acted as a big tiled terrace for relaxation and parties.

The house was in a prestigious, newly developed locality. The Orissa State Housing Board (OSHB) built 15 nice bungalows for NRIs at this place. It was adjacent to the ever-growing IT sector of the city. This project, after completion, was inaugurated by Chief Minister Biju Patnaik in 1994. It became the central hub of Bhubaneswar, the first smart city in eastern India. On the rear of the house, beyond its boundary wall, a wide, 25-foot road ran from west to east. The road separated the quarters of the state government employees from the boundary walls of the bungalows. A similar parallel road ran in front of the house. The main 200-foot-wide road was fifty feet away. There was a link connecting the front road with the main road. On the other side of the main road was the DAV school in Sailashree Vihar. I had earlier gotten the allocation of this house through the intervention of the state's minister of urban development.

In the evening, I and Rashmi drove to the nearby Bharat Petroleum Outlet to fill up on petrol. This outlet also had a merchandising section known as 'In & Out'. This section made available all daily-needed grocery items, besides a varied group of several other items of daily requirement. We purchased all our requirements for the month. I also took the telephone number of the shop so that, from next month onwards, we could order the monthly requirements for home delivery. After returning home, we sent Krishna to a nearby market with a list to purchase fish and vegetables for a week. Thus began the first day at our Bhubaneswar house.

On Monday, the fifth, I went to the BSNL office to get a landline and a broadband connection. I also applied for the connection for my cell phone. Meeting the GM of BSNL, I requested immediate action on my applications for the connections. The GM assured me that all three connections would be made available to me in two to three days' time.

The GM was true to his word. All three connections were activated by the evening of February 7. I conveyed my telephone numbers to all relatives, friends, and acquaintances. After fixing up the communication arrangements, I made a list of balanced actions that were to be taken during the next few days. The next action was to ask the manager of Tata Sky to reconnect my transferred New Delhi Tata Sky connection. It was to be connected to the three television sets at Bhubaneswar House. This was also done in time.

A maid and a driver were then engaged. Krishna found the maid, who was working in a nearby house. The driver was a retired state government employee belonging to the Athgarh area. He was recommended by our neighbours, Mrs. and Mr. Panigrahi. Mr. Panigrahi was an engineer who worked in a senior position at Nilachal Ispat Nigam, and his wife was a state government doctor (homeopathy). They were a nice couple, and it was their own house where they stayed with their only son. Dr. Mrs. Panigrahi sympathised when she learned that Rashmi was suffering from Alzheimer's disease. She advised that such patients need 24-hour attention as they have the tendency to go outside the house without any purpose and get lost due to amnesia. I had already known this and had made full-proof safety arrangements in my bungalow during its remodelling. I had also cautioned Krishna to be extra vigilant. Whenever I went out on some errands, Krishna kept the front gate locked.

In the month of March 2007, I installed five 1.5-tonne split air conditioners in four bedrooms and the sitting room. For this, I had to convert the single-phase electric connection to a double-phase. My relative, who was at that time serving as a supervising engineer on the State Electricity Board, facilitated this change. Out of three first-floor bed rooms, I had converted one into an office room with a library, a desktop computer, and a bar. This also served as an upstairs visitor room with a sofa, where I offered snacks, tea, and drinks to the guests. This room also had a big refrigerator. Bhubaneswar house became fully functional by March 2007.

Before shifting from Delhi, I had closed my bank accounts at the Alaknanda branch of the Bank of Maharashtra and had transferred the amounts to my account at the GK II branch of the State Bank of India (SBI). I had also done similar closures and transfers of my accounts from Syndicate Bank, Citi Bank, and Hong Kong Bank. A week before leaving Delhi, I instructed the bankers of my remaining two accounts at SBI GK II and Axis Bank at CR Park, New Delhi, to transfer my accounts and the fixed deposits to Bhubaneswar. SBI was requested to make the transfer to my accounts at the Personal Banking Branch of SBI at Chandrasekharpur, Bhubaneswar. Similarly, the Axis Bank of Delhi transferred my account to the Main Branch of Axis Bank at Satya Nagar. These transfers were completed by the first week of February 2007. In the last week of February, I visited these branches and made some more FDs there out of the balance sales proceeds of my Delhi flat.

During each month, I and Rashmi used to make a couple of visits to Cuttack. We stayed overnight with Badu and Baby Bhabi at their bungalow in CDA Bidanasi. Badu also reciprocated by visiting and staying with us at our bungalow. This continued for the entire period of our stay in Bhubaneswar. During this time, Natu and Menki had returned to Bhubaneswar. They were staying in their own house in Acharya Vihar. Bibhu, after his retirement, had also returned to Cuttack and stayed in his own bungalow at CDA Bidanasi. Rashmi's other two brothers and their families were also staying at Cuttack, one at his own house at CDA Bidanasi and the other at Sati Chaura Road at their ancestral house.

Budha and his family stayed on the ground floor of our ancestral Tulsipur house. The first floor of the house was with me, and I spent more than seven lakh rupees remodelling the first floor. I provided new facilities on the first floor.

A new kitchen was built at the end of the rear verandah of the first floor. A second washroom was built as an attachment to the bedroom where Maa had spent her days after the demise of Baba. A new stair case for the roof terrace of the building was also built simultaneously. The staircase from the driveway to the porch, which also led to the entrance of the first floor, was properly broadened and laid with anti-skid tiles. During this change, a three hundred-foot-deep borewell was sunk. An immersion pump inside the borewell connected it with a new overhead water tank. I also constructed a pucca garage near the second additional gate. This gate also connected the driveway through the porch up to the first gate. The first floor and the new garage I rented out to one of my acquaintances. This was rented after fixing a separate electric connection with a new metre for this floor in April 2007.

Budha, after his kidney transplant in 1999, was on heavy medication so that the new transplant was not rejected. This had suppressed his immune system, and he was likely to get infected very easily. The doctors had advised caution in his diet, restrictions on meeting outside people, and less movement outside the house. Every time I visited Cuttack, I met him with caution. It was really a painful situation for the entire family. There was hardly any social gathering or function at the Tulsipur ancestral house. The present atmosphere there appeared gloomy and very depressing. It was poisonous for any patient with Alzheimer's.

A lot of new houses had come up around our Tulsipur house. It had lost its earlier peaceful and scenic surroundings. This was one of the prime reasons for my unwillingness to stay at our ancestral Tulsipur residence. Besides, the independent, peaceful, and novel atmosphere of our Bhubaneswar bungalow could never be available at the Cuttack house. Most of my friends and acquaintances lived in Bhubaneswar. My family and I could not enjoy the stay at Cuttack after the deaths of my parents. There were also many other negative factors concerning some of our relatives that dissuaded me from staying at the Cuttack house. After giving out my portion of that house on nominal rent to an acquaintance, the problem of its proper upkeep was also solved.

I purchased a new Maruti sedan (Esteem Vxi) in July 2007. With Rashmi, I made our first journey in this car to Puri. We had the darshan of Lord Jagannath and enjoyed a night's stay at Puri Circuit House. After a long time, we both had our stroll on the beach and were fully relaxed. Next month, when my daughters Mona and Dimpy visited, all of us again visited Puri for a day. As long as we stayed in Bhubaneswar, they regularly visited us at intervals of three to four months. Dev also visited a few times when he was posted in Goa and Bangalore. The three children have always been very loving and caring for their parents. Their concern grew even more when Rashmi became a victim of Alzheimer's disease.

The year 2007 passed with visits to friends and relatives. We visited the club with regularity. I devoted most of my time to the care of Rashmi. My only diversion was to keep up with my readings and writings. Similarly, the first quarter of 2008 passed without any significant events. Towards the end of March 2008, the driver left the service as he was to settle down in his village in Athgarh. I found another immediately. Driver Ajeet joined and moved to the outhouse with his wife, Reena. They were a young tribal couple belonging to Phulbani. While Ajeet worked as the driver, his wife did the household chores of a maid. In April 2008, Krishna also left his job. He got employment in a factory in Bombay. I found his replacement in a cook provided by an ex-employee of PPL who was also staying at Chandrasekharpur. The cook's name was Santosh. He remained with me for almost ten years until I permanently shifted from Bhubaneswar to Noida.

During the year 2008, I had to go out of Bhubaneswar twice. This was necessary for the arbitration hearings in Hyderabad and Vizag. In my absence, Badu and Baby Bhabi used to stay at the Bhubaneswar house to give company to Rashmi. Dev visited his parents in Bhubaneswar in the month of November 2008. At that time, he was posted in Goa. His visit brought twinkles in the eyes of Rashmi. Like before, she doted on him. One evening, he asked his mother to prepare and give him a cheese sandwich and an omelette. While bringing these eatables from the kitchen to the upstairs lobby, the tray slipped from her hand on the staircase. The plate and sauce bottle fell and broke.

While cleaning up the mess of broken glasses, her right palm got deeply cut. There was heavy bleeding from the wound that did not stop. She was taken to a nearby nursing home, where the doctor had to disinfect the wound and put in five or six stitches under local anaesthesia. With the wound being in a delicate area, anybody else would have loudly cried when the stitching was done, even under local anaesthesia. The doctor was apparently surprised that Rashmi did not feel any pain during the stitches for the wound. Later, it was learned that, due to the effects of Alzheimer's, the brain cells do not record the signal of pain! I was very dismayed and increased my care for her because she could never attract any attention for any pain or discomfort in her body.

During February 2009, Dimpy sent a three-month-old Labrador pup to give us company. The pup was sent by air in a cage on an Indian Airlines flight on February 11. On the afternoon of that day, I received a call from the

Bhubaneswar Airport Manager. He requested to immediately take the pup away from the goods terminal of the airport. He sounded worried. This pup created unimaginable chaos at the airport goods shed. Six to seven other pups, who had also travelled with this pup on that flight, were quiet earlier. After the tantrums from our pup, they also started yelling loudly. I and my driver, Ajeet, immediately rushed to the airport to take charge of the pup. The pup was named Max—a synonym for Mad Max! The pup was later taken to a vet for injection, etc., for protection and cover under the normal procedure of care for pups.

In the month of September 2009, I had planned a four-day visit to Delhi along with Rashmi. This was as per the earlier schedule of Rashmi's check-up at VIMANS. For my stay, I had booked two rooms at the India Habitat Centre. One room was for us and the other for Dimpy, whom we wanted to stay with. She picked us up from the airport, and all three went to IHC. After our lunch, Dimpy went to the office, and her parents rested in their room. The next day was Rashmi's medical check-up.

Sanjay Patnaik of VIMANS examined Rashmi and was satisfied with the controlled progress of her ailment. He was told about the Bhubaneswar incident when her palm had several stitches and she didn't feel any pain. Dr. Patnaik said that her nervous system and its signal to the brain, along with her memory power, had reduced. It was a normal thing to happen as the disease progressed. He prescribed some changes to her daily medicines. He also told me that, if needed, I should take the opinion of the professor of neurology at SCB Medical College at Cuttack from time to time. Such action was taken later, only in July 2015, during the visits of Mona and Dimpy. Dr. Patnaik also advised me to inform him of any abnormal behaviour by Rashmi in the future. The status and condition of Rashmi could be communicated to him at any time over the phone.

In the year 2010, I could finally conclude and finish the last arbitration case. Its verdict was duly given. The Arbitration Tribunal consisted of retired justices Rao of the Supreme Court, Rangarajan, the retired Chief Justice of the Chennai High Court, and myself. The award was in favour of Vizag Steel Plant. As mentioned earlier, I have stopped accepting new engagements since 2006. To keep myself busy, I decided to start writing a book on one of the main subjects of corporate management. I commenced this writing half-heartedly in 2010. However, due to various unavoidable reasons pertaining to Rashmi's condition, the completion of the book was much delayed. It was finally completed and published only in late August 2016. The book was titled

"Financial Management for Managers". Mona arranged its publication with one of the publishers. The book was dedicated to my late parents.

Dimpy and Dev had decided to take the parents to Goa in 2010. Dimpy invited her dad and mom to fly to Delhi in September and spend some time at her residence in Gulmohar Park. She also intimated about the booking of three air tickets to fly to Goa. We were to spend a few days in Goa in the company of Dev. Both children had planned the trip to expose their mom to scenic surroundings and provide some relief and enjoyment to her dreary existence. I agreed with their idea. Our outing lasted around ten days. I had made the necessary arrangements for properly securing the house against any probable break-in by burglars. Of course, the driver and his wife were staying at the rear outhouse, but still, at Bhubaneswar, such things did happen. At that time, Max had already grown up and was the best security for the household due to the 'associated fame' of an angry, attacking dog!

We flew to Delhi on the scheduled day. Dimpy received us at the airport and took us to her apartment at Gulmohar Park. The apartment was spacious and on the first floor. It had three bedrooms besides a sitting room and a kitchen. We stayed in her bedroom. For herself, she preferred to use the sitting lounge instead of another bedroom. Gulmohar Park was a posh locality in South Delhi where the Who's Who of Delhi's legal luminaries resided. Dimpy's office, which was their law firm, was on the ground floor. The office also had the basement under its control. Dimpy could be near her parents while attending to her schedule at the office. Their law firm had already made its mark in the legal circle. I felt proud of the achievement of all the partners in giving the firm accelerated growth in spite of its stormy beginning. The list of its clientele, both Indian and foreign, was increasing year after year. It was due to the determination and hard work that its four partners had put into building its strong foundation.

Our Delhi stay was four enjoyable days. I invited Dimpy's office colleagues and one of her friends, along with their families, to party over dinner. I arranged it at the Delhi 'O' Delhi joint India Habitat Centre. It was a grand affair, and all present, including the children of the families, thoroughly enjoyed the event. Four days passed in a jiffy. On the fifth morning, all three boarded the Delhi-Goa direct flight.

At Goa, Dev had already booked our accommodation in one of the most scenic and luxurious resorts in Goa. The property belonged to the Taj Group. It was famously known as the Taj Holiday Village. Due to his being a part of the hotel industry, he had made quite a concessional tariff arrangement with that hotel. The resort was on the seafront near Taj's adjacent luxurious property, the Taj Hotel Aguada. Dimpy had all the details of the hotel booking. On our arrival at the airport, the hotel's transport picked us up and took us to the resort. We were guided to our cottage on the resort's big campus.

All the cottages were independent units. The cottage where we stayed had two spacious bedrooms. It had a lobby in the front and a wide rear veranda that led to a lawn with flower beds and a hammock to swing and relax. It was very nice for relaxation without disturbance from other guests, either in other cottages or living staff quarters. The seafront restaurant was almost fifty metres away from our cottage and was reached by walking. The path for the walk was on the seafront. At this restaurant, buffet or la carte breakfast, lunch, and dinners could be taken by the guests. There also existed twenty-four hours of room service for providing drinks and eating in the cottage.

After tea and some snacks in the afternoon, all three went walking to the seafront. We could clearly see the Aguada Fort with its lighthouse. It was a massive and marvellous citadel that defined the landscape of Candolin, a tourist hub in Goa. The fort had a historical legacy of 400 years and showcased the Portuguese heritage and architecture of the seventeenth century. The fort stands overlooking the Arabian Sea and offers mesmerising views of the surrounding areas, including the resort. While strolling on the seafront, we could see a big old ship half sunk a kilometre away from the shore. These panoramic views could also be seen from the restaurant close to the fort. In line with the restaurant and, next to the seafront, were the costly cottages of the resort. Some of them were permanently reserved by a few renowned Bollywood stars.

Since Dev was expected to come and meet us in the early evening, all three returned to the cottage and awaited his arrival. He came driving a Wagon R vehicle from his hotel and reached the cottage early in the evening. I and Rashmi met Dev five years after our Aurangabad visit in 2005. Dev promised that, henceforth, he will meet us at least once every year. These promises he meticulously kept year after year.

Subsequent to his Aurangabad posting, he was transferred to Baroda by the ITC hotel group. This was his last posting with ITC. He had resigned to join Kenilworth Beach Resort in Goa. From there, he transferred his services to the Radisson Group. While he was serving the White Sands resort at Radisson, the property was taken over by the Zuri Group, and he became the manager of that resort.

Earlier, in the first quarter of 2010, Dev had met with a serious road accident. His friend, who was driving the vehicle, died on the spot. Dev's injuries were severe. It was a miraculous recovery for him after he was hospitalised for a few months. At that time, the news of the accident was only intimated to Dimpy. She immediately went to Goa from Delhi and took full care of him until his complete recovery.

Dev had brought a packed dinner for all of us. He could feel that his mother had been badly affected since he last met her. She was hardly communicating with anybody, and, at times, she had a faraway, vacant look. He was also told that she had developed the tendency to casually move out of the residence as if in a trance. She needed supervision and care twenty-four hours a day. Almost each day of our stay in Goa, he regularly visited us. Once, he came along with his French girlfriend, who was serving in a French company in Goa. He apparently wanted to get the approval of his parents for their nuptials when they decided on marriage. Later, in 2011, when both visited Bhubaneswar and spent four days with the parents, Dev was told that he could go ahead with the future plan of marriage.

After five days in Goa, Dimpy, Rashmi, and I returned to New Delhi. The next morning, me and Rashmi left for Bhubaneswar. Our regular schedule at Bhubaneswar consisted of an alternate-day visit to the club, a weekly visit to Cuttack, and occasional trips to Puri, Ghatagaon, Gopalpur, Chandipur, etc. I tried my level best to expose Rashmi to the changing panorama associated with the new surroundings. In between, visitors from Delhi, like Solanki and others, used to come and meet me whenever they were at Bhubaneswar on an official trip.

During 2011, in every quarter, medical check-ups of both of us were done at our residence by Rajani. He was the owner of the pathological lab in the adjacent house. In that building, specialist doctors of different medical disciplines had hired spaces from Rajani to operate their private clinics. Some of these specialists were attached to big hospitals in Bhubaneswar, like Kalinga, Apollo, KIT's, and Prasad's Eye Institute.

The lives of the lonely couple were spent together. They enjoyed Dev's trip in 2011. Every quarter of that year brought joy to them when both daughters visited with regularity. This aspect continued throughout our stay in Bhubaneswar.

Alzheimer's was taking its toll on Rashmi's health and behavior. Even the visits to the club and to relations places were greatly reduced. In August 2013, Rashmi developed the problem of redness in her eyes. She was taken to the Eye Institute for a diagnosis. She was cured by their treatment. However, her overall condition was rapidly deteriorating, and there was helplessness clearly visible on my face. Towards the end of the year, her physical movements, recognition of people, control over bladder function, and speech were considerably affected. Even for her daily routine—to go to the washroom, etc.—she needed help. It became difficult for me to manage her in that condition for long. I had to hire a 24-hour nurse from one of the recommended service providers at Acharya Vihar. This agency's services were available until September 2014. Because of their below-par services for a patient like Rashmi, I terminated them and found a better service provider in a few days.

In the meantime, in the middle of October 2014, the driver, Ajeet, and his wife, Reena, left the service for personal reasons. Reena was managing Rashmi's difficult physical condition in the absence of a nurse. I ultimately hired the services of home nursing from a reputed service provider in Bhubaneswar. They provided a nurse who stayed 24 hours with Rashmi. She stayed in the bedroom of Rashmi with effect from October 30, 2014. The service provider also ensured that there was no break in nursing service while changing the nursing personnel. By this time, most of Rashmi's movements were in a wheelchair fitted with a commode. Even for her movements for any medical check-up in a clinic or hospital, she was always moved along with the wheelchair.

During the year 2014, it was found that Rashmi had stones in the gall bladder. She was having pain while taking her food. Although she was unable to cry because of the pain, it was apparently visible from the tears that she shed during her meals. On a routine examination in December, the specialist doctor advised admission to a hospital for a thorough checkup and diagnosis. It was all the more necessary, as Rashmi was unable to communicate anything on her own. The examining doctor, who was a senior consultant at Kalinga Hospital, suggested the examination at Kalinga Hospital. I decided to take Rashmi to that hospital.

Rashmi was admitted to the hospital. A good private cabin was reserved for a fortnight at that hospital. In the meantime, I informed about her hospital admission to three children and to Badu. By the time she was moved to the cabin, all three children had arrived at Bhubaneswar. Several tests were carried out, and it was found that she had stones in the bile duct. The stones needed immediate removal. The doctor planned the stone removal through a laparoscopic operation. Fortunately, Kalinga Hospital had one of the best surgeons on its roll for this operation. He was Dr. Brundaban Nahak. After thoroughly verifying the credentials of the operating doctor, I allowed the operation. The surgeon was astonished to see such big stones. He said that she must be in unbearable pain due to the stones. Except for tears in her eyes, she could not express her pain due to her disease.

Ten days after the operation, she was discharged from the hospital. Two days after her return home, both daughters left for Delhi, and the son flew back to Bangalore. Rashmi was feeling much better and could have her normal food. By July 2015, I had asked the agency to provide two nurses instead of one. This was necessary, as a single nurse could not handle all her requirements.

Subsequently, Mona and Dimpy also came to see the parents. Mona's Bhubaneswar colleague (Commissioner, Income Tax) arranged the visit of Professor Dr. Ashok Mallick to examine Rashmi at Bhubaneswar. He was head of the neurology department at SCB Medical College, Cuttack. After his examination, he said that she also had Parkinson's disease. He prescribed five more medicines. This medication created more problems for her. They were to be discontinued after a couple of months, under the advice of Dr. Patnaik of VIMANS. In hindsight, I felt that the short phase of the new medicine did more harm to her health. I had to console myself: 'What is destined can't be avoided.'

After this, Dimpy decided to put the medical care of both parents with Dr. Gita Prakash. She was a senior consultant at the Max Multi Speciality Centre at Panchsheel Park, New Delhi. The medical test reports of both parents used to be sent through email to Dimpy. She showed these reports to Dr. Gita Prakash and, after due discussion, used to send her advice to me for any action that was needed at my end. This arrangement continued for a period of almost one year. This, by and large, took care of the medical problems of that period.

Both the daughters and the son wanted their parents to shift from Bhubaneswar to Delhi, NCR, so that more care could be taken. In 2016, Dimpy and Mona made me agree to their proposal of shifting. It was decided that the Bhubaneswar house would be sold before the shift. I and Dev started the process of finding a suitable buyer for that property. The important condition for this sale was that the entire payment of the sale proceeds had to be done by bank draft or bank transfer. It was a long-drawn process. I had to get permission from the Orissa State Housing Board to affect such a sale. Earlier, I had already decided that the buyer had to run around and obtain all required legal approvals before the sale deed was to be registered. Finding a genuine buyer without the help of a middleman was really a herculean task. I had to curtly refuse the services of hordes of property dealers. I evaluated the genuineness of all the prospective buyers' intentions. In this process, many dubious buyers were eliminated.

Already, the demonetization process by the government had led to difficulties in disposing of real estate properties. Fortunately, I was lucky to find a genuine buyer in June 2017. The house was sold for a good price, and the registration of the sale deed was done in the month of August 2017. I had already discussed with the buyer that a couple of months may be required to move the family out of Bhubaneswar. The buyer had agreed and told me to take my own time for shifting. After discussing with Mona and Dimpy, it was decided that the final shift would be made in the month of September 2017. Details of such shifting were worked out in detail by both daughters. Dimpy inquired as to whether both or one of the existing nurses attending to Rashmi can come to Delhi (NCR) and continue to provide service to Rashmi. This was required so that any further arrangements could be made accordingly with the service providers in Delhi, NCR. I discussed this with both serving nurses. One of the two gave her consent to accompany Rashmi to Delhi. Dimpy then intimated the final plan of shifting. It suggested my movement along with Rashmi and our pet Max on September 22, 2017.

I learned that Dimpy was taking over a house at Sector 15A in Noida at the beginning of September. This building was earlier occupied by her colleague, who was shifting permanently to the USA. Dimpy's Delhi flat was on the second floor. It was difficult to put her mother on the second floor because of her physical condition. Hence, she had decided to change her residence so that, on the ground floor, Rashmi could stay with two nurses. In the other two bedrooms on the first floor of the proposed house, Dimpy could occupy one while the other could be with me.

I made arrangements for the transfer of my Bhubaneswar bank accounts in SBI and Axis banks to their respective branches at Hauz Khas, New Delhi. The house in Noida had all the furniture and household items. Thus, I was advised not to move these things from Bhubaneswar. We were supposed to move out to Noida only with our personal effects along with the pet Max.

Mona was to arrive at Bhubaneswar on September 18th, along with air tickets for me, Rashmi, and the nurse, Sushama. The tickets were booked for the September 22 flight by Indian Airlines. During that time, Dev too would arrive in Bhubaneswar to help. Mona would assist her dad in the packing and disposal of Bhubaneswar household effects. She was also to accompany us on the flight to Delhi. Dev would return to Bangalore after seeing them off at Bhubaneswar Airport.

I made arrangements for Max's vaccination. A cage was made to order for the transportation of the pet. The caged Max accompanied us. I gifted to the house purchaser all furniture except those in the kitchen and dining area. Five air conditioners, three TVs, and one refrigerator were also given to him as gifts. The freebies also included a bookshelf full of classic English literature and fiction, a home theatre system, and a number of feature film videos. My Esteem car was sold to him. I donated, as a gift, all kitchen and dining area crockeries, utensils, a gas stove, a washing machine, and a refrigerator to cook Santosh. It was a reward for his good service for nearly ten years. The wife of the cook got the bulk of the sarees from Rashmi. The rest was given to the maid.

On September 22, 2017, we left Bhubaneswar along with Mona and Odia Nurse Sushama. The boarding of the flight was smooth. Mona's friend Meenakshi, who then was the GM personnel of Indian Airlines, extended all help for the movement by flight. She had told the Bhubaneswar Station Manager of IA to ensure smooth boarding. With the flight taking off, left behind were aeons of our memories of the temple city of Bhubaneswar. During the two-hour flight, Rashmi sat comfortably with Mona in the front row on the right wing. I sat on the left-wing front row.

After our arrival at Delhi Airport, we had to wait for fifteen minutes for the cage with Max. After putting the cage on the rear of the SUV of Mona's friend, we drove to the house in Sector 15A of Noida. Dimpy was already waiting for our arrival. She put Rashmi in her room along with the nurse, Sushama. She guided me to my room on the first floor. Max was tied to the ground floor by the railings of the staircase near the entrance. The day was Dimpy's birthday. A small party, after the cake-cutting ceremony, was already arranged. After dinner, Mona was dropped off at her New Delhi residence by her friend.

After a sound sleep at night, I woke up around 0530 hours. I made a cup of tea for myself. After tea, I went out for a morning stroll with Max. I found Sector 15 to be a colony dotted with nice bungalows. It was a VIP colony. The residential houses belonged mostly to industrialists, big businessmen, lawyers, retired senior bureaucrats, and senior ministers of the central and state governments. The colony had several big parks, a nice club, and a good marketing complex. It was a well-protected gated sector with guards at two main entry points. I could survey the colony during my daily morning and evening walks along with Max for nearly a year and three months that we resided in sector 15-A of Noida.

The House of a Central Cabinet Minister was only three houses away from our residence. All the houses along the way overlooked one of the big parks. At times, I also used to have my walk in this park. During walks with Max, I used to cross the minister's house, which had three to four dogs of different breeds. Once, during my return from the morning walk, when I and Max were near that house, a small Pomeranian dog came charging towards Max. In the melee, I was fiercely dragged by Max. I fell on the road, and my right toenail broke. The security staff of the minister came running, lifted me up, and apologised for the incident created by the dog of the minister.

From this house, Dimpy's office in Delhi was around 22 kilometres away. The normal travel time was around forty to forty-five minutes. During peak traffic hours, it extended to almost one and a quarter hours. This was a big disadvantage for her. She had also taken a lot of trouble to provide comfort to her parents.

In my heart, I felt concerned about her ballooning monthly expenses due to us. The payment of high rent for the Noida house and the expenses of two nurses for Rashmi, among a host of other incidental expenses, must have been a terrible drain on her finances. This remained a sore point for me. She always refused any of my sharing of such expenses. The only hope was the prospect of Dimpy getting her own apartment at Jaypee Greens Pavilion Heights 4 at the earliest. For this, we had to wait until December 2018. I had already indicated my desire to purchase an apartment in the same complex. Dimpy did the needful to find one for me in her residential complex. My apartment was in Tower 4, while her apartment was in the adjacent Tower 5. Both were part of Pavilion Heights 4.

In the month of November 2017, I purchased a new Kwid Automatic RX car for my routine use. The car was purchased after Dimpy and Mona approved it. It was the first auto-transmission car that I drove. The car was used to go to the market in the sector for the purchase of groceries, vegetables, fruits, etc. At times, I also drove the car to Delhi.

Rashmi's medication and nursing care at Noida during the years 2017 and 2018 followed the pattern set earlier at Bhubaneswar. It was also continuously monitored. The advice of Dr. Gita Prakash was taken regularly. Rashmi's physical condition continued to deteriorate, like that of any Alzheimer's patient. She had, however, regained focus in her eyes after we started using coconut oil to prepare the items that she ate. Also, the Ayurvedic medicine that Mona brought from her known Ayurvedic doctor at Karnal could provide a bit more mental agility. Gradually, her intake of food was getting smaller and smaller. The problem arose due to her difficulty swallowing the food. It was due to the effects of the disease. Her body was getting thinner and thinner. Her immune system also seemed to be affected. She got coughs and colds quite easily. I only hoped that she would not be affected by her family's hereditary bronchial disorder.

In the first quarter of the year 2018, Dimpy was intimated about taking possession of her apartment and getting it registered. Years ago, she had paid in full for her apartment. The builder had taken a long time to complete it for handover. She proceeded to take over her apartment. I had earlier visited the apartment and told her to find one such apartment for me too. It needed to be in her tower or in any other tower in the complex of Pavilion Heights 4. This new deal for me was completed in May 2018.

The handover and registration of both apartments were completed in July 2018. I and Dimpy hired a contractor to fix some additional safety measures in our apartments before moving in. For my own apartment, I ordered furniture, etc. to make the living area operational. Before the date of movement, all the new furniture and accessories were received and placed in their proper places. Earlier, I had ensured that connections for broadband with WiFi and landline facilities were made operational. The connections for IGL gas and Tata Sky for the TVs in the apartment were made in time.

Finally, on December 9, 2018, I and Rashmi moved into our new apartment. The two nurses and the Nepalese housekeeper, Meena, were also moved to this apartment. Meena used to come at 9 in the morning to cook lunch and dinner. Besides, she also did other household work, like cleaning utensils, dusting, and cleaning rooms. She also served tea in the afternoon. The date of my shifting to my own apartment coincided with my 55th marriage anniversary.

A fortnight later, Dimpy too moved into her apartment. Almost a year later, Mona and her two sons (Tanmay and Aman) also moved to this complex. She, like her father, also purchased her apartment. Except for Dev, the entire family stayed in three different apartments in Towers Two, Four, and Five of Pavilion Heights 4. All these apartments were just across the golf course in Sector 128 of Noida, a part of the National Capital Region (NCR).

Rashmi's health continued to deteriorate. Her entire body had shrunk to a bundle of skin and bones. In spite of all these, she never lost a twinkle in her eyes. It used to shine when she looked at her husband, children, and grandchildren. All doted on her and used to be very sad about her condition. Her husband's grief was unimaginable. Night after night, lying awake in bed, I silently shed my tears, unobserved. My life without seeing her ever-smiling face for almost a decade was agonising. But who can change destiny's dictum?

There were no anniversary celebrations in my apartment that year. I did not have the courage to celebrate; my loving lifetime partner and doting mother of three adorable children could neither participate nor understand. Her vegetative condition was so painful that every time I looked at her, I dove deep into depression. Unobserved by my two daughters and perforced for their consolation, I had to pretend and behave normally.

The two nurses took care of her under my supervision. They, too, were feeling her agony. They never neglected their duties. Her cleanliness, her timely diet and medicines, her body massages, and moving her around in a wheelchair were their primary duties. Both stayed 24 hours with her. There was a proper arrangement for their stay in the same master bedroom, where Rashmi's double bed was kept on one side. They slept on a sofa bed. The bedroom was quite spacious. It had two floors to the roof, cupboards, and a large attached washroom. The period between December 2018 and February 15, 2019, passed without any major incidents.

In the second half of February 2019, it was my 84th birthday. All three children decided to celebrate it. Dev took leave for a week and arrived on the 22nd night, which was a Friday. His stay with his parents was scheduled to last until March 1st. He had his return flight ticket for Bengaluru on the morning of March 2, a Saturday. By the time Dev arrived, his mother had already had a cold and cough for a week. She was taking medication as well as using a nebulizer for her breathing trouble. She was responding to the treatment. As scheduled, the birthday party organised by the children went off well, and she could have a bit of the party cake and very little of the other dishes.

I and the children spent quality time with her, and she appeared to be happy, despite her physical discomfort due to a cold and cough. In the afternoon of February 28th, the children had planned to have their lunch with me at IHC Delhi on March 1st before Dev left for Bengaluru. While we were finalising this, around 6:30 p.m., the nurses called us because Rashmi was having breathing issues. At that time, she was sitting in a wheelchair. When I used the nebulizer to ease her breathing, she suddenly had two hiccups and collapsed. Immediately, she was put on the bed, and her feet were massaged. Dev tried to revive her. The ambulance with a doctor from nearby Jaypee Hospital was already on its way and reached in seven minutes. The accompanying doctor immediately examined her. At 6:50 p.m., he declared that she was no more. The family was thunderstruck. Silently, copious tears were flowing down the cheeks of all family members. The children, in spite of their intense grief, started making arrangements for preserving the body for the night before the cremation next morning.

Dimpy's office colleagues and her friends immediately arrived at the apartment. They made arrangements for the electrical freezer that preserves the body until cremation. In the meantime, Mona's friends and office colleagues also arrived to provide assistance. The body of Rashmi was moved. It was put in a supine position in the freezer with a glass cover. Over the head of her body, outside the freezer, a lighted Deepa was put as per ritual. Gloomily, I sat there and recited Bhagwat Geeta the whole night. All three children sat by my side after seeing off their friends, colleagues, and other visitors late at night. It was decided to have the cremation the next morning at the nearby crematorium in Noida on March 2, 2019, around 9 a.m. This decision was taken after Dimpy's colleague Alishan and friend Deepak had obtained the required official documents and completed all formalities during the night for the next morning's cremation.

A priest was already arranged for the morning. He was to perform necessary religious rites at the apartment as well as at the crematorium. Her body was bathed in the morning after applying turmeric paste. It was draped in a new saree by both daughters with the help of the two nurses. In the meantime, a bamboo bier was made for cremation. Her body was put on the bier after the puja in the apartment. It was then placed in an appropriate carriage and taken in procession to the crematorium. After reaching there, the priest did the puja of the last rites in the presence of family and friends. It was consigned to flames around 10:30 a.m. The ashes were collected in the evening in a kalash. It was kept in the house for its immersion on the 10th day, after the sradha ceremony, on the ghats of Ganga at Haridwar.

The kalash with the ashes was kept in the master bedroom of my apartment. A lighted Deepa was put by its side. The rituals made it mandatory to keep the Deepa lit until the ashes were taken for immersion. This was done by the three children. The rituals also required a puja and 'Mahaprasad Seva' on the eleventh day of the demise. The children had already informed all relatives and close friends of the family about the demise of their mother. They had also sent e-invitations to all for attending the forenoon event of the 11th day at the Jagannath Temple of Hauz Khas, New Delhi.

"Om Ganeshaya Namah"

With deep sorrow and profound grief we, the children and grandchildren of the family of Shree Chandidas Mohanty, mourn the demise of our beloved and loving mother/grandmother –Rashmi Mohanty. She passed away on 1st of March 2019.

For her soul to Rest in Eternal Peace at the abode of Lord Jagannath, we request you and family to Join us for prayer and "Mahaprasad Seva", on the 11th day of her demise, i.e. on 11.03.2019, at 1300 hours at Jagannath Temple, Hauz Khas New Delhi.

In grief:	RSVP:
Mona (daughter)	(Cell phones)
Dimpy (daughter)	+91 99586 45445
Dev (Son)	+91 98101 55992
Tanmay (Grandson)	+91 97422 73966
Aman (Grandson)	
	+91 99998 18054

The intense grief of the family is beyond any description. I desired to also snap the linkage from my earthly bondage. In my thoughts lurked the desire to give company to the departed soul of my lifelong partner. I felt that all the zest in my life had vanished forever; it was no longer worth living!

The children, in their grief, could not tolerate their dad's pathetic condition. In their own ways, they tried to console him and provide balm for his heartbreaking grief. The rituals and customs don't allow the family of the deceased to go outside their place of residence for nine days, except for the job of ash immersion. This ritual was observed in Toto. The family members took their food before the sunset.

These nine days, now that I recall, were the most turbulent days of my life. A host of relatives, family friends, and well-wishers visited us. Many more were contacted over the telephone (calls and messages), emails, WhatsApp, and Skype. Every call was a reminder of the beautiful, ever-smiling face of Rashmi. I could feel that she was still hovering over her dear Bobby (that's what she used to call me) and her three doting children. All through the night, I visualised her presence in my dreams. I used to feel her soothing touch and relish her soft smile and the mischievous twinkle of her eyes. During those nine days and even thereafter, suddenly I used to get up as if to search for her! Even today, I feel that all my happiness, feelings, and desires have gone along with her; my present life is no more than the life of a robot.

In spite of grief, life had to move on. For the last rites of the tenth day, arrangements for a vehicle, a hotel for a stay, and a priest at Haridwar were already made by the children. All of Rashmi's dresses and her daily items were packed in a big suitcase for giving away at Haridwar. To be at the ghats of Ganga at 9 a.m. on the tenth day, we had to move out with the Kalash on the ninth day.

Me and my three children moved with the Kalash on the said day. We stayed the night in Haridwar. The next morning, after confirming the priest's presence at the ghat, we reached there with the Kalash.

The priest had arranged all items for the pooja for immersion of the ashes and the 'Pinda Dana'. Dev performed all the rituals as per the advice of the priest. The entire event went smoothly. I, Mona, Dimpy, and Dev, while returning to the hotel, stopped in the way and gave away the old, used items of Rashmi to the needy poor. After lunch, we were driven back to our Noida apartments and reached there around 9 p.m.

After a light dinner brought from a roadside eatery on our way back, Mona and Dimpy checked about the next day's arrangements at the temple.

Next morning, around 11 a.m., I, along with Mona, Dimpy, Dev, Tanmay, and Aman, reached the temple premises at Hauz Khas. We put a large, framed photo of Rashmi in the hall where the prayer meeting was scheduled for 1 p.m. The guests and the invitees had the 'Maha Prasad Seva' of Lord Jagannath. The family joined with them in the Prasad Seva.

For almost the last five years, Rashmi borne her immense physical and mental agony without being able to communicate her sufferings. My presence by her side during this period could, to a miniscule extent, give her some moments of joy and recognition. But it was extremely difficult for me to put on a brave front and hide my perennially wet eyes for so many years. Rashmi was an indispensable part of mine. Our love, attachment, and bondage with each other were beyond any worldly imagination. We felt incomplete without each other. After more than half a century of togetherness, her departure pushed me into an incomprehensible sea of life's sorrow.

I now consider my existence a duty that I was to carry out according to the wishes of my loving, darling wife. Many times, Bubly (that's what I affectionately called her) had told Bobby to always be a shield for their three adorable offspring. I had already noted how she had waited for her entire family to be with her when she departed for God's abode.

It can't be a coincidence that Dev had joined her two sisters, coming all the way from Bengaluru, before she had her last breath! A pious soul always gets the last wish fulfilled! And indeed, she was a very caring, pious soul whose whole world started and ended with her family. She was the epitome of our traditions and culture. She had a brave heart and protected her family by building a strong shield over the 'family cocoon'!

Indeed, what a travesty of destiny! Twenty-three days after her demise, it was her 75th birthday! The family would have loved to celebrate that day with her in a grand manner, in spite of her agonisingly long illness. The family did not forget the occasion, even amidst everyone's grief. No one could imagine that destiny had already scripted her passage to the abode of the divine. Instead of celebration, the family would observe condolences. From that inaccessible abode of God for mortals, she must have observed the wounds of her husband's heart bleeding. And indeed, it did bleed. To lessen my sorrow over her remembrance in a pensive mood, I had to find an alibi in a literary pursuit. Like many times earlier, I penned a few lines in her memory. It provided a soothing balm to my spirit of depression. I remembered her 75th birthday:

Remembrance on 75th Birthday

Injustice of God badly hits me and the family,
Makes us all depressed on your 75th birthday,
Each moment over last 23 days, weighs heavily,
Your soul went to the heaven that fateful day!

Freedom from the suffering might have given
Relief and solace to your soul for moments few.
For me, there isn't any more zest in life to live.
Settings of my feelings lie scattered and askew.
Drops of tear fall from both the eyes and I miss
Your loving company sitting shaken and forlorn.
Hear the grieving heart's loud thumping beats,
It engulfs the mind to feel events of age bygone.
Eternal peace be in heaven for my beloved dear,
Shall ever carry the bouquet of sweet memories,
When I depart to go to the serene world of yours,
And recall some loving moments of old vagaries.

* * *

The Lonely Traveller

After the passing of Rashmi, I gradually tried to bring in a bit of composure in my life. This was my mask, primarily for reassuring the daughters that I was not in any depression. I took care to see that their sentiments were not affected. They were two pillars of my strength. I had always felt the pain in their eyes for their suffering mother. They tried their level best over the last one and a half decades to make their parents comfortable—mentally and emotionally. I was sure that the unbounding love, care, and concern of my three children would enable me to pass the twilight of my life without much concern till the final call came. I sincerely prayed to God that I should never, ever give them any tension on account of my health.

In mid-March 2019, Dev left for Bengaluru, and Mona returned to her Delhi residence. Dimpy also got busy with her office work. However, while in Noida, she spent most of her time at her dad's apartment. Before Dev's departure, three children decided to keep the Odia nurse back, as they did not want their father to be at the apartment alone at any time. A full-time driver was also engaged. The driver was engaged in taking me out to Lodhi Gardens for a daily walk. Besides, he was also to drive me to other places, including the India Habitat Center. They were fully aware of their dad's mental and emotional condition and saw to it that he got back some of his old spirit as early as possible. I tried my best not to disappoint them and outwardly feigned a normal demeanour.

In late March, when I had gone to a nearby market in the evening, someone dashed into my parked car and fled away after damaging it. The car, which was not even a year old, was repaired before its disposal. In mid-April 2019, I purchased a new Maruti Beleno car and disposed of the repaired Renault Kwid car. All such acts were meant to divert my mind from the terrible personal loss.

As much as possible, I tried my best to keep myself busy with reading and writing. I also gazed for hours at the golf course from the windows of my bedroom and across my study table. Time seemed to hang heavy on me in spite of my best efforts. Outwardly, I seemed calm and tranquil. My inner self continued to be tormented with the thoughts of loss—the loss of the ever-smiling and loving mother of my kids. It is never easy to bear the loss of one's ever-loving life companion of nearly six decades. Rashmi had been my inspiration and heartbeat. She had been the main source of my emotional strength at difficult junctures. She had all along been my guiding light for material and spiritual achievements. During the stormy days of my service career, she had been the zephyr of my life. The fragrance of her sweet presence, the exuberating vives of her love and endearment, her iceberg-cool temperament, and many more positive qualities were gone forever. These losses for me were inconceivable, irreparable, and beyond any endurance!

In the month of May 2019, my grief subjected me to hallucinations. I felt like a traveller in the Sahara Desert, having the illusion of an oasis. The feeling of her loss gave rise to poetic fantasy.

Her Absence

Period is now more than two months
Since you departed to the heavenly abode.
Solemnly, I bear life's hazardous bouts,
Try my best to create a normal mode.
Today's visual on the parapet of cloud,
I mistook it as you sitting in a chariot.
Woke with the sound of thunder loud
To visualise your charming silhouette!
Imagery do not leave me for a moment,
Heart gloomily ponders over the loss of you.
Prayed for your peaceful heavenly stay,
The dreamy images shall fill all the way!
The vibrant colours of life, lost and faded.
Feelings take turn to fantasy and mirage,
Lost pleasant moments of our boulevard.
Failed utterly to grab your loving image!

* * *

Life and living continued at their usual pace. The healing touch of time gradually soothes. Awakening comes to give it the stamp of destiny. Grief turns to anger, and the anger fades quickly to leave an emotional vacuum. When one has already arrived at the dusk of life, all emotions lose their significance. One can only wait for the ultimate truth of life to grab the soul for eternal peace! Till then, one has to develop patience to wait! I just could not keep track of time. The days passed into weeks, and weeks into months. Soon arrived the month of December 2019.

The month of December had special significance for me and Rashmi. It was the month of our marriage anniversary. It was also the birth month of our first child, Mona, the Christmas baby. We always celebrated both occasions in style. The absence of Rashmi on the day of her anniversary made me wish her a virtual bouquet:

Bouquet of Remembrance

On this day of the fifty sixth anniversary
Fondly remember ecstatic events array,
The path we took for our life's journey
To build our own golden nest of ecstasy!
We jelled to face life, filled with vagaries
And turned the odds to sweet memories.
Our journey was fully tuned and geared
Vibrant rides, enjoyed and remembered.
Albeit, all the ups and downs of our life,
Your support was always firmly for me.
We put our life's bell to swing and swipe,
To provide musical tunes for the chime.
Lively and important occasion of the day,
I fondly recapitulate all the care and love.
My eyes ooze copious tears to fall and lay
How I wish, both can dance and groove!

* * *

After death in the family, for a year there can be no celebrations as per the religious rituals. This was strictly followed by all the family members. Earlier, even the Deepavali celebration was avoided for this reason. The darkness of two apartments in Pavilion Heights 4 of Wish Town, Noida, was a mute witness to the gaiety around. After all, bleeding hearts can only weep in darkness!

The family hoped that the new year of 2020 would provide some escapade from the ambit of grief, but nobody knew how. The sad faces of Mona and Dimpy were never seen by me during these times. I was sure that it was only a facade to hide their grief for the benefit of their dad. They loved their mother the most. Her suffering and death had left a scar in their hearts, and hiding it before her dad required herculean efforts. They visibly succeeded, but their dad could easily see through it.

In three months, the death of my beloved Rashmi was going to complete a year. Important religious rituals at the end of a year after death were awaiting to be performed. These were to be carried out by her son and husband at Gaya. The day for this ritual was decided on the basis of *the Nakshatra* movement on the day of death. It was calculated on the basis of the Hindu calendar (Panzica or almanac). This date for carrying out the pooja and pindadan was indicated as February 19, 2020. Dev was duly informed about the date. He, with his contacts in Bengaluru, made arrangements for Pitru Pakshya Puja and Pinda Dan at Gaya on February 19. He also made hotel arrangements for our stay in Gaya. I had already booked our tickets from Delhi to Gaya on February 18th and the return flight on February 20th.

Dev reached Delhi on the morning flight from Bengaluru. From the airport, I brought him to my apartment in Noida. He met Mona, Dimpy, Tanmay, and Aman. They all had their dinner together that night. It was Dev's second meeting with his dad and both sisters after the demise of his mother. The daughters had taken their dad earlier in August 2019 to Bengaluru to stay for a week with him in his apartment. The complex of his apartment was very nice. It was near his workplace and was at a distance of five minutes' walk. He stayed alone in the apartment with a Labrador pet. He had a cook who prepared his lunch and dinner and a maid who cleaned his apartment.

In the month of October 2019, Mona also moved into the residential complex of her dad and sister. She had purchased an apartment on the 3rd floor of Tower 2. This was a wise decision for her and her two sons. Tanmay was already working in Delhi, and Aman was studying in his 3rd semester of BBA at Amity University, Noida. Now, the entire family (except Dev) stayed together in their own three apartments at the same complex. I stayed in Apartment 0807 of Tower Four; Mona stayed in Apartment 0305 of Tower Two; and Dimpy stayed in Apartment 1509 of Tower Five. This togetherness was a great consolation for me, especially after the demise of my wife. It was some relief for my depressed and broken heart.

On the morning of February 18, 2019, father and son boarded their flight from New Delhi to Gaya. At Gaya airport, a car sent by the hotel picked us up and took us there around 1130 hours. Dev checked about the next day's puja arrangement with the concerned source. He was told to reach their place at 7:30 a.m. the next morning. We were assured that everything would be done in time, and we would be released by 1330 hours in the afternoon. I remembered a similar arrangement that I had made way back in 1962. It was a similar puja for the deceased mother of Mr. Mukherjee, the divisional manager of Burmah Shell, Patna, and my then-boss.

After lunch, we went out to have a look at Gaya City. For me, it was a visit to the place where I had spent almost four of the best years of my service career. I was reminded of that golden period when I and Rashmi had begun our first journey into a happy marital life. It was five and a half decades earlier. The flashback of sweet memories rekindled the pain in my heart. I wanted to locate the old bungalow where we spent two of our most memorable initial years. It was no longer there. In its place, a big office complex of Magadh University had come.

The city had completely changed during the last half-century and was unrecognisable to me. I sat mute in the car as it moved around the city. Almost all my known people at Gaya had passed away. There was no Colonel Swamy, no Hafiz Saheb, no Bhattacharjee (with the Mogul-era title of Khan), nor were there any Sarogi, Prasad, or Srivastava. I felt like an old banyan tree uprooted by the storm of time. Dev could see the discomfort on his father's face. To divert my attention, he told the driver to return to the hotel. We had an early dinner and retired to bed.

The next morning, we did not have our breakfast as we were to sit in the pooja. After bathing and putting on white kurtas and pyjamas, we started for the trust office that arranged the puja. Reaching there around 7:30, we were given the priest and puja material. We moved barefoot on an uneven, rough path. It took us almost half an hour to reach the first place of pooja.

The pooja was performed at three places. The first place was the Phalgu River. The priest made the pinda balls and performed the ritual along with Dev and me. The place was on the bank of the river and was in proximity to the temple complex. The priest, after the first pooja, carried the pinda balls to the river and immersed them. The second place was the Vishnu Pad temple. The pinda balls for pooja were again made at the temple complex.

After the pooja, the pinda balls were carried into the temple and offered at the feet of Lord Vishnu. The Kalpataru tree in the temple complex took third place. The offered pinda balls of the temple were taken to the designated spot of said tree and were finally kept there. This was the last act of the pooja. It took almost three hours for these worships.

This ritual gave moksha not only to the soul of Rashmi but also to the souls of her parents and the souls of all past members of their family tree. The souls of my parents and the souls of all the members of my family tree too got the nirvana!

Both father and son boarded the car to return to the hotel. In the car, I narrated to Dev my previous sorrowful visit to the Phalgu River almost fifty-six years ago. I had gone there to bury, deep in the river bed, my seven-day-old first child. After birth in the hospital, she died of infantile jaundice.

We had lunch at the hotel and rested for an hour. After having tea in the hotel room, we visited Bodh Gaya. This is an important place of Buddhist pilgrimage and is only seven kilometres away from Gaya. Lord Buddha had his first awakening here when he was sitting under a pipal tree. It has a number of heritage sites full of big pagodas built by Buddhist nations like Japan, Cambodia, etc. The visit lasted more than five hours. It was quite exhausting. One has to cover a few kilometres walking inside the important heritage sites and visiting the pagodas. This place, too, had undergone a complete transformation like that of Gaya City over a period of more than half a century. I could not recognise the Tourist Guest House of ITDC at Bodh Gaya. I and Rashmi, during 1964, used to visit the restaurant of this guest house once or twice every month for lunch. The manager of ITDC had also become one of my close acquaintances at that time.

The next morning, we checked out of the hotel and went to the airport. Gaya has an international airport. It catered more to foreign visitors from the far east visiting Bodh Gaya. The return flight that I and Dev boarded had many of these foreign visitors going to Varanasi. The return flight always had a stoppage at Varanasi before landing in Delhi.

My driver was waiting at the Delhi airport to take us back to my apartment. In the evening, the entire family had their dinner together. The daughters were informed about the details of our Gaya visit. After a bit of chit-chat, the family dispersed. Dev left for Bengaluru on the next day's afternoon flight.

In the month of March 2020, the pandemic era of COVID-19 began the world over. No country could escape its grip. Governments in all countries, including India, declared a complete lockdown. The situation was more like house arrest for the entire population. It was also twenty-four hours of curfew in Noida. There could be no escape for anyone. Death and devastation continued even after a year. Towards the end of the year, the vaccines for COVID-19 were found by the scientists. Began the vaccination of a vast number of people the world over.

This ensured an improvement in the situation. The restrictions started easing a bit in August 2021. Government advisories continued to make it mandatory to follow the COVID Protocol. Efforts for vaccination of the entire population progressed. All over the world, everyone had to put on a mask, avoid crowded congregations, and follow other protocols. The trying period continued even in September 2021. A bit of relaxation to bring back normalcy in the activities of various sectors did start. But even now, it is far from normalcy. People are being advised to follow the advisories and protocol. In all honesty, people themselves have to be more careful to avoid the repetition of a third wave of the COVID-19 disaster.

During the pandemic period, I observed my departed wife's 76th birthday at home. Both daughters celebrated her birthdays at my apartment. In the midst of her fond remembrance on March 24, 2020, I expressed my love and dear feelings for her through the extravaganza of a poetic remembrance:

Remembrance

Intensities of feelings can't today be shown
By the forlorn and grieving children and me.
Time stood still forever to remind and frown
Mundane emotion of the grief won't rhyme!
We remember your ever-loving attachment,
Treasure the imagery of your sweet lovely face.
Such memories lie deep in corners of heart
And do constantly provide us a lot of solace.
For a year now your loving nearness is lost.
Graciously you flew to the heavenly abode.
The grieving made our eyes numb and moist,
Forgot the zest of living in sorrows crusade.
Your birthday is a reminder for our penance.
Crippling wound of our hearts stand forlorn,
Reminder of your sincere care and patience
Provide nostalgic melody to the endless mourn.

* * *

Remembrance flashes in the mind of all the endearing moments of the past. It provides me with reasons for thanking the almighty and the near and dear ones too! In one and a half years of the COVID-19 period, the daily routine of people was totally transformed. But my love for my wife bequeaths the horizon of infinity!

During the period of the pandemic, the economy of our country has been affected very adversely. Activities in industries, trading, and construction had either slowed down or stopped completely. Millions have become jobless. The world never faced such a man-made evil disaster. Unless one kept calm under such provocations, the end result would be mental stress and a consequent imbalance. No one understood it as well as me. That's the reason I kept myself busy more than it would have been in normal times. In virtual online meetings, I lectured on various topical subjects. I prepared many writeups on varied issues, from spirituality to social and political issues. The materials of my writing reflected my vision and opinion derived from my own experiences over the past decades.

Beginning in July 2020, when the first phase of the pandemic became dormant, I agreed to address the Group of Ex-PPLers on the second Sunday of every month. These addresses, through video conferencing, were topical subjects that shed light on the normal objectives of our society. For more than a year, I continued to address this group every month through video conferencing.

While in Bhubaneswar, I used to meet some important members of this group. Every year, from 2007 to 2011, I attended PPL Foundation Day celebrations on invitation. I interacted and addressed them as a speaker. From 2012 to 2019, I was completely tied down at home due to the serious illness of my wife.

Despite what I said in virtual gatherings, I achieved my objective of remaining busy. Remaining busy after bereavement is the only solace one can enjoy. It is not necessary to join any religious group to tamper with the adverse temperament. It can take many forms to achieve peace and solace. It can be through social work; it can be through the intense following of a hobby; or it can be anything that can provide help to the needy.

Adversity need not break one. It can provide myriad opportunities to help society while making progress. The pandemic of the present and, consequently, social distancing are burdens for the weak mind. Now, more than ever, one should broadly open all the channels of communication in this digital age. A lot of lives can be saved if one does not fall into the trap of miscommunication. One's ego should not come in the way of following the health advisories of the government's health departments. During active life, many misunderstandings are created by vested interests for short-term personal gain. In hindsight, one may feel that it could have been avoided and ignored. Maybe the human ego prevents it from being overcome at that time. Life is too short for acrimony or anguish against others. For personal solace, this needs to be understood earlier than at the twilight of life! It is appreciable to notice the zeal and tenacity of ex-PPLers to help some of their colleagues in many ways. The best help is to give encouragement and guidance for a peaceful retired life. At the same time, it is always better to avoid airing public views on religion or politics in social gatherings.

One needs to properly play a role while being active on social media. Of course, at times, the role of social media complicates some matters. During the month of September, I observed that most of what passed off as comments in such media appeared to be manufactured and not based on the relevance of the truth.

Many people misused the media for such purposes. For such people, nothing appeared to be sacrosanct or sacred—be it personal abuse, doctored quotes, edited pictures, fake news, or fake videos. For checking authenticity, the source matters. Considering the ethos of a civil society, authenticity needs to be the hallmark of all such postings. On my part, I follow this ethos scrupulously.

In September 2020, the second wave of the pandemic took a virulent form. There were innumerable deaths due to this epidemic in all corners of the country. To me, it appeared that the year 2020 was going down in the calendar of the country as a year of disaster and destruction. First, it was COVID-19, which still continued in its virulent form. Then came a number of severe cyclones, followed by unprecedented floods.

I never got depressed by these turbulent incidents in nature. My motto has all along been: "From despair, hope is born." These happen to be the two sides of the same coin. When there is no hope, there is hell, and this fear of hell gives life to the vitality of hope! I knew well that looking forward to a better tomorrow is everyone's birthright! I also know that strength of mind and a propensity to tackle difficulties are two qualities that are extremely important in prevailing situations.

Soon, the month of October arrived in the midst of the pandemic. By this time, it was medically confirmed that improving one's own immunity gives a higher degree of protection when one follows other protocols as per advisories given during the pandemic. I soon learned that the long period of continuance of COVID has gradually built up some resistance due to the boosted immunity of many in the community. This was also acknowledged by the official system for the gradual containment of COVID.

I learned that, during the treatment of COVID, the doctors try to strengthen the immune system of the patients while raising the depleted level of oxygen in their bloodstream. The hopes continued to rise further with the news that a vaccine was perfect life protection against COVID. Later events confirmed its efficacy. I always believed that one needed to find ways and means to build up immunity through natural means of exercise and a proper diet.

During the same month of October 2020, I gathered the information that a recent Physics Nobel Prize winner, British Professor Roger Penrose, solved the mysteries of the Black Holes of our universe. The professor used a mathematical equation from 1955 created by a Kolkata physicist, Amol Roy Choudhry, to arrive at his findings. While dwelling on the findings of our universe, I strangely came across certain aspects of my own life. During my life of eighty-six years, while I moved from infancy to youth and now to old age, the Earth has travelled nearly fifty billion miles around the Sun. For me, it was fascinating to learn that as I exhale just once, the sun itself travels 430 miles in its path around its own centre, with our earth in hot pursuit.

I educated myself about the interlinking of the solar system with the lives of human beings. While the solar system is a prisoner of gravity that shapes its path, we all become prisoners of our own minds. My perception has been that the real motivators in one's life are strong 'will' and 'emotion'. During my life's journey, many times I felt ecstatic, dismayed, and amazed while facing the vagaries of situations. My journey has been filled with ups and downs, darkness and light. As a senior citizen, I felt to have arrived at a stage when spirituality provided the solution for all materialistic agony. Spirituality stabilises the mind. Like a beckoning light, it shines on the path of the journey to make it smooth and meaningful. It ensures the development of a compassionate personality to propagate contentment all around.

Came the month of November and the onset of winter, which always bring health hazards to people with fragile constitutions in advanced age. People who, like me, are burdened with complications of blood pressure and diabetes needed more care during this period. Over the last four decades, I have maintained effective control through medication, exercises, yoga, and pranayama. In the winter months, I never neglect this regimen. I continue to follow this old protocol of mine even today.

During the COVID crisis, I found how little understanding people have about their own bodies. For all the intense engagement that we have with our own selves, most regard the inside of their bodies as an alien landscape! They neglect it until they face illness. They think of the relevance of their bodies while they are handed over to medical experts when things go wrong. Even then, they fail to gauge the seriousness of the medical diagnosis of the body's ailment. This is true for the majority of people. They never care to educate themselves about medical diagnostic terms. Now, the vocabulary that has sprung against a single virus in the present pandemic era is truly bewildering! All said and done, I firmly believe that prevention is always better than cure.

I continued with my fitness programme during the month of December. I again pursued my hobby of writing and took up the task of completing all my unfinished literary work. I made it a point to continue my video conferencing and attended the meetings of the F.A.I., AIMA, ICA, and PPL groups. I remembered my fifty-seventh marriage anniversary on December 9, 2020. Missing the soothing company of my soulmate on this occasion, my emotions were expressed in the form of an ode:

Fifty-Seventh Anniversary

> Like the aimless wandering of the monk,
> All emotion was lost at the altar of time.
> Missed her mischiefs and hilarious pranks,
> Lost the nuances of anniversary sublime!
> Over the harsh period of twenty-one months,
> Her invigorating smile was missing.
> Cruel destiny separated our hugging paths,
> Continued turmoil of serpent like hissing.
> Do not forget the thoughts of anniversary
> Dwelling in the distant galaxy miles away,
> The partner feels the void of his dear fairy
> In discomfort, he curses his painful stay.
> Children demand your ever-jovial nearness,
> I strive to heal my heart and rid the sorrow;
> It will strengthen my alibis and harness
> Fake profile for deceiving coming morrow!
> Hope to enjoy the existence of next incarnation,
> Keep promises in laps of mutual obligation,
> Sorrow and Joy exist in today's celebration
> To virtually mark our lifelong devotion.

* * *

While scripting the ode for my departed wife, I remembered the spirituality of our lives. We had felt that spiritual awakening had been the cause of the glorious transformation of our lives. It gave us freedom from the limited identity of our individual selves. We had felt that it was in consonance with the very core of Odisha's Jagannath Cult. This cult combines elements of several practices of different religions. It amalgamated universal brotherhood. Both of us have always believed that spirituality does not belong to any single religion. Our modern way of thinking always made us feel the consensus of opinion in all religions. According to both, the facts of the matter indicated that there was a single base of spirituality for which the paths to reach there were only different.

In a recent gathering, I was asked to speak in a virtual meeting about my perception of spirituality. *It is necessary to catalogue here, in a few paragraphs, what encompasses my spirituality.* My spirituality, as I mentioned earlier, equally embraces all faiths. It is symbolic of the true religion of mankind. This evolves consciousness where science and spirituality meet. When the light, as propagated by a scientist, is seen as the form of divine knowledge, then it will be the closest that 'Science' will ever reach to the 'Absolute'. Here, the Absolute is the Brahman or the soul. Light, or divine knowledge, is the bridge between the material and spiritual worlds. The Vedanta philosophy synchronises with all other religions as far as the concepts of *God, soul,* and *body* are concerned!

The Vedantic way to attain spirituality, or freeing the self from mundane desire, or *maya,* presupposes life's paths. These paths go by the generic name *of yoga.* Yoga means to unite *ourselves with reality.* These yogas are classified into *four systems.* They lead to the realisation of the *absolute,* where one becomes ever-free and ever-perfect. The other two systems are *Abhyasa* and *Vairagya.* The first two systems clear up ignorance of one's nature and allow the self (*Atman*) to restore its own nature. The other two are the main tools for this liberation. Abhyasa is the constant practice of the yogas, and vairagya is the nonattachment to life after freeing it from mundane bondage for true solace.

My belief is that attainment of spirituality requires one to practice four yogas. These are titled:

1. Karma Yoga.
2. Bhakti Yoga.
3. Raja Yoga and
4. Gyana Yoga.

Karma yoga purifies the mind by means of work. One must always remember and follow the teachings of Bhagwat Geeta: "*Karmanye Ba Adhikarestu, Ma Phalesu Kadachana*". Bhakti yoga indicates the natural impetus of union in the human heart. It ensures a *bridge between Atman (self) and the Absolute (soul)*.

Raja Yoga's main parts are *pranayama, concentration, and meditation*. The amalgamated three modalities ensure the lasting practice of spirituality. Gyana yoga is divided into three parts. The first is to *hear the truth*; the second is to *balance views*; and the third is to realise the ultimate truth. This is the highest and most difficult form of yoga. There can be an intellectual grasp of it, but it is extremely difficult to attain realisation. Many have tried and failed to achieve it in their lives, but it has not diminished or ended their faith in it.

The ultimate of spirituality is attained by following consciously and truly the four yogas mentioned. They are extremely difficult for a common man to attain. The best spirituality a common man can attain is through the development of good faith in others. It is easier through an ideology that supports the spirit of 'malice towards none'. As a matter of fact, whatever makes one noble and whatever expands consciousness are religion and spirituality. A truthful, joyful, and righteous self, bereft of ego and selfishness, would automatically achieve spirituality. This continues to guide my life.

It was the month of January in the new year 2021. It arrived amidst the continued gloom of last year's pandemic. Suffering due to COVID was unarguably the most consequential and painful global event of the past year. It exposed the gargantuan and historic failure of the public health system in all countries. The system totally failed to control the spread of this virulent pandemic infection.

The adverse response to this shock for the world economy was a combined fiscal and monetary negative stimulus of over 20 trillion US dollars. This amount may well cross $28 trillion in the next five years. Millions are bound to slip back into poverty. No one yet knows what other unforeseen consequences lurk in the shadows.

The cost, in terms of human life, has been astronomical. The world over, nearly 1.8 million lives were lost, and more than 80 million people were infected. In the political arena, the country of origin of the virus has already lost its position of global economic leadership. The hegemony of China in controlling the world economy has ended. Control has again moved back to the bigger democracies of Europe and America. For these countries, the degree of their naivete vis-à-vis the 'Dragon' has ended. Sooner or later, a new world order is bound to emerge.

The historically old Vedic culture, fine-tuned to modern India's advancement and ideology, shall be the new pathfinder for a glorious future for the global community.

A group of democratic nations has come forward to rescue the world. The international collaboration of these nations to develop the vaccine against the pandemic has recorded success. At the beginning of 2021, I noticed the start of hectic activities everywhere for mass vaccination of the population in all countries, including India. I hope that the nightmare of COVID-19 will be buried as soon as possible. I have faith in the blessings of divinity to save mankind.

The month of February was the month of my birth. Before my birthday comes Valentine's Day on the 14th of February. Since my Valentine has gone to the 'other world', the month of February has now lost its significance for me. But it will always remind me of the essence and significance of my happy married life. I well remember how the endearingly beautiful married life of mine over fifty-six years was built on the citadel of love, mutual respect, and trust. It was bereft of any pretensions by both. I want to share the secret of my successful, happy married life with the families of all my friends and acquaintances. Its beginning can be on any Valentine's Day.

On this day, for the members of each couple, it is pertinent to remember that one's self is the *real soulmate*. It is never possible to live your entire life pretending to be someone you are not. Truth has unique ways to make its presence felt. As a matter of fact, the person who actually gets deceived is one's own self. Greater self-understanding would help each member of all couples to progress psychologically and spiritually. The process of exploring oneself clears the mystery of one's identity. Every positive experience becomes important in fulfilling a couple's purpose in life. It would neutralise any illusions in their lives that would give rise to misunderstandings and a loss of trust.

Further, the couples need to remember that pretension is escapism; it prevents them from facing the challenges of life squarely. Pretension is acceptance of defeat; it's a defeat by which the couple would lose sight of their goal of love and compatibility. It would only be the illusion of a false ego and the exhibitionism of an empty core. There is no shame in not being able to be 100 percent compatible. But it is disgraceful to pretend and cheat. The best solution for such malady is to always speak the truth and practice righteousness. A simple act of acknowledging facts as they are is the way forward. Always listen to the dictum of the innermost soul, where the truth reigns. This spirit always solidifies the confidence of both.

Honesty and resoluteness can surmount any situation, defeat any adversary, and beat any oppressive force. The marital life attains wholeness once its opposing constituents are in equilibrium. It remains stable and whole until the bond of trust is not allowed to be disrupted by negative forces like jealousy and suspicion. The success of Rashmi and Chandi's happy married life, spanning over half a century, derived its strength from the principles enumerated in previous paragraphs. This is also the reason for me to make this advisory available to newlywed couples.

The month of March would always be a sad reminder for me. It was the month when Bobby's dear Bubly passed away. It was more poignant as her birthday also fell on the 24th of the same month.

March 1, 2021 was the *second anniversary* of her *Mahaprayan*. On this occasion, in her memory, I penned down these few lines:

Second Mahaprayan of Beloved Rashmi

Two years back, I and family lost your presence.
In abode of God, you rest in the midst of fragrance,
Missing your pristine demeanour and loving trance,
We fall back on memories filled with remembrance.

Recapitulating the dreams of our frailty adolescence,
Relished mischievous visits with your stealthy steps,
Smooth silky arms around in tight knotted embrace
Fantasy is skilfully woven ever in my memory flaps.
Your graceful gaiety acted like a balm for soul and mind.
Fairy and shapely charm always awaited filling of eyes,
Your celestial cool beauty, irresistible I do always find.
Soulful heartbeats bid for you many a thousand byes.
Being far, far away it is not easy to bend to thine eye,
Nor it's easy to woo you earnestly to capture thy love;
Oh! lord, Soulfully guide and help me to capture thee
And avoid the fall to imponderable sorrow's groove!
Fully engulfed in thy loving thoughts, I won't ever care
The surroundings and futile incongruent of life's haze;
For your sake, I will love to progress fast and dare,
With all my ingenuity, to cross all the hurdles in a daze.

With this poetic expression, I bid adieu to my ever-loving soulmate. She must be watching from heaven how I, the children, and my grandchildren terribly miss her. For me and them, time won't ever erase her memories and image. Even now, I feel that she perennially remains by my side through days and nights. My bondage with her, in thoughts and mind, stays beyond this life!

There was an intense COVID-19 vaccination drive all over the country. In Noida, too, it was in full swing. I took my first dose of Covishield on March 11, 2021. The second dose of the same vaccine was given to me in May 2021. Both daughters and the son also received both doses of vaccination during that period.

Rashmi's 77th birthday was on March 24, 2021. I wrote a few lines of poetic reminiscence befitting the occasion:

Seventy-Seventh Birthday Remembrance

A day of ever-loving remembrance
Of mine and my exuberant heart,
That sadly misses you at life's terrace,
Gives reminder of unbridled wrath.

Without fancy show of selfish motive,
You have been like a glittering brook.
With ravishing flow and tinkling dive,
The sunshine was your heavenly look.

Flavour of the day is no longer spicy,
Twilight do dampen the fading light.
Nature's grandeur aptly looks dicey,
Angel's absence douses all the spirit.

Wrinkles of body only time can grace,
My love for you can smilingly endure.
Seeing the picture of thy smiling face,
We lovingly enjoy the divine pleasure.

Waking up to a sweet nocturnal dream,
I feel of your presence lying by my side,
Our doting children's courage and charm,
Strengthens me for your love to abide!

* * *

The second quarter of 2021 passed without any major mentionable events for me. The situation in COVID was improving a bit. But the rigours of lockdown continued. I had already taken the second dose of the vaccine on May 1, 2021, along with Mona. A few days later, Dimpy too had the second dose. From the media, I gathered that, for many people, there was an impending mental health crisis due to the pandemic. This was factually true. For more than a year, citizens the world over have been undergoing isolation due to long periods of lockdown as well as fear of infection. Even small social gatherings were not permitted. It was reason enough for the mental stress and depression.

Though I advanced in age, I was mentally as strong as any young man. For me, the age of a person is just a number, provided his outlook on life is practical and positive and he remains active in body and spirit. For that, one has to approach any situation with a strong will and determination. It is not ease but effort, not facility but difficulty, that makes strong men. I always knew that there is perhaps no station in life in which difficulties are not encountered. But it can always be overcome, and the required measures of success can be achieved. For me, the difficulties have always been my best instructors, and the mistakes contributed to the best of my experiences.

I always told my near and dear ones that what looks like insurmountable obstacles can be easily crossed when approached with firmness in purpose. It requires a positive mindset to change any depressive situation during the pandemic. This is not only for myself and my family but also for members of our society. During this period, it saddened me to observe that the majority in society never rise above mediocrity. In spite of having the inclination and ability to do something positive and helpful for family and others, they become 'Cry Babies'. Though administrative failure led to a shortage of oxygen in the treatment of serious COVID patients, most resorted to the easiest method of criticism instead of finding ways and means to minimise the difficulty.

However, the presence of a few strong men in society could ultimately control the situation.

Sitting at home, I pondered the reasons for people's failures in their lives. I could clearly see that their fear of failure held them back and inhibited them from pushing forward. They always waited and waited in the hope that some mysterious power would liberate them and provide confidence and hope. This is nothing but their negative mindset! Men and women who come out of challenging situations are those who struggle and break the negative bond that handicaps and enslaves a person. This is the worst thing that has affected humanity for ages and is the primary cause of all unhappiness.

I clearly remember the occasions when I used to encourage my colleagues and juniors to shed their depression. I encouraged them to make resolutions to rise above adverse situations in life at any cost. I had the belief that only such things could bring to the forefront the true strength of one's character. Success never opens her doors to those who are lethargic and unwilling to strive hard and sacrifice their comforts. My usual quote for them was based on the famous saying: "The diamond could never reveal its depth of brilliance and beauty but for the function of the stone that grinds its facets, polishes it, and lets its light disclose its hidden wealth. This is the price of its liberation from the darkness." *Now I feel that we shall all face and bear the pandemic with its grinding and polishing for a brighter tomorrow!*

Then came the month of July 2021. Without any sign of rain and a continuation of oppressive heat, I remained indoors at home with the air conditioners running most of the time. My companion was the 12-year-old 'young' pet, Mad Max, a lovable white Labrador. Max was a gift from my second daughter, Dimpy. In February 2009, she sent Max by air to Bhubaneswar as a 3-month-old pup. Max is registered with the Indian Kennel League (IKL). In his birth certificate, IKL indicated his pedigree for three generations, beginning with his father Trek and mother Minki.

In July 2021, I was invited to speak at a gathering on the subject *'Unity versus Diversity in Social Life and Thought'*. The gist of that talk, what I hold as a philosophy dear to my heart, is elaborated here and in subsequent paragraphs.

The narration enveloped many societies of different hues that were featured all over the world. To properly understand the theme, I mentioned that one should recognise that 'dignity' is the basic tenet of civilised life. It can only be ensured by humanism. This is also the outcome of knowledge and technology. This ensures the impetus for equality and independence in thoughts, logic, and dialectics. Globalisation has attempted to implement the same knowledge and reasoning worldwide. This is irrespective of cultural differences and geographical distances.

I acknowledged the root problem of misunderstanding or mistakenly *mistaking uniformity* for *unity*. According to me, this happened due to the presumption that all human beings are the same and, therefore, their needs, aspirations, and goals would be similar. In this process, diversity is forgotten, and people lose their distinct identities to this erroneous presumption. To illustrate, I compared one group with another. The fact that one set of people believes that their lifestyle is superior to that of others and must be enforced on another group—this very idea is antithetical to the concept of equality, which, in turn, is essential for unity.

Unity is when we are one—one in mind and one in spirit. Uniformity is achieved when all believe and practice likewise. The truth is that, as human beings, we are one, but we are different individually. Realising and recognising each other's peculiarities and then existing harmoniously is unity in diversity. This does not cater to the non-realistic homogenization of the intelligent human race. Nature opposes this endeavour. Nature itself proposes diversity. No matter how accurate the technology may become, it cannot emulate the inexplicable complexities of human disposition.

Further, according to me, beliefs and views cannot bloom through imposed uniformity. This has been proven around the world by past dictatorial regimes that throttled and restricted democratic thought. Unity embraces and acknowledges the contrasts, the dissents, and the variations. It promotes prosperous coexistence. In other words, according to me, *unity* is not achievable if we aim for *it*. Unity is not about supremacy. It is respectful to all within its fold. History is witness to situations of violence when supremacist tendencies prevailed in the ruling elite. Ultimately, the ego of supremacy breaks people, societies, and countries. I also feel that the need of the hour is the *unity* that contains the effervescence of all religions in all regions of a country.

My views acknowledge that *uniformity* is not a natural phenomenon. Peace, progress, and prosperity of a nation lie in the ethos of '*Unity in Diversity*' and not in *uniformity*. Any attempt to change the social balance can only lead to chaos and disruption. It will, at the end, snap all efforts for peace and prosperity in the country. Unity in its real sense begets the era of "Sabka Saath, Sabka Vikas," i.e., togetherness leading to prosperity for all. Any idea of pseudo-uniformity would raise the head of the 'monster intolerance' between communities of different faiths. *Unity* is always better than eschewing *uniformity*. Indian ethos had the engrained philosophy of "Vasudev Kutumbakam"—the world is one family.

Towards the end of July, the weather became slightly tolerable with the onset of pre-monsoon showers. But the temperature and humidity brought in more problems. After all, I knew that human beings never get satisfied with any situation. And that has been the secret of progress for centuries after centuries. That has been the reason for the development of science and technology. Inquisitiveness and an unquenchable thirst to gather knowledge have been the hallmarks of the human race! During August, both of my grandsons completed their second dose of Covishield. I was happy that all the members of my family were now protected by vaccines against the pandemic. By this time, many had gone through the second wave of the pandemic. Due to the double dose of vaccination, I hoped that the effect of the pandemic in the future would be minimised. By following the advised safety measures, the physical wellbeing of most would be ensured.

However, there should be more focus to lessen the mental trauma of millions that occurred during the last one and a half years. My remedy to safeguard future mental health was a dose of emotional vaccination. This is most needed for remaining happy in these trying times. For elaboration on this aspect of thinking, there are three simple steps. These are elaborated on in some of the following paragraphs. It would indicate how important it is to keep one's emotions bridled to strengthen one's mental health. It will raise the level of confidence. It would be the best antidote for depression and lack of interest.

I found that, in the pandemic era, many have lost their near and dear ones. The hardest part for them was their absence from their loved ones, even during their treatment. Some even had to attend their funeral rites online! These have been rude reminders of the time that we live in. One could suddenly and intimately feel the pain of so many. This has been the unavoidable truth for all during the cursed period of the pandemic.

The prolonged and seemingly unending nature of the disruption and losses makes one routinely upset. One gets easily disoriented. For many, it develops anxiety syndrome, leading to mental exhaustion. I had all along felt that, like one needs a vaccine to protect against viruses by developing greater immunity, similarly, one will have to learn ways to immunise against emotional turmoil. Like the two doses of *the COVID vaccine, three ideas,* if implemented, will act like vaccines for one's emotions.

Firstly, one needs to cultivate *equanimity—an anchor of stillness* within us. This minimises the effects of the changing external environment. This does not mean that one is not at all affected by it. What it actually does is raise the threshold of our emotional strength, like the vaccine increases immunity. Building equanimity requires deepening one's self-awareness. One needs to know what makes him or her happy, sad, insecure, and excited. One should also learn how frequently one moves from one emotional state to another and what triggers these shifts. This knowledge provides one with the strength to explore and find remedies for an emotional breakdown or any changing emotional state.

Secondly, one of the reasons for emotional stress is attachment to specific outcomes. It can be anything: a promotion expected in a service career, moving to a recently purchased house, or, may be, the marriage of one's twenty-five-year-old progeny. The way to deal with this is to open one's heart to the possibilities of whatever may emerge. It is best for one's heart to accept reality. One need not bother as to whether that promotion comes in six months or a year or whether the progeny decided to get married in a year or three. This requires learning to let go of attachments to fixed outcomes. It will make one trust the natural process of evaluation.

Finally, it is seen that one struggles to be at peace with the uncertainty of the future. One imago fears and setbacks. One can protect against this fear by reframing the relationship with difficult circumstances. Almost nothing is as good or as bad as it seems. One can always choose to assess what the situation is trying to teach.

It is common to underestimate the innate ability to deal with any setback. I had seen many people more resilient than they often believed. In fact, invariably, in such situations, one learns and grows the most. *One simply needs to get more comfortable with being uncomfortable!*

A few days ago, I visited a friend. He was slowly recovering from an illness. It was impressive to see him so calm and focused. When asked about the secret, he said that he had only remembered and accepted the positive aspects of that situation. He described how it had brought into focus what was really important to him in life. It had made him more disciplined about his health, and now he values the relationship even more. I fully endorsed his views and termed it "emotional *"vaccination" in action.*

My advice to friends is that they should, if need be, change their attitudes in life to ensure higher immunity for emotional well-being. This will strengthen their willpower and enable them to tackle adversities in better ways.

During the whole month of August, I was aghast at the media's reporting on two topical subjects of negative nature. In normal times or earlier, when I used to have a very busy schedule, such reporting would have meant very little to me. In the present situation of the pandemic, when time is the only thing that is available in plenty, the reported subjects drew my attention for analysis and solutions, if any. I was sure that it adversely affected many members of society. No day goes by when one does not read in the news about *suicides and murders*. The cause and remedies of this social malice need immediate attention.

During the analysis, I found that death and destruction seem to be part of the staple diet of a few. Such people develop an inherent tendency for suicide or murder. They leave behind a trail of brokenness, hopelessness, and devastation. They strangely prefer the option of death as the be-all and end-all solution to the sufferings of their own or others. They feel that 'death' is a preferred 'neighbour'. They lose all hope in themselves and others, known or unknown. They perceive that the inevitable is certainly going to occur. This triggers the response of death-wish in them. Lurking in their subconscious is a world that they visualise to collapse suddenly. They assume that their world will fail to sustain itself. They believe that there is nothing more to live for.

From this perspective, it is not uncommon for such people to see death as a liberation and an escape from suffering. They often go a step further. They also wish the death of those whom they perceive as their tormentors. While the first perception leads to suicide, the second one leads to murder. In the name of divine retribution, they often take it upon themselves to accomplish the task and commit suicide or murder. This becomes their way of awarding social justice! Thus, not long before, the victim, in turn, becomes the prosecutor.

I am sure that such people often struggle with their emotional, psychological, and physical illnesses. Their suffering can best be alleviated by early diagnosis and timely treatment. Life is full of meaning and creativity; it should never be allowed to be destroyed. There is a need to reverse such situations in society. Each rational and sane individual needs to be strong—functionally and emotionally. They have to be ordained with the quality of developing an attitude. An attitude that would provide strength to fight the adversities of life and living

With our own efforts, the inner-self breakdown can be avoided at the least cost. This has always been the guiding principle of my faith in life, even when I faced unmitigable adversity! I know how much support I used to get all the time from my dear wife Rashmi for strengthening my determination.

When faced with one's own brokenness, hopelessness, or inner devastation, death is never the solution. One should never contemplate even the death of the oppressor as a means to put an end to one's suffering. The end of the oppressor is not necessarily the end of one's trouble. Others in society, by their silent presence and efforts, can provide comfort and consolation to restore normalcy to the affected. Timely counselling would save valuable lives from an untimely end.

After the narration of the depressive aspects of society, I want to put my thoughts on achieving happiness for people in the current era of depression and discomfiture. I have always held that a happy atmosphere initiates universal happiness. One often gets distracted in the quest to find happiness and contentment. That distraction comes from the perception of what is giving happiness to others. Sometimes others perceive it as ephemeral pleasure; it is often mistaken for long-term happiness.

In this context, it is important to distinguish between momentary pleasure and happiness. Leading an exuberant life keeps away boredom. It also provides a roadblock for any type of depression. Avenues are provided for varied interests. This had a varied impact on my life too. I had the satisfaction of knowing that I had used my abilities and energies to lift the level of my life and that of many others around me.

My philosophy endows me with the ability to push past all instant gratifications. It gives me the strength to disengage from hankering for momentary pleasure. This led me to the path of long-term, sustainable happiness. If one knows the difference between the two, then it would clearly denote the frivolity of a life drifting from one pleasure to another. This drifting provides only distraction, not happiness or fulfilment.

I believe that it is important to always be engaged in meaningful pursuits. It is necessary to feel that we are all responsible for positive changes. Not all our changes will be applauded or celebrated by the world. But it should not deter us from setting and accomplishing our objectives and priorities.

It is enough to believe that we matter. In whatever small way we matter to people around us, provide sufficient strength and vision to fulfil ours as well as theirs. This bestows a meaningful life with long-term happiness and fulfilment. True happiness is a mind that is at ease and peaceful. True happiness holds a heart that sings its own rhythm. True happiness belongs to a life that attains its true purpose. I always felt that, only in such an environment, all social evils would perish and have their nascent deaths.

Towards the fourth quarter of August 2021, I had planned a visit to Bhubaneswar to fulfil my last obligation to family members of my brother and sisters. I was to fly from Delhi with my daughter Dimpy and be joined by my son Dev from Bengaluru. Due to some unforeseen events, this was postponed to the future months.

From mid-August on, unprecedented downpours continued. I have always been an early riser. One morning, heavy rain continuing from the previous night made me slightly lazy. Finally, I left the bed and went to the kitchen to prepare the ginger herbal tea. I took the tea to the balcony overlooking the golf course. Though I enjoy the rain, the present fury of nature that flooded the surroundings made me philosophical.

Many questions, whose answers are hard to find, rose in their heads. The questions about the reason one is born and the purpose one exists on this planet started bedevilling my mind.

Bemused, I sat, sipping my tea. I found that the answer is multidimensional. I found that, spiritually speaking, the purpose of life is to explore the ultimate beauty that lies in experiencing inexplicable joy. This joyful exaltation provides every person's soul with eternal joy. Comprehending and experiencing this joy leads one to the ultimate beauty, even in the observance of the fury of nature! Nature's fury reminds mortals of their insignificance in the vast universe where innumerable stars bigger than our sun exist. From my knowledge of the scripture, I knew that beauty is abstract and indefinable, infinite and unquantifiable. It is beyond the realm of reason. For the beholder, it is so great that anything compared cannot match it. Factually and intrinsically, it is just beautiful and joyful to the mind. At the same time, I also knew that the mind is so subtle that it can attach to any desire. Such desire may turn out to be the greatest deceiver. Once the desire has entered the mind, one may lose everything that has been achieved in the pursuit of eternal joy.

Any sensual or physical hyperactivity may thrill one for a short time. But it would diminish self-awareness. When the thrill wears off, the hyperbole of joy crashes to its lowest ebb. It would destroy the natural creativity of concerned individuals. For mere physical and sensual gratifications, extrinsic joy as beauty does not achieve the sublime. Indulgence and consumption entail temporary relief and relaxation. They can have a far-reaching impact on the physical, mental, and spiritual well-being of a person. The altered mental state may prevent one from experiencing real joy. This joy is beyond the confines of physical or sensual pleasure. It can only be experienced through inner inquiry and a sublime state of delight. It becomes achievable by surrendering one's ego to the altar of divinity.

The downpour of rain suddenly stopped. I returned to my mundane existence without any sublimity of pain or pleasure. My thoughts veered towards today's competitive culture, which was unlike the olden days. Then the competition was fair. The winners and losers had no hard feelings between them. The situation now is: "A dog eats a dog." Now for many, it is: "Compete or perish." It appears to have produced two classes of people. One is bound to achieve success, and the other may not succeed and blame the unfavourable atmosphere more than the absence of their capabilities.

Such persons think that their failure was in the context ('*sandarbh*') of the situation in their lives. They easily ignore the teachings of the Bhagwat Gita, which mentions that *"The cause of unhappiness and misery is not the situation but more than the sandarbh; it is one's internal state that gives one the sorrows."*

According to the Gita, the intellect of such people is covered with ignorance. And, basically, this ignorance is the cause of suffering. While the situation may or may not be a unit of impact, one's inability to face any situation because of ignorance has a deeper impact on life. With knowledge alone, one can bring ignorance to its logical end. With knowledge alone, one can end the darkness in one's life. Thinking about pitfalls in life, the young generation should not be heartbroken. From my knowledge and experience, I want to share some of my thoughts with the younger generation. It will help them overcome their despair due to failures at various stages of life.

The younger generation should not accept anything at face value. It has to be remembered that nature is always at work in the background. For example, if one branch of a tree is cut off, a new branch grows back in time. The law of nature is equally applicable to human life and behaviour. The inspiration from the sermons of the Gita teaches that one's capabilities are much greater than the limitations faced in life.

One can find many examples of how these factors account for personal growth. I remembered an interesting interview that the famous Hollywood actor and martial arts expert Bruce Lee had given. When asked about his secret to success, he replied, *"I don't have a perfect body. My right leg is roughly an inch shorter than my left. That is why I put my right leg forward in my stance. Also, I am shortsighted; therefore, I specialise in close encounters. I have converted my disadvantage into an advantage."*

Understanding this will help the new generation develop a different outlook on life. They can turn their failures into successes. In today's world, the clamour to compete or perish is not the be-all and end-all of existence. It is simply an ultimatum to spur people to succeed in life. If a person has failed in the first instance, he does not necessarily perish. Everyone has the potential to take advantage of other chances and regain what was lost in the first instance. I believed in this perception, and this had relevance in my past life too. Every time you fail, learn from your failure; every time you succeed, be grateful for such an experience. When you do, personal excellence will greet you every moment.

Even after the end of the wettest August, the rains continued to bug the surroundings of the National Capital Region (NCR). On the second of September, in the apartment complex where I stay, I had an unfortunate mishap. A 35-year-old person fell from a highrise building and lost his life. It was indeed a sad incident. This type of incident always begets philosophical enigmas in my mind. It also makes me sad to think about the pressure and incidents of current challenging times on various people with weak mental endurance. I always felt that the challenging times were also opportunities to work on myself to make it strong. All changes that one wants to bring about have to begin from within. This is also the teaching of old sages.

One needs to observe one's own behaviour, attitude, and prejudices. These trigger many mixed qualities like anguish, jealousy, manipulativeness, scheming, and plotting. One has to rise above these controls to become a better and stronger self. It starts with accepting one's flaws and not overlapping them with any attempt to find the causes outside. Looking outwardly for the source of one's unpleasant conduct or impertinent behaviour would stunt one's growth. Instead, being aware of one's own weaknesses and accepting them opens up floodgates of energy and gives courage to act and work on oneself for the desired improvement.

One always has various questions, problems, and doubts regarding the past and future. These are mostly concerning work, relationships, and health. A disturbed mind can never find a solution for it. When one focuses inward and starts working on oneself with sincerity and perseverance, then all the answers will be found from within. It is essential to de-programme the preconceived notions, misconceptions, and tuning that are hindrances to growth and the inner fountainhead of knowledge. This also poses an obstacle to resurrecting oneself.

While working on oneself for improvement, one attracts incidents. These test, examine and teach something that propels one on the path to resurrect faith in one's self. It dispels layers of ignorance and fills them with true knowledge. Then comes the renewed energy for unfolding inner ecstasy. It begets the true 'karma' of intellect and knowledge of what to take along and what to dispel. That is the right time to redesign oneself because the world is beautiful and one is here to make it more beautiful. For such people, life is too precious, and there is no place for despair or despondency!

After delving into philosophy, I felt extreme happiness over the recent achievements of my two grandsons, Tanmay and Aman. Tuesday, September 7, 2021, became the messenger of good news for both of them.

The elder Tanmay had his graduation in law. He has been working as an associate at a prominent law firm in New Delhi for over four years. On the mentioned date, he was promoted as a senior associate in his organisation. All along, I knew that Tanmay would go a long way in his career and make the entire family proud. He is intelligent, diligent, caring, and sincere in all the spheres in which he operates. I had been observing him closely after Mona and both her boys shifted to their own apartments close to mine in Noida. Tanmay was working hard even during the extremely harrowing pandemic period. He served the clients of his firm through video conferencing and digital advice on all of their urgent issues. He followed the guidelines of his seniors. I have seen the sparkle of a diamond in his work and his demeanour. He will always have the blessings of his mother, Nani, Nana, Mausi, and Mama.

The younger one, Aman, is an intelligent young man. His results in the Higher Secondary Board Examination were extremely good. With the same vigour and intelligence, he completed his graduation in Business Administration (BBA) from a reputed university that has teaching campuses abroad in the UK, USA, and Australia. Like a person with farsightedness at this young age, he decided to work for a couple of years and gain work experience before doing his MBA. After obtaining his degree with an excellent score in the month of July 2021, he applied for a marketing executive's job. After an interview and selection, he joined as a marketing executive on September 7, 2021. The appointment was with a prominent, decade-old digital marketing company in NCR, Delhi. As outgoing, social, and brilliant as he is, I believe that he will progress far in life. Being the youngest in the family, he has kudos for the good wishes and blessings of all family members.

During earlier times, in my generation, there was no establishment or company that carried out anything like a digital marketing operation. My inquisitiveness made me find out and learn something about digital marketing. I found that such companies build strategies for lasting digital connections with consumers. They plan and monitor their ongoing client's presence on social media. They optimised online advertising to increase client awareness. In this, they utilise the internet and other digital media and platforms to promote their clients' products, services, and brands. Thus, the work is mostly virtual and not face-to-face like that of conservative standard marketing practices.

September is a month that revives many of my memories. In its domain, it treasures many of my sweet memories. This month marked a delightful new turn in my career at an MNC; the month was associated with the advance news of the arrival of my family's first child in a matter of a few months. This month is the birthday of my dear daughter Dimpy. At the same time, this month also reminded me of the world's deadliest act of terrorism. None would ever forget the 11th of September 2001, when three big passenger aircraft flying full load at high speed blew up New York's World Trade Centre's twin towers and Washington's Pentagon Building. It was the end of the precious lives of three thousand people.

These people never knew what struck them or what was their fault! Such acts of madness are not acceptable in a civilised society. But unfortunately, the terrorists are neither civilised nor they belong to normal society.

In the same month and day in 2021, when I think about this tragedy, automatically a question arises in my mind. Can violence, or retaliatory violence, ever be the answer to any issue? I feel that today the world is standing at the crossroads of human civilization. It is tormented by ceaseless acts of violence, bloodshed, and the sniffing out of precious lives. I sincerely feel that violence can never be a viable solution for any issue. Violence can only beget counter-violence and vengeance. Communities and countries cannot afford to carry rancour and revenge in their hearts and minds. For a better tomorrow for humanity and our future generations, this has to end. Getting rid of vengeance is the best way to keep violence in abeyance.

Human beings are inherently good. Nothing bitter can survive forever. I understand well that humanity, ultimately for survival, will recoil from violence and hatred. I remember well what I mentioned earlier. The sight of death and destruction in the battle of Kalinga transformed Violent King Ashok into Ashok the Great, a symbol of peace and tranquility. Our scriptures and history denote many such instances. They tell how the ruthless Angulimal shed his abominable ways and repented before Budha. Pandavas lamented the end of the Kurukshetra war in spite of victory. All these prove that we all have the inherent goodness to become non-violent. The world needs to emulate the teachings of great leaders from all countries. From their preaching of forgiveness and non-violence, a new world would emerge. It is everyone's responsibility to make this world a place of peace and prosperity.

The couple, Rashmi and Chandidas, have always been religious in their thoughts and actions. Their attitude towards religion had been very flexible and modern. They had respect for the teachings of all religions. They were true Hindus whose motto had been "*Vasudeva Kutumbakam*," i.e., the whole world is a family. My favourite scripture has been the Bhagavat Gita; this too espoused this philosophy. The chapter on karma yoga in the Bhagwat Gita has been my favourite. I lived by its teachings all my life. My life story would be incomplete if I failed to incorporate the inherent importance of the advice in this chapter.

Gita's karma yoga is the spiritual practice of selfless action performed for the benefit of others. Karma yoga is a path to reach *moksha* (spiritual liberation) through work. Of the classical paths of spiritual liberation in Hinduism, Karma Yoga is the path of unselfish action. It teaches that spiritual seekers should act according to *dharma* without being attached to the fruits of their personal consequences. Bhagwat Gita's Karma Yoga purifies the mind. It leads one to consider all aspects of dharma for work. The work, according to one's dharma, is doing God's work. In that sense, it is becoming and being "like Krishna" in every moment of one's life. Those who refuse to play their role incur sin. This is what Krishna tells Arjun in the Bhagwat Gita.

I elaborate on the above philosophy of karma in simple ways that an average individual can understand and follow. According to me, karma, or the activity, is as essential as food for most human beings. The mind is always active, even if one appears to be sitting idle. If one is not occupied with some useful activity, then there are high chances of falling into the trap of undesirable action.

Without some activity, one even can't take care of the body's sustenance. A person with a lot of money also needs to remain engaged in some activity. Karma is an expression of gratitude to *Creation*. God has given a beautiful world in which one can enjoy life. But, in return, one has to contribute something to maintain it and make it a better place.

By carrying out one's chosen duty, one can reduce this debt to *creation*. Those who refuse to play this role are ungrateful. To say the least, they are thieves to the extent that they enjoy others' creations without giving anything in return. A person can do his best if his chosen role in life is as per his disposition and liking. One must choose a role, keeping in mind one's intellectual abilities and inclinations. Of course, one can always inquire whether there was any qualitative lacuna in efforts. This can help with improvement.

The principles of Karma yoga are simple. One should put in their best efforts in all chosen roles without selfishness or ego. One should perform the role with top-class efficiency and a proactive attitude. One should not be obsessed with personal gains from every action. Good actions beget good results. Too much anxiety for results spoils the quality of actions.

Ego should not rule one's actions. Individual ego has no place in the overall scheme of the universe. A good result is always due to the efforts of many stakeholders. What one has achieved today is because God has given them a healthy body and a superior mind. Parents give good education, and teachers become motivators. Acknowledging all these, one must keep giving credit to others. That will sublimate the ego. Karma Yoga teaches all these and much more! These principles continue to guide me even today. I am ever grateful to my father for inculcating these values in me right from childhood. I am delighted to observe that similar qualities are to be found abundantly among all of my offspring.

I am equally thankful to my fate for giving me a beautiful wife who, characteristically, was endowed with all the good qualities of a human being. The word vanity had no meaning for her, unlike many other beautiful ladies of her time.

Humility and modesty—these qualities were synonymous with her beautiful demeanour. In her husband's stressful career, her qualities gave him reserves of great inner strength. That also became his source of unbounded happiness. Her humbleness, even for people of lower strata, endeared her to everyone. On reflection, I now understand why all spiritual traditions value humility. It is essential for a person to be humble and receive divine benediction.

From an interpersonal perspective, my wife's being so humble facilitated unlimited trust. She built a solid relationship for the entire family. She made her husband hold nature in high esteem. She made him recognise it as an overwhelming and awe-inspiring force. She made him realise how insignificant human beings are on the cosmic scale. Her absence now weighs heavily on her husband. At the same time, with her long association, I have also built a strong inner self. At any time now, I can recoup my strength just by remembering her.

My stray thoughts now hover around the following few lines:

Chandidas Mohanty

Stray Thoughts

Remembrance of the past
At the twilight of one's life,
Give vent to memories lost
Of life's struggle and strife.

Always bypass your sorrow,
Get the twilight's grandeur.
For the beauties of morrow,
One's age is just a number.

The life, precious gift of God,
Meant to give help to the needy,
And receive the Almighty's nod
For Life's adieu to be steady.

Breeze playing with coiffure,
Ravishing smiles to endure,
She always cares it to figure
Excitement and lovely rapture!

She captivates the ecstatic joy
To enjoy nature's true beauty,
Zephyr naughtily plays ahoy,
To make all the hearts frailty.

* * *

The lonely traveller misses his soulmate. In the middle of the night, he gets up suddenly to the quagmire of intolerable void. The images of his children and grandchildren capture his mind's eye and calmly take him back to the lap of a nap. He again dreams of his unfinished responsibility for the family at large. He had promised his parents that the inherited property would be distributed equally among all the siblings or their surviving successors. This too was the earnest desire of his late better half.

After completing the above task, Bobby will patiently await joining his long-lost darling Bubly.

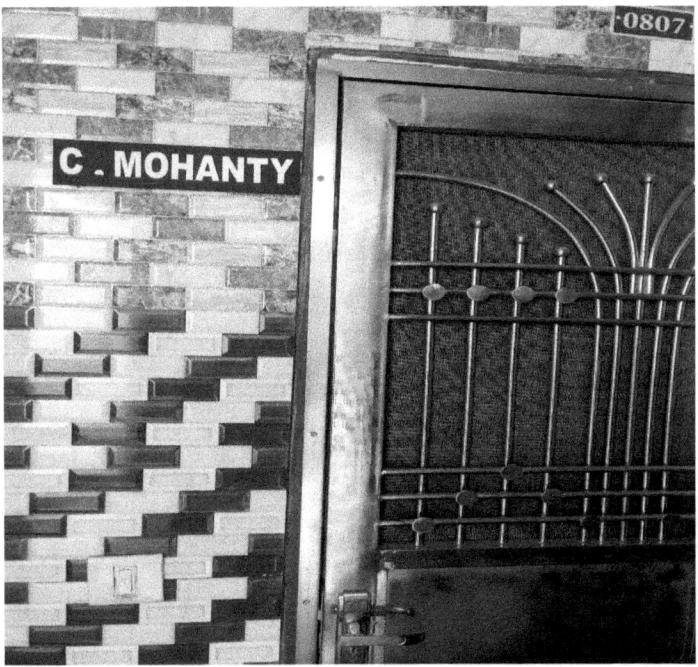

The world moves on, and so does Chandi's life!

‹ The End ›

The Author

Chandidas Mohanty received his graduation in science and post-graduation in economics from Allahabad University. Training in management was imparted to him in India and abroad. His service career, spanning over 33 years, was spent at MNCs and PSUs. He ended his service career as the managing director of a large PSU.

Post-retirement, he remained busy as a consultant and management advisor for public sector enterprises. Besides, he also continued with the work of arbitration. He is an active member of many important associations and organisations in Delhi. He was the recipient of the Bharat Gaurav Award in 2015 for his signal service to the Indian industry.

In 2006, he authored a book of English poetry titled 'Bouquet of Wild Flowers'. His second book, 'Financial Management for Managers', was published in the year 2016.

He has widely travelled to many countries around the world. His hobbies are reading and writing.

* * *

You Write. We Publish.

To publish your own book, contact us.

We publish poetry collections, short story collections, novellas and novels.

contact@thewriteorder.com

Instagram- thewriteorder

www.facebook.com/thewriteorder

www.ingramcontent.com/pod-product-compliance
Lightning Source LLC
LaVergne TN
LVHW010310070526
838199LV00065B/5506